4/05

STRIKE COMMAND

STRIKE COMMAND

The Inside Story of the RAF's Warfare Heroes

John Parker

headline

First published in 2002
by HEADLINE BOOK PUBLISHING

John Parker would be happy to hear from readers with their
comments on the book at the following email address:
johnparker@wyndham.freeserve.co.uk

10 9 8 7 6 5 4 3 2 1

Cataloguing in Publication Data is available
from the British Library

ISBN 0 7553 1058 6

Typeset in Times New Roman by
Letterpart Limited, Reigate, Surrey

Printed and bound in Great Britain by
Mackays of Chatham plc, Chatham, Kent

HEADLINE BOOK PUBLISHING
A division of Hodder Headline
338 Euston Road
LONDON NW1 3BH

www.headline.co.uk
www.hodderheadline.com

CONTENTS

ACKNOWLEDGEMENTS

As with my previous books in this series for Headline, the narrative relies heavily on personal testimony, and I am deeply indebted to those who contributed their time to bring this story to life. At the core of these pages are the recollections of more than 175 airmen, based on interviews either with myself or taped for the Sound Archive of the Imperial War Museum. I am also once again indebted to the staff of this superb resource for their help and time in searching out tapes and personalities related to specific incidents and events in the hundred-year chronology, which includes many famous missions and many famous names, some of whom are now sadly no longer with us. The IWM archive, together with research at the Public Record Office, the RAF Museum at Hendon and other excellent RAF historical sites, helps bring to life an insight into some of those heroic adventures.

PROLOGUE

From Boy to Man

Within these pages are many personal stories that will provide the reader with a close insight into a world that is both coruscating and in many ways tragic. They are told by the men who were there, doing the business for the Royal Air Force in times of war and peace through almost a century of military flight. But I have chosen one in particular as a taster for what is to come, not because it is filled with claims of great heroics. Quite the reverse. The fact is that Charles Patterson's recollections have poignant quality. They capture in essence what it was *really* like, for example, when a young man, not long out of school and who may never even have ridden a motorbike before, sat down at the controls of a Blenheim bomber that he would soon be piloting on suicidal daylight raids against German targets during the Second World War. He reveals in a matter-of-fact way the thoughts, feelings and fears that confronted himself and thousands of other young men who were expected to go out and bomb cities of the foe night after night, knowing full well that a good proportion of them would never come back.

Charles Patterson had just turned 19 when he joined the RAF at the outbreak of war and was posted to a bomber squadron a year later. The guy who was giving him tuition, Flight Lieutenant Derek Roe, was an instructor who looked 16 but was 21. He had already won a DFC and turned out to be one of the greatest Blenheim pilots of all, flying more than 50 daylight missions at a

1

time when the average survival rate was just seven.

In the summer of 1941 the Blenheim was already the talk of the RAF for all the wrong reasons. Blenheim crews, along with those flying a couple of other aircraft not up to the job, had suffered horrendous casualties in the previous 12 months. Whole squadrons had been wiped out in operations over France, Scandinavia, on the coastal beat in the North Sea attacking German ships and submarines and finally on initial sorties into Germany. The aircraft that had been Britain's big hope as the war began turned into a deathtrap. Although faster than any previous bomber the RAF possessed, the Blenheim was armed with popguns compared with opposing armoury and could not escape the new breed of German fighters. When the cry went up over the RT of the British planes – Snappers! – it would already be too late. The Messerschmitt 109 fighters would come scream-ing out of the sun to shoot the Blenheims down, which they did with alarming frequency.

One afternoon in July 1941, Charles Patterson knew his day of reckoning had finally come when his squadron, No. 114, in 2 Group, Bomber Command, was transferred to standard opera-tions over Germany in broad daylight at hedge-hopping height to dodge radar. They were to fly from West Raynham in Norfolk, where the station commander was the legendary Group Captain Paddy Bandon (the Earl of Bandon), who had already had one squadron totally obliterated. To his utter amazement, Patterson found himself promoted overnight to flight lieutenant for no other reason than he had survived his first ten operations and rumours abounded of a 'big one' in the offing:

> The nearer it came, the more alarming the rumours were. We understood it was to be a major event involving the whole group, all the squadrons of Blenheims in 2 Group. We had a new young squadron commander called Wing Commander John Nichol, who had never been on such an operation. Nor had I, but I became his deputy. I was a very inexperienced flight lieutenant but still one of the most experienced pilots in the squadron below the rank of squadron leader, and I was to fly number two to Wing Commander Nichol on his starboard in a 'Vic' of six. The atmosphere throughout the whole group was very tense, and on 10 August I learned our

fate. I was taken into the operations room to look at the target, and I'll never forget the sight that met my eyes. There was a huge map laid out on a table and there, leading absolutely straight, was a red tape from Orford Ness straight across the North Sea, through Holland and right down to Cologne. At first I just didn't believe that this was the target. And then the truth, the reality, dawned on me: that I was going to have to take part in a low-level daylight attack on Cologne with no fighter escort, in Blenheims.

Well, I can still feel the sense of shock now. However, it was no use panicking, so I listened to the briefing. The target was not Cologne itself but the Knapsack and Quadrath power stations. Group Captain Bandon told us that Knapsack was the biggest in Europe. I was shown a photograph of it. It had 12 chimneys on one side and eight on the other. No. 114 Squadron was to lead the entire operation, with Wing Commander Nichol and myself out front.

We were to fly down between these chimneys, drop our load and come back again. I went out in shock, and of course I couldn't communicate what the target was to anybody else. I had to carry this secret about with me with my fellow aircrew for two days. I also had to make up my mind: could I do this? Because statistically or tactically or from any other point of view you care to put, the chances of surviving an operation like that were negligible. How was I, a fundamental coward who'd managed to skate past it up to now, going to make myself do this operation? The next two days were spent wrestling with myself as to how I was to do it. I evolved an attitude, a philosophy, peculiar to myself. I found that the only thing to do was to stop worrying and to say to myself: You're not coming back. You've just got to go. You're caught in this situation. The alternative is to just funk it and not go at all. Completely funk it and not go at all. That seemed of the two the more impossible. So I just resigned myself to the fact that I was not coming back. I can't explain why I took that view, but I did. Some chaps did it the other way round, but I found it worked for me, every time.

And then came Sunday 12 August, when we were to go. I had a pretty poor night, hardly any sleep. We had to get up about half-past six, have breakfast and go up and be briefed on the mission. I was still saying to myself, I was just not going to come back. When we got into the operations room and all the crews in the squadron gathered to be shown the target, there was this most terrible sort of gasp of disbelief, even from the most hardened ones. Well, the operation was very comprehensively planned. We learned that there were to be diversionary bombing attacks in northern France. Everything was being done to mislead and divert the enemy fighter defences because the great dread was not only what we assumed would be tremendous flak surrounding the target, but the chances seemed pretty slim of actually getting into Germany – and certainly we wouldn't get out – without being shot down by fighters. All the experience showed that when a formation of Blenheims was actually intercepted by Messerschmitt 109s, it was unusual for more than perhaps two out of six to get away. Sometimes none got away.

We were to take off at about eight to rendezvous with various other squadrons over Orford Ness and then set off across the North Sea at very low level. Well, it's the only time in my life that I can recall seeing some of my fellow aircrew literally grey and shaking – even my own air gunner, who was a pretty imperturbable type. Curiously enough, seeing all the others looking so frightened rather bolstered me a bit, because I'd already dealt with the situation psychologically. Although one thought we were going to certain death, as we actually got involved and we were really off and we were going, somehow the scale and the element of the adventurous aspect of it began to take over and I for one was not as panicky as I had expected.

I'd always wondered what on earth enemy territory looked like and it was when we suddenly found ourselves flying over the flat, sandy Dutch islands and actually entering enemy airspace where everything looked so normal that it was in some extraordinary way reassuring: just the normality of the surroundings, of the countryside. And being so low you were able to see ordinary Dutch people in the fields and the little houses and everything just underneath us. We flew on, down south of a German fighter airfield called Woensdrecht, down the Scheldt estuary, forming up closely on Wing Commander Nichol while at the same time keeping one eye ahead, expecting fighters at any moment. We went on mile after mile, on what was a lovely sunny day, incidentally, not a cloud in the sky. Still no fighters. My navigator warned me: 'Not long now.' And then on the RT Wing Commander Nichol was saying, 'Turn to starboard', which meant a very, very gentle turn because we were only just above the ground. As I turned, there, up on the top of a long slope about two or three miles away, was this enormous industrial complex. We turned to starboard and climbed up the hill. We had to avoid the increasing maze of electricity pylons and cables which made one realise what an enormous place it was. Then the chimneys came unmistakably into view, and we inevitably flew closer and closer until the chimneys were coming right up to us. Wing Commander Nichol swung in between them and I followed. Then I became enveloped in mist and steam; we were right in the middle of them now, and there was nothing I could do except concentrate on flying the aeroplane. We had been told not to release our bombs on the water coolers but to keep them for the actual powerhouse at the far end, and so we flew on. And as we did so I saw again a lot of blue flashes from the ground – machine-gun fire – but I was past caring now.

Now, in front of my eyes amid the steam and the smoke was the target, and I pressed my tit and let the bombs go. As I did so I saw Wing Commander Nichol just ahead of me swerve sharply to starboard. I realised he was about to fly into a chimney, which he just missed. I did the same, and we came out the other side with a lot more ground fire – tracer. Wing Commander Nichol was there. He'd survived. I formed up on him, and we raced away across the cables again down past the other side of the power station. To my amazement all the other five members of our formation emerged safely, and we set off for the journey home.

Well, despite the fact that we covered the target, I don't remember any particular sense of relief because it was the journey home which seemed the most impossible part of it. We flew on and on over western Germany towards Holland. No interception yet. Then we flew into a rainstorm, and for one wonderful moment I thought we were going to get cloud cover, but it was only a shower and we emerged very shortly afterwards out into the brilliant sun again. On and on over the fields. Past little villages and hamlets with the occasional individual diving into a ditch beneath us. Then just before we got to the German border, we flew over a typical German industrialist's Victorian mansion with turrets. And in the garden, I caught a glimpse beside a cedar tree of a table, large white tablecloth, all laid out for lunch. A group of people were standing round it. As we whizzed over the top, my gunner let fly and broke up the party. He felt that any rich Germans who were living like that while the war was on deserved to be shot up, which today sounds appalling but at the time seemed right and proper.

Well, on into Holland, further and further. It seemed to me then we were going to make it. Nothing was going to happen after all, but it's always when that psychological moment comes that you're brought down to earth, and often quite literally. Suddenly, far ahead of us, just as we were coming up to the Scheldt estuary, black dots appeared in the sky. Wing Commander Nichol called out: 'Snappers!' We were flying straight into these Messerschmitts, which were circling around about a thousand feet above us. Nichol told us: 'Close in tight, close in tight.' He led us right down on to the water. The water was racing underneath, sparkling in the sun. Couldn't have been more than 10, 15, occasionally perhaps 20 feet above it. And I got as tight into him as I could. I knew this was life or death. Frankly, the concentration on the flying side of it was able to drive out most of the fear of the fighters – the sheer concentration of flying so close, so low. With my wing tip practically inside his wing tip, at that height it took all the flying concentration and skill I possessed to do it. And the others closed in, and Nichol handed over, as was the tactical drill, to the leading gunner, Pilot Officer Morton, who was a very experienced second-tour air gunner. He directed the formation because the gunners looking back could all see the fighters coming into attack. He had to decide when to open fire, when to take evasive action or when to turn into the attack. I then heard the rattle of machine-gun fire and realised our guns

6

were firing, and I could see the water being ripped with white froth from the cannon shells of these 109s. As we were turning to starboard, there was a 109 right in front of my eyes peeling off its attack, so close that I saw the pilot in the cockpit. Curiously, my reaction was simply one of interest in seeing a 109 so close. This carried on all the way up the Scheldt estuary; the attacks kept coming in and yet we still seemed to survive them. The gunners were doing a wonderful job, and unbelievably the islands to each side of us suddenly ceased and we were in the open sea. We'd hardly gone any distance out to sea when the leading gunner told us over the RT that the fighters had broken off the attack. I suppose they were running out of ammunition. We'd survived, all six of us, and as we carried on out to sea I was overcome by the greatest moment of elation I've ever experienced in all my life, with all the operations that were to come. We'd made it and we were waving to each other through the Perspex. It was just marvellous, happy relief, sheer joy flying back across the North Sea. We knew this would cause tremendous headlines. But then the reports began to come in. By the afternoon, word got round that there had been many losses . . .

There was never any room for triumphalism in the RAF, and nor is there today, because experience shows that successes were always followed by the bad news, and that day, on what had been a comparatively small raid compared with what was to come, 10 out of the 54 Blenheims had been shot down and six others had been very badly shot up and crash-landed. Two other Blenheims that had navigated British Whirlwind fighters that went out to meet the incoming raiding group to escort them home were also shot down. As for Charles Patterson, the apprehensions he and so many others shared were set aside in the business of war. He flew many more bombing missions, as well as tackling the equally hazardous role of film reconnaissance, often carried out during bombing raids. In total, 80 crew were killed, wounded or taken prisoner during the raid on the Cologne power stations, a toll that would rise dramatically as the war progressed. Bomber Command alone lost half its 110,000 aircrew during the war and another 19,000 were either wounded or taken prisoner.

But of course the Second World War, though a dramatic and destructive intervention, is only part of this story that encompasses the origins of the Royal Air Force from the beginning of the twentieth century and progressing through the decades to the nuclear age when the RAF took the brunt of European defences in the Cold War, and on into today's era of super-jets.

CHAPTER ONE

Out of the Wild West

The song said it all: those daring young men in their flying machines. And so they were. Dashing, daring risk-takers on a journey into the unknown in which there were no guarantees about returning in one piece, if at all. Down the decades the odds have improved somewhat, but the reputation of wild intrepidity, inherited by the Royal Air Force from its virgin predecessors and so amply displayed in two world wars, went way back to the beginning of the century. As will be seen from the testimony herein, the pioneering spirit that drove those young aviators, some still in their teens, to literally dance with danger thousands of feet in the air aboard flimsy contraptions was incredible. Nonchalant courage, and an ample supply of clean underwear, thus became the hallmark of the men who took to the air during the story that unfolds in these pages over what becomes a century of powered aircraft flight in the year 2003.

The start of what became known as the 'heavier-than-air' brigade needs little introduction. The 'heavy' part of the title was to distinguish powered flight from the 'lighter-than-air' faction of balloonists, who, at the turn of the nineteenth century, seemed to be making the running in the projected future of flight. That was before the most significant event in aviation history: the first flight by the brothers Wilbur and Orville Wright on 17 December 1903. They made four flights in all in their curious-looking machine at Kitty Hawk, North Carolina, the longest lasting a minute and covering just 850 feet. They succeeded where so many others had failed by making a comprehensive study of birds in flight and pioneered rudder control and other aspects of balanced flight which had been overlooked by their predecessors. Above all, they did their homework and set up a continuous set of experiments leading eventually to their famous wind tunnel trials. They sought inspiration from the work of other would-be aviators and inventors around the globe, from the Greek myth of Icarus to the sixteenth century airship sketches of Leonardo da Vinci, using records in the archives of the Smithsonian Institution and, in 1899, were especially taken by the work in Britain of Sir George Cayley. A hundred years earlier, Cayley had produced a drawing of an aircraft with a fixed wing, fuselage and tail but had never perfected an engine reliable enough to test his theories. He pressed on with his designs and eventually conducted trials with the first man-carrying glider in 1853, at Brompton in North Yorkshire, with his coachman at the controls.

Another of the pioneers whose work the Wright brothers studied was Otto Lilienthal, who progressed Cayley's ideas further by confirming that learning to glide was the first lesson in the quest for powered flight. He would launch his machines from hills, and his prolonged study of aerodynamics led the way to the next stage in the history of flight, although Lilienthal himself would not witness these developments. He was killed in 1896 when his glider was caught by wind currents and crashed. As he lay dying, his back broken, he uttered the words: 'Sacrifices must be made.'

Next, the Wright brothers took a keen interest in the important work of Britain's Horatio Phillips and his own series of wind tunnel experiments, which used steam injection to create the airflow. Phillips patented the first curved aerofoil designs, and his subsequent planes were described as 'flying Venetian blinds'. In the end, the Wright brothers beat him to the punch. It was 1904 before he completed one short flight and another three years before he managed to stay off the ground for 500 feet at Streatham, the first powered flight in England. By then, other French and British enthusiasts were already beginning to pursue the Wright's achievement in producing viable aircraft, and Lord Northcliffe, owner of the *Daily Mail*, saw both the commercial and military benefits – and dangers – of aircraft and immediately offered a handsome prize for the first person to fly from London to Manchester. In 1906 he added another challenge to the first aviator to fly successfully across the English Channel.

The interest of the British public – and military chiefs – was also aroused by the airborne activities of a flamboyant American showman, Samuel Cody, a former cowboy and gold prospector who came to Britain in 1896 to set up a Wild West show on the lines of that run by his cousin, Buffalo Bill Cody. Sam deliberately dressed like his relative, with moustache and goatee beard, stetson and silver-embossed boots, and tried pretty well everything that came along to give his show a modern flavour – including dabbling in balloons and an interest in flight. In 1902 Cody's wife, Leila Marie, became the first woman to fly, using his 'Man-Lifting War Kite'.

On the strength of that development and further experiments, he left the Wild West show behind and was awarded a contract as Chief Kite Instructor at the British Army Balloon Factory at Farnborough, on the predictions that 'lighter-than-air' craft – i.e. gas-filled balloons and airships – were about to come into their own following successful trials in France and Germany. The army's balloon section, formed three decades earlier, was concerned with using tethered balloons with chaps in the basket beneath for signalling purposes and directing artillery fire. Four balloon sections joined the British military force in South Africa in 1899, soon to be complemented by a new development – man-lifting kites. They were used in the same role as the balloons and went up when the winds were too strong for the lighter-than-air envelopes.

Cody decided the era of flight was upon the world and fast-talked his way into the confidence of the British military. He was employed on flight experiments with kites and moved on to an unsuccessful venture building the British army's first airship before deciding to build his own plane. On that journey of discovery, he became well known for his oft-heard cry: 'Imitate the birds, my boy, imitate the birds!'

Using engine technology borrowed from the Wrights and a coterie of French designers, Cody built Britain's first successful aircraft, which became British Army Aeroplane No. 1 in 1908. Although Phillips had successfully flown in 1904 and 1907, Cody went into military history as achieving Britain's first successful powered flight. His biplane, which became known as a Cody, had a 50-horsepower French Antoinette engine and twin chain-driven propellers. He flew it publicly three times in 1908, the longest at Farnborough on 16 October, when he travelled 1,390 feet before a wing touched the ground during a turn and he crashed. He escaped relatively unscathed, but he was the hero of the British army chiefs who had somewhat reluctantly assumed responsibility for nursing Britain's first military aircraft wing into existence.

The race was about to become more frantic. In that year of 1908, the US Army Signal Corps ordered a two-seat observation aircraft from the Wright brothers. The specifications were for a machine that was simple to fly, could reach a speed of at least 40 miles an hour in still air and have an endurance of at least an hour. Orville Wright met all the Signal Corps's specifications and the US army had its first airborne operation, with a machine that was listed as Airplane No. 1, Heavier-than-Air Division, United States Aerial Fleet.

The same year, Wilbur Wright set new records, staying aloft for an hour and 32 minutes and travelling 61 miles with a passenger on board. He won for himself a $100,000 patents deal with a French group, which ordered 50 of his aircraft. In the meantime, other Frenchmen were already testing their own creations and especially had their eyes set on Lord Northcliffe's prize for the first cross-Channel flight. Three of France's top aviators – Hubert Latham, the Count de Lambert and Louis Blériot – had set up near Calais for the attempt in July 1909. And of course it was Blériot who claimed the prize, taking off from Sangatte and landing near Dover Castle 43 minutes later after a flight covering just 23 miles.

With the fame and fortune that the event brought him, Blériot began building his own monoplanes, and his Mark XI model was to become one of the most effective and popular pre-First World War aircraft, capable of three hours' flying time and a fast climb to 1,640 feet in a little over seven minutes. Within the space of three years, the pace of development had reached such a pitch that the military establishments of major nations soon realised – as Lord Northcliffe had himself predicted – that powered flight represented a major threat to the security of armed forces, greater perhaps than the development of airships, in which Germany, and Count Ferdinand von Zeppelin in particular, led the field.

Although the British military and a rather reluctant political establishment were slow off the mark in assessing the options and the need to enter the arena of powered flight, entrepreneurs tended to be less faint-hearted and a number of names emerged who were to make a major contribution to the development of aeronautics and aircraft in general for the rest of the century. They included the great pioneer Alliot Verdon Roe, who went on to form A.V. Roe and become one of the foremost aircraft manufacturers. He was the first man to build and fly a triplane, in 1908, and used a new air strip at Brooklands, Surrey, built in the middle of the already famous motor racing circuit. Many other famous names made their first steps to fortunes, including the Short brothers, who had previously made balloons for the Royal Aero Club at their base on the Isle of Sheppey, the Bristol Company, formerly known as the British and Colonial Aeroplane Company, and Vickers, which came out of the Martin and Handasyde partnership. Around them came the first airfields, the most famous of which was at Hendon – known then as the London Aerodrome – which attracted large numbers of sightseers as flight began to grip the public's imagination. Hendon also became the scene of exciting air races, with machines flying around a circuit quite close to the ground, and some taking up the showmanship of Samuel Cody by offering nerve-racking joyrides for £1 a time.

Finally, in February 1911 the army was given the go-ahead to form an Air Battalion under the auspices of the Royal Engineers. Only officers were considered as potential pilots, and recruits were accepted from all regiments (and later from the Royal Navy, with its own section), but NCOs and other ranks were restricted to entrants from the Royal Engineers. The army was confronted with an immediate problem. It had no facilities, personnel or even a budget for training pilots or ground staff, and there was, at that time, only one place to go: training had to be obtained privately from instructors at the Royal Aero Club at Eastchurch, Isle of Sheppey, at a cost of £75 a time. Those officers who successfully achieved their certificate received a refund of the fee from the army. The club had been formed at the turn of the century and was initially linked to balloon flight. As the RAeC's website points out,

In 1901 three wealthy motorists, Frank Hedges Butler, his daughter Vera and the Hon. Charles Rolls, had proposed a motor tour, but this was cancelled when Vera's Renault 4.5 caught fire. The lady arranged a balloon flight with the distinguished professional Stanley Spencer, as a distraction. Over a glass of champagne during the subsequent voyage, they agreed that an Aero Club should be formed, and after landing this was done without delay. Due no doubt to the presence and personality of Vera Butler, it was uniquely – for the time – agreed that it be open 'equally to ladies and gentlemen, subject to election'. Initially confined to ballooning, when heavier-than-air flight arrived, the club embraced it with alacrity.

The club was eventually established at Muswell Manor near Leysdown on the Isle of Sheppey in 1909. Early contacts with the Wright brothers by Charles Rolls and the Short brothers, balloon makers to the club, led to the Shorts acquiring a licence and laying down the first aircraft production line in the world at Leysdown and later nearby at Eastchurch. The influence of the club in those early days was considerable. It trained most military pilots up to 1915.* From 1910 the club also took over the issuing of aviators' certificates, internationally recognised under the Fédération Aéronautique Internationale, and had administrative control in the UK of all private and sporting flying.

The army's Air Battalion was to consist of two companies, the first concerned with balloons and (when they were eventually successfully launched) airships. The other was the Aeroplane Company, which took only officer recruits who had already obtained their civilian certificate from the Royal Aero Club, or from one of the other internationally recognised bodies, at their own expense. Donald Clappen, in his memoir for the Sound Archive of the Imperial War Museum, recalled that it was a relatively short period of training with little more than two hours' flying time and a painless and undemanding test of ability to obtain that vital piece of paper:

---

* By the end of the First World War, the RAeC had trained more than 6,500 military pilots.

One had to do two flights of five figures-of-eight observed by two qualified examiners. At the end of each flight one had to land within 150 feet of a specified point – which was where the two observers themselves stood. Then came the *pièce de résistance* – the height test. We had to fly up to a height of 150 feet, cut off one's engine and land again within 150 feet of the observers. Often, if it looked as if the pupil was about to land short, the instructors would walk slowly towards the spot where they thought it would be the defined distance! I do not recall a single pupil being 'ploughed' for not landing within the specified distance. The qualities judged necessary for a good pilot included experience of aeronautics, medical fitness, clear eyesight, age under 30, good at map-reading and sketching, mechanically inclined and weighing less than 11 stone 7 pounds.

At the time, aircraft were still not envisaged as an attacking force, although Count von Zeppelin in Germany had already proved in trials that airships could be effective as bombers. This worried Winston Churchill, First Lord of the Admiralty, both in regard to potential attacks on the Grand Fleet as well as the new submarine force, which had a very limited underwater endurance, and of course civilians in urban areas along the east coast of Britain. Even so, only the most far-sighted in the military hierarchy believed that aeroplanes would be used for anything other than observation and intelligence-gathering and possibly for aerial photography. For that reason, the machines had to have a pillion seat for an observer, and those men themselves had to be trained, with a good pool of reserves to compensate for casualties among both pilots and observers.

That did not put great pressure on the military, seeing that by the autumn of 1911 the Air Battalion had only 11 aeroplanes in operation, with eight more either under repair or being converted for military use at the army's factory at Farnborough. But the army began to take note when the first recorded use of an aeroplane in conflict came on 23 October 1911. An Italian pilot made an hour-long reconnaissance flight over enemy positions near Tripoli, Libya, during the Italia-Turkish War. He completed the mission in a Blériot XI monoplane. The first bombing raid came nine days later, when a pilot dropped four grenades on

Turkish positions. The first reconnaissance photographs of enemy positions were taken on 24 February 1912, in the same conflict.

From a military point of view, Britain looked to have been left at the starting gate. Figures for the previous decade of growing interest in heavier-than-air aviation told a pathetic story as far as the British government was concerned. Germany had spent £450,000 on military aeronautics, France was substantially behind at £47,000 and the United Kingdom trailing hopelessly with an expenditure of just £5,000. The Committee for Imperial Defence met and considered. The upshot was a rapid and radical revamp of the British military commitment to air transport and the immediate creation of the Royal Flying Corps (RFC), which came into being in April 1912. One month later, three Air Squadrons formally became operational, the first still concerned with balloons and airships and the other two having the distinction of being the first fixed-wing flying squadrons to be created in the UK.

Meanwhile, the Royal Navy set up its own Naval Flying Wing to run in parallel to the RFC, and the traditional gulf that existed between army and navy certainly applied here. The two organisations were to remain aloof from each other until virtually the end of the First World War. The navy established its own training ground, the Naval Flying School, at Eastchurch, on the grounds that flying aircraft and airships for the Royal Navy required special navigational skills. In spite of the intentions of the Committee for Imperial Defence that the two organisations should cooperate to form a single air force under the banner of the RFC, that organisation remained in the sole control of the army while the Naval Flying Wing remained under the supervision of the Royal Navy. No government minister moved to end what became an embarrassing rift, leading eventually to competition for both men and machines, an unhelpful situation that continued until 1917. It became something of a contest between the army Chiefs of Staff and the navy, especially when Winston Churchill, who was very keen on flying, took over as First Lord of the Admiralty. Churchill himself penned this account of the problem he inherited:

The War Office claimed on behalf of the Royal Flying Corps complete and sole responsibility for the aerial defence of

Great Britain. But owing to the difficulties in getting money, they were unable to make any provision for this responsibility, every aeroplane they had been earmarked for the British Expeditionary Force. Seeing this and finding myself able to procure funds by various shifts and devices, I began in 1912 and 1913 to form under the Royal Naval Air Service [as Churchill insisted on calling his Naval Wing] flights of aeroplanes as well as seaplanes for the aerial protection of our harbours, oil tanks and vulnerable points, and also for the general strengthening of our inadequate aviation.

Even so, RFC commanders began to dedicate themselves to bringing some order and direction into the parlous state of its tiny air force, which was still well behind schedule for the 1912 army projections that called for a hundred machines in operation by 1915, with a full complement of trained pilots and technicians to keep them flying. The RFC also set up its own flying school at Upavon Downs and, confronted with what amounted to a firm ultimatum to equip itself with quality machines, a competitive trial of new aircraft was staged on Salisbury Plain in the third week of August 1912. Up to 15 plane makers were invited to participate, and among those who staged a demonstration was Samuel Cody. His aircraft was judged to be the winner of the trials, but there was to be no big order from the RFC for him, or the others on show that day, because, as Churchill pointed out, the army simply did not have the money. Instead, the orders went to the army's factory at Farnborough, originally set up for balloon and airship construction but was now just being re-launched as the Royal Aircraft Factory. The director of the factory, Mervyn O'Gorman, who had been hidebound by government constraints and work on airships, finally began to gather some new designers and, although progress was still painfully slow, produced aircraft that were to make a considerable impact. Among them was the Blériot Experimental biplane, known as the BE, with the propeller fitted at the front. It was this plane that the army turned to in preference to Cody's and it became the first in a line of variants, the most famous of which was the BE2c. Others followed, including the Farman Experimental (FE), which was built to the design of another French pioneer, with the engine and propeller at the rear, a setup known as a 'pusher' (as opposed to the 'tractor'

17

configuration of the front-mounted prop). The factory also made the Reconnaissance Experimental (RE) and the Scouting Experimental (SE) and those four types provided the factory with its workload for the duration of the First World War, when the number employed on production rose from just 100 to 4,860.

The private plane makers did, however, get on the bandwagon for new aircraft, and they would especially benefit from the requirements of the Naval Wing who were looking at specialist requirements for their planes, prompted by a number of innovations using aircraft at sea. This resulted from Winston Churchill's enthusiasm for combining air and sea operations. The First Lord of the Admiralty – convinced that the Kaiser was preparing for war – pursued a vigorous policy of exploring every avenue in which aircraft could be used at sea, and as fighting machines rather than for mere observation. Rapid progress was made between 1911 and 1914, in tandem with private enterprise and especially the Short brothers, A.V. Roe and another British pioneer, Tom Sopwith, who was producing a range of aircraft that found fame in the First World War. But any reticence on the part of the RFC towards getting involved in such operations was explained by the navy's official historian for the period:

> The Naval Wing paid more attention than was paid by the Military Wing to the use of the aeroplane as a fighting machine . . . The Military Wing, small as it was, knew that it would be entrusted with the immense task of scouting for the Expeditionary Force and that its business would be rather to avoid than seek battle in the air. The Naval Wing aimed at something more than observing the movements of an attacking enemy. Thus in bomb-dropping and machine-gunnery the Naval Wing was more advanced.

Experiments at sea covered virtually every possible permutation. A Royal Navy submariner named Williamson submitted proposals that the Naval Wing should discover whether submarines could be detected and attacked from the air. Air spotters did indeed see British submarines during a test run and dropped the first dummy torpedoes from a British aircraft. Williamson also came up with a design to allow machines to take off from converted ships and let them land back on board by stretching wires across the deck. An ancient cruiser, *Hermes*, was converted to carry seaplanes, and successful trials were carried out in North Sea manoeuvres in 1913.

In another experiment, a navy pilot flew a Short S27 biplane from HMS *Hibernia* while the ship was steaming at 10.5 knots. By then, also, more than half of the Naval Wing's aircraft had been adapted as seaplanes, with the wheels being replaced by floats in another series of trials. Seaplanes were able to take off from the deck of the ship on wheeled trolleys that were fitted under their floats and dropped away as the machines became airborne. The Naval Wing also began experimenting with dropping bombs from aircraft as well as night flying.

Unlike his opposite numbers in the military, Churchill had a personal passion for aircraft, although he did not apply for a pilot's certificate. He was then 38 years old and overweight, whereas 30-ish was considered old enough for fliers who also had to be at the peak of physical fitness. His instructor at that time, Ivon Courtney, left this memoir:

> WSC and I would go up perhaps 10 times in one day. He was far more keen than most learners to go up again. He couldn't bear to make mistakes. He always wanted to correct them at once. I remember the time when, on landing, he bent an undercarriage. I imagined he would want to stop flying that day. But the shock did not deter him one bit, but no one would let him go up solo. We were all scared to death of having a smashed First Lord on our hands.

Churchill's relatives were equally concerned. On 12 March 1913 the Duke of Marlborough wrote to his cousin:

> I do not suppose that I shall get a chance of writing you many more letters if you continue your journeys in the air. Really, I consider that you owe it to your wife, family and friends to desist from a practice or pastime – whichever you call it – which is fraught with so much danger to life. It is really wrong of you . . .

Danger there certainly was and fatal accidents came with alarming regularity, even claiming the life of one of the Military Wing's original and most colourful pioneers, Samuel Cody, although it was not due to his own misadventure. In August 1913 Cody had taken up a passenger at Laffan's Plain while his wife watched from the ground. She saw the machine begin to fly erratically and she could clearly see the passenger, apparently taken by fear, grabbing Cody's shoulders. The machine turned and dived before hitting the ground, killing both men. Cody was given an RFC funeral with full military honours, as James Gascoyne, DFC, recalled:

In 1913 I was a pupil with a firm of motor engineers in the Midlands, and I saw a newspaper article about the Royal Flying Corps. I had not even heard of it until then and it fired my imagination. It seemed to me a wonderful idea to have a go, and my own training as a motor mechanic was highly relevant to what was being asked for. I reported for initial training and, curiously enough, not long afterwards I was called for duty at the funeral of Colonel Sam Cody. We were told that we would all take part in the funeral. That is because we had advanced sufficiently in our training to be able to walk like soldiers. Each of us had to carry a wreath. It was a very, very ceremonial affair, which lasted about two hours.

Gascoyne was among the early chaps who joined the RFC in the expectation of becoming pilots fairly quickly, only to have their dreams shattered:

I was sent with three others to Netheravon in Wiltshire, where I joined No. 3 Squadron. The aircraft were Blériots with 70-horsepower Gnome engines. No. 4 Squadron, stationed with us, had biplanes. At the time there were only aircraft sheds, station workshops, transport sheds and a guardroom. The two squadrons were to live in tents until the barracks were completed, and the messing was in large marquees. The station was full of life. Having joined the RFC to fly, I thought the prospects were quite good because there were a number of NCOs in the squadron who already had their wings and I discovered that they obtained them by going privately to a school.

Then, when they had qualified, they would be able to draw flying pay. To my astonishment I found that none of them was allowed to fly because flying was still confined entirely to officers. One of those privately trained pilots was Sergeant McCudden, who was put in charge of the transport section. He was a funny little man, but he was very keen and he was rather inclined to be pompous.

His brother, Jimmy, later to win a Victoria Cross [see Chapter Two], came to the squadron soon after I had joined. A third McCudden brother, John, was in one of the other squadrons. Jimmy joined when he was 18, following his brothers into the corps, and was mad keen to become a pilot. When he came to our squadron, he had just come out of detention because, in his keenness for flying, he had started up an aircraft at Farnborough and the engine had pulled him into the side of a hangar and broken it up. What I also remember about him was that he had the most wonderful eyesight; with a revolver or a rifle he could always find the target. It was one of the factors that later added to his success as a fighter pilot. We used to go on the ranges, firing, mostly for revolver practice, but now and again with rifles. Later on, when we got to France, he could always spot a German aircraft a long time before anyone else. I liked Jimmy very much.

James Gascoyne and the McCudden brothers would get their chance in the coming months when eventually the rules that barred all but officers from flying Britain's much-needed and desperately scarce machines were scrapped. Soon, the British military air wings of both the army and the navy would need all the fliers they could get, and Jimmy in particular was among those set to cover themselves with fame and glory as history recorded the first exchanges of war in the air.

By the spring of 1914, as Germany's military might was expanded by the threat of bomb-carrying Zeppelins, pressure on the RFC to provide a viable air force intensified. The whole of the military wing was to be based at Netheravon with a new aerodrome under construction at nearby Larkhill. The commanders had set out their stall, pulled the British air force up by its bootstraps, instilled strong discipline and procedures, all intended to excite and inspire its pilots and ground staff, and showed the government what they could do on a shoestring budget. Even so, although its manpower and aircraft had increased dramatically in the two years since its foundation, the RFC was still two squadrons short of the targets set by the Committee for Imperial Defence. Winston Churchill was well aware that the RFC was ill equipped for the task that surely lay ahead, although he had for months remained something of a lone voice among the ministerial hierarchy in calling for immediate action to turn the British air contingent into a fighting force instead of merely applying them to the designated role of observers for the Expeditionary Forces. He had done what he could in his own sphere to at least put up some kind of show, and as the war loomed he formally launched the Royal Naval Air Service, which was, initially at least, to operate separately from the RFC. Churchill explained in *The World Crisis*:

> I had in my own hand on the eve of the war 50 efficient naval machines or about one-third the number in the possession of the army. The War Office viewed this development with disfavour and claimed they alone should be charged with the responsibility of home defence. When asked how they proposed to discharge this duty, they admitted sorrowfully that they had not got the machines and could not get the money. They adhered, however, to the principle.

Churchill was right on all counts. As the First World War began, Germany's armies swept through the Low Countries to attack France along the border with Belgium. The French counterattacked in the region of Alsace-Lorraine, and the British Expeditionary Force planned to move into position beyond Maubeuge just inside the southern corner of Belgium in accord with a deployment proposal originally drawn up a decade earlier, when aircraft were never part of the equation. All operational squadrons apart from No. 1, which was still the preserve of balloons and airships, were to gather near Dover on 12 August 1914. The mass exodus from Netheravon did not go without mishap. There were at least three crashes, one of them fatal. The mechanic James McCudden, then 19, had turned the prop and watched the plane take off. Minutes later, he had his first experience of death ahead of a war that was to turn him into one of Britain's first heroes of the air. His own words, quoted in the *Daily Mail* at the time, represent a poignant reflection of his thoughts about the incident, long before he was himself darting about the skies over France and sending many a German pilot to his death. The crashed plane was piloted by Second Lieutenant Robert Skene, with McCudden's good friend and fellow air mechanic Keith Barlow on board:

> I heard the engine stop and then an awful crash, which once heard is never forgotten. I ran for half a mile and found the machine in a small copse. I pulled the wreckage away from the occupants and found them both dead. I shall never forget that morning at about half-past six, kneeling by poor Keith Barlow and looking at the rising sun and then again at poor Barlow, who had no superficial injury and was killed purely by concussion, and wondering if war was going to be like this always.

It was, and more. McCudden went on to become the most decorated British pilot in the First World War, he survived hundreds of air battles but was dead at 23, killed in almost an identical accident to the one he had witnessed at Netheravon.

The aircraft were assembled at Dover and prepared for a grand takeoff to the war zone while the transport, stores, engineers, mechanics and spare pilots went by sea. In all, there were 105 officers and 750 other ranks from four squadrons, a minuscule figure compared with the armies now massing towards each other across the English Channel. James Gascoyne, still waiting for the chance to fly his own plane, was among the seagoing party:

> We landed at Le Havre and travelled on to Maubeuge, where we were to begin operations. The aircraft were already there, as were the Germans, who used to fly over. German aircraft came over at about a thousand feet, and we were all called out with rifles to shoot at them, but we never had any success. We were all quite hopeless. We suffered a number of accidental fatalities and a few lucky escapes. One day Captain Egerton took off with an observer by the name of Lerwell, and as he did so one of

23

his landing wheels fell away. Then another pilot took off in a Sopwith Pup, carrying the wheel which he tried to hold up as he flew over Egerton's aircraft. Unfortunately, as he flew lower over the top of him he hit his tailplane, and the two aircraft became locked together and they fell from a height of about two hundred feet and hit the ground. Miraculously, none of them was killed. All were very badly injured, but they survived to fly again. There was one song No. 3 Squadron officers used to sing in their mess. It went something like this:

> Wrap me up in my old flying jacket
> And say a poor airman lies low.
> Then six stalwart airmen shall carry me
> With steps that are mournful and slow.
> Take the crankshaft from out of my body;
> Take the piston from out of my brain,
> Then the workshop with all its mechanics
> Will make it to fly once again.

CHAPTER TWO

Aces and Heroes

Although Winston Churchill had criticised the War Office for aligning virtually the entire force of the RFC to reconnaissance tasks for the British Expeditionary Forces, there is no doubt that their pilots played a pivotal role in the early months of the war. The surprisingly rapid movement of the massive German armies across the Low Countries and into France could be observed from the air, and the strength and method of the advance towards the first British positions at Mons was plotted almost hourly by RFC observers. The RFC made continuous flights over enemy positions, and their arrival back at base was eagerly awaited by the BEF commanders. Those early sorties were generally made in aircraft that were barely suited to haste or covert flight and which attracted almost immediate fire from the ground. Some were single-seaters; others struggled with the added weight of an observer. They had very little equipment, usually just a map strapped to one knee and a pad with a pencil attached with string. On one of his first missions, Lieutenant C.E.C. Rabagliati, with No. 5 Squadron, flying east from Maubeuge, recorded stark recollections of what he discovered:

> As soon as we got over our area, instead of seeing a few odd German troops, I saw the whole area covered with hordes of field grey uniforms, advancing infantry, cavalry, transport and guns. The place was alive with Germans. My pilot and I

were completely astounded – it was infinitely more than we had been expecting. We very busily covered the area, made marks on the map and noted as much as we could. I was completely horrified. We came roaring back, and when we landed I was put into a motorcar by my squadron commander and taken off to GHQ, which was in a château some miles away. When we arrived, we were ushered into a room with a lot of elderly gentlemen covered in gold braid and the rest of it . . . all senior generals. Somebody announced us, saying: 'Here's a boy from the Flying Corps . . . come here and sit down.'

The RFC 'boy' reported what he had seen, and the generals listened intently. But as the questioning went on, Rabagliati noticed that their interest seemed to be waning somewhat and they began asking general questions about flying, such as 'What do you do if your engine stops?' In the end, the 'boy' was sent away with the distinct feeling that it had all been a waste of time. One of the generals told him: 'This is very interesting, what you've got, but, you know, our information – which of course is correct – proves that I don't think you have seen as much as you think you have.'

But he had, and further reconnaissance flights proved that the Germans did indeed have a huge presence and were bearing down on British positions fast, as the generals soon discovered. RFC warnings from those missions alone saved hundreds of lives, enabling the British commanders to order a demoralising but necessary retreat from the Belgian border before the Germans could launch what would have been a devastating attack. Even as the retreat began, German shells were already hitting the RFC's makeshift aerodrome. The backward movement of the Allies continued for 14 days before the British and French armies, with the aid of crucial RFC intelligence, halted at the River Marne to begin their counterattack and thwart the Germans' planned right turn towards Paris.

For the RFC, the continual shifting from one site to another proved a major problem, especially in the poor prevailing weather. They were glad when that halt came during the six-day Battle of Marne, but even so conditions were treacherous for the pilots and backup teams facing war on the run. There were many incidents in those early days, not least because of the weather. James Gascoyne again:

> When the British troops reached the Marne, we were stationed behind, and the first night we were there a terrific storm blew up with gale-force winds. All the aircraft were picketed out, tied down with ropes. The whole squadron was turned out, and we stayed there all night literally hanging on to the aircraft, five or six people on the wings and others holding on to the tailplane for dear life. We saved the lot, and they were able to fly again the next day. Of course, the weather affected our landing areas. The aircraft did not require a very long run to either take off or land, and we generally used ordinary meadows or fields. But by about October we found the fields were getting into such a devil of a mess it was necessary to collect cinders and ashes, anything we could lay our hands on, and French workers were employed spreading them all over the field.
>
> We had our lighter moments too. There was one outstanding character among the pilots, named Gordon Bell. He was a civilian pilot who joined No. 3 Squadron, and he was flying an aircraft called the Bristol Bullet. The first thing I remember about him, during a retreat from one of our fields, he was sent to see the doctor. In those days they were army medical officers; we had no doctor on the squadron. The doctor said to him: 'Now then, Bell, do you smoke very much?' Bell's reply was – he stuttered very badly: 'I-I-I don't drink and I-I-I don't smoke and I don't f-f-f-find fault with those that do.' Two days later, we landed at a field we were using for the aircraft during the retreat and he missed it and came down in another field. The Bristol Bullet turned up on its nose with its tail sticking up in the air. Popham, who was then a quartermaster-general, came over, saw Bell walking towards him and said: 'Where's your machine?' Bell turned round and said: 'Over there in that b-b-b-blasted field of f-f-f-fucking cabbages.'
>
> Bell was a great man for acrobatic stunts in the air, and back in England in his civvy days he'd made a habit of flying through the open hangars at Brooklands. These hangars had doors at each end, and one day Bell was doing his usual

27

stunts around the airfield and again tried to fly through a hangar. But someone had half-closed the door at one end, leaving just enough room for his fuselage to go through. Bell goes in at the open end, flies on only to find that the doors are half-closed. He hits the doors and the aircraft collapses on the ground; everybody tears up expecting to find him dead. There's Bell sitting up in the wreckage and he was saying: 'I knew this would b-b-bloody well happen one of these b-b-bloody days.'

With the Allies and the Germans now fielding some 250 aircraft of similar build and design along the battle zones, aerial confrontation became inevitable. The German pilots were under strict instructions not to engage and to pull away quickly if under attack. Their machines were quicker than the British ones and more often than not the enemy escaped with ease. There were occasions when fire was exchanged, and the first RFC pilot wounded in action by means other than crashing his plane took a bullet in the buttocks, fired upwards through his seat by an opposing flier using a handgun. The RFC pilots and observers now began to equip themselves with a small armoury of weapons: pistols, rifles and even shotguns, although some did carry hand grenades with the hopeful intention of flying above their German counterparts and dropping the bomb on them.

Pilots endeavoured to find ways of arming themselves more effectively. One of them, Lieutenant Louis Strange of No. 5 Squadron, spent hours mounting a Lewis machine-gun to his Henri Farman plane on which he was to be joined by colleague Lieutenant Penn Gaskell to work the gun. He was convinced that he would lead the way towards the day when both sides would have fighter planes. Although his prediction was correct, this episode was a false dawn, especially in the tardy Farman. In his book *Recollections of an Airman*, Strange admitted:

The enemy machine made off while we were still climbing up over our aerodrome, and I imagine the occupants must have enjoyed a good laugh at our futile efforts. But my disappointment was increased when I landed because our CO came to the conclusion that I would have a better chance of coming to grips with any aerial invaders if I lightened my machine by dispensing with my Lewis gun. He therefore promptly ordered me to unship both it and the mounting I had been at some pains to devise for it, telling my observer he would have to manage with a rifle in future.

Another young pilot who devised his own machine-gun mount – more successfully – was Lance-Corporal George Hawker, who at 23 was a major in the RFC and was the first 'ace' among British Empire pilots – a title given to heroes of the skies, from either side of the conflict, who shot down five or more enemy planes. He was known as an aggressive combat pilot whose motto was 'Attack Everything'. Flying a BE2c, he attacked the Zeppelin sheds at Gontrode in April 1915 by dropping hand grenades over the side of his plane, for which he was awarded a Distinguished Service Order. He then devised a mount for attaching a Lewis gun to his Bristol Scout, and while testing his invention he chased off one German aircraft and brought down two others. For this action, he was the first pilot to receive the Victoria Cross for aerial combat. Hawker was killed the following year in one of the longest dogfights of the war, eventually shot down behind German lines by Manfred von Richthofen.

Strange and Hawker had the right idea for incorporating machine-guns on their planes. More powerful engines and better aircraft designs were on the drawing board in all the major aircraft manufacturing centres of Britain and Europe and soon led to the emergence of fighters as a particular breed of aircraft, not to mention the equally special breed of daredevil pilots to fly them. Machine-guns were already being included in future designs, although their successful operation had thus far eluded even the best brains in the aircraft industry. The Vickers company in Britain had built a two-seater biplane of pusher configuration that was armed with a machine-gun fired by an observer, who sat somewhat precariously in front of the pilot. As Strange had found, the weight of the contraption was too great for the power of the engine, and the Vickers FB5 Gunbus, a more powerful and streamlined version, was destined to enter service in 1915.

The French had a similar aircraft already in production, called the Voisin, also of the pusher configuration, which was in action by the late autumn of 1914. But again with two men and a heavy gun on board, performance was poor, and the race was on to discover a way of mounting a machine-gun on the faster, single-seater aircraft with a front-end propeller. So far, efforts to aim the gun effectively without hitting the aircraft's own propeller had proved elusive. The solution to the problem emerged in the spring of 1915 in the form of an interrupter gear, or gun-synchronising device, designed by the French engineer Raymond Saulnier, which regulated a machine-gun's fire so as to enable the bullets to pass between the blades of the spinning propeller. The interrupter was originally designed by Swiss engineer Franz Schneider before the war, but there had been difficulties in achieving the synchronisation. But Saulnier found success working with the famous French pilot Roland Garros, a pre-war sporting hero who had won many international flying events.* They made a significant discovery with a machine-gun fixed rigidly on the fuselage. Garros found that the gun could be aimed accurately simply by pointing the aircraft towards the target and, using the interrupter, calculated that on average 18 of every 25 shots would get through the propeller without hitting the blades. Steel plates were attached to the prop to deflect any shots that hit the blades to prevent them being shot off.

On 1 April 1915 Garros made his first successful attack with his Morane-Saulnier monoplane fitted with this invention. He came upon four German Albatros observation planes and shot one of them down with his machine-gun firing through the propeller. Garros shot down two more German aircraft on 18 April. But the following day Garros himself hit trouble. He was forced to land behind enemy lines with a ruptured fuel line, probably hit by one of his own bullets, and was taken prisoner. He attempted to set fire to the aircraft, but the Germans arrived before any real damage was done and the secret of Saulnier's interrupter gear was captured along with the pilot. German designers were rushed to the scene to examine their prize, and one of them, Anthony Fokker, promptly set to work on a similar device. Combining data from pre-war experiments with the captured Saulnier gear, Fokker swiftly devised his own version of an even more efficient interrupter gear and built it into a monoplane which was virtually an exact copy of Saulnier's Morane. Thus was launched the fast and effective Fokker

* Today, the famous Paris Open tennis complex is named after him.

Eindecker (or monoplane), which was rushed into action in July 1915 and became the Germans' most dastardly weapon in the air. It marked the launch of what was christened by the media 'the Scourge of the Fokker', ranging pretty well unabated over the Western Front for months before the Allies could match it with their own modifications and faster planes.

This development marked the true beginning of the era of the aces, whose exploits gripped public imagination around the world. Pilots featured in newspaper articles, and those with the highest number of 'kills' – or victories, as they became known later – became household names. Perhaps the most enduring was Germany's Red Baron, Manfred von Richthofen, and although he was indeed Germany's highest-scoring pilot of the First World War, with 80 victories, he came late to the arena.

The world's first ace was undoubtedly Oswald Boelcke, who at 24 years old was chosen to test Anthony Fokker's new machine-gun synchronising device. He was quickly joined by others, including Oberleutnant Max Immelmann, 25, and such was their success that they were both awarded the Order of Merit on 12 January 1916, the first two pilots to receive Prussia's highest award for bravery. The two of them, and others who joined the spree, invented a new style of flying the German Fokkers, and then a fast new Albatross D series came swooping and rolling out of the clouds in the kind of aerobatics never previously seen. Before the year was out, both had been killed – a fate that awaited so many of the young aces who followed in their footsteps.

Immelmann, in his few short months aloft, became known as the Eagle of Lille and, perhaps more than most, introduced the devil-may-care courage that hundreds of fighter pilots now pursued, and paid for with their lives. He was a daring and spectacular flier who invented a number of battle techniques initially dismissed by more experienced fliers as 'stunts' but which none the less were soon in common use and were eventually taught by advanced military flying schools in the UK. The most notable and much discussed became universally known as the Immelmann turn, a half-loop followed by a half-roll.

In little more than eight months of sustained fighter attacks, Immelmann notched up 15 victories before he himself was killed in a dogfight with seven British aircraft. As with many other aces, his demise was surrounded by controversy, with the British claiming that a pilot of an FE2b shot him down, while the Germans insisted that the machine-gun on his Fokker E.III malfunctioned and he shot his own propeller off during the heat of battle.

Oswald Boelcke survived a little longer. His Albatross D.II tangled with a colleague's plane while on an infantry support mission. They both crashed to the ground. The second pilot, Erwin Böhme, survived but Boelcke was killed. In little more than a year since he led the Fokker scourge over the Western Front, he had claimed 40 victories and was established as Germany's leading fighter pilot. In fact, he wrote the manual. He set down his thoughts in what was entitled *Dicta Boelcke*, which was published by the German military as a guide to their pilots. They remained relevant in the Second World War:

1. Climb before and during the approach in order to surprise the enemy from above, and dive on him swiftly from the rear when the moment to attack is at hand.
2. Try to place yourself between the sun and the enemy. This puts the glare of the sun in the enemy's eyes and makes it impossible for him to shoot with any accuracy.
3. Do not fire the machine-guns until the enemy is within range and you have him squarely within your sights.
4. Attack when the enemy least expects it or when he is preoccupied with other duties such as observation, photography or bombing.
5. Never turn your back and try to run away from an enemy fighter. If you are surprised by an attack on your tail, turn and face the enemy with your guns.
6. Keep your eye on the enemy and do not let him deceive you with tricks. If your opponent appears damaged, follow him down until he crashes to be sure he is not faking.
7. Foolish acts of bravery only bring death. The signal of its leaders must be obeyed.

These, then, were the young pilots who led the charge of the Fokkers in 1915–16. According to James Gascoyne, a new song was being sung in the mess rooms of the RFC, adapted to the tune of 'It's a Long Way to Tipperary':

> It's a long way to seven thousand,
> It's a long way to roam.
> It's a long way to seven thousand,
> On a 50-horsepower Gnome.
> With Fokkers buzzing round you
> And the uhlans down below,
> It's a long long way to seven thousand,
> But the safest place I know.

The Allies were now desperately trying to plug the gap in terms of aerial firepower, but it would take time. For most of 1916 and well into 1917, the Germans held the upper hand in the skies with their new leading man, Manfred von Richthofen, and his 'flying circus' of death-defying stunt pilots. As a young cadet, Richthofen climbed a church steeple at Wahlstadt and tied his handkerchief to its lightning rod, just for fun. At the outbreak of war, he was a cavalry officer and saw duty on both the Eastern and Western Fronts before he requested a transfer to the flying service. He recorded his first aerial combat victory on 17 September 1916 and was infamous to troops in the trenches, who marvelled at his blood-red Fokker biplane swooping above the battlegrounds. Before his career was over, he shot down 80 Allied aircraft, became the leading ace of the war and was showered with honours. On 21 April 1918 his career ended when he was shot down over enemy lines by Roy Brown of Canada.

Much of Germany's good run was due to the effective firepower and better, faster engines, notably those designed and manufactured by Daimler and Benz. They were water-cooled, in-line engines which powered the new streamlined Albatros D.I, D.II and D.III series of fighters. They led the way in the design of compact, powerful single-seater fighters with two synchronised machine-guns mounted in front of the pilot on the upper fuselage decking and aimed with a simple ring and bead sight. The design pioneered a generation of fighters, whose concept prevailed for virtually the rest of the twentieth century.

First Fokker and then Albatros fighters gave British airmen a rough time. Some tremendous air battles were fought, and for months the RFC and the Royal Naval Air Service, who were alongside them, suffered horrendous casualties. Questions were raised in the House of Commons to establish if there was any connection between 'stunt flying' and the mounting losses among British fighter planes. There may well have been, but not for the reasons that the questioner had in mind. Quite simply, the British had never had the equipment or training to risk life and limb attempting some of the extreme examples of fighter activity. At this time, an RFC pilot needed to have only 28 hours of solo flying before joining a squadron in France. There was little chance of further training, and rookie pilots were thrown in at the deep end. But all that changed as aircraft improved and schools of advanced training back in Britain actually began teaching 'stunt flying' in 1916. James Gascoyne, with the McCudden brothers and other non-flying recruits from the earliest days of the RFC, went back to England for an advanced pilot training course at Lilbourne, Northamptonshire, that included some of the latest techniques employed by the German aces. Gascoyne recalled:

I had some wonderful instructors there. They taught me to do everything under the sun, from Immelmann turns to looping, rolling, side-slipping and everything. For an Immelmann turn you got up a hell of a lot of engine speed for a dive, then you suddenly took your aircraft up and then did a half-roll at the top and fell straight down again on to the aircraft below. A loop in my days comprised just racing your engine, opening your engine full out, putting it into a slight dive to get full speed, then pulling back the joystick, right back into your stomach, and the machine goes up, over, and then drops, and as it drops you switch off your engine and come smoothly out of it in a glide. That's the loop. It was usually done at a height of a thousand feet or more to give you time to recover in case you lost too much engine speed, and the machine came straight down.

A roll: you are flying straight and level with as much speed as you can get – and then you pull your joystick back into your stomach again and put your hand on the rudder. That causes the aircraft to do a complete turn in the air: that is to say you go upside down and you go right round, and

34

straighten up again. As soon as you've got straight again, you pull the rudder back to neutral and put your joystick back to neutral. That's completed your roll.

A spin: that's easy. You're just flying along, you shut off your engine, pull the nose up and the nose then drops with the weight of the engine and you pull your joystick back and it starts to turn you round. Now to come out of that, all you have to do is to centralise the joystick, put your engine on and you're out. All very simple movements. Another thing I enjoyed: in those days biplanes had wires that braced the two wings together on struts. These wires used to run across the aircraft. They were tapered to avoid air resistance, and we would turn these wires flat in a dive, especially in ground attacks, so that you got a terrific whistling noise going through, and they reckon that used to scare the Hun to death.

At Lilbourne we had three types of aircraft: the Avro, the Sopwith Pup and the SE5. The Avro was an absolutely magnificent machine; you couldn't go wrong with it. It had a Gnome engine, and you could do every stunt in the world without any difficulty whatsoever. The SE5 was the best machine so far as I was concerned. You could do just anything you liked. It was as strong as an ox, and you felt that you were more or less armour-plated right through, although you weren't. That was fitted with a Vickers gun, firing through the propeller. On the top of the centre sections you had a Lewis gun. To get it down to reload it, you had to pull it down on a rail, take a drum out of the side and bang it on, then push it back. This was all supposed to be very easy, but the wind used to catch this thing as you turned it to put it on, and if you weren't careful it shot out of your hand. I lost one and I saw it go back behind my tail and it very nearly hit it.

The Fokker biplane and triplane fighters were more than matched by the SE5 to meet the Germans on their own ground – and beat them. The two air forces became more evenly matched as 1917 progressed, with the Allies slowly taking the upper hand, having introduced the SE5, the Sopwith Camel and the French Nieuport. They were now also taking their aircraft to heights of up to 15,000 feet, an astounding achievement, considering the pilots were still in open cockpits and had no creature comforts whatsoever, nor oxygen. By the autumn of 1917 the Allies were gradually taking control of the air, supported by a massive increase in the production of fast, reliable machines from the factories of France and Britain, although many famous battles and high honours were to be won in the months ahead.

The Fokker D.VII came on stream in 1918, with a power-packed Mercedes engine. Armed with two machine-guns, it had a top speed of almost 120 miles an hour. Britain matched and bettered it, and at the same time introduced two-seater fighters. These included the highly praised Bristol F2b, with its superbly reliable 220-horsepower, Rolls-Royce Falcon V-12 engine and armed with a synchronised machine-gun for the pilot and two movable machine-guns for the observer. The Sopwith and Nieuport series were also upgraded, and then Britain delivered its own *pièce de résistance* with the most awesome fighter of the war, the SE5a. Although it did not reach the battle fronts until 1918, it brought what many have viewed as the final impetus to the Allies winning the war in the air. It had an endurance of two and a half hours, had a manoeuvrable machine-gun on the upper wing that could also be pointed upwards and had a ceiling in excess of 19,000 feet.

The improved range of aircraft was vital, but equally important were the courage and skill of the men who flew in them, both pilots and observers. Many more heroes and aces emerged as the aircrews were abundantly prepared to take risks. A leader among them, although by no means the most popular, was James 'Mac' McCudden, from Gillingham, Kent, whose progress we have followed thus far in these pages. Although he did not get his pilot's certificate until 1916, three years after he joined the RFC, his skills were such that he began instructing new pilots immediately. Already a medal-winner for downing enemy aircraft from his position in the observer's seat, he now went on to become the most decorated pilot by April 1918 just after his twenty-third birthday.

The list of honours was capped in that year by the highest accolade that could be afforded, the Victoria Cross, when McCudden's number of victories had reached 54. 'Of these,' the citation read, '42 [enemy aircraft] have been destroyed, 19 of them on our side of the lines. Only 12 out of the 54 have been driven down, out of control. On two occasions, he had totally destroyed four two-seater enemy aeroplanes on the same day, and on the last occasion all four machines were destroyed in the space of one hour and thirty minutes. While in his present squadron, he has participated in 78 offensive patrols, and in nearly every case has been the leader. On at least 30 occasions, whilst with the same squadron, he has crossed the lines alone, either in pursuit or in quest of enemy aeroplanes. On 30 January 1918, he single-handedly attacked five enemy scouts, as a result of which two were destroyed. On this occasion, he only returned home when the enemy scouts had been driven far east; his Lewis gun ammunition was all finished and the belt of his Vickers gun had broken. As a patrol leader he has at all times shown the utmost gallantry and skill.'

Three months later, with his victory total standing at 57, McCudden was killed, though not by enemy action. His aircraft stalled after takeoff and crashed to the ground. His younger brother, John, also became an ace before he, too, was killed in 1918. It was during the final months of the war that saw the demise of many of the pilots whose exploits had thrilled the British public, their stories recounted endlessly in the newspapers of the day. Many, like McCudden, were to receive the highest honours their nation could bestow – including numerous awards to pilots who had joined the RFC from British Empire nations, such as Australia, Canada and New Zealand.

Not long after McCudden's death, his star pupil, Edward Corringham 'Mick' Mannock, from Aldershot, also succumbed to enemy fire while still only 21 and having attained the rank of major. He had also beaten McCudden's total by four to make him Britain's leading pilot of the First World War in terms of victories. He already had an interesting history. When the war began, he was interned in Turkey while working as an inspector for a British telephone company. After an unsuccessful escape attempt, he became deathly ill and was repatriated by the Turks in 1915. When he recovered, he joined the Royal Army Medical Corps before transferring to the Royal Engineers. Despite a congenital defect that left him virtually blind in his left eye, Mannock was accepted by the Royal Flying Corps in 1917, training under the scrutiny of James McCudden. Often physically sick before going on patrol, Mannock routinely shared victories with other pilots or didn't bother submitting claims for enemy aircraft he'd downed in combat. After selflessly sharing his sixty-first victory with Donald Inglis, a newcomer from New Zealand who had yet to score, Mannock was killed when his aircraft was shot down in flames by machine-gun fire from the ground. Inglis was also brought down by ground fire but survived.

Undoubtedly the most popular of the British heroes, however, was Albert Ball, from Nottingham, who was still only 19 when he began to notch up his 44 victories. He was perhaps the first of the daredevils to experience the hero-worship of the British public. They idolised him. But he was no extrovert pilot full of bravado, and in fact he hated the war. He was deeply religious and known as 'a quiet little chap'. In the air, he was fearless. So keen to become a pilot, he joined the French Air Service in the spring of 1916, flying two-seater biplanes in France with No.13 Squadron. He quickly tired of this and requested a transfer to fighters in No. 11 Squadron, flying Bristol Scouts, and was soon in the headlines, earning a Military Cross in July 1916 and the Distinguished Service Order in September. After a short break, suffering from battle fatigue, Ball transferred to No. 56 Squadron in April 1917. It became known as 'Bloody April' because of the excessive number of British casualties on the ground. But it was also the month in which Ball scored many of his victories. He was noted for developing the tactic of diving on an enemy aircraft and coming up under its belly while blasting away with his machine-guns. He was also the first pilot of the war to attach a mirror to his plane so he could see behind him without turning his head, a practice soon followed by many Allied and German pilots.

Although Ball himself was shot down six times, he always managed to get his plane back to friendly territory. But on 7 May, while on patrol, he was confronted by Manfred von Richthofen's Flying Circus. Alone, he fought bravely, but in the end his plane plummeted to earth. He died in the arms of a French farm girl who found him. He was 20 years old. The details of his demise were unknown for a number of years until the Germans claimed that Ball was involved in a duel with Lothar von Richthofen, the Red Baron's brother. Both crashed to the ground but Lothar survived. Albert was posthumously awarded the Victoria Cross. The day before he was killed, Albert had written in a letter to his fiancée: 'Won't it be nice when all this beastly killing is over, and we can enjoy ourselves and not hurt anyone? I hate this game.' His VC citation read:

> For most conspicuous and consistent bravery, from 25 April to 6 May 1917, during which period Captain Ball took part in 26 combats in the air and destroyed 11 hostile aeroplanes, drove down two out of control and forced several others to land. Flying alone, on one occasion he fought six hostile machines, twice he fought five and once four. When leading two other British planes, he attacked an enemy formation of eight. On each of these occasions he brought down at least one enemy plane and several times his plane was badly damaged. On returning with a damaged plane, he had always to be restrained from immediately going out in another.

William 'Billy' Bishop was another loner, so much so that he gained fame as 'The Lone Hawk' and notched up 72 victories. Born in Owen Sound, Ontario, in 1894, he joined the 8th Canadian Mounted Rifles at the beginning of the war and transferred to the Royal Flying Corps, receiving his pilot's certificate in 1917. Flying the Nieuport 17 and SE5a, his extraordinary eyesight and consistent practice earned him a reputation as a crack shot. He had already been awarded the DFC after scoring 25 victories in just 12 days. On the morning of 2 June 1917, his single-handed attack against a German aerodrome on the Arras Front earned him the Victoria Cross, making Bishop the first Canadian flier to receive this honour. Before the war ended, he found time to write *Winged Warfare*, an autobiographical account of his exploits in the air over France. Because Bishop flew many of his patrols alone, most of his victories were never witnessed. After years of controversy, a television broadcast entitled *The Kid Who Couldn't Miss* led to an inquiry by the Canadian government in 1985. The Standing Senate Committee on Social Affairs, Science and Technology discredited the film and said it was an unfair and inaccurate portrayal of Bishop, who had died in 1954.

The citation for his Victoria Cross in August 1917 recorded

that Bishop had come across an enemy airfield where seven machines, some with their engines running, were on the ground:

> He attacked them from about 50 feet, and a mechanic who was starting one of the engines was seen to fall. One of the machines got off the ground, but at a height of 60 feet Captain Bishop fired 15 rounds into it at very close range and it crashed to the ground. A second machine got off the ground into which he fired 30 rounds at 150 yards' range, and it fell into a tree. Two more machines then rose from the aerodrome. One of these he engaged at a height of 1,000 feet, emptying the rest of his drum of ammunition. This machine crashed 300 yards from the aerodrome, after which Captain Bishop emptied a whole drum into the fourth hostile machine, and then flew back to his station . . . with his machine, which was very badly shot about by machine-gun fire from the ground.

Another Canadian, William George Barker, from Manitoba, had 50 victories. He joined the RFC after a year in the trenches with the Canadian Mounted Rifles and qualified as an observer in August 1916. He shot down his first enemy aircraft from the rear seat of a BE2d. He then went solo after 55 minutes of instruction and received a pilot's certificate in January 1917. By the autumn, he was in Italy where his Sopwith Camel B6313 became the single most successful fighter aircraft of the war, logging more than 379 hours of flight time. Barker shot down 46 enemy aircraft before his aircraft was retired from service. On 27 October 1918, flying alone in a Sopwith Snipe, he found himself facing a massive enemy formation – 60 Fokker D.VIIs flying in stepped heights. Barker did not shy away and in an epic battle shot down four enemy aircraft before he was himself badly shot up, with severe wounds to both legs. Passing out from loss of blood, he managed to crash-land his Snipe behind British lines, an action for which he was awarded the Victoria Cross.

This is but a brief sojourn with the many who received the highest honours for their bravery in the First World War, and at the same time were part of a defining period of aerial combat, inventing techniques that were to be used and expanded on decades later.

CHAPTER THREE

Balloons and Airships

The exploits of the fighter pilots captured public imagination at a time when all nations involved in the appalling slaughter desperately needed heroes. But there were many other emerging airborne operations that were less glamorous but requiring equally innovative skills of those engaged. Large numbers of them were to be drawn from the ranks of the Royal Naval Air Service, whose creator, Winston Churchill, it will be recalled, laid claim to air defences at home. He did so largely by default, when virtually the entire assets of the RFC were hurriedly commandeered by the British Expeditionary Forces in France at the outbreak of the First World War. On 3 September 1914 the War Office formally handed day-to-day responsibility for the aerial defence of the United Kingdom to the Admiralty. The army naturally retained the provision of standing troops, anti-aircraft positions and all other ground cover.

Churchill, meanwhile, was ready for the task and immediately pulled from his briefcase a well-prepared edict on how the First Lord of the Admiralty planned to ensure the defence of the British Isles, given that a new terror in the skies – namely bomb-dropping airships, known after their maker as Zeppelins – was anticipated at any moment. Other forms of aerial bombardment were also expected, especially if – like the UK – the Germans were beginning to perfect the launching of aircraft from the decks of ships. Advance knowledge of the Zeppelins and their actual payload was limited, but enough detail was known to create a huge worry for citizens and politicians alike. Just like the air war in France, a whole new dimension of warfare was about to be launched on the world, although it must be said that the fear eventually proved greater than the reality.

Although the RFC provided the bulk of attacking aircraft as the war developed, ranging through fighters, bombers, ground attacks through strafing enemy positions and even humanitarian missions,* the RNAS pioneered many of the techniques in other forms of aerial combat, including airships, night-flying bombers, aircraft-carrying ships, seaplanes with floats replacing wheels, airborne anti-submarine patrols and torpedoes launched from aircraft. At that moment in time, however, there were no home defences in place to match what was undoubtedly the most feared and formidable aircraft ever seen – the huge and physically frightening airships designed and built in Germany by Ferdinand, Count von Zeppelin, each capable of carrying a substantial load of high-explosive bombs and incendiaries.

Hot-air and hydrogen balloons had been a feature of numerous military campaigns since 1793, when the French formed a company of Aérostiers, the first ever lighter-than-air brigade using the balloons with baskets attached for observation purposes. Zeppelin himself became fascinated by them when he witnessed a balloon flight while serving as a volunteer cavalryman in the American Civil War and spent the rest of his life experimenting with lighter-than-air flight. During that time, three main types emerged into international use: non-rigids, semi-rigids and rigids. Non-rigids were simply balloons with baskets or gondolas for a crew of two or three and used for observation, usually tethered to the ground by cables. Semi-rigids also relied on lighter-than-air internal gas to maintain the balloon's shape, but also had a metal keel that extended along the balloon's base to support a gondola or car – initially the fuselage of obsolete aircraft – suspended beneath. Rigids consisted of a framework of light alloy girders covered with fabric but not airtight. Inside this framework were a number

---

* One of which was to drop food to 13,000 starving British, Indian and Gurkha troops who were besieged for 143 days at Kut-el-Amara, Mesopotamia, in 'the other war' against the Turks in 1915 and whose commanders finally surrendered after a relief column of British troops was itself heavily outgunned, suffering 21,000 casualties.

of gas-filled balloons, each of which could be filled or emptied separately, and it was the internal balloons the airships relied on to stay afloat. Rigids kept their shape whether or not they were filled with gas. The first successful airship was built in France in 1852. It was a cigar-shaped, non-rigid gas bag 143 feet long, driven by a screw propeller from a three-horsepower steam engine. It flew over Paris at a speed of about six mph, and its operation was totally reliant on calm weather. Count von Zeppelin, however, took the designs further than any one of his predecessors and completed his prototype airship in 1900. It was about 420 feet long and 38 feet in diameter; the hydrogen-gas capacity totalled 399,000 cubic feet, and the ship was steered by rudders fore and aft and was driven by two 15-horsepower Daimler internal-combustion engines, each turning two propellers. Two light aluminium gondolas suspended forward and aft carried passengers and crew.

The British army had previously experimented with large airships without great success, including one flown by Colonel Samuel Cody, and had since built and tested a number of smaller models, but it was well into 1915 before satisfactory designs of the semi-rigid type were approved, and only then after considerable pressure from the Admiralty, which inherited the airship development programme from the army when Churchill took over responsibility for home defence. The Admiralty produced its own specification for an airship capable of speeds of 50 mph, carrying two crew, a wireless and 160 pounds of bombs.

They were minuscule compared with the giant Zeppelins, the most famous of which was the LZ70, which was 740 feet long, could reach a height of 16,000 feet and had a range of 7,500 miles. The Zeppelin statistics sounded startlingly impressive, but in fact they were not as good as their publicity, and a large number of German crews had been killed in disastrous accidents even before the craft finally became operational for military purposes. Even so, their very appearance was enough to scare the living daylights out of the British when, by the end of 1914, Germany had nine Zeppelins in operation. Even Kaiser Wilhelm II was afraid of them and stipulated that they were not to overfly his own towns and cities or the royal palaces (especially his own) when, for the first time in history, aerial bombardment of civilian populations and property became a possibility, and then quickly a reality.

The first air raid was carried out by two Zeppelins on 19 January 1915. They hit the east coast without warning and dropped their bombs on Great Yarmouth and King's Lynn. Outrage and panic gripped the nation, and demands for protection by strengthening anti-aircraft defences were demanded by the media and public alike. The best that could be done in the time available was to cobble together a hurried early-warning system, whereby ships and aircraft would keep a special Zeppelin watch and warn by radio of their course. Newly formed mobile anti-aircraft units with searchlights were also increased in numbers so that they could swing into action when warnings were received. The RNAS, who were already manning most of the east-coast airfields, were given priority to open more, and to set up a system of being able to get attacking planes in the air quickly as soon as Zeppelins were spotted.

Hasty proposals were also drawn up to take the fight to the source – to carry out attacks on the Zeppelin bases – and the RNAS set up an immediate programme of concerted missions to that end from a new forward position at Dunkirk. Within a month, some of the first bombing raids ever staged from aircraft were being made against Zeppelin sheds in Cologne, Düsseldorf and Belgium, but it was insufficient to deter future attacks. A number of Zeppelin attacks over Britain followed, leading up to what was considered the most outrageous of all: the bombing of London, first on 10 May – two days after a German U-boat sank the Cunard liner *Lusitania* off the coast of Ireland, killing 1,400 innocent passengers. Little damage was caused by the first Zeppelin raid, but a second, on 29 May, was more successful. In that attack, Zeppelin LZ38, commanded by Hauptmann Erich Linnarz, arrived over Stoke Newington just before midnight and dropped hand grenades and incendiaries on to the houses, killing four people, injuring many more and damaging property. Residents ran out into the streets, crying: 'The Germans are here.' The anti-aircraft equipment that was supposed to bring them down proved useless because Linnarz kept his Zeppelin out of the range of the guns. Nine aircraft took off in a bid to shoot him down, but in spite of the airship's size they were unable to find him in the dark and cloudy skies.

Seven days later, the Zeppelins reappeared over the east coast and launched an attack on Hull, killing 24 people, wounding 40 and damaging a good deal of property. Once again, attacks on the source of the Zeppelins were launched by RNAS squadrons, and on 6 June Erich Linnarz's LZ38 was destroyed while taking on emergency repairs at its shed at Evere, Belgium. A day later, a new navy pilot, Lieutenant Reginald 'Rex' Warneford of No. 1 Squadron, spotted her sister ship, LZ37. Warneford, who was 20, had only recently won his certificate from the Royal Aero Club. He was not especially well liked among his colleagues, and indeed Ben Travers (later famous for his farces) said his 'cocksure and boastful nature annoys us all'.

Be that as it may, at 01.05 on 7 June 1915, Rex Warneford, in a Morane aircraft carrying six 20-pound bombs, caught sight of the LZ37 as it prepared to land near Ghent, Belgium. He recalled at the time: 'I came from behind, but well above the Zeppelin height then 11,000 feet, and switched off my engine to descend on top of him. When close above him (at 7,000 feet altitude) I dropped my bombs, and, while releasing the last, there was an explosion which lifted my machine in the air.'

Unfortunately, the blazing remains of the Zeppelin fell on a convent and killed two nuns and two children. The explosion also turned Warneford's plane upside down, the engine cut out and he had to make a forced landing behind enemy lines. Fortunately, he managed to get it started again and take off before the Germans could reach him. But he acquired a unique accolade – as the first British pilot to shoot down a Zeppelin – and came back to a hero's welcome. For this, he was awarded the Victoria Cross, though sadly it had to be collected by his mother at the ceremony in July. Rex Warneford was by then already dead and buried, killed while on a test flight for a new Farman F27, along with his passenger, Henry Beach Needham, a reporter for an American newspaper.

For the time being, the Germans were undeterred by critics of the Zeppelin force who were now pointing out that these gigantic craft had made no real impression against the infrastructure of British industry. Thus, in the first months of 1916 a massive new attack was launched with nine Zeppelins, all bound for Liverpool and the shipbuilding yards. In fact, they began to unleash their bombs over the Black Country. Seventy people were killed and 113 injured. Public anger was revived, and the government was forced to act. The RFC, which had improved substantially in both men and machines, began moves to regain its responsibility for home defences. The RNAS, on the other hand, would undertake prime responsibility for dealing with enemy aircraft attempting to reach Britain.

The RNAS was also rapidly expanding its own fleet of airships, which began in modest terms in the autumn of 1914. They were not on the lines of the giant Zeppelin-type airships in which field Britain had not been especially successful. Instead, the Admiralty went for the small non-rigid airships, which were to be used throughout the First World War for anti-submarine patrols, convoy escort and coastal reconnaissance. In all, 200 airships would be built, and they maintained a quite remarkable record of protecting coastal convoys from German submarines. They began with the SS model, or Sea Scout, specifically designed for coastal patrols. The RNAS thus assumed full responsibility for airship development from the army and transferred all its airship operations from Farnborough to RNAS Kingsnorth when it took over control in 1914. Captain Thomas Williams was among the early pioneers and went on to become one of Britain's foremost military airship pilots. He placed his memories on record at the Imperial War Museum:

At the outbreak of war I was engaged with a shipping company in the City of London and was exempted from service. This galled me. I didn't feel I was doing my duty or my job. I felt I ought to be fighting with the others and so eventually my father took me up to the Admiralty in November 1914 and found an old crony of his who was an admiral. To my delight the admiral turned to me and said: 'We are starting to build some small airships to fight the submarines. Would you like to command one?' My trembling voice replied: 'Oh yes, sir'.

I was fascinated with flying. But I was put into airships. I was told to report to Wormwood Scrubs, which was practically the only airship station we had then. It was just common land. We used to take off very often with the prevailing wind so that we had to fly over Wormwood Scrubs prison and we could see the prisoners walking round in circles and felt very sorry for them. Every now and then we'd see a white face looking up and hastily dropping their heads there because they weren't supposed to look up.

Our main centre was being completed at Kingsnorth, and it was treated as if aboard a ship; we used naval parlance all the time. We would ask permission to go ashore when we left the station and used naval language. Everything was described as on the starboard or port side. The airships were naval ships of war carrying the White Ensign. The discipline was distinctly stricter, and training was intensive. As soon as a man showed any ability at all he was put in the pilot's seat. When I achieved my pilot's certificate, I was posted to the Royal Naval Airship Station at Anglesey. It was situated in an ideal spot to do the work we were supposed to do, which was to go out over the Irish Sea, or to the south of Ireland, and escort the convoys into Liverpool. It was a small station; one shed accommodating four Sea Scouts, and I was immediately allocated SS25, which was a BE2c airship. They were crude contraptions; they simply had aeroplane bodies hanging underneath the gas bag on wires. But having said that, they were very efficient indeed. We could keep up long hours, but our bomb capacity wasn't very great. We had no armaments at all to begin with and merely carried out observation and issued alerts if we spotted any German submarines. In fact, my first armament was a Webley Scott pistol hanging on a brass hook on the side of the fuselage. Then we had quite small bombs, which were more or less lying loose, rolling about on the floor.

We hung them over the side on bits of string and carried sheath knives to cut the string to drop the bomb. We had no bomb sights; we simply knocked a couple of nails in as a rough indication of the trajectory. So everything was very basic. It had the usual uncomfortable open cockpits – no comfort whatsoever. You had all the rain pouring down your neck, a continual draught everywhere and no sanitary arrangements whatsoever. Some people carried cans and some carried bottles. I evolved my own system which, I believe, became standard in the end. I bored a hole in the floor and attached some rubber hosing to it at the other end – the business end – a petrol funnel, which I hooked on the side of the fuselage. I found that was a distinct home comfort.

Our task was to get out to sea and be at a spot where we'd pick up the incoming convoys, which often meant scores of ships led by a battleship or cruiser and at least four destroyers running around like dogs chasing chickens. But if there was nothing special on I aimed to get airships out on the routes because not every ship was in convoy; there were some stragglers, particularly foreign vessels, and we'd be out looking for them and mothering them as far as we could. And to do that meant that we wanted to be out at sea by dawn, particularly as that was the time when German submarines would come to the surface.

New improved versions were on the way as the Admiralty began to set great score against the potential of airships for home defences and for patrolling the vital shipping lanes that gave passage to vital supplies. The Coastal Class airships were slightly larger and appeared at Kingsnorth in May 1915. They carried a four-man crew and a useful payload of bombs, although the engines were soon upgraded to allow the airships to stay aloft for a patrol lasting a full 12 hours, carrying nearly a half-ton of bombs or depth-bombs. They were armed with two Lewis machine-guns for self-protection. The car was better too. It was covered with plywood with four portholes and a glass floor panel. The cockpit, however, remained uncomfortably open to the elements. Further improvements were introduced the following year in a model named Zero, and Captain Williams put this at the top of his list as the finest aircraft ever made:

It had what we'd been pleading for all the time: a boat-shaped body that could float on the water. It had seats for three men. Up in the bow was a man who had dual duties; he doubled as a wireless operator – a very simple Morse outfit in those days – and was otherwise engaged as a gunner. He had a machine-gun, which he could fire over the bows. In the middle sat the pilot, whose job was to fly the airship. He would do the elevation with his right hand on the wheel, steer with his feet, control the engine with his left hand and with any other hand he could spare at the moment, operate the gas controls and pressures, and so on. And in the rear, just in front of the engine, because it was a

48

pusher type, sat your engineer, whose job was to make sure the engine was running efficiently. We had a sea anchor, a canvas bag on a grommet, which we could run down the trail rope, and that would anchor us in the water – if we were lucky. We could run down a grapnel for land work, and on striking the ground the prongs would spring out.* So that if you trailed through a hedge, the prongs of the grapnel would hook into it, which was very useful indeed. It had the feeling of a real airship instead of a botched-up job of half an aeroplane and half an airship as we'd had before.

Even larger airships were introduced as the war progressed, including one non-rigid in 1917 which had an endurance of 20 hours and could travel at 55 mph when the engine worked properly. The car was fully enclosed and carried a crew of 10, who now had a few home comforts aboard, including a hotplate for cooking. None of the British-built ships, however, could be compared in size with the Zeppelin, and in a move towards larger airships and longer patrols and endurance Britain had ordered a semi-rigid airship from Italy at the beginning of 1918. Captain Williams was informed that he had been given the 'honour' of flying the huge craft to England in what would be the first flight of any kind between Italy and the United Kingdom. He took with him a crew of eight and five VIP passengers.

The semi-rigids were in their infancy, and this was Britain's first – and called SR1. The whole party travelled to Rome – four officers and ten other ranks. Captain George Meager and myself were the flying pilots. It was of the medium size, about half a million cubic feet of hydrogen. It had two main engines, and in order to give us a little bit more speed to get home a smaller aeroplane engine was put over the top of the control car – which proved to be a pest. The two main engines had reversible blades to the propellers which could act as brakes, so that you could come up at speed, put your main engines in reverse and pull up standing. The Italians –

* Numerous chimneypots, chicken coops, washing lines and farmers' fences went missing, especially during training sessions, when young pilots tried to anchor their craft.

rather to our surprise – came in to land much faster than we were used to because they were able to brake. Matter of fact, they had a hospital at the aerodrome where they would put damaged landing parties. They'd knock men over, you see, as they made a grab for the ropes. They'd get dragged along and they were going rather faster than we thought was right.

We waited several weeks there to get the ideal weather and eventually set off in October 1918. The journey home was a nightmare. The first thing that happened to us after the first day's flight was to find that the shed that was supposed to be waiting for us in France was too small. And that applied throughout the whole journey. In other words, we had to moor out in the open the whole way home, and it took us four days. We hit thick fog at Paris and passed the Eiffel Tower so closely I could have thrown a biscuit on the top of it. Some time during the day, still in this awful thick fog, I eased the ship down and down and down to get a view of our position, hopefully near the coast, and suddenly I found I was looking right in the face of a cow.

Very soon we came out over the sea at Dieppe and then, in contrast to our previous dearth of wireless messages, the air was now full of them; every wireless station in the country seemed to be looking for SR1. 'Where the hell have you been?' Everybody was looking for us. We had instructions to land at Kingsnorth, and a shed was being cleared for us. A number of familiar faces in the people waiting to receive us, and they were looking at us in amazement; we must have looked a dreadful sight. We were all soaked in black oil; we hadn't shaved for four or five days and our eyes were bloodshot; we were pretty well stone-deaf from the roar of the engines all the time. We crawled out of the ship and got on the ground and our own friends didn't recognise us. We were taken into the shed and everything tied up and then we more or less collapsed. We were taken and fed like children and put to bed.

The army had, in the meantime, retained its own balloon sections for observation purposes and they saw valuable service on a number of fronts. But they were precariously dangerous, as Walter Glenn Ostler recorded:

When the war broke out the railway exempted me. I was in what they called a key job. They thought they just could not carry on without booking clerks. I was six feet two inches tall and very soon patriotism built up very intensely around London. On alternate weeks I used to meet my fiancée at Finsbury Park. Being so tall and fairly conspicuous, I suppose, I was soon made to feel that my place would be in the forces. In fact, on one or two occasions I was given white feathers. One I well remember was in a very crowded tramcar, going home to Wood Green one night. This lady simply pushed up alongside me and stuck this white feather in my buttonhole, much to my embarrassment. So I applied for release to join the service and got it after an argument. On 30 August 1915 I went up to the main recruiting office in Whitehall and was pleased and excited to be accepted for the RFC, which they were pushing as the esprit de corps. I reported to Farnborough for four weeks' square-bashing. Recruits were coming through in great numbers: hundreds, each afternoon. You would see them marching up to the camp gate in their civvies, and there just wasn't room for us in the camp. We were under canvas; the barrack blocks were full. I was selected for training at the British School of Telegraphy at Stockwell, London, and after that I found myself quickly on the train to Barnes and Roehampton, the actual place you were equipped for an overseas posting which, in my case, was to Salonika and the Struma Valley with the 17th Kite Balloon Section, which had 120 men. My first base there was Mikra Bay, about six miles outside Salonika along the coast.

Ours was a self-contained unit with its own cookhouse, its own gas-making squad, its own MT drivers, its own telephone exchange and telephonists. The gas-making squad was responsible for making the gas from silicon and caustic soda and I don't know what other ingredients – but highly dangerous. It was a piece of machinery on a lorry. They used quite a lot of water, so they had to be near a river. They used to make the gas and put it in a nursery balloon, which was tied off and manhandled down to feed the gas into the main balloon. An officer with experience would signal when it had sufficient gas for buoyancy.

There were far more balloon hands in the squadron than anywhere else. It was their job to see that the balloon was topped up and to move the balloon from its normal bed, where it was held down by sandbags hooked in the rigging and tied down to corkscrew stakes twisted in the ground. It would be manhandled from its bed to the winch. There were winch operators too. It was a normal winch on a lorry, and the balloon would be fastened on to the cable from the winch and the buoyancy of the balloon would pull out the steel cable as it went up to 5,000 or 5,500 feet. The observers were all officers; we had about six or eight of them, and they would go up in rota and keep watch over the entire front for any untoward movement of the enemy. They were connected from the balloon basket down to our own telephone exchange by a telephone cable, which ran down through the winch cable. From our own telephone exchange we were in communication with all the batteries around. In fact, one battery was eight miles from our position and the telephone line needed patrolling every morning to make sure that there was not a break in it. Because whenever that battery wanted to fire, or whenever we saw anything that could be fired on, we could get in touch immediately with the batteries. The first night we were there, we bedded down under canvas and our battery started to fire. It shook the ground from under us. We then realised that this battery was barely a stone's throw from us, but so beautifully camouflaged that we hadn't seen it. This quite quickly drew fire from the enemy, too, and we were soon under fire. One thing the Kite Balloon Section did not like was being shelled, as there is no retaliation.

What we usually did when Jerry had got us pinpointed on the ground was flit. And we flitted. Everything was packed on the transport; the balloon was manhandled by the balloon hands and we simply walked across country. At our new point, we had to get set up quickly, rig up our telephone exchange so we were operative by eight the next morning. Our mission was spotting artillery batteries. Our observers each specialised in one part of the front, and when a target area had been selected, that particular officer would go up in the balloon basket, the height anything up to 5,500 feet and with a pair of binoculars. The balloon basket was about three feet high and each side were walks on a wooden frame. On the front and the rear were two parachutes hanging outside the basket. These parachutes were rather interesting in that they were the Guardian Angel type and were packed in a casing rather like a big fat umbrella. The silk of the parachute was pushed to the top and was very carefully packed and ended up in a rope, which was held into position simply by an elastic band, which could be broken at a pull. The other end of the rope finished up in an eye-splice, which was trailing in the basket.

The parachute harness was got into by putting one's legs through two loops of canvas; it crossed over the back and came over the shoulders with a belt. They were to be used in cases of emergency, such as the balloon getting shot down and you had to jump out. The observer had a microphone slung around his neck and, looking down on the target, he pinpointed enemy positions by telephone to the gun pit itself, which might be miles away.

Before I went up in the balloon I was given no training at all. I knew the country from the map. Once up there, the whole panoramic view of the front lay before you, almost under your feet, as it were. We had no special clothing. We were just dressed normally. It was very nice to get 5,000 feet above the earth on a blazing-hot day, where the air was that much cooler. By the middle of the summer, the heat was so intense on the ground that from about ten-thirty in the morning until about three in the afternoon, everything packed up; dead quiet. The war stopped. The war started again between three and four in the afternoon, as it was getting cooler. One gun would go off and then they blazed away all over the shop.

Of course, we also had to be on the lookout for German fighters, not just for the people on the ground – for our own sakes. We had a good deal of trouble with them on our next posting to a station called Orijak Gulley. Increasingly, we began to get reports of hostile aircraft flying around over our lines. It was sent down in code from various observation posts way back, and I would get it on the wireless. But we were not troubled until one day Lieutenant Thrower, who was second in command of the section, was up observing and we were under notice that a German fighter was around. Thrower would have been up about 5,000 feet and, as a bolt out of the blue, came this Albatross with a fixed gun firing through the propeller. He came out of a wisp of cloud, straight down on to the balloon, and in seconds the whole thing was ablaze. Thrower jumped, and the burning balloon passed his parachute on the way down and scorched him. He landed quite safely, looking very white and needing a stiff whisky. This certainly put the wind up all of us. It happened so suddenly. For several days no one went up. It took us a couple of days to fill a new balloon with gas, and we decided to send it up with ballast to see what happened. Sure enough, a German fighter – later identified as ace pilot Leutnant Rudolf von Eschwege, known to his German colleagues as the Eagle of the Aegean – comes down again and shot up the balloon. We lost three or four balloons in a row, and this put an end to all our work on observation, and such a state could not continue.

So Captain Gimmingham went up. He was the CO. He went up one afternoon and again von Eschwege comes down. Although it was in standing orders that observers in the basket must be tied on to their para-chutes, we imagined that Gimmingham was not tied and, in facing the front of the balloon and tying on his parachute, he was shot through the jaw; the bullet had gone clean through the balloon. The German fighter sheered off and Gimmingham jumped. As soon as the parachute took his weight, he fell away, and the parachute floated down to earth quite gently while he fell like a stone. I suppose he fell over 3,000 feet. We all rushed up to where he fell, but of course he was dead.

In the next week or so, we had our own two Lewis guns and seven other machine-guns from one of the regiments, and in the last one or two raids from von Eschwege, where he had shot down an empty balloon, all this lot had blazed away at him without success. He was a most clever fighter. He would come straight down over the top of the balloon, set the thing alight, side-slip, and at low level he would streak off. Something had to be done, and so we approached a Royal Engineers explosives expert for advice as to how to get rid of von Eschwege. The first I knew of it was when an officer came to me and said: 'We must make this balloon basket look as realistic as possible. I'll have a dummy made representing the officer. We'll dress him in Flying Corps uniform. We'll have maps, a sheet of paper, anything, it won't matter, as long as it looks like a map hung from the sides of the basket.'

Little by little I pieced together what was happening. They were putting 200 pounds of high explosives into the basket. It was going to be fired by electrical contact. We put it up again the next morning. It hadn't been up long before the hostile aircraft warning was received. Then all at once von Eschwege came streaking out of a wisp of cloud, straight down towards the balloon with its dummy officer. As he got over the top of it, the man in Operational Post No. 1 said, 'Now', and the man in Operational Post No. 2 depressed his plunger. I have never seen, nor expect to see again, such a huge ball of fire in the air. The result was that it blew the plane's tail off, one wing, and threw von Eschwege out of the cockpit. They all fell in several directions, and the steel cable that had been tethered to the balloon came whistling down.

A huge cheer went up and all started to run towards the spot where von Eschwege was falling. I saw him lying on the grass in his German flying outfit; he looked a young fellow in his early twenties, just a fair-headed boy. We gave him, as we had given Captain Gimmingham previously, a military funeral, and that same night from the Constantinople broadcast of German news came the message: 'In successfully completing his twenty-first victory in the air, Leutnant von Eschwege met a sudden and violent death.' We had no more trouble from German fighter pilots through the whole of the winter, until the following March.

Even so, balloons thereafter were judged to be too vulnerable to attack, with many deaths through accident or fighter action. They were never again used for such purposes after the First World War, although in the Second World War unmanned barrage balloons were used to hamper enemy aircraft. As for airships, the performance of the Zeppelins by no means matched the fear of mass destruction, although in the 1920s and 1930s airship construction went on at pace in both Europe and the United States with some notable successes.*

* The British rigid dirigible R34 made a round-trip transatlantic crossing in July 1919. In 1926 an Italian semi-rigid airship was successfully used by Roald Amundsen, Lincoln Ellsworth and General Umberto Nobile to explore the North Pole. In 1928 the Graf Zeppelin was completed by Zeppelin's successor, Hugo Eckener, and in August 1929 the massive airship flew around the globe in 21 days with a crew of 37 and 16 passengers. In nine years of operations, it had made 590 flights, including 144 ocean crossings. Britain's answer to the Graf Zeppelin was the R101, launched in 1929 with 52 people on board. On the ground, everyone looked skywards as she made her maiden voyage over London. On 5 October 1930 the R101 crashed and exploded into a fireball in heavy rain on a French hillside near Beauvais, killing 44 people on board. Germany pressed on with its own airship services and in 1936 began regular transatlantic passenger flights with the new Hindenburg. These achievements were, however, outweighed by cost and disasters, the last of which ended airship travel for more than half a century. The hydrogen-filled Hindenburg exploded into a ball of flame coming in to land at New Jersey, killing 33 of her passengers and crew.

CHAPTER FOUR

The First Big Bombers

Airships apart, bombing operations from aircraft had a fitful beginning, largely because of the lack of engine power and equipment. Those pilots and observers engaged in such missions in the early days had to run a terrible gauntlet of anti-aircraft fire and enemy fighters, quite apart from having to launch their cargo with their frost-bitten hands. Robust attempts were made in the early stages of the war at utilising existing aircraft for bombing operations over both land and sea but specialised bombers were slow in arriving. The war had reached its fifteenth month before aircraft powerful enough to be designated as bombers were in use by either side. In the meantime, those charged with the task found it very much a make-do-and-mend situation, in which heroics were necessary for survival, and the casualty rate was alarmingly high.

This tardiness in developing a specialised bomber was not for the want of trying. In 1910 the navies of several countries began to experiment with launching torpedoes from low-flying aircraft, usually seaplanes and, later, slinging large bombs underneath aircraft. The problem with a heavy payload, however, was that the plane's performance was severely hampered, thus cutting the pilot's chances of dodging any trouble on the approach. In any event, there was widespread disbelief that any nation would actually use such weapons to attack civilian populations without the risk of reprisal. The Zeppelin raids over the UK brought an end to that misapprehension. As we have seen, the first aeroplane bombing raids were simply grenades tossed over the side. In early 1915 the French Voisin's L-type carried the largest ever bomb cargo, taking around 130 pounds of small bombs that simply lay in the bottom of the cockpit until the observer was ready to throw them at the target with his bare hands. The RFC were also experimenting. James Gascoyne, of No. 3 Squadron, recalled early attempts at daylight bombing when the BEF needed aerial support over the trenches on those appalling battle fronts:

> We began using ordinary army shells, converting them with a fuse cap which exploded on contact with the ground. These bombs were inserted into aluminium tubes made in the station workshops, and a pin was pushed through to hold the bomb in position. When the pilot wished to drop the bomb, he leaned over the side, pulled the pin out and away went the bomb. It was a very primitive affair, and it was all done by eye and guesswork. The bombs were also extremely volatile. On one occasion, Lieutenant Cholmondley was in his aircraft, and the mechanic was busy putting the bombs in. On one of the tubes, the pin hadn't been properly secured and the bomb slid through. The mechanic put his knee under it to stop the bomb going, and the whole thing went up. Four people were killed, including Lieutenant Cholmondley.

The RFC continued its efforts, and indeed the first Victoria Cross to be awarded to an officer of the RFC was the result of similarly crude bombing runs in April 1915, just after the Germans had unleashed a deadly new weapon, a massive cloud of yellow-green gas over the trenches at the Second Battle of Ypres. The Germans had broken through at St-Julien, and aerial observation of the enemy's movements became imperative. Bombing raids were ordered in conjunction with the reconnaissance patrols, particularly against concentrations of German troops in the Ghent region, along with attempts to put rail and road links out of action to prevent reserves being brought up. RFC No. 2 Squadron, then based at Merville (Estaires), near Hazebrouck, a dozen miles from the Belgian border, was given three specific railway targets which the BEF commanders considered vital to the German advance. Most importantly, they wanted a busy Belgian rail junction serving Menin and Courtrai, 35 minutes' flying from base, put out of action. The man tasked with this mission was Second Lieutenant William Rhodes-Moorhouse, an experienced 28-year-old pilot who had trained privately with the Royal Aero Club and had his own aircraft before the war. He and his colleagues were flying solo in their two-seater aircraft so as not to reduce the performance of their aircraft. Each had a hundred-pound bomb slung under the centre section of the fuselage.

Flight Commander Maurice Blake advised his pilots not to go in too low because the wind resistance to the additional load beneath would reduce manoeuvrability and the maximum speed would be cut to less than 70 mph. An unpredictable factor, too, was the possibility of damage to the aircraft as it pulled away from the explosion of the bomb as it dropped. To that point in time, there had been little experience of the blast effects on the aircraft that had dropped powerful explosives. They were to release their bombs as soon as they had a good sight of the target, but the final decision was left to the pilots themselves.

When he reached the vital railhead, Rhodes-Moorhouse made a shallow dive down to 300 feet to ensure a direct hit. As he approached the target, he was met by a hail of machine-gun fire from an elevated position, which turned out to be a German emplacement in the belfry of a local church. The damage to his aircraft and himself was already severe, but Rhodes-Moorhouse held the plane steady and pressed on, leaving the moment of releasing the bomb until the very last. Fresh gunfire from the ground ripped into the fuselage, and Rhodes-Moorhouse, already in difficulty controlling the plane, let the bomb go only to be hit by the effects of the blast itself and from the splintered wreckage as it rose up into the air.

Wrestling with the controls, he pulled away in the face of another barrage of machine-gun fire that ripped into the plane and into himself. In the 40-minute return journey, weak from loss of blood, he struggled to remain conscious, but in spite of his injuries he made a good landing with the engine turned off. Colleagues who rushed to assist him were visibly shocked by what they found, with the plane shot through with holes and the cockpit awash with blood. Rhodes-Moorhouse was lifted from the plane and taken for treatment. Medical Officer Gale discovered, to use his own words, that 'the bullet has ripped the inside of his stomach to pieces'. Rhodes-Moorhouse died the following day, clutching a photograph of his wife and young son. Unusually, the pilot's last request to have his body returned home to England was granted, and there he was given a military funeral with full honours. A month later, it was announced in the *London Gazette* that King George V had approved the posthumous award of the Victoria Cross, the first to be won by an airman.*

The success of the bombing mission, and others in similar vein, were followed up by both the RFC and RNAS. The latter used the same technique to launch torpedoes during the Gallipoli campaign in August 1915 when a British Short Type 184 seaplane sank a Turkish vessel in the Dardanelles, another 'first' in bombing missions.

A hurried reassessment of the use of bombers was under way and designs for heavier attack aircraft, more powerful and with some form of bomb-aiming device, were already on the drawing board. The RFC took delivery of its first aircraft designed specifically as a bomber in 1916, the de Havilland DH4 with a 375-horsepower Rolls-Royce Eagle engine, which gave the aircraft a top speed of 135 mph at 6,500 feet. Although quickly superseded by the DH9, almost 1,450 DH4s were produced in Britain and another 4,846 in the United States. The importance of strategic bombing and accurate attacks on both military and civilian targets had finally been recognised. Initially, they were seeking to carry a payload of 660 pounds of bombs or fitted with a 37-millimetre gun on the nose.

The Admiralty, with Churchill still at the helm prior to his departure in the wake of the Gallipoli disaster, went one step further and commissioned the development of the first specialised heavy night bomber, the Handley Page HP0/100. It was to be operational by January 1916. At the same time, conventional

---

* In May 1940 William Henry Rhodes-Moorhouse, the boy whose photograph was in the hands of the VC hero as he lay dying, was himself 28 years old and a flight lieutenant in the RAF. By sheer coincidence, he was posted to Merville, the same airfield at which the father he never knew was based in the First World War. After the retreat from Dunkirk, he was engaged in the Battle of Britain. In September that year, with the DFC to his credit, he, too, was killed, shot down in combat in a Hawker Hurricane near Tunbridge Wells.

land-based Sopwith Pups made the first ever takeoff from the deck of a merchant ship. It was the first step towards the arrival of true aircraft carriers, culminating in the formation of a squadron of Sopwith Cuckoos assigned to HMS *Argus*. Although the squadron did not become operational until the end of the war, this development alone marked the beginning of the end of battleship dominance at sea and, like all innovations in the nursery of the First World War, the repercussions down the decades of the twentieth century were immense.

All these new procedures demanded an ever increasing degree of professionalism and skill on the part of the men who were at the sharp end. And although the atmosphere of a high-octane sport that had pervaded the early days of flight still miraculously remained, new recruits were for the first time facing a far more intense level of training and discipline, with a meaningful curriculum that entailed rather more than a few flights in an aeroplane. As recounted by James Gascoyne in earlier pages, stunts were very much part of that training from 1916 onwards, so that the new fliers were exposed to all the tricks and techniques that might confront them. This was only a beginning. The prospect of flying the new, powerful – and big – aircraft of the bomber squadrons, needing crews of three and later four, or the peculiarities of night flying with very basic visual aids, such as a map and a torch, all had to be dealt with. The need was urgent.

Germany, like all the air forces of the major nations, were developing bigger aircraft specifically for strategic bombing campaigns, and if anything were ahead of the game. The new threat of formation flying for mass bombing raids had also suddenly appeared on the horizon. Although the big formations did not begin to appear until towards the end of the war, calls for greater preparedness to meet this threat were being voiced loud and clear as early as spring of 1916. The *Daily Mail* picked up the mood of the politicians and public alike when it began a resounding campaign: 'Hit Back! Don't Wait and See!'

The threat became a reality in 1917 when the Germans began rolling out their brand-new twin-engined Gotha pusher biplane bombers to begin a series of daylight raids over London, followed soon afterwards by night-time bombing. They began with lone aircraft, and then for the first time in formation. The first major effort in May of that year saw 23 Gothas bound for London, only to be turned back by poor weather. A month later, 20 bombers set off from Germany and 14 of them reached London to dispose of a total of 72 bombs concentrated on a single square mile of the city, killing 162 and injuring 432. Great damage was also caused to property.

The earlier airship raids had already forced the War Office to step up its defences, which even in late 1915 consisted of only a handful of fighters to intercept the raiders and fairly basic anti-aircraft capability on the ground. By mid-1917 the RFC had to divert men and machines badly needed elsewhere into home defences, deploying a force of 12 squadrons with 110 aircraft, while the RNAS was fully deployed around the coast, running observation and fighter squadrons against both air-borne and seaborne attacks. When the next big German raid of bombers occurred on 7 July 1917, 78 aircraft of the RFC and 17 from the RNAS took off to intercept. The defensive force included 21 different types of fighter aircraft, including some of the very latest. Even so, only one of the attacking bombers was shot down because the bombers were able to maintain greater height.

Over the summer months, bad weather affected the Germans' performance, and in September they switched to night-time bombing, the first of these running on six consecutive nights. As the war ran its course, the casualties on the ground mounted: 557 killed and 1,387 wounded in 51 airship attacks; 857 killed and 2,058 wounded in 52 aircraft bombing raids. The figures were not huge, perhaps, but frightening, and more so because for the early months of bombing missions the Allies were coming second. Finally, the War Office began to get a grip, but it was well into 1917 before organisation and ingenuity took hold among the Allied attacking forces across the Channel to begin serious bombing raids on German targets, although not, as yet, on cities. Major W.E.D. Wardrop had previously served at one of the RNAS coastal stations, at Felixstowe, handling the first flying boats out hunting submarines before he was posted to France in the summer of 1917 as an observer in bombers, for which he had undergone intensive training at the newly created Air Gunnery School. He and his colleagues were kept hanging about in Calais for weeks before they were finally posted to their respective squadrons. He joined No. 7 Squadron (soon to become 207 Squadron, RAF) at Coudekerke:

I was allocated to one of the Handley Pages, No. 3130, the largest type of aircraft I had been involved with. It was still fairly open. We had no oxygen of course, but we had sheepskin boots and leather clothing, and fur-lined gloves and helmet. I personally used to wear a silk stocking on my head before I put my helmet on. I also used to have silk gloves underneath my fur-lined gloves. They were most effective. We were supposed to have whale oil to combat frostbite of the face but I never saw any. I used to put Vaseline on my face and found that very effective until we came back and then you suffered. Frostbite was a regular injury.

Otherwise, the plane was a joy, absolutely secure, like a dreadnought. You immediately realised the power of the Rolls-Royce engines. One felt absolutely confident that the Germans or anybody else could never bring it down, what-ever you did. But of course we would be brought down in due course.* At the time, and like everyone else, we did not consider it possible. We had a three-man crew: the pilot and the observer sat side by side in the front, and a gun-layer sat in the rear. He had two platforms, one higher and one lower. He had three Lewis guns, one for firing back underneath the tail and two at the top. The observer had two Lewis guns in the front cockpit and also had responsibility for the bomb-dropping equipment.

To drop the bombs, he would lie almost prone, and he had five pushes, like bell pushes, and five lights – two red, two green and one white – to guide the pilot to whatever the observer wanted him to do. The two green meant veer to the right, and so on. The pilot was thus able to see exactly what the observer wanted to get him lined up on the target. One also had to calculate the height and the wind drift and take

---

* They were hit by anti-aircraft fire but landed the plane in no man's land. Wardrop and his two colleagues were rescued by Belgians just as German artillery blew the plane to pieces. They managed to get back to base and resumed operations in a new aircraft.

account of the speed of the machine. We carried bombs of various sizes, depending on the target, from 25-pounders, which were sighting bombs, up to, eventually, just one 1,660-pound bomb, a massive thing that did an awful lot of damage. The smaller bombs were stored vertically, tail downwards and nose upwards under an eyebolt. When we were ready to drop, you pulled a lever and released them. The big bomb, the 1,660-pounder, was slung horizontally underneath and you just released it.

Each crew was independent, although if one of us got a good fire going, others would follow in. When we went deep behind German lines, say 250 miles or so, we had to carry more petrol and thus perhaps only three or four 250-pounders. The first time we used the 1,660-pound bomb, the target was a railway siding full of ammunition and we had trouble getting a good sighting. With such a big bomb we were not supposed to go lower than 4,000 to 6,000 feet for the drop, but we were so determined we were going to do something with the wretched great thing that we went down lower than we should and we all got slightly concussed [from the blast]. We woke up over Holland; the machine was more or less flying itself. Agents generally reported on the success or otherwise of a bombing raid, and if you said in your own report that you dropped the bomb on a target and they found it three or four miles away, we had to answer for the misdeed. And of course they now had aerial photography for both targeting and verification.

When we began night bombing, it was a different kettle of fish in so many ways, not least in navigation, where so much depended on your knowledge of the surrounding country-side. You also had to be very careful about lights in the plane. We had torches but we had to remember we could be seen by other aircraft and, if we were low enough on a clear night, from the ground. People lighting a cigarette could often be seen on a dark night. We used to have to try to memorise the landscape [from maps and aerial photographs], especially for precision bombing of docks and railways. When it came to bombing their aerodromes we didn't pull any punches. At night, it was virtually impossible for ground staff to recognise what plane was coming in, although some could identify the engine noise. We'd pretend we were coming in to land and they even put the lights up for us and I would promptly give them what I'd got left in the machine.

By the autumn of 1917 the numbers of aircraft available to the Allies had increased substantially to around 7,500 of some two dozen different types. America's entry into the hostilities brought an additional 1,481 combat aircraft over the coming months. With this additional capacity, special training in night flying was set up for both bomber pilots and observers and their fighter pilots flying with them for protection. Short-distance, low-level bombing runs were also introduced using a variety of aircraft fitted with racks of bombs and guns to hit enemy transport, communications, supplies and, a little later, the troops them-selves. Navigation was still a problem, especially in darkness, and as Dr J.C.F. Hopkins explained in his memoir, the systems were still very basic:

> Although the training we'd had before had made us quite proficient, it hadn't really done much to improve our accu-racy at bombing. It was never easy by any means to pinpoint the actual objective. At that stage of the war, we had no proper bombsights so one can understand it was rather hit or miss. In fact, there were times when the pilot hung the bomb over the side and dropped it with his hands. I shall never forget the awful dismay when I released my big bomb on what I thought was going to be a direct hit on a large building only to see it drop at least three-quarters of a mile or a mile away, even from a matter of about 3,000 feet. It was an awful shock to me to think that one could be so inaccurate. The strong wind had deflected the bomb, which is awfully shattering to somebody who thought they were rather good at bombing.
>
> As to actually finding our targets, we had a mapping officer who did his best. He used to go out with machines at night and fly over sections we operated in. He'd come back with a whole picture of it in his mind. And he would get big sheets of blue sugar-bag paper to paint in the various landmarks and roads, railways, lakes, woods. We found this a great help because it was surprising how realistic these

pictures were when we actually got over the spot. By that time, our objectives were nearly all against transportation. It was the theory that if we could harass the Germans, it was bound to affect their efficiency in the lines, which was found in the end to be quite correct. We could carry enough fuel for only two and a half hours' flying time. So really we could only do 150 miles. We would make two of these trips on one night something like 30 to 40 miles behind the lines; not much more.

In March 1918 a big new German offensive began [after Russia's exit from the war, freeing up massive German troop reinforcements for the Western Front] and the nature of night bombing operations changed dramatically from bombing enemy communications to direct operations against the enemy's ground forces. The operations were very much intensified. We attacked anything where we saw troop movement. But the principal target for attack just for the few days was the main road on which the Germans were advancing rapidly, and we simply concentrated on that. The weather, it so happened, was very fine; bright moonlit nights – we could see almost individual vehicles on the road, and troops. And we just went straight out there, dropped as many bombs as we could, mostly anti-personnel bombs. We'd return as quickly as we could to our aerodrome and there'd be intense activity, loading up the machine, filling up with petrol, oil, getting ready for the next show. We did a great deal of damage; we stopped these columns from going along the key route of their advance, and more or less halted a new breakthrough.

By early 1918, therefore, the RFC/RNAS alliance, along with the Allied air forces, had introduced heavy-duty bombing raids into Germany itself, put up effective low-offensive day and night bombing raids on enemy communications, transport and troops and had greatly increased its stock and range of fighters as they came off the production lines in their hundreds. Already, for some of the more inventive minds in the higher echelons of command, a vision of air power was emerging that saw an independent air force attacking the enemy far from the front lines, destroying essential elements of the enemy's war capability by mass bombing of factories, transport networks, supply units and even centres of government.

By August 1918, as the Battle of Amiens began, the British and French had between them 1,800 aircraft available for that sector alone, and the Royal Air Force (as it had now become with the merging of the RFC and RNAS) was able to provide unprecedented support for the army. In just one section, No. 5 Brigade of the RAF fielded 17 squadrons with 332 aircraft to support the BEF along a front of just 25 miles. After months of German air supremacy, the odds and the action had swung heftily towards the Allies. The RAF, whose creation will be described more fully in Chapter Five, acquired the stock-in-trade of the two organisations, amounting to a vast array of machines, manpower and airfields scattered across the United Kingdom, Europe, Asia, the Middle East and Africa. This greatly enhanced the Allies' ability to put up increasingly larger formations of fighters and bombers in the skies, separately or combined, which once again set new standards and innovations of considerable proportions. James Gascoyne, whose wartime experience we have followed in these pages so far, was in action to the final stages of the war, when so many new techniques came into use. He recalled:

In July 1918 I was in the pool of pilots, which was just outside St-Omer. There were up to a hundred pilots and observers there, all of whom were being held to fill up vacancies caused by casualties in other squadrons. I was eventually posted to No. 92 Squadron, a very mixed outfit, with Americans, Canadians, New Zealanders, South Africans and one or two Englishmen. We were also a very happy lot. You felt you had joined something worth joining. The main duty with 92 was two-hour patrols in which you went normally in a flight of five aircraft. You patrolled at any old height, 5,000 feet, 10,000 feet. Your purpose was to attack any German aircraft doing observation over your own troops or directing artillery fire. If you came across a fighter squadron, you would engage and fight it out. When the fighting had finished, you would each go home. We had no means of direct communication between each other. It was all done by signals.

If the Germans were below us and the flight leader,

usually a captain, waggled his wings, that signified that he was going down. Then you prepared to go down to join in his scrap and it was everyone for themselves. As soon as your leader wanted to break it off, he did so, again by a wing waggle, and off you all went together. Supposing, for example, you see a big German squadron coming towards you – say 10 or 15 aircraft – and you are only five, you obviously break it off rather than be shot down, which would be bound to happen to you.

One evening we took off on an alert, but the other pilot who was coming couldn't start his engine, and I went up alone. I spotted a German observer and I chased him. I was so keen on the chase that I went about 15 miles over the line. Anti-aircraft shells began bursting up all around me and suddenly it stopped. It occurred to me that there was something wrong, and I looked up and there were nine German aircraft in layers of three. The first lot came down, and I went through cloud and managed to evade them. The second lot came down, and just then I heard shots and I looked up and it was one of our squadrons doing a full squadron patrol – 12 aircraft – and they came charging in. I promptly dived straight down, got down as low to the earth as I could – spinning down – as they attacked the Germans and shot two of them down. I didn't want to get shot by my own side.

Identification was always a problem, especially in the clouds. You had to make sure it wasn't an Allied aircraft you were firing at. It was all going along so quickly you just didn't know who you were shooting at, and formation flying, which was in vogue towards the end of the war, was a big help. You'd fly in echelon in three flights; the first of five aircraft, the second of five aircraft and the third of five aircraft. We flew with one in front and one on either side. But when you got into a fight it all broke up. There were also bigger units for formation flying, which could involve several squadrons flying as a wing.

They were used when the army administration had picked out a particular German combination they wanted to attack, ground targets, and they'd send the bombers to attack them and our job was to see they were not pounced on by the Germans. We each had our positions allocated, ready to come down in the event of a big scrap. The Germans were using the same formations, 50 or 60 aircraft together in the air, all spinning around each other and making a lot of noise, tracer bullets flying all over the place. It could get very messy and confusing. The two sets of pilots were about equal in their efficiency by this stage of the war, except that the Germans had one major advantage in the tactics they employed. They generally fought the big air battles over on their side of the line, leaving us to do the attacking. Thus, if an aircraft got hit or the engine stopped, or the pilot got wounded, their pilot could go straight down and land in their own territory and they'd live to fight again, whereas if we were shot down we were prisoners of war. I had some experience of that. I once had my engine shot up when we were about 10 miles behind the line, flying somewhere between 15,000 and 17,000 feet, and I just shut my engine off and planed down. I landed behind our line. But if we'd been flying about 7,000 feet I would have been a prisoner of war.

This was especially likely in air operations in the last months of the war, during the general Allied offensive, when they introduced widespread ground strafing behind the enemy lines. It was for the individual pilot to select his own ground strafing. We just went over the line and looked for anything to shoot up. If you could shoot up transport and block the road, that was a fine thing; you stopped the whole lot. We just went along firing at will and dodging bullets coming up from the ground. By then, we were also armed with Cooper [25-pound] bombs, four on a rack, and you just pulled a plug and away they went. They were very effective when you had a line of transport or a block of stuff. If you tried to bomb a solitary moving target, you wouldn't have much chance hitting it. We had a lot of fun chasing transport columns, which might be 200 yards long.

Few knew it, or even contemplated it, but the war was heading towards its conclusion. There was still violence, death and destruction aplenty in the remaining weeks, but poignant moments too. Ronald Sykes joined the RNAS in April 1917, had 15 hours' flying time and then qualified for his certificate. In September 1917 he was assigned to No. 9 Naval Squadron and a week later scored his first victory before he himself was shot down near St-Pierre-Capelle. He escaped capture by swimming the Yser River. He joined No. 201 Squadron in August 1918 and remembered scenes of high drama as he recorded his reflections of those final months. They included two remarkable stories of demonstrating humanity and a sense of comradeship between opposing airmen that, in their own way, summed up the futility of the slaughter of a generation of young men, which was by then thankfully drawing to a close:

> Captain Sam 'Kink' Kinkead* took five Sopwith Camels to escort bombers on a raid. When the bombers finished their attack, they headed for home . . . putting their noses down and throttles full open to go as fast as fighters. So off they went, and we trailed along behind them, keeping up high because we had a bunch of enemy aircraft up behind us, Fokkers to the north and to the south, but the way to the west was still quite open. We counted 36 enemy aircraft, and to our amazement they just flew alongside us and escorted us back towards the lines. I think Kinkead was just wondering what to do next when a lone Fokker D.VII came out of the formation to our right and flew straight underneath us, fairly asking for a fight. So Kinkead pointed at me, and I dived down, and as soon as I got on top of him and close to him, he just went into sharp turns, and I realised he was very confident that he would keep out of my line of sight. I'd got a bit of speed left from the dive, so I pulled up to do the Immelmann turn, which I liked doing: pulled up to do a half-roll, and then just pulled back hard on the stick and then came down on to him.
>
> As I went up, Kinkead streaked down past me and straight on to the German's tail and there he stuck. They were twisting and turning and half-rolling; vertical banks this way

---

* Kinkead, a South African, joined the RNAS in 1915, saw service in the Dardanelles with No. 3 Naval Wing, and then saw action on the Somme and at Ypres. Flying a Sopwith Camel, Kinkead scored 24 victories and ended the war as 201 Squadron's highest-scoring ace. Described in his DFC citation as a bold and daring airman, he became a distinguished flier after the war but was killed in a crash as he attempted to break the world air-speed record in a Supermarine S5 in 1928.

and all over the sky. I made a few attacks, but he was able to deal with my attacks quite easily. And so I thought my best duty was to guard the leader's tail. To begin with there was a big dogfight going on. The other three Camels stayed up high, and there seemed to be enemy fighters all around them, all over the sky. There were the three of us sticking together in this little compact bunch, going down and down. Well, we went on for a time like that, and then I discovered that the sky had cleared. There were no more German fighters about because we had crossed the line and they had turned back. There were just the three of us: the German and Kinkead with me guarding his tail. We were now down at ground level. Then they were in vertical flight, but Kinkead gave an extra-hard turn on his stick and just managed to get his sight on the German's rudder. He hit that and put it out of action. So the German levelled up and landed and found to his disgust that he was among Australian troops. Kinkead waved and we went back to base. As soon as we landed, Kinkead got a car and drove back to where the Australians were. By that time the German pilot had been taken away to a prisoner-of-war camp, but he'd left a gold cigarette case with the Australians, with the instructions that they were to give it to his victor.

The Australians were very excited about this fight that was going on, and had even got the numbers of our Camels, with Kinkead's number as the winner. So they gave him this gold cigarette case. It was quite a fine thing, with the badges of the German's family and the German Flying Corps on it. That was a wonderful thing for me to witness, as an aerial spectator of this fight with a famous German pilot. We learned later he'd got a squadron of trainees with him. His idea was that he would show them how to break up a British formation and start a real dog-fight. Fortunately for us, it didn't come off that way.

The second incident recalled by Sykes happened soon afterwards, when he was brought down while on a low-offensive mission:

We were doing ground-strafing attacks and had been straf-ing the German infantry. The smoke over the battle area was clearing away, and I could see the trenches. I went back and spotted one advance trench with some Germans in. I dived on it and fired and then I stopped shooting because they were all running down the trench. They seemed to have their hands up, and some British soldiers were just arriving. The Germans were starting to climb out over the parapet at one end of the trench and going off to the west in single file as prisoners. A friend, Nick Carter, who was flying close got hit by something and came down among some bursting shells. He climbed out of the machine and got into a shell-hole and there was a German soldier there, disarmed, waiting to be taken prisoner. This German soldier had got the Iron Cross, which he pinned on my friend's tunic, shook his hand and walked away . . .

Sykes's fighter squadron, like many in the latter stages, was also involved in a significant development: the arrival of air armadas of bombers protected by fighters, huge formations for mass attacks on the battle fronts and eventually on cities. One of the most ardent proponents of such a scheme was Billy Mitchell, the US army officer who was later to be famously court-martialled in 1925 for insubordination after daring to criticise the military hierarchy of his country and suggesting that the United States should build a massive air force, totally independent of the army.

Mitchell was more or less branded a heretic when he prophesied a major shake-up in the use of ground forces, allied to huge strategic bombing operations, mass airborne disbursement of troops and equipment and the eclipse of many of the traditions of warfare still held to be true and sacrosanct by the ageing generals. He became air adviser to General John Pershing, commander-in-chief of the American Expeditionary Force on the Western Front, and his theories were briefly put to the test in September 1918 when Mitchell commanded the largest concentration of Allied air power ever assembled – a French–US force of almost 1,500 planes. In the Meuse-Argonne campaign he used formations of up to 200 planes for the mass bombing of enemy targets. After the war, Mitchell was appointed assistant head of the US air service and continued to propound his expansive theories about the future of air power and transport. Many said he was a dreamer, exaggerating the impossible, but of course he wasn't. Another fan of persistent mass attacks was Major-General Hugh Trenchard, head of the RFC in France, and it was he who, in 1918, organised the first Allied Independent Bomber Force of heavy bombers to raid targets in Germany. This was significant, in that Trenchard was about to become head of the newly formed Royal Air Force and what was tried out then, in the last days of the First World War, would hold important connotations for the next one.

CHAPTER FIVE

Afghan Wars and Action in Iraq

The Royal Air Force was officially born on 1 April 1918 with great pain and apprehension, the unwanted offspring of its parental senior services, the army and navy, and hustled into the world by the War Cabinet against a backdrop of fear and panic among the British public at large. The beginning of the Gotha bombing raids over London and talk of experimental armadas were defining events, confirming once and for all that the island status of the United Kingdom was no longer a relevant factor in the nation's defence against aggressors. Although invasion of her shores was by no means unheard of, Britannia still ruled the waves and by and large maintained control of the great moat that surrounded fortress UK. Suddenly, almost without warning or comprehension, the Grand Fleet, with its battleship-led dominance of the nation's coastlines, had lost its claim to being the sole provider of defensive measures. Far greater dangers were now imminently possible unless Britain could have control of the air too.

The shock waves from that realisation were immense, and the War Cabinet demanded an immediate inquiry into home defences. A committee was appointed to make the study, under the chairmanship of the respected South African politician Lieutenant-General Jan Christian Smuts, who had arrived in the country recently to attend an imperial conference.

The first report appeared within three weeks and criticised the totally inadequate anti-aircraft defences in Britain's major cities. It also suggested that London's position as imperial centre should be given priority protection from the bombers and its most populated areas equipped with air-raid sirens to give the civilian population a chance of survival. (In most parts, it was still left to policemen to race around on their bikes blowing whistles and carrying placards proclaiming the message Take Cover.)

A follow-up report shortly afterwards dealt exclusively with the organisation of Britain's air forces and Smuts pulled no punches. He assessed that they were an organisational mess, riven by backbiting and rivalry among the top brass. He also examined the topical issue of the bombing of enemy cities and, like Billy Mitchell, had no hesitation in saying that aviation was on the brink of playing a much greater role in war. Britain, he insisted, should aim for nothing short of air supremacy, just as she had maintained supremacy at sea, and he prophetically outlined his vision of future combat:

As far as can at present be foreseen, there is absolutely no limit to the scale of its future independent war use, and the day may not be far off when aerial operations with their devastation of enemy lands and destruction of industrial and populous centres on a vast scale may become the principal operations of war, to which the older forms of military and naval operations may become secondary and subordinate.

Of course, there was uproar, acrimony and disbelief among the officers and men of the said military and naval forces. Smuts's theories were tantamount to heresy – much the same reaction, incidentally, as many naval commanders had given to the arrival of submarines. Nor was there even the slightest hint of alacrity, as a result of Smuts's report, when the RFC and RNAS were conjoined in their forced marriage to bring the Royal Air Force into being. Even its new Chief of Air Staff, the army's former RFC stalwart, Major-General Hugh Trenchard, warned the government that they should not expect too much of the new service, and privately told army commanders in France that 'ministers are quite off their heads as to the future of possibilities of aeronautics for ending the war'. He would subsequently change his tune, and once in the job he made the RAF his baby. That did not, however, bring an end to the sniping from the competitive commanders of the army and navy.

Both had kept tabs on the creation of the RAF in the last months of conflict, but when the war was over a resounding turf war broke out and the two senior services again began to fight tooth and nail to prevent the RAF from remaining a solo operation in peacetime. Having failed to have the infant drowned at birth, efforts continued at the highest levels in the ensuing decade to get the RAF disbanded and allow the army and the navy to resume control of their own separate air wings.

The end-of-war figures demonstrated the dramatic progress of the Royal Air Force in the last months of conflict, although it had barely had time to establish itself operationally before the war ended and wholesale demobilisation began. It had inherited 30,000 officers, 260,000 other ranks, 23,000 aircraft (and many acquired under Germany's surrender of arms), 401 airfields across the United Kingdom and another 271 overseas, including those in India and the Middle East. It had more than 180 active squadrons, and the great emphasis placed on training in the latter stages was demonstrated by the 200 training squadrons. It also possessed a range of equipment that had not been invented when the war began, such as synchronised machine-guns, bombsights, onboard wirelesses, aerial cameras, crude night flying aids and other new technologies. But what use was such a vast force in peacetime? And furthermore, with Britain all but bankrupted, who could justify anything but drastic cuts in the defence budgets now that the threat to the United Kingdom had evaporated with the signing of the Treaty of Versailles?

In common with the massive cuts across all services, the RAF provided good business for the newly created aircraft disposal companies. Within a couple of years, it would be slimmed down to a complement of 3,250 officers and 28,000 other ranks, with a stock of around 1,250 aircraft, of which half were classed as non-operational, meaning for transport, training or broken. There were, for example, 70 supposedly operational aircraft in India in the early 1920s, but on one famous day, when a survey of working machinery was conducted, only seven could be classified as being airworthy. Although that was not the norm, it demonstrated in a nutshell the infirmity of a large number of the

77

aircraft. There would be no rush to buy new, either, and so the army and the navy persisted: what is the point of having an independent air force?

Fortunately for the RAF, a great ally returned to the political stage in the general election that followed the Armistice. Winston Churchill came back into government as Secretary of State for War and Air and immediately asked Major-General (later Lord) Hugh Trenchard, who had resigned as head of the RAF a few months earlier, to become Chief of Air Staff. An army officer with Boer War experience, Trenchard had taken command of the Royal Flying Corps in France in 1915. He became the RAF supremo on 15 February 1919 to begin what would become a 10-year stint at the helm, with more or less carte-blanche for moulding and creating the air force that matched his own theories with great emphasis, first and foremost, on training. His ideas were not to everyone's liking, but it is possible that without such a strong character at the top the RAF may well have succumbed to the sniping of those who favoured disbandment, as Sir William Dickson, then a young officer (and later to become Chief of Air Staff), well remembered. Promoted to a staff appointment as ADC to one of Trenchard's senior lieutenants at the Kingsway, London, headquarters, Dickson was close at hand:

> He had this dominating personality, one with a terrific sense of mission. His presence was felt by everyone around him, and much farther than that, too. We were really all running around trying to give expression to his ideas or obey his commands. He was just like Churchill himself. You hadn't time, in a way, to be fond of him or pay attention to whether he was going to be nice or not. You were caught up with his terrific drive which was very infectious and imbued him to all of us. Those who didn't get on with him were got rid of pretty damn quick.

Outside, the Kingsway headquarters were nicknamed by its enemies in other government and military departments as Bolo House (Bolo standing for Bolshie, derived from the leaders of the ongoing Bolshevik revolution in Russia). But Trenchard had an ace up his sleeve, and it was handed to him by Churchill. In private discussions, they formulated ideas about the future of the

RAF that would prove to be of major significance for decades to come, and they were set out in a concise paper for ministerial approval. They were to a large extent anchored in Trenchard's theories about bombing the enemy into submission. Apart from his own pet scheme of setting up schools of excellence to train both aircrew and ground staff, Trenchard included in his projections for the future the first seeds of an idea that the RAF could undertake the role of rapid intervention in far-flung parts of the British Empire whenever trouble arose. The suggestion had immediate appeal: it would be fast and cheap to base bombers overseas to bring unruly groups to heel rather than sending thousands of men in dozens of ships it had needed to this point in history.

Trenchard did not overstate his ambitions. His vision was limited to small wars and outbreaks of unrest, and he maintained there was a clear role for the RAF to step into the breach. It was of such interest to government that a White Paper, *An Outline of the Scheme for the Permanent Organisation of the Royal Air Force*, was rushed into print, put to Parliament by Churchill and rubber-stamped in November 1919. There would be no great expansion programme. Quite the reverse. The new RAF was granted a budget of just £15 million (or £550 million in 2001).

Among the small but hugely significant possibilities buried in the paper were suggestions that 'before long it will prove possible to regard the Royal Air Force units not as an addition to the military garrison but as a substitute for it'. It also discussed establishing bases and airfields 'within easy reach of the most probable centres of unrest'. This one sentence, as will be seen, contained major implications – the scale of which were unimagined at the time – in that military air activity overseas would begin the process of unfolding air routes across national borders, and especially over the many colonial territories in the hands of the British, French, Dutch, Belgians and, late to the game because of the Versailles Treaty restrictions, the Germans. From these beginnings, commercial air travel would soon follow.

Operational opportunities for Trenchard's colonial policeman theories presented themselves within a matter of weeks, and the results were to form the launch-pad for experiments in air warfare that were to resound down the remainder of the twentieth century, and indeed into the twenty-first, when distant, half-forgotten places like the North-West frontier, Kabul and Quetta were suddenly blasted into the headlines at both ends of that time spectrum. The British army in India had been intermittently engaged for decades on the infamous North-West Frontier, reaching into the mountains that separate the subcontinent from Afghanistan, extending 400 miles from north to south, and populated by a raw and ruthless population, divided into many tribes with no central ruler or authority.

The RAF's involvement had been limited so far, merely assisting the army in reconnaissance in 1915. Four years later, things began to get serious again when what was known as the Third Afghan War erupted. Two RAF squadrons, already on hand to assist in whatever way they could, were joined by four others to begin bombing raids against Afghan towns and villages. One of the attacks launched on Kabul was from a Handley Page V/1500, which had already made history by completing the first ever through flight from Europe. It seemed to prove Trenchard's theory about the effectiveness of such missions. Four bombs hit the palace of the local ruler, who immediately put up the white flag and asked for peace terms.

Not every group gave up so easily, if at all. Pathan tribesmen, a murderous breed of fanatical Muslims, saw the arrival of aircraft in the skies above their villages as a new challenge. They were well known for their treacherous, bloodthirsty ways. Tall, lean guerrillas, they enjoyed torturing their British captives, gouging out their eyes, slicing up their flesh while still alive, cutting off their testicles and stuffing them into their mouths, and dreaming up the slowest of unspeakable deaths, sometimes at the hands of their women. To be captured by them meant a slow, agonising draining of life, and British soldiers were warned in advance that if they ever fell into the hands of Pathans, they should kill themselves at the earliest opportunity.

The Pathans and other hostile tribes continued their uprising, and further air attacks were ordered in an attempt to bomb them into submission. The RAF squadrons ran bombing missions every day for 28 days, but after the first week observers reported clear acts of defiance. During the second week, the tribesmen could be seen standing fully in the open on high rocks and outcrops firing rifles at incoming planes, a number of which, surprised by the attacks, were hit. On 14 January 1920, during a raid on the Pathans in the Ahnai Jangi Gorge, six aircraft were severely damaged by a barrage of rifle fire. Three were brought down instantly, and three others managed to limp back to safety but were beyond repair. The revolt eventually became serious enough to merit a full-blown counter-movement by a force of almost 30,000 men from the British army in India. The RAF was heavily used during the offensive and, once the uprising had been contained, remained on station to continue its police activity from the air for many years, as outbreaks of guerrilla warfare continued over this unforgiving landscape. Among those to become involved was William Dickson, who, anxious to get back to flying after his term at Kingsway, was posted to India as a staff officer with No. 1 Indian Wing at Kohat:

The Royal Air Force station at Kohat was a two-squadron wing. It had two operational bomber squadrons, and my appointment was to be the air staff officer under the group captain, who not only flew with the squadrons but was also responsible for their flying training and their direction for whatever operations we were engaged on. We were a general-purpose squadron, bomber and reconnaissance, but primarily there to carry out the policy of what was called in those days air control of the frontier. That, in a nutshell, really meant using air power or the deterrent threat of bombing on recalcitrant tribesmen as a means of preserving order in tribal territory.

It was really a relationship between the political officer and the air force. If a tribe raided into administered territory or committed some other offence, the political officer would then convey a warning to the tribesmen that unless they stopped doing it or unless they paid a fine for their misdemeanour, then punitive action would be inflicted on them. If they persisted, then they would get a warning. Leaflets would be dropped over several days that by a certain date they must evacuate their villages, get into a place of safety with their women and children. On the given date, their village would be destroyed unless their leader paid the fine. Often, this worked without any bloodshed or bombing, but sometimes you got a pig-headed leader and the village was destroyed by our bombers. They soon got tired of living in caves and being bitten by fleas and they would come in and pay the fine and the bombing would stop.

This was felt by Hugh Trenchard and others as a more economical way of preserving order on the Frontier than by the old-fashioned way of sending in a column or brigade of troops, which was of course fighting the tribesman at his own game. Although the army did exactly what we did – burn the villages down and come out again – the tribesmen regarded it as a victory if they killed a few soldiers. Our bombing raids were a very much quicker and more scientific way of controlling them.

We flew everywhere of course. It was the whole beauty of being in the air force, flying right down not only in the Frontier but into Afghanistan to Kabul, or down to Quetta or flying up to the Himalayas to help take supplies to our battalion up in Chitral, where they were inaccessible. One battalion used to go up to Chitral once a year and then was relieved by another battalion. It was a major military operation to get it there and get it back. While they were up there, the only link they had, apart from messengers, with the outer world was the Royal Air Force. And of course great accuracy of bombing and navigation was vital over this very difficult country, where the maps were very poor or even non-existent. We had a detachment at a place called Miramsha in Waziristan which was always much sought after as a place to go for a couple of months in charge of a flight, working in conjunction with the Waziristan scouts. That was also where Lawrence of Arabia was based while trying to escape from publicity after his escapades and got Trenchard's approval to be posted out to India as a leading aircraftsman. He was the orderly room clerk. His whole object was to get away and avoid media interest – but you couldn't get more publicity by doing exactly what he did.

The use of the RAF elsewhere in Britain's colonial empire was similarly expanded to engage them on a number of fronts and involving other legendary figures. One of the first such campaigns was experimental in concept but proved to be a significant starting point for future operations. The Mad Mullah of British Somaliland, as tribal leader Muhammad bin Abdullah Hassan was known to soldiers and the media, had long run a guerrilla campaign against British interests in that country and had successfully evaded four military missions to seek him out and arrest him. When a fifth army operation was planned, involving the deployment of two divisions of troops and the building of a railway to support their movement across country, the hard-up British government balked at the cost. Trenchard was approached by the Colonial Office and the upshot was a scheme to launch air attacks against the Mullah supported only by a relatively small ground force, a battalion of The King's African Rifles along with 500 members of the Camel Corps and 1,500 levies.

Ministers jumped at the suggestion, and an RAF team were taken aboard HMS *Ark Royal* from their base in Egypt with eight DH9 aircraft to sail to Berbera. From there, they moved to attack positions and launched daily bombing raids against the Mad Mullah's stronghold at Medishe. Ground troops moved in to provide additional support, and as the rebels took flight they were chased by the aircraft. The Mullah's own fort at Tale was similarly attacked and captured. He had made his escape to Abyssinia, where he was killed a year later.

The success of the RAF's first major peacetime task outside India was welcomed by the new Colonial Secretary, none other than Winston Churchill, who took over in 1920, and he was naturally keen to expand on the RAF's role as colonial policemen. It was in his mind to reduce the enormous cost of maintaining a British troop presence in troublesome areas by whatever means possible – especially in the Middle East. There, in addition to British troops already *in situ* at bases in colonial possessions and other interests such as Egypt, another 86 battalions of British and Indian soldiers were currently garrisoned in tented cities across Mesopotamia (Iraq), Persia (Iran), Palestine and Transjordan (Jordan) ostensibly to bring stability to territories bequeathed to Britain by the League of Nations at the end of the war. They would all prove to be difficult and volatile and would remain so throughout the twentieth century and beyond. Straightaway, the British simply became the targets of local uprisings that soon swelled into considerable forces, armed with leftovers from the war.

Even more worrying for the ministers back in London was the enormous cost of funding these armies. Churchill called a conference of his Middle East military and political officials in Cairo. The main item on the agenda was how to reduce the British troop commitment. One route chosen and adopted was to pay 'fees' (or bribes) to local leaders to keep their people subdued. The second new and important factor was to employ Churchill's own theory, to let the RAF take the brunt of policing and provide them with the barest minimum of ground forces. His proposals were quickly approved in London, Churchill already having cleared his scheme with Hugh Trenchard, who would be given an increase of one-third in the air force annual budget to take control in the first of the regions targeted for RAF policing – Mesopotamia, or Iraq as it became known in 1922.

The country was still a vast arena of rumbling antagonism, especially around the Kurdish strongholds, and the Turks were staging renewed incursions, trying to regain a foothold in the country they had lost. Even as approval for the new scheme was being won, a major uprising was taking place. Rebel forces numbering 150,000 were moving against British positions, and further British troops were rushed in from neighbouring bases to hold the line. It was almost another year before Trenchard could get his own scheme under way, but once *in situ* it began to run successfully, much to the chagrin of the army generals whose own operations he had replaced. They were even more put out when, for the first time in history, military command of foreign territory was handed to an airman, Air Vice-Marshal John Salmond, whose brother Geoffrey was subsequently to run the RAF in India.

Salmond was initially given eight squadrons to set up shop in Iraq, along with just nine battalions of troops supplied by the British army in India, a contingent of Iraqi levies and six armoured car companies. The results were entirely successful. Iraq was calmed and the British were able to pull tens of thousands of troops out of the region, all of which was achieved against a backdrop of bitter inter-service disputes and back-biting. The response of some senior figures in the British army was ferocious, even to the point of refusing to oblige with resources for the new RAF garrison in Iraq. The comments of some generals was tantamount to wishing that the RAF would crash to earth in what they were convinced would be a futile exercise that would blow up in their faces. Well, it didn't and for the next 16 years the RAF dealt efficiently with local intermittent skirmishes, even to the point of gathering its own intelligence.

By the mid-1920s, air control of the Middle East was more or less established. While obviously not a universal solution to all problems, the theory of air policing had been successfully advanced and was seen as the first steps towards the kind of military activity later to fall into the hands of the parachute regiments and other airborne troops. Even then, the need for new and heavier aircraft for overseas operations brought about some of the most important developments in aviation history.

The most dramatic was the switch from wood to metal for the aircraft mainframe. Then came bigger, faster engines, fully retractable landing gear, enclosed cockpits, gyroscopically driven flight instruments, electrical cockpit lighting – the list of technological innovation was growing by the month. Yet amid this welter of improvement and discovery, the RAF remained fairly anchored to the era of make do and mend. The only limits were set by equipment and machines, and in a post-war decade that saw great social upheaval and industrial unrest in Britain, there was no great rush to re-equip the armed forces.

Even so, some remarkable achievements were made, using relatively old machines. Not least among the side-effects of setting up in India, the Middle East and North Africa came the process of establishing air routes, transporting men and equipment across continents, paving the way for commercial aviation and literally forcing governments and the military to acknowledge the pace of change by adopting new and better aircraft coming off the production lines. Without commercial flight, fledgling manufacturers could not survive, and the progression of both was vital to the continued development of military aircraft. Crucial to all was the development of air routes, enabling aircraft successfully to traverse continents without being shot down for encroaching on national boundaries. Sir William Dickson recalled a significant step when he was ADC to Britain's Air Officer Commanding-in-Chief in India, Air Chief Marshal Sir Geoffrey Salmond:

His brother Sir John Salmond inherited the post of Chief of Air Staff from Lord Trenchard, who (although he had

85

merely moved on, and not died) left a sort of will an testament on how the air force should be developed. The two Salmond brothers, one CAS in the UK and one in India, were under a special obligation to press this idea of greater use of the air. Out of that came many things which were vital to the development of air power. It led eventually to the creation of the bomber transport aircraft because you had to have the ability to bomb tribesmen or recalcitrant elements, as well as a suitable conveyance of supplies up to the area of their command. We also carried a certain number of troops and supplies and then, in turn, it led to the question of air routes. Geoffrey Salmond was a pioneer of that, along with his brother. They were at the fore in establishing the air routes across the world, which were followed by civil aviation in due course.

It began in India itself. We had a magnificent sapper, Colonel [later Sir] John Turner, who was responsible for all the airfields on the subcontinent. They were being developed all over India every 300 miles or so. An airfield was carved out of the mud or the grass and a guard put in charge of a little hut there with some petrol supplies. You could fly all over India with a little red handbook, which described the whole network of airfields. Then it was decided to extend this to Singapore. Colonel Turner, with the people from Singapore, established airfields all the way from Calcutta to Singapore, all about 300 or 400 miles apart. Then the Viceroy of India got an invitation from the King of Siam to send a flight of the Royal Air Force to Siam on the occasion of the annual royal celebrations. Geoffrey Salmond persuaded the Viceroy to accept this invitation as a double thing, not only to accept the invitation of the King of Siam but also to open up this route which he'd been developing to Singapore.

The flight was full of incident, something I will never forget, using just two Wapiti aircraft with open cockpits, Geoffrey Salmond flying behind myself as a pilot. We had a spare Wapiti with Flight Lieutenant Anderson just in case our Wapiti went unserviceable. Then we had a twin-engined transport aircraft which followed up independently with John Turner in it and the luggage and some fitters and riggers. There was just one incident which rather illustrates the conditions of flying in those days. It took place between Calcutta and the town of Akyab, which is along the Burma coast before you get to Rangoon. Everything was done by map-reading. We flew from Dum Dum airfield at Calcutta to the stage at Akyab. But when we were about 60 miles short of Akyab there facing me in the Wapiti was a storm, a huge black cloud the like of which I'd never seen before, absolutely completely black, right down on to the sea, extending inland to the mountains in Burma and right our seaward as far as you could see. There was no way round it and no way above it. It was going up very high. But we'd reached the point of no return because we had insufficient petrol remaining to get us back to Calcutta.

We really had only one choice . . . to follow the coast, which was made up of mangrove swamps and inlets. We plugged our way through this with the rain coming down literally in sheets. Luckily, the engine kept going and we churned our way through, the wheels almost touching the water. After what seemed hours the weather began to lighten up and we came through it. There, a bit off course, away to the left, was the coastline. We turned east and found Akyab and landed. I've never been so relieved about anything in my life. I was about to taxi in to where the hut was when Geoffrey Salmond tapped me on the shoulder and he stood up in the cockpit and I turned round and he held out his hand and we shook hands. It was that kind of experience. We were both absolutely soaked, and all our luggage inside the fuselage was soaked. Even the letter to the King of Siam from the Viceroy was wet. But on we went; flew to Bangkok over the mountains. Nobody had ever flown there before, over the teak jungle. We attended the celebrations at Bangkok, which were very impressive, and went on to Singapore afterwards, and we were there about a week and then flew back again.

In the Middle East, meanwhile, the first ever air route was established between Baghdad and Cairo, a journey of almost 900 miles over extreme terrain of sands and mountains. If journeys were to be completed with worthwhile loads, then a route had to

87

be worked out at ground level providing regular suitable landing places with fuel dumps. This was achieved by sending survey teams in convoys, and so began the difficult task of laying airstrips with white-painted markers. By 1922, converted wartime Vickers Vernon bombers were making the run, capable of carrying 12 passengers in considerable discomfort.

On the strength of these pioneering experiences, Britain went on to establish a network of air routes across its colonial interests which subsequently became the route maps for fledgling airlines. Britain also negotiated agreements with other European countries to reach the Mediterranean – instead of shipping aircraft around the Bay of Biscay – and once there to project outwards using as stepping stones the colonies and protectorates of Malta, Cyprus, Palestine, Transjordan, Iraq, the Persian Gulf protectorates, India, Burma and, later, the Malay protectorate. As endurance was increased, the stepping stone theory made it possible for Britain to establish long-distance hauls without flying over hostile territory. The French forged its air routes through Algeria, home of the French Foreign Legion, which provided access to the French Sahara, French Equatorial Africa and Madagascar. The Belgians and the Dutch, with their respective colonial ties, had similar stage-posts, and by exchanging routes and landing rights those nations opened up the routes for both military and commercial aircraft to their far-flung empires. Many regions would be served by flying boats or seaplanes, which were widely used by the RAF in the Middle East during 16 years of stop-go activity. These planes had the distinct advantage of not requiring landing strips and were used for virtually every purpose, including bombing, patrolling and transport.

In 1935, for example, when the Italian dictator Benito Mussolini began to flex his muscles towards Ethiopia, new flying boats were ordered for delivery to squadrons based in Iraq. They were all moved down to Aden and were supported by additional squadrons brought in from England. The Italians invaded Ethiopia in October and several RAF squadrons were shipped to the Middle East, while some of those already in the area were moved nearer to the war zone, though there was no direct intervention in the conflict.

Flying boats were also deployed, with the squadron of

Singapores from Iraq moving to Aden; Rangoons and Stran-
raers were stationed in Gibraltar with a squadron of Supermarine Scapas, with another of Singapores based in Egypt. All
these remained at their new bases until October 1936, some
months after the Italian invasion had been completed. Airman
Herbert Arnold, who had been stationed at Basra for almost
three years, was among the crews to receive the new boats:

> Our squadron was getting six new flying boats. The ones we
> had previously were Rangoons, which were an adaptation of
> the civilian Calcutta flying boat, and they were not really a
> war plane at all. They were a straightforward adaptation, the
> only six ever built for the RAF, and apart from the military
> equipment inside the boat and the three gun positions which
> had been added, they were virtually the same as the civilian
> Calcutta. We were to take these old boats back and pick up
> our new boats from the factory. The flight commander for
> the trip, Squadron Leader Clift, was retiring, and he was
> determined that he was going to have a good trip home. So
> we had a leisurely ride up the Persian Gulf. We called at
> Kamaran island, Port Sudan, Alexandria, Athens, Crete,
> Corfu, Bizerte, Algiers, Malta, Gibraltar, Lisbon, Hourtin in
> France, and eventually back to Plymouth. But of course it
> wasn't all easy going. Refuelling was something of a prob-
> lem, especially up the Persian Gulf. The fuel was in four-
> gallon drums, which had been previously carted to particular
> points, buried in big mounds of sand and marked on our
> charts. If we called at one of these fuel dumps, we had to get
> the rubber dinghy out, pump it up by hand and row it ashore
> trailing a line. When we got ashore, we would have to dig out
> the drums, take them down to the water's edge one by one,
> tie them to the rope and float them out to the boat. We
> would have to pump the drums out by hand, one man on
> each side of the pump handle.

When we landed at Piraeus in Athens, the Greek air force
came out to escort us and to take us for an evening's enter-
tainment in town. And they'd ordered a meal in the Britannia
restaurant for all of us, officers and airmen. And as we
walked in this restaurant, every customer in the place stood
up and the band played, 'Rule, Britannia!'. Do you think the

Greeks would do that today? I don't think so. We eventually arrived in England and went to the Short brothers factory at Rochester to collect our new machines, the Singapores. We flew back to Felixstowe and put the radio and equipment in them and accepted them for Royal Air Force service. They were much better, sturdily built. They had four engines, two pushers and two pullers. And they were equipped for self-maintaining service. You could leave base for weeks at a time and all you needed was fuel and food.

They were totally self-contained. You had your own bunks and bedding. We carried spares of all sorts on board, even two spare propellers. There was a wardroom at the front for the two officers. One was a pilot and the other was a pilot navigator. Their compartment was divided from the rest of the crew with curtains. And then there were four bunks in the back. We then had to restart our journey back to Aden again. By the time we got back, the emergency was over so we returned to Basra to resume our role as the airborne policemen.

Our normal duties as a squadron were to patrol the Persian Gulf. We had one flying boat in the Persian Gulf pretty well all the time. As one came back, another one went away. No. 84 Squadron was responsible for the southern half of Iraq; No. 30 squadron was at Mosul, and they patrolled the oilfields and the north. And then at Hinaidi, which was just outside Baghdad, No. 70 Squadron was responsible for any transport that was required. Patrols used to go off for about three weeks at a time. Every time we went, we drew ration money in cash. This was six shillings a day for everyone. The officers and airmen were the same; all drew the same amount of money. We bought our own food from the canteen stores, enough tinned food for three or four weeks or as long as the trip may be. This was carried on board and stowed below the floorboards in the bilges of the boat. We always carried a crate of beer as well – 48 bottles of McEwan's Red Label beer. Drinking water was unobtainable around the Gulf, so we carried five-gallon drums of that too.

Our main duties were to check out all the populated places around the Persian Gulf. As we moved from one place to another, we would signal to the navy, which maintained a sloop at Bahrain if we saw any suspicious-looking dhows. They would send the sloop out and intercept the dhow. There was still slave trading going around the Persian Gulf. They would go across and pick up people on the Persian side and take them over to the harems of the Saudi-Arabian side. We'd also carry political agents around the region as well as the sheikhs, from Bahrain, Dubai, Abu Dhabi, Muscat and all the smaller sheikdoms. Basically, we were keeping a profile around the whole region.

Ironically, before long the Singapore flying boats and their crews from Basra were destined for the place that was their namesake – Singapore itself. With the Japanese becoming increasingly belligerent after their invasion of China, the defence of Britain's most important colony in that region suddenly became paramount.

CHAPTER SIX

Woefully Ill Equipped for War

While the RAF's efforts overseas had been well praised, the grave weaknesses in home defences in the United Kingdom, combined with a general lack of resources for its air-force squadrons across the board, caused growing anxiety as tensions across Europe gathered momentum in the early 1930s. In a nation laid low by the General Strike and economic depression, the rearming of the RAF – or the military as a whole, for that matter – had been seriously neglected. Politicians hid behind the supposed hand-cuffing of Germany through the 15 parts of the Treaty of Versailles, the principal feature of which banned Germany's rearmament. This degenerated into an ongoing rule of thumb adopted as a matter of convenience: that no major war could therefore be anticipated for 10 years after 1918, and that thinking was extended and turned into a kind of rolling excuse against Britain's rearmament. Thus, the British government became the laggard of Europe in re-equipping its armed forces, and this woeful inaction continued into the first half of the 1930s. As Air Chief Marshal Sir Michael Armitage wrote: 'Those five years had been permeated by an almost wilful blindness to the dangers facing the country on the part of the British government and an electorate intent on pursuing disarmament, and further eroded by severe economic crisis.'*

* *The Royal Air Force*, Michael Armitage, Cassell, 1993.

The British airmen had to look on enviously as new machines that incorporated some very worthwhile advances in design and performance came into service elsewhere. The truth was that in 1933 – the year of the Nazi takeover in Germany – the RAF possessed only 827 operational aircraft, and more than half of them were already obsolete. Its manpower was virtually the same as the slashed-down total in 1919, and new designs for all types of aircraft were proceeding through the system at a snail's pace. France possessed 1,650 machines, while Italy and Russia had 1,500 each. That year, too, Hitler tore up what remained of the Versailles agreement and was soon boasting that the Luftwaffe would be restored to its former glory by 1938.

With Winston Churchill warning at every opportunity of Britain's inadequate defences, Prime Minister Stanley Baldwin announced in 1934 that the RAF would undergo a complete review. This was prompted by a report on Britain's air defences which concluded that enemy bombers crossing the coast of the United Kingdom at speeds in excess of 200 mph and at a height of 10,000 feet would reach their targets over the nation's capital and industrial heartland before RAF fighters could intercept them. The penny was beginning to drop that the Royal Air Force was ill equipped to meet modern warmongers, i.e. Hitler. Bombing Arabs in Palestine, Kurds in Iraq and Pathans in Afghanistan was all very well, but real war it wasn't.

The change of mood happened almost overnight. Mussolini was on the march, and tens of thousands were seen doing their 'Heil, Hitler!' bit at Nazi rallies. The swastika flags were out and waving. Germany was rearming fast and, when the realisation finally dawned, Baldwin had to make the humiliating announce-ment that a major expansion programme for the RAF would seek to guarantee that Britain would have parity with Germany's new air force by 1938. Here, a mere 17 years after the end of the First World War, was the British Prime Minister admitting that the defeated nation would have an air force better than his own if he was not careful. The truth was that it was already too late. Timidity in government – afraid of upsetting the Germans – and a confusing, unfocused series of expansion plans merely delayed matters further. The ultimate aim was to triple the number of pilots, add 50 new airfields throughout Britain and at least double the stock of operational aircraft. In reality, those figures would soon be seen as a gross underestimation of what was truly required. Worse still, Britain's rediscovered ambition for air supremacy was, for the time being, tied to aircraft being built to 1930–32 specifications and were largely out of date even before they went into production.

However, organisational changes were made to streamline efficiency and to shake off some of the remaining vestiges of the Trenchard legacy, which to some extent had created a class-driven Air Staff in which ability was not necessarily the key to promotion. In 1936 control of air operations was wrested from a single body and handed to four separate commands – Bomber, Fighter, Coastal and Training Commands – each with its own headquarters. New younger men were promoted and an eagerness to get on thankfully began to emerge. Those in Britain who, like the many Hitler appeasers in the upper strata of British society, were still convinced that the increasingly warlike Nazis had no desire to take on Britain again were soon to witness a horrific demonstration of Britain's blatant shortfall in air power. It arrived with two events in 1937 which caused apoplexy among British military planners. The first came on 27 April, when a new dimension to the Spanish Civil War opened up when Hitler sent in the Luftwaffe to help the Fascist dictator General Franco. The Nazi intervention into the Spanish conflict provided, in Churchill's view, a spectacular opportunity to test efficiency and equipment. It was, he would record later, nothing short of a dry run for the future, and this news report vividly captured the moment:

Guernica, the cultural and spiritual home of the Basques, was destroyed yesterday by the bombers of the German air force sent to help Franco by Adolf Hitler. It was market day and the square was crowded when the bombers, Heinkel 1-11s and Junker 52s, escorted by fighters, appeared and pounded Guernica with high explosives; they then set it alight with incendiary bombs and strafed it with machine-gun fire. Eyewitnesses told correspondents of the death that rained down on them. 'They bombed and bombed and bombed,' said the mayor. One reporter, who arrived in the city soon after the planes had left, said: 'As we drew nearer, on both sides of the road, men, women and children were sitting, dazed. I saw a priest in one group. I stopped the car and went up to him. His face was blackened, his clothes in tatters. He couldn't talk. He just pointed to the flames, still about four miles away, then whispered: "Aviones . . . bombas . . . mucho, mucho." In the city soldiers were collecting charred bodies. They were sobbing like children. There were flames and smoke and grit, and the smell of burning human flesh was nauseating. Houses were collapsing into the inferno. It was impossible to go down many of the streets, because they were walls of flame. Debris was piled high. The shocked survivors all had the same story to tell: aeroplanes, bullets, bombs, fire. Today, those who can are leaving Guernica, their possessions loaded into farm wagons pulled by oxen, victims of a calculated act of terror. There were military targets in Guernica; it is a communications centre and it has a munitions factory, but there is no evidence that the German bombers aimed for them. They simply unloaded their bombs indiscriminately on this undefended town.

Even more cruel in its application was a second bombing outrage halfway across the world in the summer of 1937. The incident that finally rammed home the potential of modern air warfare – if such confirmation was still needed – occurred on 29 August, when waves of Japanese bombers and fighters barnstormed out of the sun over the historical city of Shanghai and dropped thousands of tons of incendiary bombs and strafed the city's streets. The air attack to clear the way for Japanese troops advancing across China was the greatest ever slaughter of civilians by attack from the air, with 2,000 instant casualties.

The key feature of both these appalling air raids was the indiscriminate bombing of populated areas regardless of the innocent victims who would be caught in the firestorm. The Germans were testing the capability of their bombers, and especially the noisy, frightening Stuka dive-bombers, which were highly damaging in attack. Bomber escorts also strafed the populace. Me 109 fighters, with lethal wing-mounted machine-guns and aerial cannon, came line abreast in *Rotten*, or pairs, about 200 yards apart. Two of these *Rotten* formed a *Schwarm*, and this flexible formation – called a 'finger-four' by English airmen because the formation matched the splayed fingers of a hand – was eventually adopted by all the major air forces in the Second World War. Noting the German and Japanese techniques, Sir Edgar Ludlow-Hewitt, Commander-in-Chief of Bomber Command, turned on its head the thinking central to the foundations of the RAF when he wrote in a memo: 'Experience in China and Spain seems clearly to indicate that with the aircraft in use in these two theatres at present, fighter escorts are considered absolutely essential for the protection of bomber aircraft. So far as I am aware this policy runs counter to the view long held by the Air Staff.' Indeed it did.

Bombers selected for production in Britain were chosen at a time when the actual designated role of the bomber was the subject of a confusing array of opinions, which were merely exacerbated by the intervention of Sir Thomas Inskip, Minister for Coordination of Defence, who was influenced by cost. The types of bombers selected, therefore, were either single- or twin-engined light bombers. They included the Bristol Blenheim series, which led Britain's new generation of monoplane bombers. It was noted for its speed of 285 mph, which could outpace most fighters at the time of its delivery, but not for long. It maintained its speed by carrying only a small payload. The first edition of Blenheim was virtually obsolete even before the war began, and production was halted by 1942. Although many Blenheims remained in service, they were eventually demoted to distant stations that were glad of anything.

Another new entrant, the Fairey Battle, was powered by a single engine and did not impress. When it came into service in 1937, the Battle was classed specifically as a day bomber to replace the old open-cockpit Hawker Hind, the last biplane bomber in the RAF. The Battle itself was unwanted by the RAF even before it went into full-scale production; but it was at the cheap end of the bomber range and easy to manufacture. It therefore became a key element in the expansion programme, and more than 3,000 were produced before it was finally discontinued at the end of 1940, by which time the RAF was lumbered. The aircraft had a cockpit design that gave little protection to the crew, and its guns were simply no match for marauding fighters. It suffered catastrophic losses in the early stages of the war – including five shot down while on a reconnaissance mission over the French border on 30 September

1939, thus recording the first RAF planes destroyed by the enemy in the Second World War. Better, but limited in its use, was the Vickers Wellesley, but it had no internal bomb bay, the munitions being carried in nacelles under the wings. It did, however, perform well and was used to establish a new distance record of 7,162 miles in November 1938, when two Wellesley bombers flew from Egypt to Darwin, Australia.

Other bombers in service included the Handley Page Hampden, the Armstrong Whitworth Whitley, a not very popular plane that was used to re-equip the bomber squadrons in 1938, and of course the popular Vickers-Armstrong Wellington – but even that was initially built to a 1932 specification. Unlike most of the afore-mentioned types, the Wellington was built through 18 different marques right to the end of 1945. These, then, were among the aircraft that would equip Britain's bomber squadrons at the start of the war, all commissioned against this backdrop of future planning that had been hampered by an out-of-date philosophy and constantly changing 'best guess' scenarios, which, as we will see, fell well short of reality with disastrous consequences. The manufacturers were also desperately short on technology, such as basic navigational aids and bomb-aiming devices, which really did not improve until two years or more into the war. Although the expansion programme quickly and substantially increased the RAF's inventory of combat aircraft, most were, as Sir Michael Armitage described it, 'of dubious operational value . . . they were being produced because they were better than the alternative, which was to halt production altogether and leave some of the production lines idle until designs and then the jigs for more modern aircraft were complete, and meanwhile leaving the squad-rons with nothing to fly'.

The story was rather more hopeful at Fighter Command. In 1937 the RAF's standard fighter was still the Hawker Fury II, a sporty little open-cockpit biplane which had been a good servant but was completely obsolete. A new fighter, the Gloster Gladiator, with an enclosed cockpit, an aircraft designed to 1932 specifications, entered service in 1937, and that, too, was already a has-been before it fired a shot in anger. It was the last in Britain's long tradition of fighter biplanes, and, in the rush to re-equip, eight fighter squadrons received Gladiators in 1937–8. It was among the first in action at the outbreak of the

Second World War, but production ceased in 1940 when 531 had been built, thus plugging the gap until the fighter range was fully augmented by the magnificent heroes of their time, the Hurricanes and the Spitfires, which were about to make their entrance into RAF service.

Powered by a Rolls-Royce Merlin engine, the Hawker Hurricane was first introduced towards the end of 1937 and was the RAF's first fighter to exceed 300 mph in level flight. It had an impressive armoury of four Brownings in each wing and so, finally, the RAF possessed a machine truly capable of offering determined defence against attacks by the new high-speed bombers and the escorts being assembled in copious numbers in Germany. This capability would be further dramatically improved with the arrival of Supermarine's classic Spitfire Mk 1, delivered first to an excited No. 19 Squadron in June 1938. Although more advanced versions quickly followed, even the Mk 1 proved to be all that the pilots of No. 19 Squadron could have wished for at the time: top speed 355 mph from the Merlin II piston engine and a rate of climb to 15,000 feet in six minutes.

The increased manning of the RAF had, in the meantime, met the original targets and more. As war approached in 1939, the total strength had risen to almost 200,000 officers and other ranks, although well shy of the wartime requirement, which, at its peak, rose to almost 1,300,000 that would include the much-valued and re-formed Women's Auxiliary Air Force and an expanded RAF regiment.

This was all very well, but the aircraft were slow coming through and all the strategists immediately recognised that the bulk of RAF personnel had little operational experience, and those being trained up were doing so on old and obsolete machines. At the time of the Munich agreement, for example, when the outbreak of war was seen as a strong possibility, the RAF possessed only enough Hurricanes to equip three of its 19 operational squadrons. The rest were flying biplanes that would have been no match at all for the latest German aircraft. This lack of decent hardware and adequate training facilities became an immediate issue, and was especially true in Bomber Command. With so few planes available, those put up for training purposes were both few and old. The result was that men were going into bomber squadrons in 1939 with little training in vital areas such as navigation and air-to-air gunnery. Few gunnery crews had any experience at all on the turrets that came with the latest bombers.

The situation in Bomber Command was such that four months before the outbreak of hostilities, Sir Edgar Ludlow-Hewitt, who was by then Air Chief Marshal, bluntly stated in a letter to the Air Council that he could not foresee 'within any predictable period' his command attaining the strength or efficiency to declare itself ready for war. This proved to be an entirely accurate assessment, and when war came Bomber Command was hard pressed to launch any effective bombing offensive against Germany. It was Britain's good fortune that initially both sides responded to President Roosevelt's appeal for restraint in the bombing of civilian targets, Germany agreeing only after concluding the aerial onslaught in Poland on 18 September. In that breathing space, hurried measures were taken to improve the chances of Bomber Command with the formation of the Central Gunnery School, the Bombing Development Unit and the Armament Experimental Establishment, although all these facilities came too late to have much effect on the first year or two of warfare.

In those early months, the British bombers spent their time dropping warning leaflets over German territory and attacking ships in the North Sea. Even in this limited campaign, unacceptably high losses were incurred from the very beginning. On 3 September 1939 a single Blenheim from Wattisham took off for a reconnaissance flight over the port of Wilhelmshaven. It produced intelligence to launch a force of 27 bombers – Hampdens and Wellingtons – for an immediate attack on German naval units located at the port but, hampered by bad weather, they returned without a bomb being dropped. On day two of the war, 14 Wellingtons were sent out to attack German shipping, and 15 Blenheims made a second run to Wilhelmshaven. The raids caused no great damage to German assets, but Bomber Command lost two Wellingtons and five Blenheims. Similar sorties went on through increasingly difficult weather conditions until December. In that month alone, 233 sorties were flown and, if nothing else, gave the crews experience of both night flying and confrontations with enemy fighters.

Losses, however, began to outweigh the questionable benefits of these raids. On 14 December, five out of a posse of 12 Wellingtons hunting German shipping were lost to enemy fighters; on 18 December 12 out of 20 Wellingtons were shot down and three others were so badly damaged they had to make a crash-landing on return to base. As winter set in, these raids became fewer, until a diversion to the main thrust of the oncoming battle suddenly produced a definitive target.

After Poland, Hitler ordered his High Command to begin the advance on the Low Countries and France before winter set in, but his generals asked for time to prepare for what they envisaged was an unprecedented *blitzkrieg* of troops and heavy metal moved by land and air. And so very little happened, and the only sound of military activities outside territory already secured by the Germans was the clump, clump, clump of British soldiers' boots footslogging towards a front line across the English Channel which did not, in truth, exist. There was so little activity in the first months after the declaration of hostilities that the American newspapers dubbed this period the Phoney War. The thousands of young men being drawn into military service were either en route with the BEF in France or marching up and down the parade grounds of British military bases and generally preparing the defence of the nation's beaches. They called it the Bore War, and it was only partially enlivened by some side action to the main event which suddenly loomed in Scandinavia.

Taking advantage of the impending conflict in Europe, Russia invaded Finland in October 1939. The Finns stood their ground and kept the Red Army at bay well into the New Year. The attack temporarily diverted the interest of the European contenders towards that region, and specifically to Kiruna in northern Sweden, which was Germany's main supplier of iron ore. In winter, the ore was shipped through the ice-free Norwegian port of Narvik on the western seaboard and then through neutral Norwegian waters to Germany. On the pretext of supporting Finland against the Red Army, the British had, with French acquiescence, worked out that on the way they could occupy Narvik and Kiruna, the two key centres for the shipping of iron ore, and halt the flow of vital supplies into Germany.

It would require the cooperation of both Norway and Sweden. Both nations refused, in the hope of maintaining their neutrality. By then, it was too late. Prevented by bad weather and adverse intelligence reports, the German High Command delayed its invasion of the Low Countries still further and instead focused on the developing situation in Scandinavia. The upshot was Hitler's approval of an incursion into Denmark and Norway on 7 April 1940, the latter through eight ports from Narvik and on down around the western and southern coastline to Oslo and, for the first time ever, using airborne troops to secure inland sites. A British task force, having laid mines around Narvik, was at that moment sailing home and actually passed the German ships without seeing them, leaving the way clear for largely unopposed landings on the morning of 9 April.

As German warships appeared off the Norwegian coast, the airborne invasion began inland. Within 48 hours, the Germans had landed seven divisions and captured all the main ports, while the airborne troops secured their position in Oslo and major airports. The weather halted planned parachute drops at Oslo airport, and infantry troops were landed in a succession of Junker 52s to take possession. Five companies of parachute troops did, however, drop at other key airports. The Germans established a firm hold on the southern half of Norway.

Oslo was overrun by noon that day, yet the Norwegian government decided to make a stand and moved to Elverum, there to send word inviting the British and French to dispatch troops immediately to their assistance. The terrain was rugged and difficult, and with more than 350,000 troops already committed to the BEF to confront the German invasion which must soon surely come, the British army agreed at last to the formation of 'guerrilla forces' backed up by a naval task force and an RAF fighter force consisting of bombers and fighters. The former went first – 83 aircraft set off from British airfields on 12 April 1940, the largest bombing action so far of the Second World War.

It consisted of 24 Hampdens, 23 Blenheims and 36 Wellingtons. In their first attack on German positions, the RAF lost six Hampdens and three Wellingtons in one day. Once again, daylight raiding had taken its toll. The first-day losses caused deep anguish at Bomber Command headquarters back in Britain, and for the rest of the Norwegian campaign raids focused almost entirely on attacks on enemy airfields and mine-laying operations. Meanwhile, No. 263 Squadron, equipped with Gloster Gladiators – the last biplane fighter in British service – were moved up aboard the aircraft carriers *Glorious* and *Ark Royal*. The Gladiators hit trouble immediately. They flew off the host ships to a makeshift landing strip on a frozen lake which proved an almost impossible surface from which to scramble, and 20 hours later, on 24 April, 10 of the newly arrived aircraft were still on the ground when they were attacked by Ju88s and Heinkel 111s. All were wiped out. The remaining five were flown off to another airstrip located 20 miles away, but in dire conditions and poor visibility, all were damaged or crashed on landing. The pilots and ground crews were all withdrawn on 2 May, leaving the bombers to make occasional long-range raids.

But that was by no means the end of the story. No. 263 Squadron was immediately re-equipped with Gladiators and were to link up with No. 46 Squadron flying Hurricanes. What happened next represents one of the first wartime stories of great heroism, courage and tragedy for which I will defer entirely to the words of Sir Kenneth Cross, one of the two airmen who survived it out of the 41 pilots who set out on the mission on 18 May:

I was posted to Digby to command 46 Squadron in November 1939. Absolutely first class. The pilots were all very young, but they had had seven or eight months together on Hurricanes. They were, without any doubt, one of the best squadrons in Fighter Command. They were the first squadron to engage an enemy formation in any numbers in the beginning of the war. On Trafalgar Day in October, they intercepted some Heinkel float planes off the Humber and shot down five or six. So for a short time they were the top-scoring squadron in Fighter Command. We were, I found, what was called the No. 1 Reinforcing Squadron. I got instructions from Fighter Command to go to France to look at an airfield there that we would go to if reinforcements were required for France. But by April, May the north Norwegian expedition was mounted. We were switched from France to going to Norway . . . the instructions that we were to go to Narvik.

Various preparations had to be made. Our Hurricanes were fitted with variable-pitch airscrews. We were given a certain amount of Arctic clothing and other equipment. Our establishment was increased so that we were entirely self-contained, with cooks and everything for the campaign. We were then told that we would be ferried to Norway by the aircraft carrier HMS *Glorious*. We were told it wasn't possible to land on the carrier because tests which had been done at Farnborough indicated that the deck was not long enough for the Hurricanes to come to a stop. They had no hooks, as the Fleet Air Arm aircraft had. So we flew off 18-strong from Digby up to Abbotsinch near Glasgow and landed there. The next day we taxied the aeroplanes through fields to a jetty, put them on a lighter and went down the Clyde to where the *Glorious* was anchored. I insisted that each pilot should go with his aeroplane, which was fortunate because the bargees had no idea that the wings would not take a bit of buffeting on the side of ships, and so on. Anyway, we got all 18 aircraft hoisted aboard using cranes. The 18 pilots had seen their aircraft stowed in the hangar. The next day we went up to Scapa Flow with the other aircraft carrier, the *Furious*, which now contained No. 263 Squadron with its Gladiators, then set forth for Norway. When we got into position there, we received a signal to say that 46 Squadron was to go to an airstrip called Skaanland on a fjord near Narvik. We understood that 263 Squadron was to go to another airstrip further away at Bardufoss.

Bardufoss was ready, but Skaanland was not ready. After two or three days waiting, it was necessary for us to return to Scapa Flow to refuel the aircraft carrier. Then we set out again for Norway. This meant that we were in this ship for something like 10 days. Finally, we were ranged on deck in sixes. I, as the squadron commander, was the first to take off with a Hurricane, which had never been done before from a carrier. We didn't know whether the Hurricane would do it or fall over the edge. But in point of fact, with our variable-pitch airscrews and full power of the Merlin engine, they leaped off the deck without any difficulty at all. We reached Skaanland and found a muddy strip on the edge of the fjord covered with coconut matting. I landed first. As I went in, the wheels sank and the aeroplane tipped gently forward. I bent about two inches of the airscrew. I was furious because it was apparent that the airfield was unfit for landing.

The first person who approached me was some old reserve officer. I let him have it and said the airfield was not fit for landing on. Such was the strain of the times up there, which we were to appreciate later with 24 hours of daylight and no respite from enemy action, the poor man burst into tears. However, the wing commander, who was the CO of the air force, then appeared. The next aircraft that came in after me landed successfully. It was apparent that the CO thought that it was perhaps me not the airfield that was at fault. However, the third aircraft dug in even more than I did and did a complete somersault on the runway and put it out of action. There was nothing for it then. I climbed back into my aircraft and called the 46 Squadron aircraft still in the air and said: 'You must go to find your way to Bardufoss. This airfield is now blocked.' It was a tribute to their training and ability that all the remaining aircraft, with very inferior maps, found their way to Bardufoss and landed successfully. I followed the next day, my aeroplane having had the airscrew straightened. We operated from Bardufoss for the rest of the time we were in Norway.

The attack on Narvik started the next day. We patrolled Narvik alternately with 263 Squadron. The whole of the time the assault was taking place, no German air opposition was successful and Narvik was captured in 48 hours. In the process, the odd German aircraft, Ju88s or Heinkel 111s, appeared. We shot down several. We were there at Bardufoss for about two weeks when the attack on France started.

We listened to the news of the German advance there, and it was a great disappointment to us when the following day the commander of the RAF force told us that the government had decided to evacuate from north Norway, because at that time we'd actually captured Narvik and we'd pushed the Germans right back to the Swedish border and in another two weeks the whole of north Norway would have been ours. But we understood perfectly well the amount of shipping required to sustain an expedition of this size. So the entire British and French force was to be withdrawn immediately, and we were to cover the evacuation of the troops from the various fjords by destroyers.

[During the 14-day Narvik campaign, the two squadrons had flown 638 sorties and claimed 37 enemy aircraft destroyed. On the last day, eight Gladiators remained operational and were flown back to HMS *Glorious* for the journey home. No Hurricanes had ever landed on an aircraft carrier, and so No. 46 Squadron was ordered to destroy the remaining 10 Hurricanes so that the Germans could not get their hands on them.]

When the evacuation was complete, we were told we would have to burn the aeroplanes as the last thing at Bardufoss. But the Hurricanes were valuable, much-needed aircraft, and we were determined to get them home and 10 pilots stepped forward to make an attempt to land on the *Glorious*. Farnborough figures said it was impossible; my pilots didn't believe it was. At three o'clock in the afternoon we'd been flying hard all day, but there was very little interference with the evacuation by the Luftwaffe. I sent my most experienced flight commander, Flight Lieutenant Jameson, with two of his pilots out to the *Glorious* to see if the Hurricane could in fact land. They were to signal if successful, but no signal was received. At three in the morning I decided to make the attempt. We had been flying for 24 hours solid when we flew to the ship. It was a very welcoming sight. We saw the blinking light which these carriers always carried on the horizon. Then it was time to try. We didn't know whether Jameson and his two pilots had been successful or not (and in fact they had).

I did the first landing and it actually turned out to be a relatively simple operation. My Hurricane stopped little over two-thirds up the deck. I was standing on the brakes pretty hard all the time. All seven came on successfully, so in fact we saved the 10 remaining aeroplanes in the squadron. We went down below, for some hot cocoa, then the fact that we had had no sleep for 24 hours eventually caught up with us. We were all exhausted, and we all fell into the bunks which were allocated to us. Nobody woke up really until mid-afternoon the next day, which was 8 June. I woke up at about half-past three. I went along to the wardroom and was sitting in the wardroom where tea was being served and having a cup of tea when the action stations was sounded on the ship's Tannoy. I went along to my cabin and put on my padded Irvine jacket.

For some unknown reasons I put the squadron funds,

amounting to £200, in an envelope in my inner pocket. I don't know why I did that but I did. Then I went to my action station, which was on the quarterdeck at the extreme stern of the ship. When I got there I saw on the horizon two patches of smoke. As I looked at them I saw flashes. I went up the starboard gangway on the starboard side of the ship, on to the flight deck. As I stepped on to the deck, a second salvo hit the ship, demolishing the gangway I'd just come up. The third shell of the salvo hit the deck about 10 yards in front of me making a large hole. But it didn't explode. The ship was then hit by a number of salvoes.

The intercommunication system failed, so that the only information we had from the bridge on the quarterdeck was by runner or messenger. For the next half an hour or 40 minutes the ship was steadily hit by salvoes. One of the first salvoes after I'd left the flight deck hit the island where the bridge was. We understood it killed the captain. After about an hour or perhaps a little less, the ship began to list very badly, although we were still doing quite a good forward speed, some 12 to 15 knots. We were zigzagging. I thought she would roll over, she had such a list on. Then eventually the order was given to abandon ship. Carley floats were thrown over the side for the crew and us passengers to swim to when we'd jumped over the side. I asked a naval pilot who I'd got to know quite well in our trip out, Ginger Marmont, what was the form on abandoning ship. He said: 'As you see, when they drop these floats, we're still doing quite a considerable speed. When they drop a float, you want to go pretty quickly afterwards otherwise you'll have a very long way to swim.' So when they dropped a float from the quarterdeck I had my Mae West on, I went over the side, came up like a cork, swam about 10 yards and scrambled aboard the Carley float. Very soon we had 20 or 30 people aboard. To my great delight, Flight Lieutenant Jameson, my number two in the squadron, came swimming along and scrambled aboard with me. We sat side by side.

Eventually, the *Glorious* came to a halt about half a mile away from us. One moment she was there. When we looked round again, she had gone. Then the two German battleships came up. I didn't know at that time that they were the

Scharnhorst and the *Gneisenau.** However, the two ships steamed up, did not stop to pick up survivors and went straight on. Within quarter of an hour we were alone 40 miles inside the Arctic Circle and about 200 miles off Norway. It was rough and very cold. Within a short time some of the men began to die. Within three hours the first died. We had between 20 and 30 aboard our float. But within a few hours there were only seven of us left. They were just dying of exposure. It was extraordinary, really, those who survived, because one was a marine who was wounded. He survived. One was an old warrant-officer of considerable age. He survived. Some of the youngest did not survive. It was wet and it was cold, but I had an Irvine jacket. Jameson had got nothing but a tunic and a roll-necked pullover on him. But it was light the whole time. There was high cloud, no sun. We had no idea of the passage of time. By next morning the sea became absolutely calm. So then, there we were, nothing to eat, nothing to drink. I said to Jameson: 'How long do you think we can stick this, Pat?' He's a New Zealander, a particularly tough New Zealander. He knew a lot about survival. He said: 'I think about six days.' The fact that we'd lost a great many people in six hours didn't shake Jameson's view at all. So we just sat there.

We passed most of the time being asleep, always with one on watch. At the start there were hundreds of Carley floats, but the next morning there wasn't a sign of anything at all. They all got scattered. Of course, we were quite confident that at any time now the British fleet would come over the horizon and we would be picked up. What we didn't know was that nobody had received the message from the *Glorious* when she was attacked except one cruiser who didn't pass it on. No one knew what had happened until the Germans announced it.

Eventually, somebody called out: 'There's a ship.' Sure enough, there, 10 or so miles away, was this ship. It was an

---

* Two destroyers, the *Ardent* and the *Acasta*, which were escorting the carrier, were both sunk by the two German warships in the preliminary stages of the battle.

agonising business watching it. We could see its masts. When its masts were in line they were coming towards us. Eventually, it came on . . . it was a little Norwegian tramp steamer, the ss *Borgund* running away from Harstad and making for the Faeroe Islands. They'd come right through the area of the Carley floats. They picked up one or two here, one or two there. Eventually, on this little ship they had a total of 37 people. So, of the three crews of 1,500 men, 37 in the *Borgund* were all that were saved. [In fact, Cross and Jameson were the only two survivors of the 41 airmen who initially set out on the Narvik campaign on 18 May.] We were the last float to be picked up. There was a splendid old Norwegian engineer who understood the situation very well. We were absolutely parched with thirst. We asked him for a drink. He gave us a drink out of a little mug, which he never filled more than a quarter full, which meant you had about three sips only. Then he would say, 'No', would give you no more. Then 20 minutes later you could have three more sips. This was very sensible because some of the people who drank more than they should have done had very great problems with their stomachs later on.

Eventually, when I was a bit better I was moved up on deck until we reached the Faeroe Islands and were taken off on stretchers by a British army contingent, which was defending the place, to the local civilian hospital. By this time we realised that our legs up to our knees had been afflicted with what I can only describe as a mixture of frostbite and trench foot. They hurt more and more every day. So we were taken aboard the destroyer *Veteran* commanded by a legendary naval officer by the name of Jackie Broome, who pre-war was a great caricaturist. We went slowly down from the Faeroes to Rosyth then, when we were getting near there, we were told we were going to Gleneagles. The golf hotel I once knew had been turned into an army general hospital. We were there then the whole of the rest of June, July and part of August. We eventually left Gleneagles in mid-August. With sticks, we could walk. But our feet were still very much enlarged. We could only wear soft carpet slippers. We went down by train back to Digby, where we'd started from, sadly. Then the doctors sent us off on sick leave. I went back to my home at Hayling Island, near Portsmouth, arriving there in the middle of August.

When I was in Gleneagles hospital I found once again the squadron funds, which was a very considerable sum in those days. I wrote to the CO, who had re-formed my squadron at Digby, and said I'd got this money and I proposed to send it to him. He wrote back and said they didn't want it. They had everything they wanted. Why didn't I keep it and spend it on a party? I didn't think this was correct. When I was better from Gleneagles, I wrote to Fighter Command and said I'd got the balance of the money, which had been given me by Fighter Command in case I needed it during the expedition. I think I had about £192 out of the £200 because we'd been able to spend a little bit on buying salmon and things from the local people up at Bardufoss to augment the ration. So I sent the £192 back to Fighter Command.

They wrote back to me and wanted to know what had happened to the other £8!

CHAPTER SEVEN

Three Weeks in May

Aircraft and engine factories were working flat out to produce new machines, but Britain actually began the war with an inventory substantially below the targets set in the mid-1930s, while Germany had exceeded hers. On 3 September 1939 the RAF had just 536 bombers against an estimated 2,130 in the hands of the Luftwaffe and 608 front-line fighters against Germany's 1,215. Even that disproportionate comparison did not represent a true picture in view of the fact that the British bombers – and indeed some of the older fighters – still in use were soon to face challenges that went well beyond their capabilities. Production of newer marques was stepped up to quite incredible levels as the war progressed, necessarily spurred on by the fact that in the early months RAF losses in aircraft and personnel soared off the graph of expectation. The brunt of these disasters was taken immediately by an Advanced Air Striking Force sent across the Channel with the British Expeditionary Force and stationed at airfields in north-eastern France under the command of Sir Arthur Barrett.

He was given 10 squadrons of the light bombers, Battles and Blenheims – 160 aircraft in all – ostensibly to bomb German positions along the Allied front, if and when the time came. They were the same aircraft that had already been shown to be totally unsuited to daytime bombing operations in the Norwegian campaign, where so few survived. Barrett was also provided with four squadrons of Hurricane fighters for their protection. In addition to the AASF, there was also an air attachment eventually reaching 19 squadrons of bombers and fighters operating as the BEF's Air Component Force, including 10 squadrons of Hurricane fighters. These aircraft were to operate only from areas under BEF control, principally for reconnaissance, photographic surveys and defence. Further support was available from Bomber Command sorties flown directly from the British mainland. On the face of it, it seemed a fairly substantial response, given that France, Belgium and Holland had their own air forces in a state of readiness. But it soon became apparent that the bulk of the effort would fall on the British with almost immediate effect. Doubts were already being voiced about whether Britain had enough power to repel the might of the Luftwaffe from her own airspace, let alone take the lead role in the defence of Western Europe. Only days before the Germans began their charge across Europe towards France, the whole issue of bomber/fighter deployment in France boiled into a major – if hidden – controversy, through differing beliefs and expectations among the RAF hierarchy, politicians and the public. As evidence of Germany's strength in numbers and efficiency mounted, there were more people than dared speak out who were worried about the British bombers and the potential for serious miscalculations of their worth.

To even mention such matters at that moment in time might well have brought accusations of defeatism. Some senior figures went on record, however, to urge extreme caution. Sir Richard Peirse, Vice-Chief of Air Staff, gloomily surmised on 29 April 1940 that it would be foolish to provoke the Germans needlessly unless Bomber Command could promise decisive results, which it couldn't. This was more or less admitted by an equally worried Sir Charles Portal, who had just taken over as Commander-in-Chief, Bomber Command, and was quick to voice his concern that the two chief components of Bomber Command's squadrons in France – Fairey Battles and Blenheims – were simply not up to the task at hand. On 8 May 1940 he wrote:

> . . .the proposed use of these units is fundamentally unsound, and that if it is persisted in, it is likely to have disastrous consequences . . . It can scarcely be disputed that at the enemy's chosen moment for advance, the area

concerned will be literally swarming with enemy fighters, and we shall be lucky if we see again as many as half the aircraft we send out each time. Really accurate bombing under the conditions I visualise is not to be expected, and I feel justified in expressing serious doubts whether the attacks of 50 Blenheims based on information necessarily some hours out of date are likely to make as much difference to the ultimate course of the war as to justify the losses I expect.

Portal knew well that to fly these planes on daylight raids would be suicidal, because – as it was soon proved – they would be cut to pieces by German anti-aircraft flak and fighters. To fly them by night was equally barely worth the risk because the likelihood of pinpoint accuracy on specific targets after dark was remote to an air force designed and trained on the Trenchard edict of 'area bombing' and still without the basic navigational aids, bomb-aiming equipment and ground-to-air communications. Coupled to those shortfalls were the disadvantages of crews being rushed into action on the barest minimum of training. All of this was soon to become so very evident.

10 May 1940: Hitler began the long-expected assault on the Low Countries and onwards to France, and Winston Churchill became Prime Minister. The temper of the war was irrevocably altered by the Nazis' overland charge accompanied by a massive and brutal air campaign that gave no quarter to supposed 'moral restraint' to which the British had adhered. The German ground forces were fewer in number than the combined British, French, Belgian and Dutch armies that faced them. They were, however, better equipped and had the ability to move with unprecedented swiftness. The crucial element in the German attack, however, was the strength of its airborne assault and a hugely superior air force which, unlike the Allies, was directed by a unified command structure. The most vital statistics came in the overwhelming strength of the Luftwaffe's attack. It would later be shown that they had their airfields stacked with 3,824 warplanes ready to go, including 860 Messerschmitt Bf 109s, 350 Bf 110s, 380 dive-bombers, 1,300 bombers, 300 long-range reconnaissance and 340 short-range reconnaissance aircraft. As the German *blitzkrieg* across the Low Countries began, the Dutch and Belgian air

113

forces crumbled in an instant along with their ground troops. The French air force was also deeply in the mire, fielding an ancient fleet with little backup from its chaotic nationalised aircraft industry. New aircraft failed to reach the front in time, the crews were ill trained and there was a dire shortage of spares and maintenance services. The Luftwaffe's intelligence had provided chapter and verse on these shortcomings and barely bothered with the French. They went instead straight for the British planes, and aimed a heavy bombardment at nine of the RAF bases in France and Belgium on the first day, destroying many aircraft on the ground.

Thirty-two Battles went into the air that day. Thirteen were shot down and every one of the rest were damaged. In a separate mission, a squadron of the AASF Blenheims was assigned to attack a German-held airfield near Rotterdam. En route, they were counterattacked by Bf 110s, and five Blenheims went down. The misfortunes of that first day were to be repeated over and over again and, like a bad dream for the RAF squadron commanders, the situation got worse as each day progressed, particularly for the Fairey Battles, which were virtually wiped out within two weeks.

11 May: Six Blenheims were lost or damaged in operations against German positions, seven Battles were downed and all the Blenheims of No. 114 Squadron were destroyed on the ground by German air attack. The RAF's eight Hurricane squadrons in France, Nos. 3, 79, 501 and 504 Squadrons, were in the air constantly and had to reinforce the beleaguered BEF's Air Component Force, which was in dire trouble as the Germans broke through the Belgian lines. Further support was needed, and No. 11 Group had to send in more fighters, flying patrols directly from squadron bases in the south of England.

12 May: Nine Blenheims of No. 139 Squadron took off to bomb an enemy column near Maastricht and only two returned. Twenty-four Blenheims from Bomber Command flew to attack bridges over the River Maas; ten failed to return. Fifteen Fairey Battles were also lost in various operations on the same day. And finally in that horrific 24 hours, No. 12 Squadron stepped forward en masse when their commanding officer asked for volunteers for an exceedingly risky mission to hit a German supply route by bombing crucial but well-protected bridges over the Albert Canal near Maastricht. Only six Battles were available for the task; five made it to the target area. Led into attack by Flying Officer Douglas Edward Garland, a 21-year-old Irishman, they took out one bridge in particular that was being used by the invading troops accompanied by hefty protection from fighter aircraft and anti-aircraft and machine-guns. In doing so, all five Battles were shot down and four crews killed or captured. The five ill-protected Battles ran a gauntlet of what has been described as an 'inferno of anti-aircraft flak' and attacks from German fighters. That the mission was accomplished successfully was judged to have been largely due to the expert leadership of Flying Officer Garland and the coolness and resourcefulness of his navigator, Sergeant Thomas Gray. Both were posthumously awarded the Victoria Cross – the first such awards of the war for the RAF. The third member of the crew, L.A.C. Reynolds, received no recognition, a fact explained away by his lesser role and the fact that the award to even two members of the same crew was, historically, an unusual occurrence. By the end of that day, also, the AASF bomber force had been reduced to less than half its original strength. Worse news was yet to come.

13 May: Churchill's War Cabinet met to discuss bombing policy. The Prime Minister, known for his strong views on specifically targeted bomber operations, discovered that a number of those around his table were sternly opposed to any bombing of Germany for the time being, reiterating warning voices expressed earlier by Portal and others who feared the worst. Churchill's predecessor, Neville Chamberlain, claimed that if British planes bombed the Ruhr now, the Germans would be forced to retaliate . . . 'and our defences are not as strong as they might be'. Sir Archibald Sinclair, from the Air Ministry, agreed and said 60 or 70 fighter squadrons were needed to defend Britain and the RAF had only 39. Others made similar observations, and Churchill bowed to their opinions. He was particularly disappointed that he could not send more fighters to France but said it was impossible under the circumstances and, similarly, 'we should not allow our heavy bomber force to be frittered away and thus deprive ourselves of its deterrent effect and of the ability to deliver its heavy blow'.

14–15 May: Daylight bombing raids by the AASF were finally halted when 28 out of 37 bombers sent out that day failed to

115

return home after a terrible battle while launching a mass attack on German pontoon bridges near Sedan. That night, a further nine Blenheims from a Bomber Command dispatch of 28 aircraft were shot down. This, added to other operations involving Fairey Battles, represented a loss in that one 24-hour period of 42 out of 76 aircraft that took off that day. The AASF alone had now lost three-quarters of its original force. That day, also, the air war took another dramatic turn when the last vestige of moral restraint was thrown to the wind when the Luftwaffe launched a heavy bombing attack on Rotterdam, with thousands of civilian casualties. Within hours, restrictions of bombing raids on Germany were lifted and Portal was authorised to send his largest force so far to attack rail and oil installations east of the Rhine.

15–16 May: A force of almost a hundred of Britain's so-called heavy bombers – Wellingtons, Whitleys and Hampdens – took off from British airfields bound for the industrialised area by the Ruhr on what was Bomber Command's first strategic campaign of the war. It was not a success. They were to hit 16 targets, which turned out to be not quite as visible at height as the crews had been led to believe. As they came within range, poor visibility cast a shadow on the mission, and barely a quarter of the crews found their designated targets. Reports from the region next day confirmed that the damage would not cause the German war machine any great difficulties, but reprisals could be anticipated. On the 16 May, also, eight additional half-squadrons of Hurricanes were flown to France in response to a request from the French to bolster defences as losses on that front continued to mount. In addition, three different squadrons would fly daily from British airfields to join the fray as the bombers continued to suffer substantial reverses as the Allies attempted to slow down the German advance, without success.

17 May: At 4.50 a.m. 12 Blenheims of No. 82 Squadron of Bomber Command left Watton, Norfolk, to attack German columns on the move through central Belgium. They never reached their goal, having been themselves intercepted by 15 Bf 109s before they could link up with a protection squad of Hurricanes. Only the Blenheim of the squadron commander, Wing Commander the Earl of Bandon, survived the attack to return to base; the rest were shot down. Paddy Bandon was ordered to close the squadron down, but within 24 hours he had mustered enough crew to get the decision reversed. The same day, Barrett's AASF lost another nine Battles, and as the German advance continued he was forced to move his entire stock of aircraft to bases to the south.

19 May: Virtually no air base in north-eastern France was now considered safe for RAF or BEF operations, and the order went out for withdrawal to the UK. Only a limited number of fighter squadrons of the AASF would remain, and they would be supported by Hurricane squadrons flying directly from airfields in the south and east of Britain. The emphasis was now firmly on the ability of the Hurricanes to keep the Germans at bay. The Hurricane squadrons in particular had already caused immense damage to the Luftwaffe. Since 10 May, no fewer than 27 Hurricane pilots became aces, and overall Hurricane pilots claimed 456 kills, but the cost to themselves had also been high. They now had the task of helping to save their comrades in Bomber Command and troops on the ground from an even greater catastrophe as the final days in the Battle of France began to unfold.

22 May: Sorties across the Channel continued from dawn to dusk for the fighters as British army units retreating towards the Channel ports came under heavy aerial bombardment. For a week, the BEF troops, who had been heading for their only avenue of escape, came under repeated attack from waves of German bombers and screaming low-flying fighters raking them with machine-gun and cannon fire. RAF sorties were now being flown from bases in southern England. Fighter squadrons were being rotated for duty in France, and those based in the Midlands and north of England were relocated to overcrowded airfields in the south. Even then, the range presented almost impossible odds of warding off the German attacks. By then, the withdrawal of troops was under way. All roads leading towards the French coast were crammed with soldiers and every possible form of transport. Blown-up vehicles littered the routes as they headed towards the sea for what now became the only route to possible survival and even that possibility required something of a major miracle.

27 May: Operation Dynamo, the great evacuation of Allied forces from the beaches of Dunkirk, began to save more than 400,000 British and Allied troops from annihilation or captivity.

For this, 222 naval vessels and 665 other craft of varying shapes and sizes famously began the journey across the Channel and eventually brought out all but about 60,000 men, who were either killed or taken into captivity over the next six days. The RAF were already running round-the-clock sorties in an attempt to put up an umbrella of protection, although not without some controversy and criticism of what was considered – both at the time and in retrospect – an inadequate response to the great human drama now being played out beneath them. But unknown to anyone outside the War Cabinet, Fighter Command under Air Vice-Marshal Keith Park had fewer than 250 aircraft at his disposal specifically to deploy over France. The difficulty of range also remained an immense problem, given that even on the shortest run across the Channel, fighters would be left with less than 30 minutes' flying time before they had to return to refuel, and of course a good deal of the action was well beyond the coastal areas in an attempt to intercept the German aircraft before they reached the escaping troops. The question was asked, then and later: should not the RAF have sent far more aircraft? It was debated within the War Cabinet at the same time that Air Chief Marshal Sir Hugh Dowding, then head of British air defences, was under pressure to assure ministers that he was conserving sufficient aircraft to meet air attacks on Britain which, Churchill warned in the House of Commons, 'will certainly be made very soon upon us'.

Park had done his best to improvise and, with no further aircraft available, he had to juggle those aircraft he had to meet the seemingly insurmountable task by putting up a large force, with up to four squadrons flying over the Dunkirk area and beyond at any one time. These went up in staggered time to keep a presence of RAF fighters in the air for up to 12 hours every day for the remaining days of the evacuation, as one of his Hurricane pilots, Alan Geoffrey Page, recalled:

When the war started, I was in fact still a student at London University where I'd learned to fly with the University Air Squadron. We were immediately called up and I personally was sent to Cranwell, the Royal Air Force College, to polish up my flying training before being posted to a fighter squadron, No. 56. Our squadron was sent over to France to try to help the evacuation from Dunkirk. Despite the fact that the army said 'Where are the RAF?' the answer's quite simple. If we'd been over the beaches where the soldiers could see us, we wouldn't have been doing our job. Because you've got to intercept the enemy before he gets to the target. So we were out of sight and going deeper meant we had about 20 minutes of fighting fuel after we'd crossed the Channel and then we had to come back. We were based at North Weald just near Epping Forest in No. 2 Group, which was the fighting group both at Dunkirk time and of course during the Battle of Britain.

We were young, enthusiastic, had nice aeroplanes and no fundamental problems. How well were we prepared for combat? Not very. One learned the hard way. When I was at Cranwell, we did a little dive-bombing and air firing but it wasn't really as good as it should have been. So you learned the hard way – actually doing it. You saw an aeroplane with an iron cross marked on the side of it and you attacked it, and through experience you learned to hit it more often than you did at the beginning. We'd go over to France, one or two squadrons together, and we would sweep all the way round behind the beaches and try to intercept any German aircraft coming to attack the soldiers on the ground. That was one role. And the other role was to escort Blenheim bombers and be their fighter escort when they went to bomb targets that were related to the evacuation from Dunkirk.

But our shortage of fuel wouldn't permit us to remain there very long. People didn't understand this. I think our ground crews got into fisticuffs in local pubs and taverns because after a few beers the soldiers would say: 'Where were you?' And our ground crews knew very well that we'd gone off there. Imagine yourself being a soldier and dive-bombed and machine-gunned on the ground and with no RAF around that you can see personally. You don't realise that they are probably 30, 40, 50 miles away trying to stop the Luftwaffe getting at you. But the man on the ground isn't aware of that, and he automatically is very bitter and twisted about the fact he was not being looked after.

Also, the RAF had pre-war standard methods of attack which time proved were completely ineffectual. Later on in

119

the war, we copied the German tactics which they had developed during the Spanish Civil War. They were ahead of us in the way they flew their fighter formations. But one learns quickly and, for example, the basic formation in 1940 was three aircraft. Well, learning from the Germans we realised that your basic unit is two aircraft and not three, and a formation was eventually developed called a 'finger-four', which if you stretch out your hand with your fingers splayed, forgetting the thumb, you'll see that those were the relative positions of the fingertips to the way we flew our aircraft.

There was one incident where we intercepted a formation of German fighters, with Stukas, the Ju87 dive-bomber. A Stuka was an easy target. The only trouble was when they went into a dive, they were so slow and you followed them down with your Hurricane, you caught them up so rapidly that you only had a very short time – literally one or two seconds – to fire at them because you were accelerating so rapidly at the dive that you'd go past them. [In fact, the Germans withdrew the Stuka from the Battle of Britain because they were just decimated.] Well, the Messerschmitt 109 fighters came down on us to help their Stukas. It was quite funny, because I was running out of fuel and it was touch and go whether I would get back to England. Because when you get into a fight, obviously you're putting on much more engine power and your fuel consumption really shoots up. So there came a point where you had to pull out and head back for home, otherwise if you stayed around any longer you weren't going to get home. So I levelled out just a few feet over the sea and streaked towards Dover with two Messerschmitts chasing me. I think they, too, probably had a fuel problem because they left me alone after a while. The next enemy was when I got near Dover harbour, and the Royal Navy started opening fire on me thinking I was an attacking incoming aircraft. But I managed to avoid that one.

Over Dunkirk, it looked like masses of ants on this large sand-dune area. One felt desperately sorry for the troops down below, and I think it's important to remember that Dunkirk was not a glorious victory as far as the army was

Britain's first military aircraft, British Army Aeroplane No 1, was designed and flown by former Wild West cowboy and showman Samuel Cody – Buffalo Bill's cousin.

This FE2D was among the early 'pusher' types with the propeller mounted at the rear to allow forward firing by the precariously positioned machine gunner, here in France in 1916, prior to synchronised firing through the propeller. (*Left*) James McCudden, one of the first heroes of air combat, who won a Victoria Cross after shooting down 54 enemy aircraft. He was himself killed three months later.

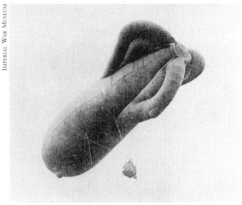

Balloons formed a vital part of early military flight, used for observation of enemy lines and to guide artillery ground fire with map references relayed by telephone. They were tethered by metal cables to around 5,500 feet and were ready-made targets for enemy fighters.

Only slightly less precarious were early airship operations, although both these models were of a later, more sturdy design.

Between the wars, the RAF took on the role of international policeman. Here, the lively Westland Wapiti of No 60 Squadron bombs rebels on the North West Frontier.

Many revolutionary designs were inspired by popular air races, such as the Schneider trophy. Advances are evident in the Short Brothers Southampton flying boat (*left*) and the Supermarine S6B (*below*), a variant of the 1927 version that won the Schneider trophy.

Britain's fighter aircraft were sadly lacking as World War II loomed. The mainstay was the Gloster Gladiator (*above*) a sporty biplane built to 1932 specifications. War was already a reality before the brilliant Hurricane (*below*) began to appear in any number.

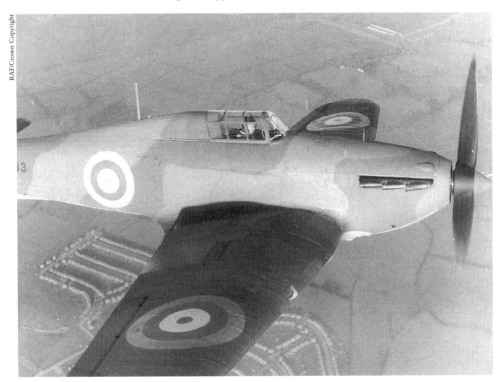

And then came the Spitfire, speeding away on its Rolls-Royce Merlin power pack and firing eight Browning machine guns at 1,200 rounds a minute.

(*Left*) Some of the pilots who flew the Hurricanes and Spitfires in the Battle of Britain, with Douglas Bader (*centre*).

A later but equally brilliant addition was the Hawker Typhoon fighter bomber which helped put the Germans to flight in France.

Some of the staff who plotted the course of the air battles over Britain and the rate of incoming bombers.

The Blenheim bomber, built to 1930s specifications, proved unequal to the task when the offensive against Germany began. The aircraft saw exceptional service but losses were heavy. The anti-aircraft fire that met all bombers, British or German, was tremendous as these dramatic pictures below demonstrate.

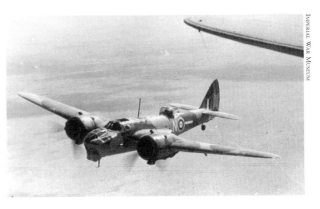

The bomb masters – but not always in agreement: Sir Arthur Harris, head of Bomber Command (*above*), Don Bennett, founder of the Pathfinders Force (*centre*) and Leonard Cheshire, boss of the famous No 617 Squadron and present at the A-bombing of Japan (*below*).

British crews faced a wall of flak over Brest on the night a VC was won and (*below*) a German anti-aircraft battery in operation.

The great workhorse of Bomber Command, the Lancaster, takes its place in history with the largest bomb ever carried by a British aircraft.
(*Below*) A ten tonner is dropped on Arbergen Railway Bridge over the Weser on 21 March 1945.

The lead crew of the famous Dambusters raid by No 617 Squadron prepare for takeoff, with Wing Commander Guy Gibson (on the ladder) who was awarded a Victoria Cross for his command of the expedition.

A torpedo-carrying Beaufort bomber of Coastal Command, engaged throughout World War II on vital defence of home waters and the crucial supply convoys. Flying low into attack, they were hugely vulnerable to ship guns.
(*Below*) A Beaufort scores a direct hit.

concerned. I feel it was a glorious victory for the Royal Navy, the way they got so many troops off. And I think it was also a glorious achievement for the people in the little boats. But let's face it, the army were in full retreat and they were relying on the navy and the RAF and the little boats to get them off. We had a glimmer of the military situation, but we weren't really kept informed as a fighter unit of what was going on on the ground. Our lives consisted of sleeping as much as we could because there was a great shortage of that. And then there were just several 'Tomorrow morning, first light, you're off on a fighter sweep', or to escort the bombers to certain areas. Even so, morale was tremendous, because the routine was that we would be flying many, many times during the day, having taken off in the darkness and then, as the dawn came up, we'd fly to a forward base such as Manston or Hawkinge or Rochford, and then we'd be at readiness all through the day and then in the evening, just as the light was beginning to fail, we'd fly back to our base at North Weald. There'd be a mad rush to get down to the local tavern before the pubs closed. Don't forget we were all 19, 20, 21 years of age. We were just overgrown schoolboys.

I flew over the Dunkirk area probably a dozen times, I suppose. It all folded pretty quickly and we'd go sort of twice a day. We were trying to give constant support, and in fact I think the Germans probably got a shock. After Poland and the Low Countries, where they only got token resistance from rather antiquated aircraft, at Dunkirk they suddenly came up against an air force with sophisticated fighters. We were also disciplined as an air force in the Royal Air Force and we never looked on the Germans as being superior to ourselves – except in numbers.

During the Dunkirk rescue operations, a deployment of Spitfires was allowed. They had previously been barred from flying over France for reasons of security, so that the Germans were not able to get their hands on Britain's newest and most potent weapon in air defence. Among the pilots was Air Commodore Al Deere, then a 21-year-old flier who became a much-decorated pilot of the war and was a pioneer in one other respect. He was born in Auckland, New Zealand, and joined the Royal Air Force just before his twentieth birthday under the British government's direct commissioning scheme for the dominions of South Africa, Australia, Canada and New Zealand. They invited applications from young men in the age bracket of 18 to 25, and they sent out selection boards to each of the countries to sign up recruits. It was a scheme that brought hundreds of much-needed recruits from the dominions. As Al Deere said:

I was one of the lucky first 24 selected in New Zealand. I just wanted to fly, and I don't think it really occurred to me that war was on the horizon. After training, I went to No. 54 Squadron, based at Hornchurch in Essex. We were equipped with Gladiators at the time. Our first piece of excitement was the Munich crisis. We were all brought up to a state of readiness. We had lovely silver Gladiators with our squadron crest on. Then we spent days painting all the silver off and camouflaging them ready to go to war. Of course, later we were equipped with Spitfires, and I personally believe and have always believed that that saved us. Because we could never have coped with the Germans in Gladiators, as was proven in Norway when the Gladiator squadrons were sent in. At the time we thought: 'We'll be able to take these chaps on'. We were very proud of our squadrons. We were a mixed bunch of chaps who were all pretty young. I suppose our average age was 21 or something like that. Some were younger, some a bit older. We thought we were good. It didn't occur to us we'd be shot out of the sky. But we were pleased when we became the third squadron in the Royal Air Force to be converted to Spitfires. We hadn't had any experience on monoplanes of course, and there was no such thing as a dual aircraft in those days. So you just learned the cockpit drill and read the pilot's handbook carefully – and you flew it. Right from the word go, it felt right as an aircraft. It was amazingly tough. It looked fragile, with a narrow undercarriage, and you had to get used to cross-wind landings. But it was an amazingly tough aircraft really, as it was to prove later on.

When the British army started retreating and Dunkirk was going to be the point of evacuation, we fighter squadrons in East Anglia were sent out on patrol to cover the beachhead, the evacuation there up and down that coast. We did two or three trips a day. It was the first time we as fighter pilots had crossed the Channel to make combat and then come back. Because the endurance factor on a Spitfire was fairly critical, you couldn't stay that long. We weren't accustomed to finding our way back across the Channel. We patrolled the coast from Boulogne to Dunkirk and up as far as Antwerp trying to support the evacuation from the air. Dunkirk itself was on fire; I think there must have been an oil storage tank. It was just completely overcast by black smoke that mingled with lowish cloud. So from miles away you knew where Dunkirk was. It was just black smoke over the town. Of course, we got in combat with the Germans, who had by that time had moved some of their bases forward. They were able to get their fighters as far as the bridgehead. We had preset attack patterns which we had practised. But they soon went by the board against fighters. The tactics we had practised were strictly evolved for attacking unescorted bombers. But we were never able to put them into practice against fighters.

I have some very specific memories about that because I think it's recorded history that I was the first Spitfire pilot to have combat with a 109. That was over Dunkirk. Some 109s appeared. There were two of us at the time and we got into combat with them. I got on the tail of a 109 and managed to shoot him down. He went down into the sea on the coastline. I put in a lengthy report about it when I got back, because I was able to stay behind this chap for a long time. He tried to shake me off and I put in a report to the effect that, except initially in the dive, the Spitfire was superior. That was pooh-poohed at the time, I don't mind telling you, by those at the top. They said: 'All our records show that the 109's better than a Spitfire.' And I said: 'Not in close combat, it isn't.' Eventually, I was proved right.

Later, I shot down a Dornier and a Heinkel and then, I regret to say, I was myself shot down by the rear gunner of a Dornier which eventually came down itself. This Dornier appeared out of a fairly cloudy sky over the bridgehead. We chased him. I got on to his tail and was firing a burst at him. I could see return fire from the rear gunner and suddenly I felt a juddering. I think it was probably fairly lucky. A bullet from the rear gunner went into my glycol tank. That's my coolant system, gone. That meant I was *hors de combat*. I had to come down. I crash-landed on the beach between Dunkirk and Ostend and the Dornier came down over the top of me, smoking, and glided away inland. I wasn't injured until I landed. I hit my head on the front of the cockpit and it knocked me out cold. I landed wheels up, right on the edge of the water. The tide happened to be coming in. When I came to, I scrambled out and got my parachute out and walked up the beach towards a café. By that time the tide was gradually coming over the Spitfire anyhow. It was never recovered, so I imagine it sank into the sand in the course of time. I had a badly cut eye. In the café a woman stuck my eye together with plaster and put bandages around it. I then set off to get to Dunkirk. I expect it took me two or three hours because there was a lot of refugee traffic. Eventually, I collared a bicycle and rode the rest of the way. I met a couple of British army tommies inland a bit. I said: 'Where are you going?' They said: 'You tell us.' I said: 'You're evacuating, aren't you?' They said: 'We don't know. We're just what's left of our thing.' So we headed for Dunkirk and it was an absolute shambles, a lot of strafing and the bombing.

The beaches were a mass of human flotsam, which was every now and again sent diving for cover as the fighters swooped low, guns blazing. There were many injured and many bodies, but between the times of bedlam, order and discipline was restored and lines of men waited, as one said, like orderly cinema queues to get aboard the ships and boats as they came in and out of the harbour and the shoreline to snatch another bunch to safety, and even that wasn't guaranteed. Scores of boats were sunk by German bombers, including seven destroyers. The medics, meanwhile, stayed back to help the many wounded who would be among the hundreds left behind. Al Deere was among the lucky ones who got away:

You got into line and waited. Others were already swimming out to boats. Then a destroyer came in and I managed to get on it. The ship was absolutely stuffed to the gunwales with soldiers. We were bombed not far after pulling off, but we didn't get hit. And yes, there were some sarcastic remarks about the RAF. They said: 'Where the bloody hell have you been?' I, who had been flying 10 days non-stop up to the time I'd been shot down, two and three sorties a day, and I was pretty tired.

I answered in no mean manner and said: 'We were there but perhaps you didn't see us.' I told them. They weren't very pleased with me. I was the only airman on board. It was a bit unpleasant, but I suppose one couldn't blame them. They were pretty worn out. When I got back I went straight to my squadron, which had moved from Hornchurch to Catterick for re-equipping because we'd lost quite a few. We'd started with 17 pilots, I think, and finished with eight. Some were shot down and didn't come back. Some were badly injured. We lost both our flight commanders. In fact, our casualties for the amount of flying we did and the time spent were greater at Dunkirk than in the Battle of Britain. We were operating so far from home. I was shot down but I managed to get back. So many others didn't.

Although short of planes and often manned by inexperienced crews, the Royal Air Force flew a staggering number of sorties over France during the 10 days surrounding the evacuation of the BEF: 2,739 fighter sorties, 651 bombing missions and 171 reconnaissance flights. The cost had been high. During May and early June, losses to all units were horrific: almost 1,000 aircraft of all types lost, including 66 lost in the Norwegian campaign, and most of the crews killed or captured. Among these disastrous figures was an even more depressing subtotal: of the 261 treasured Hurricanes sent across the Channel to be based in France, 75 had been lost or so badly damaged as to be irreparable. Another 120 Hurricanes had been parked up on bases awaiting repairs but, on the evacuation of all airfields from France, these had to be destroyed, along with machinery and vehicles, to prevent the Germans from getting possession of them. Put together with the losses suffered by squadrons flying out directly from England, and the depressing total was 432 Hurricanes and Spitfires. Britain's most important assets in the looming battle for air supremacy over the United Kingdom had been lost in the battle for France.

On 3 June, with the evacuation from Dunkirk almost complete, Britain had just 331 fighters classed as operational. It was a grim picture. That day, Dowding told the War Cabinet that the heavy losses had substantially weakened air defences and he could not guarantee air superiority over Britain for more than 48 hours in the event of a German air attack. He produced a graph which showed the losses of Hurricanes in the 10 days from 8 to 18 May: 250 had been lost, an average of 25 a day compared with four a day received from production. If this had continued throughout May, he said, the entire Hurricane force would have been wiped out. As it was, the number of fighters serviceable as of the previous day was 224 Hurricanes and 280 Spitfires. Even this low figure did not represent the true picture. Dowding told the War Cabinet:

A number of the pilots already with their squadrons have not yet completed their first solo on eight-gun fighters and need up to six weeks to become sufficiently proficient to take part in active operations.

Dowding ended his summary by declaring that quite apart from the tremendous drain of sending any large numbers of fighters to France, he was faced with the formidable task of reconstructing the home defence squadrons, which had suffered heavily as a result of recent operations in France, and that this had to be done at a time when he had to be prepared for an air attack on the British Isles. The War Cabinet now accepted that no further squadrons could be sent out to France, but this situation remained within the top-secret confines of the cabinet room, and those still trapped in France were left to ponder their plight with what they saw as a poor RAF response. With the Germans heading onwards with Paris in their sights, limited operations continued, especially to cover evacuations from Normandy and western France of both troops, civilians and others seeking refuge within the United Kingdom.

The RAF, meanwhile, continued to provide air support for the French right to the moment that the French government agreed to an armistice deal with Hitler on 17 June. H.A.C. Bird-Wilson, then a 20-year-old pilot with No. 17 Squadron, based at Croydon, who was to become Air Vice-Marshal, had just returned from operations over Dunkirk:

We were informed that we'd be moving to the north of England in 24 hours. We were down to our third commanding officer by this time, and we had lost a flight commander and several of our pilots. We were due for a rest and retraining, really. Instead, our orders were changed at midnight and we were told we were heading for Le Mans in France. This was a great surprise to us, but off we went. We landed in France the next day, and the squadron took on the retreat through western France. We were sent on numerous patrols around places like Le Havre and Rouen and by sheer eyeballing – using our eyes – we managed to intercept quite a few German aircraft. It was difficult, because the smoke from burning oil tanks at Rouen went up thousands and thousands of feet. There was a great deal of tension because we didn't know really what to expect. Every time we took off we just went into the unknown. We had quite a few raw pilots at this time, people who had only got 10 hours on Hurricanes. I remember the squadron taking off in formation, and these inexperienced pilots were overtaking the squadron commander on takeoff because they didn't really dare throttle back. It was up to the more experienced pilots who had been through the northern part of France, fighting, to try and look after these chaps. We didn't have time to give them any further training, because every sortie we made, we were going into a fight. And the only lessons we could teach them were verbal lessons, to tell them to throttle back, that their aircraft wouldn't stall and that they shouldn't be frightened of it. But it's a picture that stays in my mind of seeing these young chaps just wouldn't throttle back, and they really led the squadron off the ground. Even so, pilots with only 10 hours' experience of Hurricanes didn't have much chance of survival. They couldn't turn their Hurricanes tight enough, and they were just raw meat to the more experienced German pilots. But likewise, vice versa; so 50–50, I suppose, really.

For the final stages of the RAF operations in the Battle for France, No. 17 Squadron was moved to Dinard, down the coast from St-Malo, and flew sorties from there until 17 June, when the armistice was about to be signed. Bird-Wilson recalls the surprise

that now awaited the squadron commander from the French
people they had been supporting:

> The French station commander called our commander in
> and told him we had just one hour to get off his airfield,
> otherwise our Hurricanes would be destroyed. Not a very
> friendly gesture, considering we'd been trying to help France,
> but at any rate those were our orders and, quite honestly,
> I've never seen a squadron scramble so quickly. We were
> ordered to land on the Channel Isles and patrol Cherbourg
> while the army were being evacuated from there. We eventu-
> ally left the Channel Isles on 27 June 1940, and the possibil-
> ity of invasion and occupation was already feared by the
> local population. The only experience we had was from
> young ladies coming up to us pilots and asking if we would
> fly them back to England. Well, in a single-seater fighter it
> was a pretty tight squeeze and of course against the rules. I
> can't say that everybody obeyed the King's Regulations and
> didn't succumb to a request from a pretty young lady,
> because later I did meet a lady at a party who said she'd
> come from the Channel Isles in a Hurricane. It was quite
> possible, but the pilot would have had to fly without a
> parachute and – not complaining, I would think – sitting on
> the girl's lap.

With the Germans now firmly ensconced across the Channel, the
British War Cabinet contemplated the immediate future and
prospect for air supremacy over Britain that Churchill considered
'essential' if a German invasion was to be held back. Other
pressing matters concerning the RAF, also being discussed,
exposed another great vulnerability. The first dealt with what
Churchill described as the 'muddle and scandal' of the aircraft
production branch, which had failed to ensure that aircraft were
coming off the lines in timely fashion and that the emphasis had
been placed on the production of the types of aircraft that would
be most suited to the tasks ahead. Churchill considered that the
Air Ministry had failed on both counts.

He had personally harnessed the brutish entrepreneurial tal-
ents of Lord Beaverbrook, the Canadian owner of the *Daily
Express*, to aircraft production. He, said Churchill, had made 'a

surprising improvement in the supply and repair of aircraft'. But now it seemed that there were not enough pilots to fly them. At a War Cabinet meeting in the first week of June, it had been disclosed that the RAF was so short of pilots that it could become a 'limiting factor' in performance in the weeks and months ahead. Churchill immediately fired off an angry memo to Sir Archibald Sinclair at the Air Ministry, stating that this was the first time this particular admission of failure had been made by the Air Ministry, and he wanted to know why, especially as 'immense masses of aircraft are devoted to the making of pilots, far beyond the proportion adopted by the Germans. How then is this shortage explained?'

He added that it would indeed be lamentable if machines were standing idle for want of pilots to fly them. The scandals, the shortcomings, dire losses, duff planes, inexperienced fliers, not enough aircraft and then not enough pilots: in short, the sum total of years of neglect had come home to roost at a time when Britain had her back to the wall. The RAF, hoisted on its own outdated principles and non-applicable doctrines, undermined by outmoded aircraft, some lousy managers and serious competition that it fought with one hand tied behind its back, had clearly suffered the age-old effects of being a political football, a situation, incidentally, that was not left behind that first year of the 1940s.

Dead ahead was the challenge of a lifetime for hundreds and then thousands of young men, who would soon find themselves flying by the seat of their pants, because there would be no other way. Churchill set the scene in the House of Commons on 18 June: 'the battle for France is over . . . I expect that the Battle of Britain is about to begin'.

CHAPTER EIGHT

On a Knife's Edge

After the surrender of France, the Germans began to amass the accoutrements of their planned invasion of the British Isles on the very edge of the English Channel and there, in a famous scene, Reichsmarschall Hermann Goering stood eyeing up the 22-mile span and declared that his Luftwaffe would crush Britain in a matter of weeks. Some across the water would not have argued with him. The British, he said, were now at the mercy of his air force, and he had every reason to voice such optimistic bravado. The British home defences had been weakened, as we have seen, by putting up a better fight for France than France herself managed. The Germans had been keeping a close account of the RAF losses and boasted that Britain was short of trained pilots, which was also true. It was likely that they were also aware of another crucial element that seriously affected Britain's future strategy in dealing with incoming bombers that would soon be dispatched in their hundreds to knock the daylights out of the RAF. Britain's air defence plans had been worked out on projections for air combat based on the straightforward issue of fighters attacking bombers. But that was old thinking, based on the belief that only bombers would have the endurance to reach British mainland targets. All that changed when the Germans side-stepped France's first line of defence, the supposedly unimpregnable Maginot Line, and marched on. As Air Chief Marshal

Sir Theodore McEvoy pointed out in retrospect:*

> When France fell, we realised that the Germans could now
> send bombers over escorted by their very efficient fighters –
> yet we had based all our earlier calculations on unescorted
> bombers. And although we didn't much mind losing what
> was left of France, which didn't count for much, we were
> horrified at the thought that Messerschmitt fighters would
> be watching their backs, which we hadn't calculated on at all.

Across the Channel, the heavily mechanised and exceedingly
well-equipped German army was literally zooming across France
to march down the Champs-Elysées on 14 June and stick a
swastika on the Eiffel Tower. The Luftwaffe began to take
possession of airfields close to the Channel, some of which the
RAF had vacated only 24 hours earlier. At sea, barges and
landing craft were being ferried by the hundred to the Channel
ports to carry German troops forward for the launch of Operation Sea Lion: the invasion of Britain. The German army, 120
divisions strong, had no other diversions after its triumphs in
Poland, the Low Countries and France. It had yet to begin
sending troops into North Africa, where Mussolini's army was on
the move against British possessions and could focus on the
forthcoming battle with the British army.

The latter was a mere 25 divisions strong in June 1940, which
included some enthusiastic but ill-trained and barely equipped
county regiments that were by no stretch of the imagination
ready for war. And of course there was the Home Guard,
officially launched on 23 July with 250,000 volunteers armed to
the teeth with home-made weapons such as broomsticks made
into pikes by attaching carving knives, cutlasses, shotguns, cata-
pults and the like. With such a dire state of affairs at the back of
him, Churchill even called for a report on the possibility of
spreading mustard gas on Britain's most vulnerable beaches.

The Luftwaffe, as everyone knew, had built a superior force by
then consisting of almost 3,000 fighters and bombers. At best,
the RAF could muster only a joint force of around 1,200 aircraft,
of which around 600 were fighters, and not all by any means were

* Memoir, Sound Archive, Imperial War Museum.

fit to fly. The odds were stacked heavily against Britain, and ironically only the skies themselves were cloudless in a brilliantly sunny summer. Churchill had learned from the First World War to take a positive view – that tomorrow the tide might turn, or at the very least an action might be taken tomorrow that would assist in the turning of the tide. He leaped on ideas and immediately promoted the benefit of three positives as the War Cabinet weighed up the pros and cons of the forthcoming onslaught:

1. The British still had overwhelming naval superiority.
2. There were 20-odd miles of clear blue sea in which to attack an invasion force.
3. Beaverbrook had rampaged through the tardy Ministry of Supply and pushed the planemakers into doubling then trebling the delivery of Hurricanes and Spitfires and instigated moves to take delivery of a large number of aircraft built and purchased in the US which were to be flown to the American border with Canada, pulled over the border by horses (so as not to upset America's neutral stance) and then flown across the Atlantic to Britain (see Chapter Nine).

The Royal Navy had already played an ace. The French had been given the opportunity to surrender its naval fleet into British or American hands to stop the Germans from taking possession. When no response was forthcoming, the British sent flying boats to block the exit of the Mediterranean port of Mers el-Kebir, Algeria, where French warships were at anchor. When a final ultimatum expired on 3 July, the French ships were sunk by an aerial and naval bombardment launched from a flotilla of Britain's own warships and an aircraft carrier, with the loss of 1,280 French sailors. On the same day, all French ships then lying at British ports were seized, and that night Churchill, apprised of latest intelligence traffic, issued a rallying call to 'all persons holding responsible positions in government, the fighting services and the civil departments':

On what may be the eve of an attempted invasion or battle for our native land, the Prime Minister desires to impress [their] duty to maintain a spirit of alert and confident energy . . . there are no grounds for supposing that more German troops can be landed in this country . . . than can be destroyed or captured by the strong forces at present under arms. The Royal Air Force is in excellent order and at the highest strength it has yet attained. The German navy was never so weak nor the British army at home so strong as now.

As history shows, that assessment was, understandably, something of an overstatement, but Hitler was taking no chances. He personally demanded that no seaborne invasion should begin until the RAF had been neutralised. Goering assured him that it would not present a problem and that he planned to achieve mastery of the air by the relentless bombing of airfields, aircraft factories, fuel dumps and every industry that helped keep the RAF in the air. Furthermore, his own fighters would shoot the Hurricanes and the Spitfires out of the skies. In making these dangerous assumptions, he had overlooked two crucial factors that were soon to show their worth as the Battle of Britain commenced: the sheer heroic tenacity of the British fighter pilots and the instant success of a home defence system that had been dramatically upgraded in the months since war was declared and was only now fully operational. At its heart was the new radar early-warning system invented as recently as 1935 and which was not only far better than the German equivalent, but was the most advanced in the world.

By mid-1940, Dowding had overseen the erection of a chain of radar stations that were able to detect aircraft flying up to a hundred miles away as well as providing a fairly accurate assessment of the number of aircraft and their height. A second chain of stations detected aircraft travelling at less than 3,000 feet, and in early 1940 another development by the British scientific team working on the project produced a transmitter that crucially detected 'friendly' aircraft. Dowding's own operational control headquarters sat atop a structure of four home defence groups. Each group had its own command and control, and each command was subdivided into sectors for more localised control. The largest group was No. 11, which covered an area stretching from East Anglia to Dorset and which controlled 22 combat squadrons, 13 of them flying Hurricanes, six with Spitfires and three with Blenheims. Dowding's operations room, star feature in many a film on the Battle of Britain, built up a minute-by-minute picture of air activity over Britain gleaned from the chain of radar stations. These were combined with reports derived from visual contact by members of the 3,000-strong Observer Corps operating from 1,000 posts across the UK, providing front-line information on incoming raids. Reports from these sources were collated by the Fighter Command operations room and simultaneously read by the operations rooms in the four group command sectors. Based on the plotting of the incoming raids taking shape on the boards in front of them, the local operational controllers decided on their group's response by scrambling the necessary squadrons.

They were the key figures in the Fighter Command system of, hopefully, being able to put enough planes in the air to seriously deflect any incoming raid of German bombers and fighters. Additionally, Dowding's home defence operations had, by the end of June 1940, just completed installing the final batch of almost 1,100 heavy anti-aircraft guns and 480 light pieces along with 3,000 machine-gun posts and around 4,000 searchlights. One further hazard for attacking Germans was the re-emergence of balloons, which had virtually disappeared during the inter-war years. Now, 2,000 were being rushed into operation as barrage balloons tethered over ground installations at a height of 5,000 feet and were especially effective in causing grief to dive-bombers.

The German air attacks began on ports and airfields along the English Channel, where convoys were bombed and the air battle was joined. At that point in time, the Luftwaffe had 1,480 bombers, 989 fighters and 140 reconnaissance aircraft lined up for the battles ahead and positioned in an arc around England from Norway to the Cherbourg peninsula in northern coastal France. Against this oncoming force, Britain had just 660 combat-ready fighters and another 500 or so in various stages of repair in maintenance units. On 9 July the British war planners were again expecting the invasion to begin at any moment. Instead, the following night the first mass attack of 120 German bombers and fighters was launched against a British convoy between Dover and Dungeness. At the same time, 70 planes raided South Wales, bombing dockyards in the first large-scale attacks on the British mainland, and the pressure on the British fighter squadrons began to mount. Air Commodore Al Deere, whom we met earlier in the battle for France, recalled:

In July we went from convoy patrols to being more defensive in that the Germans at that time started sending formations of fighters across with the intention of drawing us up into combat, hoping to destroy the fighter force before they themselves launched the invasion. So gradually through July the tempo of the whole thing built up so that we were doing three and four sorties a day and the Germans were getting more and more aggressive as they built up their forces on the other side. Their penetration at the time was only 20 to 30 miles inland, so they were trying to get us up and have as few losses as possible themselves – knock us out, that's what they were trying to do. Fortunately, Dowding and his group [No. 11] commander, Keith Park, realised this would probably be their aim and therefore the number of fighter squadrons committed to battle at any one time was fairly severely restricted so that we always had a reserve.

Eventually, they started then to send over the bombers. Their first targets were the coastal airfields such as Manston, Hawkinge, Tangmere, and so on. Originally, we were at Manston, which was hell because we were getting strafed and bombed there on a twice-daily basis, being the first airfield that the Germans would sight and the last one they would see on the way back, so they got it both ways. Then the real fighting started in that we were not only coping with bombers but fighter escorts as well. Gradually, they moved their penetration further and further until eventually they were bombing the London airfields, and my squadron had been moved to one of them, Hornchurch. In one of the raids on Hornchurch, for example, I was caught taking off, blown up taking off by a German raid on the airfield. I was held up from taking off by a pilot who'd got himself in the takeoff lane and didn't know where to go. He delayed me. By the time I'd got him sorted out, I was last off and caught the bombs and was blown sky-high. Three of us were. We all got away with it. My Spitfire was blown up. I finished up on the airfield in a heap. I got pretty badly concussed. My number two finished on the airfield with his wing blown off. A doctor bandaged me up and I just went back because we were under tremendous stress at the time and we were still desperately short of pilots.

Rescuing pilots became vital. Special operations were put in force by both sides to save pilots downed over the sea. The Germans were running air patrols with planes marked with a red cross, while the British were using patrol boats to pick up pilots, their own and the Luftwaffe's, who had baled out. In that, the British held the advantage. German pilots went straight into captivity, while British pilots who came down either over sea or on land and were successfully rescued generally returned quickly to battle in double-quick time, but the balance tipped in Germany's favour with the large number of Bomber Command losses on the Continent.

Either way, casualties across the board were mounting at an alarming rate. On 14 August Churchill was apparently visibly shocked to learn of the latest figures for the RAF covering the two months of June and July: 526 killed or missing, 629 injured or captured. At that moment, 4,496 young pilots were in training, although there was a desperate need for aircraft in which to train them, inasmuch as every airworthy Hurricane or Spitfire was needed for the battle. Civilian casualties were also beginning to mount. In the second week of August, as the Battle of Britain began to be fought in earnest, 1,419 civilians had been killed in air raids, 90 per cent of them in London. The casualties would of course soon spread to other cities and, even as Churchill received these figures, bombers were being dispatched from Germany that day to hit Southampton. On 15 August 100 bombers with 60 fighter escorts attacked shipping ports, aerodromes, aircraft factories and air-force installations throughout Tyneside, the accuracy of the attack giving much credence to the rumours of fifth columnists and spies operating widely through the countryside. By some sixth sense or sheer brilliance in strategic insight, Dowding had earlier transferred seven squadrons of fighters to the north, and the counteroffensive they launched meant that during the Tyneside attack 30 bombers were shot down with only two English pilots injured.

On the same day, a further 800 bombers hit targets across the east and south of England. Depleted by the cover for the north,

137

Dowding had to put every single squadron he had into the air that night, and Sir Anthony Eden, who was visiting Churchill in Downing Street, would later record:

> I sat in the Cabinet Room with him while reports came in of the air battle that was developing. Squadron after squadron of the Royal Air Force went up to engage the enemy and still the Luftwaffe kept on coming. The news was scrappy at first and still more squadrons were called for until it seemed they had all been committed. We listened and conjectured; things looked very stern and the odds were against us.

Churchill could stand it no longer and ordered a car to take him immediately to Fighter Command headquarters to keep abreast of what was happening as it happened and was 'joyously ecstatic' as he learned that almost 100 German aircraft had been shot down, with the loss of 25 fighters that night. The scene was repeated again the following day, and Churchill returned to the command centre of Keith Park's No. 11 Group, which became a regular port of call. This time Lord Ismay was there with him and witnessed the reaction as another day of heavy bombardment began. Ismay wrote:

> At one moment, every single squadron in the group was [again] engaged. There was nothing in reserve and the map table showed new waves of attackers crossing the coast. I felt sick with fear. As the evening closed in and the fighting died down, we left by car . . . Churchill said: 'Don't speak to me; I have never been so moved.' After about five minutes, he leaned forward and said: 'Never in the field of human conflict has so much been owed by so many to so few.' The words burned into my brain.

On 18 August the Air Ministry estimated that the Luftwaffe were now sending over in excess of 1,000 planes a day and that day was no exception; wave after wave of bombers and fighters arrived to be met by the Hurricanes and Spitfires of virtually every available squadron. Seventy-one German aircraft were destroyed on that day against 22 British fighters shot down, 16 pilots lost and 15 aircraft destroyed on the ground, bringing the tally in the previous 10 days to 694 German planes shot down with the loss of 150 British fighters.

Britain's own bombing operations against German positions had continued, although in the case of Bomber Command there were more crews available than planes. On 25 August, however, a squadron of Wellingtons took off in two waves to bomb Berlin. It was the RAF's first bombing mission over Germany in this phase of the battle and was ordered by Churchill himself, more as a propaganda and morale-boosting exercise than one designed to inflict heavy damage on the German population. The tactic had unexpected results. Hitler ordered that a heavy revenge bombardment of London itself should begin, and this change of target for the bombers, though unfortunate for the residents of London, had the immediate effect of taking the pressure off the airfields of Fighter Command. Al Deere again:

> I've always believed if they'd have stuck to attacking our airfields and our radar stations they could have well beaten us because without the radar stations we were in no position in terms of strength to keep squadrons in the air. We had to have advance warning so that we could stay on the ground until the last moment and therefore conserve our strength. They did knock one out down on the south coast. A whole raid, a very big raid into the Isle of Wight went undetected. At that time, August going into September, new aircraft had started coming in. Beaverbrook had got cracking, and we were having them flown in. But we were still short of experienced pilots. We were getting pilots who had not been on Spitfires because there were no conversion units. They came straight to a squadron from their training establishments. Some of them did have a few hours on Hurricanes but not on the Spitfire. There were also many fresh to England, and some who could barely speak English.

In fact, volunteers from the Commonwealth and elsewhere made a vital contribution. No. 242 Squadron was almost entirely made up of Canadians in 1940, and No. 1 Squadron of the Royal Canadian Air Force came to Britain en masse. American volunteers formed the Eagle Squadron, which operated until the United States joined the war. There were also South Africans,

139

Australians and a large contingent of New Zealanders. Pilots from the French and Belgian air forces also came over, as well as Czech and Polish. The Royal Navy sent 58 experienced fliers and two squadrons from the Fleet Air Arm to join the battle so that, all told, almost 2,900 aircrew were engaged in the Battle of Britain. Pilot losses remained one of the most serious problems facing Dowding, and it was something of a chicken-and-egg situation, as Al Deere explained:

For example, we got two young New Zealanders into my flight. Chatting to them, I found they'd been six weeks at sea coming over. They were trained in some very outdated aircraft out in New Zealand. They were given, I think, two trips or something on a Hurricane and then were sent to the squadron. We were pretty busy, so we gave them what was known as a cockpit check. They'd go off for one solo flight and circuit. Then they were into battle. The problem was of course that they didn't last. Those two lasted two trips and they both finished up in Dover hospital. One was pulled out of the Channel; one landed by parachute.

All I used to say to them was: 'Look, don't do anything by yourself. Stick with your leader and just watch and, unless you're attacked yourself, just stay out of trouble until you get the feel of things.' It's pretty hard for a young chap to follow that dictum. In fact, generally what happened was they'd follow their leader and the next thing they knew they were in the parachute because a 109 got up behind them or something. By then, the raids were becoming so big you could see them from miles away when you got up there. These German armadas were frightening. You'd see this great mass of aircraft in the distance, just black spots. You'd see the bombers first, obviously, because they were in close formation and bigger. As they got closer, you'd see little black specks weaving all around them. Those you knew were the 109s. It really was a frightening sight. There seemed no way of stopping them. We were always overwhelmingly outnumbered.

As for tactics, we just got in what we hoped was the best position. My squadron, the Spitfires, would engage the top fighter escorts, which I think we did fairly successfully. At least we drew a lot of them off from the Hurricanes, which couldn't get the height and were down below attacking the bombers. The 109 was the most feared. The 110, which was a twin-engined, was very easy because it was slow. They had a rear gun but it was pretty useless. The Germans in the end withdrew it from escort. The 109 was a tough customer, and they were well flown. They had a 0.5 cannon in the nose which was pretty lethal. We only had .303 Brownings at that time, eight of them, admittedly. Yes, they were good, they were damned good. No question about that. So, really, when you became engaged with a German formation it was every man for himself, Spitfires and 109s going round and round in circles, swooping and diving.

Once you got into combat, there wasn't time to be frightened, but we *were* frightened, of course we were, the whole bloody time. If you're in combat you're so keen to get the other guy and save your own skin that your adrenalin's pumping and there's no room for fright. I'd often wonder why there weren't more collisions. There were probably more than we knew about, because if somebody collided you didn't know about it. There was, in the initial engagement, a danger of collision. Then, I had a collision with a 109 because we were both trying to come at each other head on. The closing speed was such that neither of us could get out of the way and we collided. I crashed in Kent on fire. He went into the sea. I crashed into a cornfield. Got a bit burned but I got away with it. I was in East Grinstead, the burns place, for two days, then I was back on the squadron. They were just burns. I had to have stuff on them and that sort of thing. The next morning there was an air raid. The hospital was evacuated to shelters. I evacuated myself to the railway station and got a train back to Hornchurch. The doctor was furious with me. I was flying the next day.

I was in East Grinstead twice. On the other occasion, I had an encounter with some 109s which made a mess of my Spitfire. I jumped out at 10,000 feet and came down in a field in Kent and was picked up by a passing ambulance on its way to the hospital. I escaped with a sprained wrist, which they taped up, and went back to work.

The weather was, we used to say, rotten weather because it

141

was fine almost every day. We'd get up at five in the morning, get down to the dispersal and say, 'God, another fine day', knowing that the Germans would come. We used to pray for cloud. If it was cloudy over their target area, it would stop them because they had no way in those days of accurately locating the target. On an average day, we would go up perhaps as many as five times in a day and get into combat on three occasions. The sorties lasted 40 to 45 minutes, depending on combat and that sort of thing. It was just dawn till dusk, non-stop. You'd go perhaps 10 days without actually seeing the mess in daylight. We'd go off at first light if we were operating from the forward base, which was Manston, and similarly we'd come back in the evenings at last light. You were either in the air or at readiness, sitting in the dispersal hut. We used to have meals brought out to us.

Even so, I don't think the average fighter pilot had any sense that the Battle of Britain was an historic event, except to say we knew that if the Germans got air superiority it would enable them to invade without much opposition from the air. Air superiority was vital to the Germans to guarantee reasonable safety of their troops across the Channel. They still had to beat the navy, and our navy would have done a marvellous job, but without air cover we would have been pretty much at the receiving end of the full might of the German air force. We knew that, but we didn't really think about it, to be honest. I did, however, seriously contemplate the fact that the Germans might win. Yes, my word, I did. You see, pilot shortage was acute in the end. I always thought they would invade provided they could establish a reasonable air superiority. They were much closer to it, I think, than they thought they were. In my squadron, by the end of August we were reduced to maybe three of us who were experienced and had gone through the whole show, Dunkirk and the lot. Other squadrons were similarly placed so you were virtually fighting at that time a war with very inexperienced chaps. That could only get progressively worse . . .

Al Deere's mention of the East Grinstead burns hospital was of special significance to his good friend, Geoffrey Page, whom we also met in Chapter Seven describing his early adventures over Dunkirk. Though Deere's burns were not serious, he was eventually made an associate member of what became known as The Guinea Pig Club. It was formed by a group of early patients – Page among them – at the Queen Victoria Hospital, East Grinstead, where the surgeon in charge, Archibald McIndoe, won fame for his unsurpassed skill in plastic surgery. Born in Dunedin, the 40-year-old New Zealander, formerly of the Mayo Clinic and St Bartholomew's Hospital, London, was later knighted for his pioneering work in remodelling the faces and limbs of injured airmen – McIndoe's guinea pigs. Geoffrey Page, still flying Hurricanes with No. 54 Squadron and who had come through many early skirmishes when the Battle of Britain commenced, said:

> I don't think we had any sense that the fate of the country depended on us. We were so occupied with our daily task as the main fighter airfields in the south-east area were being hit daily. The ingenuity of the ground crews and the fact that we hadn't got concrete runways meant that we kept on flying. There was always enough grass somewhere that you could take off on in between bomb holes, which were immediately marked with coloured flags. So Fighter Command was still very much in commission when the big air raids on east London began. Even so, our squadron by then was losing quite a lot of people. We were supposed to muster 12 aircraft for one attack, but in fact we only had 10. So the 10 of us took off to meet this incoming raid, and as we climbed – the usual procedure – the controller said there were 90 bandits approaching from the south and they were at about 15,000 feet.
>
> We could see what looked like a swarm of little insects beginning to take shape. It was a large formation of Dornier 217 bombers escorted by Messerschmitt 109 fighters. Well, the 10 of us were catching up slowly with the bombers, who by that time had unfortunately been able to drop their load. They flew northwards out over the Thames Estuary and we chased them. I was in the leading section of three, and the one nearest to the German bombers. Then I could see all this tracer ammunition coming from the whole formation.

They'd singled me out as the target. Probably they had a radio control gunnery officer who was saying: 'Pick out that particular fighter and shoot at him.' All these things that looked like lethal electric lightbulbs kept flashing by until suddenly there was an enormous bang and then the whole aircraft just exploded. The scientists reckon the temperature goes up from a cool room temperature at 15,000 feet to 3,000 degrees centigrade in about 10 seconds. When you consider that water boils at 100 degrees centigrade you've got quite a temperature change there on your hands. So if you don't get out in virtually just a few seconds, you're not going to get out at all. I instinctively carried out the drill of releasing the harness that strapped me to my seat and I slid the hood back, rolled the aircraft on to its back and virtually kicked the flying control column so the aircraft pointed its nose upwards. But as I was upside down that sort of popped me out of the aircraft like a cork out of a toy gun. Stupidly, and no one really knew in those days, I wasn't wearing gloves, although later on it became mandatory to wear them. My hands and face got a terrible burning. My mouth and nose were saved by my oxygen mask. I found myself tumbling head over heels through space.

I remember seeing my right arm extended and I sort of looked at it and my brain ordered me to bring it in and pull the metal ring of the ripcord on the parachute. And that was agony because of this cold metal ring on a badly burned hand. It's like an electric shock. Anyway, you don't have a choice; you've got to pull the thing otherwise the parachute won't open. I then found myself floating down.

My first natural instinct was to look up to see if the parachute was on fire but fortunately it wasn't. Then I took stock of the situation. I noticed quite a funny thing had happened. My left shoe and my trousers had been blown off completely by the explosion. I was naked from the waist downwards. My legs were slightly burned and I could hear the fight going on all around me because when you're on a parachute there's no engine noise. It's surprising how sound travels. Well, it took me I suppose about 10 minutes to float down into the water and there were various problems. First of all, when I hit the water I had to get rid of the parachute.

This is done by turning a metal disc which is just about over your stomach. It is necessary to turn it 90 degrees and then give it a hard thump and all the parachute harness breaks away. That's the theory of it, but when your hands are very badly burned it's difficult to turn the buckle. So I found myself in the water still connected to the parachute, which had come down on top of me, so I was really inside a tent with all these cords from the parachute rather like an octopus's tentacles. I knew that if I didn't get away from the parachute quickly it would get waterlogged and sink and take me with it.

So again desperation comes to the rescue and you know that if you don't turn that metal disc and if you don't thump it that's the end of you. So you do turn it, you do thump it, and I must say it was exceedingly painful. I got rid of that and then the next thing now was to blow up my life-saving jacket. You have a little tube which is just over your left shoulder. I got hold of this and started to blow into it after I'd opened the valve and all that came out the other end were bubbles because the life-saving jacket had been burned through. My face was beginning to swell up from the burns by this point. I couldn't get my helmet off. The leather strap under my chin had melted and I just couldn't undo it. So I set off for the distance, but my swollen eyelids were beginning to close up so the distant view of England which I could see quite a few miles away was getting more and more blurred. I knew the vague direction and I started swimming and then a happy thought came into my mind that in my jacket pocket was a brandy flask that my dear mother had given me which I'd filled with brandy, thinking that on some occasion or other there would be an emergency and I'd need the brandy.

Quite often in the mess over the previous weeks when the bar had closed, my fellow pilots had said: 'Come on, Geoffrey, you've got a brandy flask there. Let's have a tot.' But I said: 'No. One day I may have an emergency.' And now I had one, and I rolled over on to my back and went on swimming, kicking my legs. It was another painful business, getting my hands under the useless life-saving jacket and undo the tunic flap, which had a button.

145

Eventually, I got the brandy flask out but I couldn't hold it properly in my hands, so I held it between my wrists and undid the screw cap with my teeth. Just as I was about to take a swig, a dirty big wave came along and knocked it out of my wrists. The whole lot went to the bottom of the Channel.

I continued swimming towards England and then after a while I heard more than saw a boat. I could hear the chug, chug of its small engine. It turned out to be a whaler, which was a sort of small lifeboat put out by a Trinity House vessel, which has seen me come down. There were two men in it and it was interesting, they kept asking me questions. By this time I'd been swimming for about half an hour and I was a bit tired and fed up with the whole affair. So when they said to me, 'Are you a Jerry?' I'm afraid I let loose with every rude four-letter word I could think of and that immediately assured them that it was an RAF officer they'd picked out of the water. They took me to the ship, where the captain dressed my burns with lint, and they gave me a cup of tea. Margate Lifeboat came out and took me off the Trinity House vessel and they were going to transfer me to Margate hospital.

For the first time for about I suppose an hour or more by then I was able to laugh, because waiting on the quayside was the mayor of Margate dressed in a suit and a top hat which, you know, when you've been in an air fight an hour before, you're in dire pain through burns and then there's a chap in a top hat and a tail coat saying 'Welcome to Margate' was something of a test of one's patience. I spent a few days in Margate hospital and then I was taken up to the Royal Masonic Hospital in London, and then later on I found myself at East Grinstead in the hospital of plastic surgeon Sir Archibald McIndoe, where I spent two years undergoing plastic surgery before going back to flying in November 1942, in time for the D-day landings.

McIndoe was fantastic. He was so far ahead of his time, both as a surgeon and as a humanitarian. He was quite unique. There would be many pilots passing through this place, and those of us there at that time were the first. Among them was a famous name, Richard Hillary, who wrote a book called *The Last Enemy*. When we were allowed to get out of bed and walk a few yards, there was a little hut we used to go to where we could have a glass of beer and get away from the ward for half an hour or so. Six of us got together and formed a little club. We called it The Guinea Pig Club.

Eventually, all patients of McIndoe were invited to join the famous club, which was kept in existence after the war for well-attended annual get-togethers. One of McIndoe's earliest patients was Air Vice-Marshal Harold Bird-Wilson, who sustained his injuries in September 1938. He was a 19-year-old trainee pilot when his Swallow aircraft crashed through a mechanical fault and his head smashed into the control panel and windscreen. He suffered terrible facial injuries, including the loss of his nose. His subsequent treatment, which included four operations, was concluded with plastic surgery at the East Grinstead hospital when he became McIndoe's second patient – and 'number two guinea pig' – in January 1940. Within two months, he was on a conversion course to fly Hurricanes and became operational with No. 17 Squadron in March in time to join the battle for France and subsequently the Battle of Britain. His recollections of that period deal honestly with an oft-ignored aspect of impending battle – fear:

The squadron was based at Debden but moving forward on a rotating basis to Martlesham Heath. We were initially on convoy patrols, and we used them to train our pilots and keep them on the alert. It was obvious that a fight was going to come and we knew that our days of reckoning were ahead of us. We were scrambled against a gradually increasing number of enemy aircraft. We usually went up in flights and then it grew into squadrons. You read many stories of pilots saying they weren't worried and weren't frightened when they saw little dots in the sky which grew in size as they came from the French coast towards us. If anyone says that he wasn't frightened or apprehensive at such an occasion, then I think he's a very bad liar. You look ahead of you and you see, as the battle went on, hundreds of aircraft coming towards you. I don't believe any man is that tough not to be a bit worried at the odds the RAF were fighting or that we had insufficient squadrons to take on this horde of aircraft, which gradually built up during the battle.

I openly admit that I was worried and I was frightened at times. Fatigue also broke into a chap's mentality in the most peculiar ways. Some really got the jitters and facial twitches. Others, as I did, had nightmares. I used to wake up dreaming I was night flying my Hurricane. This went on quite a long time. There was nothing you could do to control fear at all. It's in a man's make-up whether he's a brave chap or whether he's not so brave, or whether he worries or he doesn't worry. It's human make-up, but you did see people who had really taken shock extremely badly. They'd come in the bar and they'd have a terrible facial twitch or a body twitch, and there was nothing you could do to help them except to act back again the same twitch, so they realised that they were doing it. It was a very cruel way to be kind. I had cases of chaps coming up to me and saying: 'I can't take it.' Usually, they hadn't been with us very long. You would try to help them, take them under your wing, but in the end some would ask to be posted. There was an awful place called the 'lack of moral fibre unit', LMF, at RAF Eastchurch, on an island in the Thames. And if a chap had a nervous breakdown he was sent there. I'm sure many a squadron commander or wing commander did their utmost not to send a chap there. Personally, I would have tried to talk him out of it or have him posted elsewhere.

No. 17 Squadron flying Hurricanes was among the busiest and took a number of casualties as the battle intensified:

We had a lot of success in the squadron. Being at Debden, we were scrambled against hordes of bombers coming in with their fighter escorts. We seldom knew what other squadrons were being sent out with us, or what protection we ourselves would get from the Spitfires – if any. Basically, we were 12 aircraft being sent up to hit the German bombers. Our radar and our controllers were excellent. They really told us what was happening but very seldom did we have a chance to get above the bombers. We were told to go to a certain height. We were the bomber-hitters; that was our role regardless of the glamour of the Spitfires.

They should have been there to protect us, the Hurricanes, as we hit the bombers. We were usually fed in from the side at more or less the same level as the bombers, although it was hard to define exactly which way one would go in to attack a large formation. The ideal was to break up the leaders who were the pathfinders for the bombing raid. The fighter formations generally flew somewhere above the bombers, and they used to come hurtling down at us and through us and then up again. The tactics came to be named 'yo-yo tactics'. They'd be above us and they'd come down and then bounce back again to altitude and then down again. They learned it in the Spanish Civil War and were very flexible in their formations. I think the Germans did a very good job in protecting their bombers, but we, likewise, managed to get through to their bombers, and the Spitfires were meant to protect our tails. Therein lay another problem. Hurricane pilots became very worried about Spitfires accidentally shooting down Hurricanes. It had happened in the recent past, and we had that in the back of our minds the whole time. You had only a matter of seconds to identify an aircraft before deciding whether to shoot or not to shoot. I myself recall intercepting a raid coming in when an aircraft came down right in front of me. I was just about to press the trigger when I realised it was a diving Spitfire. And you put hundreds of rounds of ammunition into an aircraft that you couldn't miss. The Germans had the same problem.

When I was shot down on 24 September, we were scrambled a bit late and we were about 15,000 or 16,000 feet, chasing the bombers in an area south of the Thames. Suddenly, Spitfires came diving down through our formation. And we – oh God – we were a bit worried about that, but we didn't realise they were being chased by 109s who came through behind them. The next thing I experienced was a terrific bang in the cockpit and flames coming up from my fuel tank. I looked up and I found I hadn't got any Perspex left in my hood and it was getting fairly hot. So I baled out immediately. The first thing one notices is the quietness having baled out. The battle was going on and you could hear the rat-a-tat of guns going off in the distance and the noise of engines of fellow pilots of the squadron circling round, to make sure one got down safely. I was slightly wounded with shrapnel and stuff, and as I floated down I saw a naval torpedo boat coming out to intercept me in the mouth of the Thames and this they did. I splashed down in the water, and the naval chaps gave me a shot of rum and a shot of morphine and they rushed me to Chatham Naval Hospital and then from there I was moved the next day down to Haywards Heath. It was 42 years later, in 1982, that I read in a book that I was the fortieth victory of Major Adolf Galland, the famous German fighter ace. He became a lieutenant-general of the Luftwaffe. I wrote to him and congratulated him on receiving his Knight of the Iron Cross for his fortieth victory and that I happened to be the sucker he shot down. He wrote back with his story, which tallied accurately with mine. He came across for Sir Douglas Bader's memorial service, and we spoke on the telephone. The Battle of Britain had more or less petered out and moved on to the next phase by the time I was hit, but I don't believe we had any sense of victory at the end of it because the battle was ongoing and the only victory one got was in watching scoreboards of the number of Germans that had been shot down. It was rather like a cricket match, really . . .

The scoreboard for the 'few' accommodated 2,353 young men from Great Britain and 574 from overseas, pilots and other aircrew officially recognised as having taken part in the Battle of Britain. Each flew at least one authorised operational sortie with an eligible unit of the Royal Air Force or Fleet Air Arm during the period 10 July to 31 October 1940.

The number of aircraft lost in the Battle of Britain combating the invasion threat was as follows: 718 from Bomber Command; 280 from Coastal Command; and 34 from the Fleet Air Arm and other RAF Commands. This in addition to the 448 lost in Fighter Command. The total number of names listed in the Westminster Abbey Battle of Britain roll of honour is 1,503. Germany lost 1,700 aircraft during the same period.

Across the Channel, meanwhile, the invasion barges and the troops on standby had been receiving a daily dose of British bombs, and hundreds of craft that were to have carried the German ground forces to the shores of Kent were now lying on the bottom. Furthermore, as September edged itself on the calendar, Fighter Command had overcome some of the shortages of machines and manpower and were now shooting the attacking bombers out of the sky faster than the German aircraft industry could replace them.

The Battle of Britain was won.

Goering failed to deliver air supremacy and Hitler's much-vaunted invasion plan was abandoned for the winter, never to re-emerge. It was, however, just a first instalment of what was to follow and just a taste of the Blitz that London and other cities would face in the weeks and months to come.

CHAPTER NINE

Bombers with No Punch

'The few' had prevailed in the short, sharp and heroic aerial cannonade, but the battle itself went on. In the first week of September, the Luftwaffe began the Blitz, nightly bombing raids over London and then outward to key British cities, which in the first three weeks of operations claimed 15,000 civilian casualties. While Fighter Command continued as before, going up to meet the incoming raiders, the focus of expectation now switched to Bomber Command as ambitions rose for a significant response. Churchill was in no doubt about that, as he wrote on 3 September: 'The bombers alone provide the means of victory.' Therein lay the next glaring challenge, but the pertinent question was: could it be met?

The hapless optimism among some at the Air Ministry of Bomber Command's ability to provide that impetus was but a thin veil that could not hide the truth: Bomber Command did not at that time have the aircraft to carry such an offensive forward or the ability to make any real impression against German targets. Little had changed in the preceding months since the disastrous losses among the bomber squadrons and the consequent demise of their crews. The losses would have been marginally more acceptable if the bombers were causing great harm to the Third Reich, but they weren't. A bombing raid towards Berlin in August 1940 by 129 British aircraft, for example, caused little destruction on the ground, many of the bombs hitting the

153

countryside well short of the military and civil installations they were aiming at. Few doubted the courage of the pilots and airmen which was on display every hour of every day that passed. Their lives were being risked – and taken – by raids that were ill-conceived by a Command influenced by the aspirations of the superior level of administrators who wanted to demonstrate to the War Cabinet that something was being done. The problems still lay in the serious inadequacy of the available aircraft. It was a declining inventory combined with a shortage of crews. Equally as important, however, was the lingering confusion among the hierarchy of the RAF, the Air Ministry and even the War Cabinet itself over targeting policy: whether to go for precision bombing on industrial and military targets, which Churchill wanted, or expand the area bombardment and risk the lives of civilians, which he did not want. Since the former could not be achieved under present arrangements, area bombing was really the only alternative until new equipment and targeting management systems were in place.

In the immediate aftermath of the Battle of Britain, the bombers had been trekking back and forth to northern France to hit airfields, army settlements and, most importantly of all, the hundreds of German barges and other craft being assembled at Antwerp and the Channel ports in readiness for the invasion of the British Isles. Some 2,500 craft were either already moored or on their way, and from 7 September repeated bombing raids had sunk most of them. The bombers were always met by a barrage of flak and strong opposition from the German fighters, sustaining a high proportion of losses. There were many stories of great heroism emerging, none more poignant than that of an 18-year-old Scot, John Hannah, who became the youngest airman to be awarded the Victoria Cross. Hannah, born in Paisley and educated at Glasgow Secondary School, was a shoe salesman when he joined the RAF in August 1939. He trained as a wireless operator and then took an air gunnery course at West Freugh before joining No. 83 Squadron, flying Hampdens from Scampton, Lincolnshire, where he was promoted to the rank of sergeant.

On 15 September 1940 Sergeant Hannah was wireless operator and air gunner flying in Hampden No. P1355, 'Betty', on a successful raid on German barges at Antwerp. As they turned for home, 'Betty' was hit by heavy anti-aircraft fire, which set off a fierce fire inside the aircraft. The rear gunner and the navigator had to bale out and Sergeant Hannah could have done the same. Instead, he remained to fight the fire as the pilot flew the severely damaged aircraft on out of the flak to give the crew a better chance. The heat was overpowering, and ammunition inside the aircraft began to explode. Sergeant Hannah fought the fire with two extinguishers and then with his bare hands. In doing so, he took severe burns to his arms and body. After 10 minutes he put out the fire, and the pilot nursed the badly damaged aircraft back to RAF Scampton. John Hannah's bravery earned him the Victoria Cross but, weakened by the burns and inhalation of smoke and fumes, he contracted tuberculosis a year later, leading to his eventual discharge from service, with full disability pension, in December 1942. Debilitated by the effects of his injuries and illness, he was unable to take up a full-time job to support his wife and three small daughters. His condition gradually deteriorated and he died on 7 June 1947 at Markfield Sanatorium in Leicester. His was but one of many stories of heroism.

Bombing raids were also carried out on German military installations in Denmark, although again with considerable losses. Twelve Blenheims from No. 82 Squadron were to attack a German airfield at Aalborg, Denmark. One aircraft had engine trouble and turned back. The rest were shot down by 109s and were lost. These losses angered and upset Churchill greatly, and then with a passion as the Blitz continued on into the autumn. Night after night after night, hundreds of German bombers, reaching armadas of 500 aircraft by November, rained thousands of tons of bombs and incendiaries on the civilian populations of London, Coventry, Southampton, Liverpool and other major centres and factories. Among those hit was the Vickers Supermarine Spitfire factory, killing 30 and halting production for a time.

The fact that the Germans could hit such targets and knock out a vital factory merely pointed up the fact that Bomber Command could not reciprocate with such precision. Churchill was by then insisting on a strong retaliation, and on 20 October 1940 even he was now forced to change his mind about precision targeting when he blasted the Air Minister, Sir Archibald Sinclair, with a memo:

I am deeply concerned with the non-expansion, and indeed contraction, of our bomber force which must be expected between now and April or May next, according to present policy. Surely an effort should be made to increase our bomb-dropping capacity during this period. I ask that a wholehearted effort shall be made to cart a large number of bombs into Germany by a second-line organisation such as I have suggested, and under conditions in which admittedly no special accuracy could be obtained.

It was fortunate indeed that bad weather set in for what would become a harsh winter of 1940, which hampered both sides. The need to hit the Channel ports also evaporated when Enigma decrypts revealed that Hitler's invasion plans for Britain had been postponed to the spring of 1941. That did not pacify Churchill's demands for attacks on Germany, and when Air Chief Marshal Sir Richard Peirse took over as head of Bomber Command he was given a clear mandate to step up attacks on specific German targets such as railways, oil installations, industrial areas, factories, electricity plants and the like. How exactly this was to be achieved was still something of a problem for the incoming chief. He took over a force of just 500 aircraft made up of Blenheims, Wellingtons, Hampdens, Whitleys and a number of Battles that no one wanted to fly. Of those, a quarter were generally under repair, and less than half the total aircraft available to him were suitable for night flying. On a good day, Peirse could realistically put up fewer than 170 aircraft and increasingly was being asked to support operations of Coastal Command in the Battle of the Atlantic now opening up when Germany, as in the First World War, invoked a policy of trying to starve Britain into submission by U-boat and warship attacks on her vital supply convoys. Although the Admiralty assumed operational control of RAF Coastal Command in April 1941, joint operations were still necessary, and the whole simply increased the demand on available aircraft across all three Commands. Lord Beaverbrook, who had secured a very substantial improvement in the production of fighters, was already looking at bringing new bombers into the arena at a faster rate. He admitted to Churchill that there would be no significant improvement to the bomber force until mid-1942 at the earliest, when the new Stirling, Halifax, Manchester and finally the war-winning Lancaster bombers would be coming through in significant numbers. He had, however, set in motion a stopgap solution which would entail setting up a front company in the US, buying aircraft from American suppliers and smuggling them into Britain via Canada – so that America would not violate her neutral status. Australian Don Bennett, still in his twenties and a commercial pilot with Imperial Airways, rejoined the RAF in 1939, and was a man – like many antipodeans in the RAF – with a thrusting personality who spoke his mind. He had already been engaged on a couple of secret missions for the RAF when Beaverbrook sent for him, and the meeting resulted in a true-life adventure into the unknown:

> He asked me if it would be possible to fly the North Atlantic in winter.* I said it would. And he said: 'Well, I'm making up a little team of Imperial Airways pilots who believe we can do it. The Air Ministry under Sinclair are absolutely adamant that it's completely impossible. They say it would be suicide in wintertime to try and fly the North Atlantic.' Beaverbrook was very, very anti the Air Ministry because of it. Anyway, he appointed myself and Wilcockson, Humphrey Page and Ian Ross, four of us who'd been Imperial Airways pilots. We went to Montreal on a ship where we were greeted by Beaverbrook's representative, who simply said: 'Anything you want, you can have. You must get all the aircraft you can flown over to England.' So I had to rush round and test new American aircraft that were offered to us, and advertise for crews. We employed civilian Americans to start with, but the quality was absolutely beyond contempt so we got eight Imperial Airways pilots over from London by sea. There was no other way of getting them. Everybody was very helpful, and the spirit was so right and things like installing extra fuel tanks for the 13-hour flight were done straightaway. Within a matter of weeks, myself and Humphrey Page delivered two Hudson bombers from Burbank, California,

---

* At the time, the only air service across the Atlantic was the Pan American Clipper, a flying boat that flew from New York to Southampton via Bermuda and Lisbon.

up to the Canadian border, where we towed the aircraft across the frontier with horses. We were not allowed to fly them over because of America's neutrality. We towed them over to a place called Pembina, near Winnipeg. From there we flew along to Montreal, where we landed at St Humbert, which was to be our base. Wilcockson took on the job of training controller and I was operational controller.

All of us came under the Royal Bank of Montreal's boss, who was representing Beaverbrook, and he was the man to whom we were responsible. They were terribly helpful. They did everything they could in the way of facilities and money and cars, and so on, and the training and selection of the civilian crews, who came as a result of our advertising, worked extremely well when you remember that we only started at the time of Dunkirk. We did the first delivery flight of seven Hudsons five months later. They all arrived safely at Aldergrove, to the surprise of everybody, where we were received by the air force with open arms.

Psychologically, it was very important. We gave confidence to the air force by the fact that America was helping indirectly. But to me it was operationally important, because we had achieved a winter crossing of the Atlantic which nobody else had ever done. It was tough going, for several reasons. The early American pilots just wouldn't have been looked at in ordinary airline work simply because they just didn't have any qualifications. But they had all the courage in the world and some eventually stayed on in England and joined the RAF. They were willing to stick their necks out and trust me, roughly speaking. That's what it was, it was sheer trust, to go and do the job. We gave them de-icing paste on the leading edge, which they had absolute faith in because I said so – things like that. It was quite a revelation in human nature.

In the next 12 months, Don Bennett's team delivered 360 Hudson bombers, 21 long-range Liberators, the big four-engined bombers, and 57 Catalina flying boats. Many of the Liberators and Catalinas were assigned to Coastal Command as the Battle of the Atlantic intensified. In the first year of operations, Bennett lost only one of his aircraft during the crossing, due to a mechanical failure. When the American Congress passed the Lend-Lease Act, the Atlantic ferry became a legally recognised operation and both America and Canada wanted to take it over. The Air Ministry beat them to it and turned it into an RAF concern, under the operational name of the Royal Air Force Ferry Command. Many of the pilots were graduates of Canadian flight-training schools who after a brief conversion course became known as North Atlantic ferry pilots – at a time when it was still considered a hazardous adventure for land-based planes to make the journey. As for Bennett, he was already working on another scheme, which he called the Pathfinders, to lead British bombers directly and more accurately to their targets. He'd written a very detailed paper on it and understood that it had been well received by the top brass. When he returned to England, however, he walked into the Air Ministry to find bad news waiting. Peirse had decided to cancel the project. Bennett said: 'He told me that there would be no Pathfinder Force for Bomber Command while *he* was in charge.'

In the event, that would not be for long, and in time Bennett's Pathfinders would flourish. But for the present he was posted to take over No. 77 Squadron, flying Whitleys, which he described as 'the worst aeroplane they could find for me'. His story continues in the ensuing pages. Another Bomber Command inmate who also had early ideas about marking enemy targets and the safety of British bombers was Geoffrey Leonard Cheshire, a brilliant young pilot later to become famous beyond the Victoria Cross he would be awarded in the course of his outstanding four-year wartime experience. He recalled in his tape-recorded memoir for the Imperial War Museum:

When I got to Oxford in 1936, Hitler was rising. And somehow everything changed. Without understanding it, you felt that there was a threat to peace. Come 1938 [when he was 20], I felt convinced that war was going to come. I applied for a permanent commission direct entry from Oxford. It didn't take effect until 1939 and war had broken out. I was called up at the end of September. My first thought was . . . the bombing. Everybody had a sort of mania about bombing. We were convinced we were going to

159

be bombed from every side. Otherwise, I think I just took war as a matter of course. It had come. We couldn't picture what it was going to be like. I remember very vividly asking myself the question: what will happen under gunfire? And I couldn't picture myself coping under gunfire. I didn't take to rifle shooting, but the moment I was in an aeroplane I just felt at home. So I was lucky. I wasn't an especially good pilot. But I just liked it, and I especially like low flying. I liked fast cars. I had an Alfa-Romeo. I liked speed. And it was only low down you got the sensation of speed. I liked flying under high-tension cables, and so on. It wasn't a rational thing. I just liked it. I used to do it whenever I thought I'd get away with it. In fact, it stood me in good stead later.

I had it firmly fixed in my mind that I did not want Bomber Command because they were doing these daylight Blenheim sorties. Of course, they posted me to heavy bombers. So I converted on to Whitleys and on to No. 102 Squadron, Driffield, in June 1940. I was very fortunate because I had a very good captain, Flight Lieutenant Lofty Long, a New Zealander. He'd already got a DFC. He was very severe in a disciplinary sense, as regards knowing the aeroplane, yet very human. He used to let me in the flying seat quite early on, over Germany. Captains seldom did that with their second pilots. My first mission, at the time of Dunkirk, was to bomb the bridge at Abbeville. And I don't blame the army for saying: 'Where's the RAF?' Fighter Command didn't have the range and night heavy bombers had no accurate navigation. We had no night bombsights. It made me think from an early time that we should be bombing low level, or anyway marking low level, and bombing an accurate marker. I started putting papers up to that effect, but they didn't get any further because we were bombed out from Driffield and events moved on. That day, the sirens went just at the end of lunch. The station commander dived under the mess-room table. I decided to head for the shelter at the end of the mess. When I got to the door, one of the pilots was standing there transfixed, looking upwards. And I looked upwards. There was a Stuka coming down and his bombs had left him. You could actually see them coming down towards us. I pushed this fellow's back and shouted 'Run', pushing him as hard as I could while I dived the 15 yards into the shelter. But he never moved. The bomb landed right on top of him. It was then I realised that people can get transfixed by a threat or fear. He just couldn't move. There were a large number of casualties. They completely razed the station, and many planes were hit.

One of the problems that both Don Bennett and Leonard Cheshire – along with many other frustrated young pilots – identified very early on in their missions was that of finding the target at night. Each aircrew was responsible for its own navigation and confirmation of arrival over the target. The system was a real hit-and-miss affair, based either on the ETA (i.e. the expected time of arrival) at target or what was known as 'dead reckoning'. The expression was an abbreviation of 'deduced reckoning', through which the aircraft's position was plotted from its heading and the forecast winds, the latter being finally arrived at from measurements during the flight. Both methods required a high degree of accuracy which, on a long flight was often interrupted by the weather, fighters or flak and was seldom achieved. Not only were results unsatisfactory, but bomber crews were being put to extreme risks searching for their target while wading through a maelstrom of flak. This became even more crucial in the early months of 1941, when the Air Ministry issued a series of directives to Peirse as to where the bombers should be targeted. The three most vital were considered to be:

1. A 'hit list of nine of the most important synthetic oil production plants were to receive immediate attention. Their destruction, it was calculated, would severely disrupt Germany's oil supply.
2. U-boat pens, shipyards and aircraft factories in an attempt to stem the rising German onslaught against Atlantic convoys of between 40 and 60 ships carrying vital supplies to Britain. Bombing raids were also requested against shipyards in Kiel, Bremen, Hamburg and U-boat operational bases on the French Atlantic coast.

3. Heavy bombardment to cause great dislocation to the German railways and arterial roads and to 'destroy the morale of the civil population as a whole and of the industrial workers in particular'.

This represented a major change of policy for Bomber Command, although it was still rather gentlemanly, if not pathetic, in comparison with the ongoing German Blitz on British cities. In the four months to July 1941 the Command flew more than 12,000 sorties in pursuit of those directives, 80 per cent of them at night, and in doing so took a loss of 321 aircraft and crews, most of whom were killed and the rest went into captivity. Furthermore, the damage to the German infrastructure that had been targeted proved to be disastrously ineffective. In August, Lord Cherwell, scientific adviser to the War Cabinet, instructed a team of analysts to study the results of bombing raids over Germany during the previous eight weeks, examining more than 4,000 photographs taken by camera-equipped bombers at the time of their raids. The results were a terrible indictment against British bomber effectiveness when, at the same time, so many crews were being sacrificed.

First of all, it was discovered that more than 60 per cent of the crews had not managed to get within a 75-mile radius of their given target at night. Of those crews that claimed to have reached their targets, only one in four had actually dropped their loads within five miles of the target. On nights without a moon or in bad weather, only about one in 20 crews dropped their loads within five miles of the target. Yet the raids continued in much the same vein for months ahead. On the night of 6 November, the largest British bomber force ever mounted – 392 bombers – took off from their British bases to hit German targets in spite of bad weather, 170 of them bound for Berlin. In fact, because of the weather conditions, 96 of the Berlin force did not even reach their target, and those that did caused relatively light damage.

On that night, however, 21 aircraft were lost, proving once again that until new aircraft came into service along with technological innovations, there was little point to these missions. Churchill said as much after Peirse had been summoned to attend a War Cabinet meeting to provide an explanation and to give his projections for the future. The result was that major bombing raids into Germany were to be substantially curtailed to conserve strength and to train aircrews in readiness for a new offensive in the spring of 1942. The one piece of significantly good news was that the first of the Avro Manchester IIIs had passed all its test flights with flying colours. This was the aircraft that many were convinced was going to make all the difference: a magnificent plane with four Rolls-Royce Merlin engines in place of the two Rolls-Royce Vultures used on the earlier Manchesters.

It was ordered into immediate production, to be known as the Lancaster, and as such to become the most famous bomber in the history of the Royal Air Force. Its arrival in sufficient numbers was months away, but the makers were working flat out to get this giant up and running. Bomber Command, meantime, had been trying other tactics. Running parallel to the night bombing raids to Germany throughout 1941 were daylight missions and, closer to home, the launch of 'circus' operations using both bombers and fighters. They were led by some of the stars of the Battle of Britain, and among the younger pilots was Johnnie Johnson, later to become Air Vice-Marshal and who became one of Britain's most famous pilots of the war, yet who maintained the enviable record of never being shot down. Johnson had joined No. 616 Squadron just as the Battle of Britain was ending:

It was an auxiliary squadron, South Yorkshire Squadron stationed at Kenley. It was very badly led, as a result of which, on the day I joined, six or seven people were shot down and killed and several others wounded. The squadron was taken out of the front line that very day, because they'd been decimated. Morale was very bad. I was one of several newcomers. And the veterans kept themselves to themselves, very aloof. They didn't want to discuss their experiences and shut themselves off. I think Stuffy Dowding realised that the squadron had been so badly knocked about that we shouldn't really be at Coltishall. So we went further north to Kirton in Lindsey, in Lincolnshire, to re-equip and retrain because there were, by then, only four or five of the original pilots left. We carried out patrols over the convoys travelling through the North Sea, which were being attacked usually at first light and last light. As a squadron, we had a little more time and better equipment to prepare ourselves, and early in 1941 we moved south, to Tangmere, which was vastly different from the relative peace and quiet of Lincolnshire. Tangmere was very much in the front line. As we got out of our aeroplanes, sirens were sounding, squadrons were landing and there was an operational air about the place. It had been bombed the day before. The sergeants' mess was down and the NAAFI had been hit. So we were suddenly put back in the front line, as it were. We were expecting to renew the Battle of Britain but the emphasis had changed by then and Fighter Command – it was Sholto Douglas at the head then – started to send us out. Reaching out, he called this philosophy; reaching out over the Channel in wing strength, with Douglas Bader leading the Tangmere Wing and [Adolf] 'Sailor' Malan leading the Biggin Wing. There were various other famous people: Tuck and Deere, and so on. Douglas Bader was an excellent leader. He had time to teach young people. He had the ability to impart his knowledge to young people, and so on. And the morale in the Tangmere Wing was very high.

Our mission was to try to entice the German fighter force to come up and have a go at us. But they took little notice of us, because we weren't doing much damage at 30,000 feet. So we started taking a few bombers to bomb them – they were called circus operations – in the spring and summer of 1941. And that succeeded in bringing them up. The Luftwaffe responded in some strength, especially before they were drawn off to the Russian Front in July. There were some quite stern fights, and we lost quite a few experienced people from the squadron. Several Battle of Britain pilots were shot down, some killed, some taken prisoner like Bader. It was quite a busy time, and in many respects a more dangerous type of flying than the Battle of Britain. You'd got the Channel to cross, both ways. And you were over enemy territory with most of your fighting so that if you came down and survived, you were in the bag.

I think there was a certain amount of chivalry at that time, a spillover from the first war, if you like, during these skirmishes. It will be recalled that when von Richthofen was shot down, the Royal Flying Corps flew over and dropped a wreath, regretting the death of somebody they called their most worthy enemy. When Douglas Bader was shot down, Adolf Galland, who was commanding on the other side, took him to the mess and wined and dined him. You wouldn't get that in the army, I don't think, or the navy. The Luftwaffe even said that if Bader wanted a new set of legs they would guarantee safe conduct for a Red Cross aeroplane to come and bring a set to St-Omer. So that was rather a nice thought.

Douglas Bader went down after a collision with an enemy aircraft over Béthune on 11 August. He baled out but was forced to leave one of his 'tin' legs in the aircraft. He became a prisoner of war for the remaining three and a half years, ending up in Colditz Castle after two attempted escapes. Within five months, Robert Tuck was also at Galland's dining table. Tuck had led the Duxford Wing over France until October 1941, when with fellow aces Adolf 'Sailor' Malan and Group Captain Harry Broadhurst, leader of the Hornchurch Wing, he joined a propaganda mission to the United States to share experiences with Britain's allies. When he returned in December, Tuck commanded Biggin Hill Wing. Less than a month later, he and Canadian Flying Officer Bob Harley took off for France, flying at low altitude to escape radar to a particular target 21 miles inland at Hesdin. After a successful attack, Tuck was brought down by anti-aircraft fire and was soon invited by Oberst (Colonel) Adolf Galland to have dinner with him and his pilots at St-Omer. Tuck had encountered Galland during a fighter sweep in 1941. Tuck's wingman was shot down; then Tuck had downed Galland's wingman. 'So that was you?' Tuck said. 'I got your number two as he passed in front.' 'And I got yours,' Galland replied, 'which makes us – how do you say it? – even stevens.' Tuck was taken under guard the next day and eventually to Stalag Luft III prison camp south of Berlin to be reunited with his old squadron leader, Roger Bushell, and other captured chums. He made numerous escape attempts but remained in captivity until 1945.

The Blenheim squadrons also flew the circus raids, as well as carrying out limited daylight raids, and various methods were used to try to stem the appalling losses in this type of mission. Air Chief Marshal Sir Ivor Broom, then 22 years old, had been one of the bomber pilots in the circus operations and survived to tell the tale. He also flew low-level missions into Germany:

The Blenheim was really the only aeroplane that was able to carry on daylight bombing right through 1939, '40 and '41. The Wellingtons, Whitleys and Hampdens had to concentrate at night because they were so much slower. My first squadron was No. 114 at West Raynham, flying Blenheims. At that time the squadron had two particular roles: mast-high attacks on German shipping, particularly off the Dutch coast, and low level into Germany. Both attracted a good deal of flak, and losses were high. Then we went into the circus ops, where we would fly in a squadron formation of 12 aeroplanes. We attacked targets in northern France from heights of about 8,000 feet, all bombing in formation. When the leader dropped his bombs, you all dropped your bombs. We were very much bait to get the German fighters up into the air for our fighter escort to attack them and put them on the defensive. So we did circus operations for many months before 54 Blenheims were briefed to carry out the first proper deep penetration by a major force into Germany in daylight – seldom done before. It was to attack the power stations at Cologne.* We had a fighter escort to the Dutch coast, but then of course they couldn't come any further with us. We then hedgehopped all the way across Holland. It was the first time lots of people in Holland had obviously seen the RAF, because they waved like mad as we flew over their rooftops and fields. You knew when you'd passed into Germany, because they no longer waved; they dived for cover.

We were still flying at around 50 to a 100 feet until we got within a mile or two of the power stations. We carried bombs with 11 seconds delay, so those that dropped at very low level didn't blow themselves up, which gave about 1,000 yards clearance before the bombs exploded. But getting 54 aeroplanes over the target you couldn't have them all going quickly at low level or some would have been blown up by

* As described in the Prologue by Charles Patterson.

the ones in front. So one group would go over at 50 feet, the next group go to 1,000 feet, and then quickly back down to ground level. So you did it in very quick succession. And then back all the way across Holland and the North Sea. It gained a lot of publicity. A photograph of my aeroplane taken by the gunner of another aeroplane appeared in all the press at the time. There was some fighter interception, but fortunately it was very difficult for them to get their guns on you if you were right down among the treetops.

Intermittently throughout 1941, Bomber Command and Coastal Command were also placed on alert to attack the most feared of German warships operating against British convoys in both the North Sea and the south-western approaches, notably the giant battleships *Bismarck* and *Tirpitz* and the battle cruisers *Scharnhorst* and *Gneisenau.* Their names became as well known to the British public as their own famous ships. The Royal Navy declared it would hunt them down, and, indeed, in one of the largest operations ever mounted against a single ship, British warships chased, trapped and finally sank the *Bismarck* in what was recognised as a brilliant manoeuvre 630 miles off the coast of France in May 1941.

At the same time, the *Scharnhorst* and *Gneisenau* had been located using Brest harbour. Both Bomber and Coastal Commands were regularly assigned to attempt bombing raids on the two battle cruisers over a period of several months. But they were always well protected, and between January 1941 and February 1942 no fewer than 127 aircraft were lost in the specific attempts to sink these two ships. There were incredible stories of crews flying into a storm of flak on these raids and none more so than one of the earliest, led by Flying Officer Kenneth Campbell of the Royal Air Force Volunteer Reserve, from Saltcoats. A graduate of the Cambridge University Air Squadron, he had trained at RAF Cranwell and RAF Abbotsinch before joining No. 22 Squadron flying Bristol Beauforts, a relatively new generation of maritime attack aircraft which came into service as torpedo-carrying bombers in 1939, largely used by Coastal Command.

On 6 April 1941 Campbell's squadron was tasked to mount a torpedo attack on the *Gneisenau* lying in Brest harbour. On

167

arrival over the target, Campbell found himself alone yet told his crew to prepare for attack. They went in 50 feet above the protective mole of the inner harbour, dodging between the masts of the flak ships that surrounded the battle cruiser. He launched his torpedo at point-blank range inside the harbour, and the *Gneisenau* was hit below the water line. Every flak gun in the harbour now turned on the lone aircraft, which was shot to pieces and crashed into the harbour. All the crew were killed. The battle cruiser was out of operation for over eight months, and the story of the bravery of Kenneth Campbell and his crew became known later only through reports from the French Resistance. Campbell was posthumously awarded the Victoria Cross. Quite naturally, emotions ran high about the attacks on these warships, and so it was with great anguish to all concerned, months later, when the two battle cruisers *Scharnhorst* and *Gneisenau*, along with the heavy cruiser *Prinz Eugen*, slipped away from Brest as things became too hot. Surrounded by no fewer than six destroyers, a ring of small torpedo boats and air cover of a dozen fighters, they made a dash for safety of their home port in Germany. Their escape in poor weather conditions was discovered too late, and they became engulfed in the murky night before British naval intelligence realised they had left. All three air Commands – Bomber, Fighter and Coastal – were ordered to put up a search and attack force immediately, and every British ship in the area was alerted to be on the lookout, but in spite of the size of the protective ring the warships sailed home without incident. British aircrew flew almost 250 sorties in the search but never managed to get a sniff. Churchill was furious and the serious tactical error was roundly criticised in the British newspapers the following day.

With that failure still fresh in memories, news arrived about the *Tirpitz*, the most feared of all German ships that was like a monster haunting naval intelligence. When she was discovered to be lying in the shadow of a mountain in Trondheim Fjord from which to sally forth into northern waters, Bomber Command was ordered to mount an immediate attack to sink her. The honour, in April 1942, went to No. 10 Squadron, which was flying newly acquired Halifaxes. Along those dispatched on this task was the founder-member of the Atlantic ferries, Don Bennett:

The Royal Navy intelligence boffins believed that although a torpedo or a bomb couldn't touch the *Tirpitz* because the armour plating was too thick, they thought the construction of the bottom was less strong. They'd dreamed up this scheme to roll spherical mines created by Dr Barnes Neville Wallis [later to devise the bouncing bombs of the Dambusters' raid] down a mountainside and under the soft belly of the *Tirpitz* to burst the hull from below. Each of my squadron carried five of these things, which weighed 1,500 pounds each. The ship was moored very close to the shore, and all we had to do was drop these mines and they would go down and do their stuff while a second squadron bombed from height – that was the story. We know now that nothing would touch the soft belly of the *Tirpitz* but, anyhow, we set off to make the attack. I led the raid in at low level in bright moonlight, over what turned out to be the worst possible planning route you could ever have – over heavily defended islands and coastal defences and close to supporting ships.

Forty miles from the target, I became a flamer [flames emitting from the engine], and I was picked on all the way. It was to be an exact stopwatch run, exact speed, height and timing, and then we would drop our load. It would have been perfect but for the fact that when we arrived there was man-made fog filling the whole of the fjord. It was a very clever thing. They sprayed a chemical on the water and it produced a fog about 200 feet thick. You couldn't see a damned thing. The drop wasn't very accurate, and guns were opening up all around us. It was pretty hopeless. Anyway, the result was that the ship was undamaged.

Naval intelligence had done it again . . . letting us go into an area where they knew there was going to be this fog without telling us. We lost half the aircraft, hacked down by the flak guns and defending ships – myself included. We were burning up and everybody had baled out. I got out with half a second to spare as the starboard wing folded up and I hit the deck just as my parachute opened. Fortunately, I came down in deep snow, over my head. It took me three days and nights to get across country and into Sweden, dodging the Germans out with dogs looking for us. On the way, I picked up one of my crew who surrendered to me

169

thinking I was a Hun. We were interned in a camp there, Sweden being neutral, but fortunately I managed to get a message to London and was out within 30 days.*

That was just as well, because Bennett would soon be needed elsewhere, on the Pathfinder project that he had previously floated.

Bomber Command also had to find resources during these critical months to join Coastal Command in operations against German shipping and U-boats around the coasts of the UK and further afield as the toll on supply convoys began to mount. Churchill had ordered the formation of a Battle of the Atlantic Committee to look at every possible way of halting the losses among shipping bound for British ports carrying much-needed materials from the colonial nations and America. In a memo dated 7 May 1941 he indicated that the defence of ships 'now has first priority', having earlier declared that 'in order to win this war, Hitler must either conquer this island by invasion or he must cut the ocean lifeline which joins us to the United States'.

As in the First World War, the Germans were making a pretty good stab at the latter ever since the invasion had been put on hold. And so now the focus turned to Coastal Command, which had been the poor relation in terms of equipment from the outset. It was quickly revamped and re-equipped to provide a force of 480 aircraft, although it was a thoroughly mixed fleet that included Liberators, Wellingtons, Beauforts and Beaufighters as well as the

---

* Various attempts were later made to sink the *Tirpitz*, including a major operation using eight midget submarines, two of which actually managed to get under the ship and explode massive charges, for which two VCs were awarded. The *Tirpitz* was put out of action for months. But still she had failed to sink. On 3 April 1944 she was attacked by a joint force of Fleet Air Arm bombers and fighters. Two waves of aircraft, consisting of 42 Fairey Barracuda torpedo bombers and 80 American-built Grumman Wildcat and Hellcat fighters, dodged 68 anti-aircraft guns to score a number of direct hits to put her out of action again. Four more attacks were launched that year, including one by 28 Lancaster bombers of the famous No. 617 Squadron, launched from a staging post at Archangel, Russia. Finally, the pride of the German fleet was done for and towed to Tromsø Fjord to act as a coastal defence battery. The RAF made one more run at her and this time she went sky high – blown apart when her own ammunition store was hit, and fewer than 90 of her trapped crew of 1,000 survived.

Catalina flying boats that Don Bennett and his colleagues had brought from the United States. The last were particularly useful, having a range of 4,000 miles and capable of carrying 4,000 pounds of weapons, although they themselves presented a problem in that there were few crews who had any experience of flying them. Even with this additional manpower, Coastal Command resources were fully stretched, especially as they had to provide cover to the extreme limits of aircraft endurance for the Atlantic convoys prior to the arrival of American support.

This cover, allied to surface operations, was fairly effective initially. In the first two years of the war, 12,057 ships arrived at British ports in 900 convoys. Only 291, or just under two per cent, were lost to enemy action. A good deal of the credit for these relatively light casualties could be claimed by Coastal Command for their constant vigilance around the coasts. Although success in sinking any U-boats eluded them, in the six months from June 1941 Coastal Command, with supporting action from Fighter and Bomber Commands, attacked 698 enemy vessels, sinking 41 and damaging many more. The cost, however, was unacceptably high. Very quickly, the Germans began arming their merchantmen and providing heavy escorts. The RAF's tactics of low flying to achieve accuracy in the distribution of their payloads meant they presented something of a duck shoot for the maritime guns, and during that six-month period 115 aircraft engaged on anti-shipping patrols were shot out of the sky. Given the dire shortage of both crews and aircraft, which affected Coastal Command as much as anyone, it represented another questionable sacrifice. The doubts brought about a serious study of these operations, and in the late spring of 1942, all low flying over enemy shipping was abandoned, with the result that accuracy in attack also faltered.

This coincided with another development that put the Allied shipping under even further pressure. One of the 'priority' tasks that had been endowed on Bomber Command by the Air Ministry was the destruction of heavy-duty concrete pens being built for U-boats in the French Channel ports. The theory was that if the pens could be blasted apart before they were completed, the U-boats would have difficulty in operating. But in spite of some near-suicidal attempts by bomber pilots dodging a wall of flak, the building programme went on pretty well

171

unaffected. This gave the U-boats a secure haven from which to receive fuel and repairs and return quickly to their attacks on British and neutral shipping with a murderous capability that was amply demonstrated by the sinking of the *Arandora Star*, an independent ship of 15,000 tons carrying German and Italian refugees from Liverpool to Halifax, Nova Scotia. This was followed by the sinking of the Dutch liner *Volendam*, carrying 320 refugee children, off Malin Head. Only good fortune and an excellent rescue operation saved them. The 200 children and adults on the *City of Benares*, sunk by a U-boat in September, were not so lucky.

At the beginning of 1942 the attacks became more premeditated when Admiral Karl Dönitz introduced his wolf pack hunting system for U-boats, first tried out in September 1940 against convoy HX72 coming in from Nova Scotia. It meant that U-boats operating together could have a more devastating effect than single boats and was especially useful at a time when German naval vessels were diverted to the north during the invasion of Russia. As time went on and more became available, Dönitz perfected tactics whereby he would personally direct the packs, typically between five and a dozen U-boats, to attack the Allied convoys. Between 1941 and 1943, almost 140 wolf packs were formed for operations to hit Allied supply lines, the largest, in November 1942, consisting of 20 U-boats. With America now in the war, the wolf packs operated against shipping routes from the east coast of the US right across the Atlantic. They targeted convoys of between 40 and 60 ships travelling in, say, 12 columns extending to five and a half nautical miles in length. Although the convoys were under the protection of naval surface ships and submarines, as well as Coastal Command aircraft when they came within range, the U-boats could weave in and out of convoys virtually at will, and they made a point of going for stragglers. Some benefit was to be derived by the expansion of Coastal Command's air-to-surface-vessel radar equipment (ASV) which could detect submarines on the surface at seven miles. It was only a temporary advantage. By the end of 1942 the Germans had developed ASV detectors, which were fitted to all their submarines. As each month passed in 1942, the Allied shipping losses mounted until by the end of the year the tonnage of shipping lost was running at 800,000 tons a month. A new

Strike Wing of Coastal Command became operational in December 1942, principally staffed by Beaufighters equipped with bombs. But, as with Bomber Command itself, there was no quick fix, and it would be towards the end of 1943 before Coastal Command, in conjunction with the Royal Navy surface operations, were able to combat the U-boat menace.

CHAPTER TEN

Heroes of the Storm

With the London Blitz still ongoing and with problems on virtually every front, Winston Churchill produced one of his brilliant rallying oratories in the House of Commons in May 1941: 'When I look back on the perils we have overcome . . . When I remember all that has gone wrong, and remember also all that has gone right, I feel sure we have no need to fear the tempest . . . let it roar and let it rage. We shall come through.' He ended with a warning to the people of Germany, that they should prepare themselves for the war of 1942, a threat he made repeatedly as he looked to Bomber Command to take the battle to the Germans. The message barely hid the unpalatable truth that Britain was hanging on by a thread and 1941 would, at best, be a holding operation in Europe. There was also an 'at worst' side to the situation as that year of tension progressed: worrying reverses in the Mediterranean and the Middle East and the beginnings of a rout in the Far East. The very regions that had been the hub of RAF activity in the 1920s and 1930s were now to be in the front line against the tripartite forces of Germany, Italy and Japan, a deal that was cemented by 27 September 1940, converting the Berlin–Rome tie-up into a triangular axis of aggression.

In the very places where, back in the good old days, the RAF took on the role of flying policemen of the Empire, the pressure was mounting. Unfortunately, RAF bases at the forefront of these key flash points were virtually running on empty with a setup dating back to that long-gone era, so steeped in old traditions that dozens of serving airmen still had their families with them. In all the three main overseas theatres, aircraft and men were not only in short supply, but the machines they had were by and large made up of tired rejects from the UK. RAF squadrons were still flying fighters of early 1930s vintage, and some of their bombers were even older. Reinforcements, as the going got tougher, would be few and far between from the UK, and that meant some disturbing and, in the end, catastrophic sacrifices in which the RAF played an incredibly courageous but costly role in attempting to prevent. The first test in these new arenas came with the Italian invasion of Egypt, which was to be ably met by what was then known as the British Army of the Nile with RAF support. The Italians had entered the war with around 1,850 front-line aircraft, whereas Britain had a combined force of fighters and bombers numbering fewer than 300, spread across the whole of the Middle Eastern command. The territory under Air Chief Marshal Sir Arthur Longmore covered a vast region taking in the whole of the Middle East, North Africa, the Mediterranean, the Balkans and East Africa, overlooking the vital Red Sea access.

There were 14 bomber squadrons to cover this area, five of which relied entirely on Sunderland flying boats of varying ages. Nine of the squadrons did possess some modern (i.e. 1937) but short-range and well-used Blenheims, while the rest of the inventory in the region was made up of a varied mixture of old stock. At that time, there was not a single Hurricane or Spitfire to be seen, and all the fighter squadrons were still flying the Gladiator biplane. About half the entire force was based in Egypt, watching over key military bases and the Suez Canal, in which Britain was a majority shareholder, providing access to the Indian subcontinent and the Far East. The RAF also had establishments in the long-standing British protectorates of Aden, Palestine, Iraq, Kenya, the Sudan and Gibraltar. There was a base of sorts at Malta and three airfields – but no aircraft, save for three used by the local administration.

That was the unpromising picture as Mussolini ordered his troops into Egypt, although they did not prove to be beyond the limited resources of British forces. Even so, RAF commander

Longmore now had to adopt a strategy of extreme caution. He knew he would get precious little in the way of extra planes and men from the UK, and initially they could be counted in single digits: six Blenheims along with six Hurricanes shipped out in packing cases. To add to Longmore's woes, some additional action sprang to life in the eastern Mediterranean when Mussolini invaded Greece after the government there refused to allow his troops free passage.

Again, the Italian dictator's delusions of grandeur were not matched by the performance of his armies, and the Greeks gave him much more trouble than he had expected. Longmore was ordered to assist the Greeks by sending over what aircraft he could spare. That amounted to a joint force of Blenheim bombers and Gladiator fighters, which were flown to Athens to help defend the city against the Italian attack. Three more squadrons were dispatched in November amid rumours of German activity towards the region, leaving Longmore even more desperate for aircraft over the Middle East.

He managed to maintain his air superiority in the North African campaign with many creditable bomber raids, although the Italian fighters seemed loath to come up and challenge their British counterparts. By the end of the year, the Italians were on the run. General Archibald Wavell led his army towards swift and decisive advances, capturing Tobruk and taking 100,000 prisoners. The euphoria of the British successes was to be short-lived. In February 1941 Hitler sent General Erwin Rommel with the advance party of what would become the mighty Afrika Korps, which began landing at Tripoli to rescue Mussolini's army, and the real battles began. RAF bombers and fighters would soon be facing a strong contingent of the Luftwaffe's Fliegerkorps X. As Rommel began his move against Wavell, Hitler played his trump card – launching a devastating *blitzkrieg* against Yugoslavia and then onwards to Greece with a massive invasion force of ground troops supported by around 1,250 aircraft, including Stukas and the deadly Messerschmitt 109s. Longmore was ordered to send in four additional squadrons to support the Greeks, including Blenheims and his newly arrived Hurricanes, but even as the gallant pilots took off, it was already a lost cause. Axis columns moved ahead with pace, and in the air the RAF put up a brilliant show – highly praised in London – against a far superior German air force. But in less than 10 days the Allied force was down to fewer than four dozen aircraft. Greece was as good as lost, and Cairo ordered the withdrawal of all British troops as the Greek army surrendered on 23 April. The last remaining seven British Hurricanes were moved to Crete along with thousands of Allied troops and all the guns they could carry to stage what would become a last hopeless stand in the eastern Mediterranean.

The RAF also joined the British fleet in a Dunkirk-style operation in the evacuation of troops from Greece, using flying boats, but, as at Dunkirk, substantial amounts of vehicles, equipment, ammunition, fuel and heavy guns had to be abandoned along with a number of damaged, but reparable fighters and bombers. Even so, some 43,000 troops and civilians were successfully evacuated. The heroics of the navy and the air force in this operation could not mask this further setback: the immolation of much-needed troops and, from the RAF's standpoint, the loss of 189 aircraft during the Greek campaign. Worse was to come. Enigma decrypts from Bletchley Park revealed that the Germans were planning a massive invasion of the strategically important island of Crete, which at that time had a mere 14 Hurricanes and seven Royal Navy aircraft available to defend the enemy's onslaught.

Churchill ordered Wavell to send reinforcements: more guns, more tanks, more everything. The commander wired back that he could spare only six tanks, 16 light tanks and 18 anti-aircraft guns, although the Allied manpower on the island was bolstered after the fall of Greece to around 30,000 Australian, New Zealand and British troops under the command of General Bernard Freyberg. Churchill, having viewed the Germans' precise order of battle – courtesy of the Enigma decrypts – still had grave concerns that they had sufficient firepower to hold on. His worst fears were realised on the morning of 20 May, when Stuka dive-bombers and artillery aircraft screamed out of the sky and began pummelling the Allied troop positions. They were followed by wave after wave of stinging aircraft attacks and landings, including Ju52s towing huge DFS 230 gliders packed with troops, vehicles and guns. Suddenly, the skies were filled with the greatest airborne invasion force ever mounted in the history of warfare.

By late afternoon, almost 5,000 men had been dropped or

landed on the island, and one of the most costly battles of the war to date was under way as more German paras and mountain troops were delivered to the island hour after hour, eventually totalling 22,040. They met spirited Allied resistance, whose strength had been hugely underestimated by German intelligence. The RAF never stood a chance, given that in the preceding two weeks the Germans had assembled a force of 650 combat aircraft, 700 transports and 80 gliders in Greece. For more than a week, the Luftwaffe bombarded Crete until the remnants of Longmore's fighter contingent was down to just a handful of Gladiators and Hurricanes, whose immediate evacuation was ordered. The lack of credible air cover also exposed the British fleet to grave danger as it began the evacuation of Allied troops. Three cruisers and six destroyers were sunk and an aircraft carrier, six cruisers and eight destroyers were hit by varying degrees of damage and many sailors were killed or drowned. The final toll showed the extent of the disaster: 4,600 Allied troops killed, 2,000 wounded and 11,000 taken prisoner. Longmore lost all but four of the aircraft sent to the aid of the vastly over-powered Allied forces.

Back in North Africa, the picture was no less encouraging. After the rout of the Italians, Rommel had reinstated the Axis advance backed up by a hefty Luftwaffe force. He launched a full-scale land offensive in April and put to flight the British Army of the Nile, which was forced back towards Egypt, and in the process 9,000 Allied troops and three British generals were captured. Longmore's bombers and fighters took a pounding as they tried to provide the answers to a multitude of increasingly difficult operational objectives.

By the end of May the British could call on just 189 aircraft across the whole region, although relief of sorts did arrive somewhat unexpectedly for the tired-out RAF when large numbers of German aircraft were pulled away to attend the invasion of Soviet Russia on five separate fronts, which began in July. Temporarily, the pressure was less challenging in the air, but the Allies' ground forces now dug in for a long, hot summer of pounding artillery and oceans of blood and sweat. It was in this period, too, that attention of both the Axis and British turned towards the island of Malta, the British base whose role in the oncoming Battle of the Mediterranean was to become crucial.

In the spring of 1941 the Royal Navy re-established its submarine base at Valletta, which had, until then, operated on a shoestring. Six submarines had been transferred from the Far East, and within a month of arrival three were sunk by Italian torpedo bombers. Four new T-class submarines were transferred from convoy protection duties, and two of those were sunk en route. The new commander on the Malta station, Captain G.W.G. 'Shrimp' Simpson, was promised a prompt delivery of additional submarines to administer his priority directive: to stop all Axis supplies and troops from Italy to Tripoli. Since the major naval base at Alexandria was 1,000 miles along the coast, Malta became the key operational base for Britain's submarine force. Over the coming months, the submarine service in the Mediterranean went to great lengths to achieve the ambitions of the war planners in causing as much grief as possible to the Axis powers, and for that they needed the urgent and effective cooperation of the RAF. As Captain Ronald Mills, commander of *Tetrarch*, one of the first submarines to arrive at the base, recalled: 'From the moment we arrived, the Italians were bombing daily, but we didn't have much fear of them even though we had just three aircraft on the island piloted by the governor's own staff. When the Luftwaffe set up shop on nearby Sicily it was a different ball game altogether.'

Longmore had absolutely no aircraft to send to Malta and they had to come direct from the UK. Four Sea Gladiators were sent, still in their packing cases, as a temporary measure, while the Italians were bombing the new submarine facilities even as they were being built. Then four Hurricanes on their way to Egypt were held back at Malta during a refuelling stop, and they were the sum total of Malta's air defences until another batch of 12 Hurricanes arrived in July. The trouble was that in an environment that was becoming exceedingly heated, there were a lot of rookie pilots. Among them was William Nurse, who was 19 in the early summer of 1940, when he trained in Tiger Moths. He completed his course at Montrose in single-engine Miles Masters aircraft in January:

Thirty-six finished the course, the remaining four having been killed in the process. I was among 12 who came out as sergeant pilots, and after a few days' leave we were sent to No. 56 Operational Training Unit at Sutton Bridge to get out first taste of flying Hurricanes before being posted to No. 185 Squadron under Squadron Leader 'Boy' Mould. In March 1941 we and our aircraft were taken aboard HMS *Furious* heading for Gibraltar. There we transferred to the *Ark Royal*, the machines being pushed across on planks. We flew off the carrier, and this is something I feel bitter about. Of the 11 of us, nine were trainees straight from OTU. The twelfth, Flying Officer Pike, had been flying Battles in France and had gone up to learn to fly Hurricanes. He and I were the only two who had squadron experience. It was a fiasco. Pike took off and I went second. A Blenheim came in from Gibraltar and we were told that we were to form up behind him and he would guide us to Malta. He only circled once; we were still all over the sky, and then he decided to climb through cloud. When we came out of the cloud there were only four of us following the Blenheim and two of those were in difficulties. Anyhow, this small group struggled on to Malta as best they could and should have landed at Hal Far, but as the Blenheim got to Malta he waggled his wings and so the others followed him to another airfield. I was the only one who landed at Hal Far, where the station commander was waiting to meet us and had arranged breakfast. Two others then came in, then a fourth. Pike and one other came soon afterwards, so now we had six. Half an hour a later, four more came in. Three of them had found themselves above the sea and formed up behind a sergeant pilot, who led them in. The eleventh never did show up and was apparently shot down.

The point was, nobody had any map-reading experience over water and certainly no operational experience, and there they were going out to Malta. We became No. 185 Squadron, and we were the defence of Malta. The Italians were much better than people gave them credit for and, anyway, our Hurricanes were clapped out. They still flew beautifully, but when the Italians came in you were fighting for your life. When the Germans arrived, it was hopeless. The problem was that our aircraft were old and both the Germans and the Italians could outrun us and out-climb us.

They used to come down out of the sun, fire and go through and never stopped for a fight. It was a very good way. We had a lot shot down. We also lost quite a few on the ground. The 109s would come sweeping across the airfield. It was a very stressful time. You were flying three or four times a day, and it became worse and worse as the casualties mounted. Reinforcements were few and far between. Two squadrons came in November and then went on to the Middle East, and they were the only reinforcements we had during the whole time I was there.

This state of affairs continued, with fighters attempting to hold the increasingly vicious Italian air attacks at bay. At the end of November the Luftwaffe, having temporarily switched to the Russian Front, returned with a vengeance as Rommel stepped up his own campaign to meet the renewed vigour of the British forces, now called the 8th Army and under the command of General Sir Claude Auchinleck. The RAF was also under new management. Air Chief Marshal Sir Arthur Tedder had taken over the North African command and by judicious management and the arrival of reinforcements he had put together 27 operational squadrons for work in the Western Desert, 11 in the Suez Canal zone and four in Malta. The last included day and night bombing squadrons of Blenheims and Wellingtons. Among the Blenheim pilots was Ivor Broom, whom we last met flying light bombers over Germany. He recalls:

I was sent down to Portreath, Cornwall, to a unit there for dispatching aircraft to the Middle East. I had about 230 hours' total flying at the time and believe it or not I was considered to be the most experienced of the group which I was asked to lead. A group of six. We flew to Gibraltar, which took seven hours. The runway there was literally a graveyard of wrecked aeroplanes where inexperienced crews had not been able to cope with landing. We rested overnight and took off for Malta the next day, flying time seven hours forty minutes. Now, when we got to Malta I thought it was just a refuelling stop. We had the maps to take us all the way to Singapore if needs be. But the air marshal in charge of Malta was Air Vice-Marshal Hugh Pughe-Lloyd, and he had a reputation for replacing his losses by hijacking crews who were in transit. Next day I found I was with No. 105 Squadron. At the time, Blenheim squadrons were going out from England for three weeks' detachment at Malta and then back. So when 105 went home I was transferred to No. 107 Squadron. And when 107 was due to go back they didn't have any replacements to send out, so it had to stay on for the next four and a half months. The other bomber squadron was No. 18, also flying Blenheims. Our main role was to attack shipping taking supplies to Rommel in North Africa, all in daylight. Few of us had any night flying experience. We'd go out searching for shipping and if we couldn't find any ships, and we went down by the North African coast, then we would go inland to find a target of opportunity on the Tripoli–Benghazi road area and then back to Malta. This was all at low level, 50 feet stuff. One day the squadron was asked to attack some very important big ships in a Sicilian harbour. The harbour was so defended that it was decided it had to be done at night, a moonlit night. So they picked the two most experienced crews in the squadron to do it and I was one of them.

Now, my total night flying was seven and a half hours. I hadn't flown at night since my training conversion six months earlier. We had to go in low again, in the moonlight. All this bombing at low level was done by pilot release, not a navigator, or bomb aimer. At night. I mentioned my lack of experience to the CO of the squadron at the briefing. He said: 'Would you like to do a couple of circuits and landings before you set course, so you've had a look at what Malta looks like at night, with no lighting for when you come back?' Before I could answer, my gunner said: 'Not ruddy likely. Let's do the op first. We don't want to do any circuits and bumps with that load on.'

Italian air defences were also surprising: no flak ships but lots of little coastal ships, which were bristling with guns, and they tended more to have naval support for the ships going down to particularly Tripoli. I believe we sunk or damaged 24 ships during my time with 107 Squadron, and we lost 24 crews in that time. I suppose in war you'd probably say that's not bad arithmetic. We'd lost virtually all the officers. I was a sergeant pilot when I went to Malta and I was commissioned there. That did not deter us from taking our targets where we could find them in accord with Hugh Pughe-Lloyd's directive: 'You are to attack the enemy at every opportunity.' But this was only possible because of the marvellous work the fighter pilots did in their air defence role. Their sole job as fighters was to defend the island, not to escort us at all. I was never escorted by a fighter during my whole time at Malta. You couldn't afford it. They were there to defend and beat off the attacks from the Germans and Italians. And we were very complementary to one another.

At the turn of 1942, however, the attacks, dive-bombings and airdrop mine-laying deployed against the island and its military guests began to take a turn for the worse. Four hundred Luftwaffe and 200 Italian fighters and bombers had been moved to bases in Sicily for what became a relentless blitz. The attacks continued day and night, and on 13 February 1942 the Lazaretto submarine base was badly hit, with the sick-quarters and mess-decks flattened. Another wave of attacks on 17 February brought a deluge of armour-piercing bombs, several submarines were seriously damaged and the island's main airfield, already heavily pockmarked, took more sustained attacks. A recently arrived flight of Wellingtons, used as night bombers, was withdrawn to the Middle East because of the lack of safe airfield facilities. In fact, the airfields of Malta were being ripped open almost as soon as they had received emergency repairs.

In the third week of March the joint forces of the Luftwaffe and the Italians were hitting the island with up to 300 sorties a day. This continued at such a pitch that on 16 April King George VI announced his award of the George Cross collectively to the island of Malta, which had been under constant attack for four and a half months. By 18 April there were only six serviceable fighters on the island. A flight of Spitfires came in as reinforcements but ran into trouble even before they became operational. Sergeant William Nurse, wounded after being blown up (ironically in a building in Valletta on his day off from flying), remembers:

The Germans always seemed to know when we had reinforcements coming in. The first lot of Spitfires that came in were knocked out on the ground almost as soon as they landed. In May we had a re-supply of 47 Spitfires, which came in from the aircraft carrier USS *Wasp*, but they had it better organised and didn't hang about. As soon as they landed, they refuelled them and got them straight up.

Quite a few of the Spitfires were quickly damaged, but the remainder kept up a spirited defence until reinforcement came in periodically. Partly because of mounting submarine damage and partly because the very presence of the base was attracting heavy bombing activity, the submarine operations from Malta were abandoned and the remaining boats took temporary refuge at Alexandria to regroup and await new arrivals from the UK. They would return 10 weeks later, with a new Malta force in support of the famous mercy mission to relieve the besieged island, the convoy codenamed Pedestal. The convoy faced fierce bombardment from the Luftwaffe, which sank all but five supply ships out of 14 that set out and dozens of the escort vessels and aircraft that were amassed to accompany the convoy in to Valletta.

Although by no means ignored by the Italians and the Germans, the pressure was lifted from Malta slightly when in June more Axis aircraft were deployed in support of Rommel's advance against the 8th Army in the Western Desert and on towards Tobruk. Within the month, the battles began to take on the appearance of a rout against the British and Commonwealth forces, and before long command of the 8th was changed again, this time with General Bernard Montgomery in command. Over a three-month period, Montgomery built up his force while holding back any further advance from Rommel's Afrika Korps and finally had mustered around 200,000 troops, including Britons, Australians, New Zealanders, Indians, Frenchmen and Greeks. In the six months since the siege of Malta, the island had been heavily reinforced with both Spitfires and bombers, which were being deployed against Axis supply lines and troopships. In North Africa itself, the RAF had brought together a force of almost 800 planes, pulled in from every quarter of the region, as well as getting reinforcements from the UK, where new Stirlings, Halifaxes and Manchesters were freeing up the Wellingtons,

Blenheims, Whitleys and Hampdens for use overseas.

The build-up was under way for the reclamation of North Africa and, with such a vastly superior force than any previously assembled in the Middle East, Montgomery turned the tide, and the church bells were ordered to be rung across England after his famous success at the Battle of El Alamein on 30 October 1942. Seven days later, the Allies launched their first invasion of the war with Operation Torch, which put 65,000 American troops on to the North African coastlines, landing around Casablanca in Morocco and Oran in Algeria. They were followed by three battalions of British paratroops, two of which went by ship and the remainder flown from Cornwall to Gibraltar and then on to an airfield at Maison Blanche, near Algiers, from which the first major British paratroop airdrop was launched on a vital airfield at Bône. The battle was by no means over, and although Axis troops had been evicted from a vast swath of territory and diverted Hitler's attention from other pressing theatres, the follow-up to Operation Torch's initial success faltered. The Germans had not been dislodged from their footholds in Bizerte and Tunis, and the campaign quickly became bogged down by a long, very wet and miserable winter.

The British paras, under severe pressure, needed reinforcing, and the RAF had to keep up both a strong fighter cover and concerted bomber effort across the whole region through the winter. There were some particularly tough encounters, especially for the bombers as they were confronted by 109s. Twenty-five-year-old Wing Commander Hugh Malcolm of No. 18 Squadron of Blenheims had flown numerous missions over the area throughout November 1942. At the beginning of December he led attacks on Bizerte airfield, which was base to troublesome German aircraft. He and his squadron were successful in putting it out of operation, and on 4 December he led an attack on another enemy fighter base near Chougui, Tunisia. On reaching the target, however, the squadron was intercepted by an over-whelming force of German fighters, which began swooping in and out of the advancing bombers. One by one, Malcolm's squadron were shot down as they repeatedly came under attack until he himself was shot down in flames. His 'skill and daring of the highest order' were recognised with the posthumous award of a Victoria Cross.

★　★　★

The fightback in the Middle East was overshadowed by nothing but bad news from the Far East, where tragedies and losses of immense proportions were unfolding as the Japanese launched simultaneous offensives on three fronts to coincide with their attack on Pearl Harbor on 7 December 1941. On that day, a massive Japanese offensive was launched against Hong Kong and the Philippines, Malaya and on towards Burma in the north and, going south, Singapore and Sumatra. By the end of the month, the Japanese had made significant advances across the whole of South-East Asia, and on Christmas Day the hopelessly out-numbered force of 6,000 Allied defenders in Hong Kong were ordered to lay down their arms by the colony's governor, Sir Mark Young. In the parallel actions, the Japanese landed sub-stantial forces at Kota Baharu, on the east coast of Malaya, just short of the border with Siam (now Thailand), and while the thinly spread RAF defenders were drawn to cover that area, the main Japanese invasion was occurring a hundred miles north at Singora to begin their lightning thrust north towards Burma and south to the British jewel of Singapore. At the same time, Japanese bombers hit Singapore city, where the RAF had noth-ing in their inventory to match the invading air fleet.

Singapore was defended principally by two squadrons, Nos. 36 and 100, flying Vickers Vildebeests, an old biplane of late 1920s specification originally intended for patrolling home waters as a torpedo bomber. There were also two squadrons flying the very same Short Singapore 1935 flying boats whose delivery to the Middle East and beyond was described earlier in these pages. But with so much activity now confronting the Allied air forces across the whole, vast panoply of Far Eastern activity, the RAF com-manders could call on fewer than 250 serviceable aircraft, less than half the number available to the Japanese and which bore no comparison in efficiency, age and speed.

The fact that the tired old Vildebeest biplanes made up the front line in Malaya was well known to the Japanese. The bomber strength was equally stretched, with just four squadrons of Blenheims, backed up by two of Hudsons flown by the Royal Australian Air Force and three Catalina flying boats. The British fighters were even less of a match. They were made up of four squadrons of Brewster Buffalos, which had gone into service in the Far East after being rejected in the UK for poor performance. The Buffalo also had only a limited fuel capacity, all of which did not augur well for Singapore when the kamikaze crowd came over. Japanese invasion tactics also put the RAF into a spin. The key landings and subsequent air attacks were staggered, so that the hard-pressed Allies had little room to manoeuvre with such a meagre selection of defending aircraft available.

The first Japanese attack at Kota Baharu, for example, drew in several squadrons based in northern Malaya and, thus diverted, the Japanese went in pretty well unhindered with their main landing at Singora. By nightfall, almost half the 110 British and Australian aircraft defending Malaya and Singapore had been destroyed. There was a hasty attempt to get an Allied air attack going over that region, and two squadrons of Blenheims scrambled from the Butterworth base near the Siam border to make a raid on Singora at daybreak on 9 December. Squadron Leader Arthur Scarf, of No. 62 Squadron, RAF, as leader of the raid, had just taken off when enemy aircraft swept in, destroying or disabling all the rest of the machines destined to join him. Scarf decided nevertheless to fly on alone to Singora. Despite attacks from roving fighters on the outward journey, he completed his bombing run and was on his way back when his aircraft was again shot up by marauding Japanese fighters. He was severely wounded and although bleeding profusely managed to crash-land the Blenheim at Alor Star airfield without causing any injury to his crew. He was rushed to hospital, where he died two hours later. He was posthumously awarded the Victoria Cross five years later when the full facts of his heroism were established from homecoming prisoners of war.

Singapore island was now to be subjected to concentrated bombing and strafing by Japanese aircraft and navy guns, while all through Malaya airfields were bombed with fragmentation bombs and anti-personnel mines clearly designed to kill or maim ground crews and support staff. At the end of that day, 9 December, losses across the board had been such that the regional RAF commander, Air Vice-Marshal Pulford, had no alternative but to halt daylight bombing operations. Reinforcements to relieve Singapore were supposedly on the way. The battleships HMS *Prince of Wales*, the battle cruiser HMS *Repulse* and an escort of four destroyers were steaming in, but they were spotted by Japanese reconnaissance and attacked by a force of 88 aircraft, sent out to find and destroy. Within an hour, the convoy had been scattered and sunk. Eleven Buffalos, scrambled after receiving an SOS from the *Repulse*, arrived in time to see the last of the ships disappearing beneath the waves.

Additional aircraft for the RAF did get through, however, in the form of 17 Hudson and Blenheim bombers, followed by 50 Hurricanes packed in crates, along with 24 pilots, brought in aboard ships carrying troop reinforcements for the equally stretched 14th Army. Even so, by the third week of January 1942 the Japanese were within 50 miles of Singapore, and an RAF reconnaissance aircraft reported that enemy troops were 'swarming like ants' after more landings at Muar. The Vildebeest squadrons, along with the Buffalos and Hurricane fighters, were running dawn-to-dusk sorties against the ever-growing and fast-moving invaders, but they were no match for the Japanese fighters, the Zeros. On 28 January Pulford ordered the remaining aircraft to pull back for the final defence of Singapore. There they battled on in the face of a tremendous 10-day onslaught from the air, land-based artillery and naval batteries until finally Pulford halted all RAF operations over Singapore and sent the handful of aircraft still operational to Sumatra. Pulford himself followed by boat on 13 January but never made it, believed killed trying to avoid capture. On 15 February the great naval base of Singapore, once considered impregnable, surrendered to the Japanese. Announcing this grave development to the nation, Churchill described it as a 'heavy and far-reaching military defeat'.

As he spoke, the Japanese were ramming the attack further, to complete the rout of the Allies. Sumatra was next, where a last-stand force of around 50 bombers and Hurricanes was bolstered by 30 Hurricanes that arrived aboard the carrier HMS *Indomitable*. With Singapore taken, the Japanese were able to throw their full weight into Sumatra, and within two weeks the enemy captured Palembang airfield, destroying three dozen Hurricanes in the process. By March the Allied forces had been pushed back into Java with their backs to the sea. On 3 March the remaining 18 Hurricanes and 17 Hudson and Blenheim bombers were ordered to evacuate to Burma. Two Vildebeests still flying also went north, but neither made it. Three Hudsons of No. 1 Squadron, RAAF, were sent home to Australia. Allied forces remaining on Java surrendered the next day.

The aircraft going north were too late to save Rangoon, where the RAF had just 36 aircraft left: a ragtag bunch made up of 15 Buffalos and 21 Chennault 'Flying Tigers', part of the American Volunteer Group serving with the Chinese. Blenheims and Hurricanes were sent in from the Middle East in January, and they were further reinforced in February. But the Japanese advance had been so swift that much of southern Burma had been occupied by the beginning of March, and that included all the airfields. Rangoon, by then a smoking ruin, was taken on 8 March and surviving Allied aircraft were now pulled back to the west coast. Later in the month, the Japanese, with total air superiority, began their thrust to push the British out of Burma, having already completed the rout of French Indo-China. The Allied forces, consisting of two small infantry divisions, had to make one of the longest retreats in British military history to reach a solitary railway bridge across the Sittoung river to get clear and back into India. Five battalions of Gurkhas were among the British troops in retreat, and four of them were engaged in fierce rearguard action in which they lost over 2,000 men. Many of the troops were left stranded on the wrong side of the bridge when it was blown up to prevent the Japanese, in hot pursuit, from crossing into India.

India and Ceylon (Sri Lanka) were now in the firing line and urgent appeals were sent for air defence reinforcements. Four squadrons of Hurricanes, including two from the hard-pressed Middle East campaign, were dispatched to Ceylon, bringing the air force on that island by the end of March up to a strength of 50 Hurricanes, 14 Blenheims and a handful of flying boats. A Japanese attack on the island was expected at any time, the principal target being the large British naval base on the island at Trincomalee, currently home to three aircraft carriers, five battleships, seven cruisers, 15 destroyers and five submarines. The fleet was moved out to avoid the bombing raid that was sure to follow and to seek out the Japanese naval force that had been reported heading towards Ceylon. The air attack came on 5 April, and during almost three days of battle more than 40 enemy aircraft were shot down, to the loss of 30 defending fighters. At sea, the British task force encountered the oncoming Japanese force and substantial battles ensued. Over the coming week, the Royal Navy lost the aircraft carrier HMS *Hermes*, two cruisers and two destroyers just off the east coast. Twenty-eight merchant ships also went down, but Ceylon was saved from invasion.

Overall, the first six months of the war against Japan in South-East Asia had been an unmitigated disaster. Many airmen were among the 138,700 Allied troops killed, wounded or taken prisoner in this campaign. Thousands were never to be seen again in this scenario of monstrous cruelty at the hands of the Japanese, lost in remote jungle camps, starved, tortured, beheaded, experimented on or forced to work on the Railway of Death, along with 45,000 other Allied prisoners, 18,000 of whom died. Luckier during those final days in Burma were 8,600 civilians airlifted to safety by Dakotas of No. 31 Squadron and the USAAF.

CHAPTER ELEVEN

1,000 Bombers over Cologne

Two and a half years into the war, an effective British bombing offensive against Germany remained as elusive as ever. The best minds among the strategists, planners and scientists were being employed and some solutions were already in the pipeline, along with the much-anticipated Lancasters, but they were still months away from being able to make a difference. In the meantime, a firm and decisive change of direction was just about all that could be done. This came with two dramatic developments in February 1942, as Churchill and the War Cabinet viewed the woeful results of the bombing so far, for which the manpower of Bomber Command could not be held to blame. Quite the reverse. The campaign so far had maintained only one consistent element, which was the appalling sacrifice of the bomber crews themselves.

Just as disconcerting was the failure of the hierarchy to get to grips with firm direction. To date, there had been 22 separate directives from the Air Ministry on bombing policy towards Germany as the war planners attempted to find a route through the joint hurdles of inadequate machinery and the morality minefield of blanket bombing. The frustration of the men lower down the batting order – those who had to do the business – was all too evident. Then, at a stroke, the confusion was ended. On St Valentine's Day 1942 the latest directive gave an unambiguous signal: start bombing again. A list of priority targets was drawn up: to hit German industry, especially the U-boat yards, along with the harassment of Berlin and other major cities to maintain a fear that would induce the need for greater numbers of home defence personnel. Ten days later, the second ingredient in this major revamp became known when the boss of Bomber Command, Sir Richard Peirse, was dispatched to India and in his place came Air Chief Marshal Sir Arthur Harris, a strong proponent of area bombing. He arrived with firm ideas and objectives, and not for nothing would be become known as 'Bomber' Harris (although 'Bert' to his colleagues and 'Bunny' to his wife). He had been in America since December, briefing his opposite numbers there as the mighty 8th US Air Force prepared to launch its own massive campaign against the Nazis from British bases. Within a month, a detailed plan had been drawn up to station no fewer than 115 USAAF groups in Britain, and aircraft soon began to arrive in substantial numbers to begin their own daylight campaign to run separately from Bomber Command's night raids.

Harris inherited a Command still relatively weak in both strength and true ability. On the British airfields and available for operations at that time were an unimpressive selection of fewer than 600 aircraft, including 78 Blenheim and Boston day bombers, 221 Wellingtons, 112 Hampdens, 54 Whitleys, 29 Stirlings, 29 Halifaxes, 20 Manchesters and just four new Lancasters. Just to recap, the Avro Lancaster, originally called the Manchester Mk III, did not actually enter service officially until June 1942, when deliveries began to No. 44 Squadron at Waddington.

Nothing much changed since the bombing of Germany had been discontinued before the onset of winter. None of the aircraft in Harris's inventory had any new equipment that would aid accuracy in attack, and British bombers still had to fly individually without navigational aids at night well into 1942. Bomb-laden twin-engined Hampdens, Whitleys, Wellingtons, Blenheims and Manchesters – some of them quite slow – also had to fly much lower than the 20,000 feet or more achieved by their four-engined successors. As we have seen, they were particularly vulnerable to radar-linked concentrations of both light and heavy anti-aircraft fire, as well as new German night fighters. Weather was almost as dangerous as enemy flak, causing dangerous icing in winter and upsetting navigation.

Even so, very soon after taking over, Harris began planning some very big hits and a totally new strategy, starting with the biggest ever raid to be launched from Britain: 1,000 aircraft to bomb a single city on a single night. It seemed an impossible task, given that the number of operational bombers at that time was well short of 500. Harris reckoned that by calling in all available planes from both Coastal Command and the training units, and putting rapidly into working order all the unserviceable aircraft around the country, he could – for one night only – send up the required number.

The date was set for the end of May, and in the meantime lesser raids were planned for immediate execution, mainly to try out a new navigational aid called Gee (see below), which was to be used operationally for the first time in March 1942, with a small number of aircraft equipped with it using flares and incendiary bombs to mark targets at Essen for the main force to follow. Initial results were disappointing, with only one bomb in 20 falling within five miles of the town. On 28 March, in a second raid guided by aircraft using Gee, 234 planes were sent against the Baltic port of Lübeck with far better results. Thousands of tons of high explosives and incendiary bombs ripped through the harbour and the city, overwhelming the German firefighters. Hitler ordered immediate retaliation, and on the night of 23 April Germany launched the first of what became known as the Baedeker raids – targeting British towns and cities of real historical interest selected from the Baedeker tourist guidebook to Britain: Exeter (23–26 April), Bath (25–28 April), Norwich (27–29 April) and York (28–29 April), killing in all 938 British citizens.

Within the month, Harris was ready to exact his own revenge with a blanket attack on Cologne. He had finally cobbled together his 1,000-plus bomber force by the third week in May. That total did not include any from Coastal Command, whose aircraft were under heavy pressure themselves over the seas around the British Isles. So Harris went ahead, rolling out all available planes, including all those held by the training units, such as the Wellingtons, Halifaxes and Stirlings, plus all those in hangars under repair on which ground crews had been working 24 hours a day to get serviceable, and a large number of old bangers that rattled and shuddered their way towards takeoff, plus some with built-in air-conditioning through the number of flak holes that hadn't yet been properly patched up. The logistics of the operation were equally daunting, not least to get the bombers over the target in good order without crashing into or dropping bombs on one another. It required precision planning and timing of nightmarish proportions.

On the night of 30 May, 1,046 bombers took off in waves and went en masse to devastate Cologne. Once again, they were led towards their target by the aircraft with Gee, but on this occasion accuracy wasn't the key issue – the sheer impact of the bombs would be sufficient. The bombers would drop 1,800 tons of incendiaries and high explosives on the city that night – four times larger than the worst raid on London to date, which was 440 tons dropped on 16 April 1941. Two hundred factories were destroyed or damaged, 600 acres of the city laid waste, 469 people killed, 8,000 injured and 45,000 people made homeless. The RAF's tally was: 910 of the bombers reached the target and 39 were lost. A gleeful Churchill wired Roosevelt: 'I hope you were pleased with our mass attack . . . there's plenty more to come.'

The Cologne raid was the first major attack on what was to become the Battle over Germany, and the reaction inside the Third Reich was one of disbelief, best summed up by the words of Hitler's architect and Supply Minister, Albert Speer:

We were given a foretaste of our coming woes when the British gathered all their forces for an attack on Cologne. By chance . . . I was summoned to see Goering on the morning after the raid. He was in a bad humour, still not believing the reports of the Cologne bombing. 'Impossible! That many bombs cannot be dropped in a single night,' he snarled at his adjutant. 'Connect me with the Gauleiter of Cologne.' There followed, in our presence, a preposterous telephone conversation. 'The report from your police commissioner is a stinking lie!' Apparently the Gauleiter begged to differ. 'I tell you as the Reichsmarschall that the figures cited are simply too high. How can you dare report such fantasies to the Führer? I tell you once more they're many times too high. All wrong! Send another report to the Führer revising your figures. Or are you trying to imply that I am lying? I have already delivered my report to the Führer with the correct figures. That stands!'

Despite the relatively light losses, many of Harris's pilots struggled home on a wing and a prayer. Leonard Cheshire was among them:

I got badly shot up over Cologne. I took a direct hit, which blew a ten-foot hole out of the fuselage and set fire to the aircraft. The wireless op was very badly wounded. But at least we managed to get her back. I was given a field DSO for that and taken off for 10 days for a course. I returned to carry out several more raids over Germany before I was posted to No. 35 Squadron with the new Halifaxes. The aircraft was so new, there wasn't as yet a conversion course to Halifaxes and you had no dual in those days. You just did one trip standing behind the CO. Then he got out and said: 'Over to you.' And that was it. So in a sense you didn't quite get to learn the aircraft as well as you did doing a conversion course on a Whitley, for instance. The Halifaxes carried a heavier bomb load but in my opinion didn't have the same safety margin. They went higher and obviously they'd moved into a new level of bombing. The thing that sticks out in my mind from that time was the need to be totally professional. The odds on surviving a tour were very much against you. So if you wanted to survive you had at least to cut down the possibility of not getting through because of a mistake on your side. The rest you could only leave to providence. Every mission that we did was an important mission. I felt that at all costs we had to hit the target. And the equipment and the weather and the whole technique was against you finding a target at night. So it needed a total commitment of mind and of heart to mastering your aircraft and your bombing technique.

Cheshire and many of his colleagues did exactly that, but also the technical innovations coming into use were a godsend and contributed heavily to turning the fortunes of the Command. Gee was the first of three systems which were introduced progressively in 1942, the result of months of round-the-clock effort by teams of some of the finest scientific brains in the country. Gee relied on measurements between pulses received from three synchronised transmitters on the ground. The aircraft's position could then be determined from a lattice of intersecting lines overlaid on the plotting chart. Range was limited to 350 to 400 miles, and it was subject to jamming by the Germans. It was used operationally in a small number of aircraft in March 1942, but by the end of the year the device had been installed in 80 per cent of bombers flying into Germany.

The next system was Oboe, which measured the range of the aircraft from two ground radar stations very accurately, and instructions were given to guide it to the target. One maintained the aircraft on a track passing over the target, and the other determined the correct moment for bomb release. The third and most important was called H2S, a radar device carried in the aircraft which scanned the ground beneath and formed an 'echo map' on the indicator tube. Pyrotechnics were also developed to mark the aiming point for the main bomber force, and thus radar and target markers would, by early 1943, prove invaluable to the British offensive. Other innovations included equipment known as Mandrel, which jammed German Freya early-warning radar, and another system codenamed Tinsel was introduced to jam radio communications between German night fighters and ground controllers.

As the uncommon successes of the British bombing campaign began to mount, however, some unseemly and at times exceedingly bad-tempered infighting broke out between Bomber Command and the Air Ministry's Directorate of Bomber Operations. Air Ministry advisers to Chief of Air Staff Sir Charles Portal had become pressingly interested in resolving the problems of achieving a greater degree of accuracy by the bombers through target identification and marking. Group Captain S.O. Bufton, former commander of No. 10 Squadron, had risen to Director of Bomber Operations and was an outspoken supporter of precision bombing. He saw Harris's move to area bombing as merely a stopgap measure until a target-finding force could be set up. With the new technical aids now in place, the time had come for Bufton to make his move, much to Harris's disgust. Harris went on record to state his objections and said that Portal 'had no right to overrule me on the advice of a junior staff officer whose only qualification was that he dropped a few leaflets on Europe at the beginning of the war'.

But Harris lost the battle, and the decision was taken to form what would become known as the Pathfinder Force (PFF). He did, however, successfully reject the Air Ministry's candidate for the job, the commander of 2 Group, Basil Embry. If he had to have the Pathfinders, he wanted his own choice of commander and successfully fought off strong internal objections to appoint the young Australian group captain, Donald Bennett, who had run the Atlantic ferry service and whom we last met bombing the *Tirpitz*. Still only 32, Bennett was highly regarded in the service as a fine technician and brilliant flier, but cocky with it. He had thousands of hours of flying, held a First Class Navigation Certificate, a GPO Wireless Operator Licence and every Civil Ground Engineer's Licence. He had already expressed his own theories on the subject of target-finding, which had been rejected by Harris's predecessor. Bennett recalled:

I was never more convinced about anything in my life. You must have navigators. They must be good navigators and they must have a lot more than an airspeed indicator to get them there. And that's what started it. From there I had all sorts of people supporting me. They were so keen on getting it right that they just simply supported somebody who was himself a navigator, and remember I had a book in being on navigation which was the leading world book, so they knew me as such and they backed me. Now that went for almost everybody, but not of course for Sir Richard Peirse, and I'm also sorry to say that it also did not go for Bert Harris, who fought tooth and nail to try and stop it. I found myself commanding Pathfinders with his blessing but with his open opposition to the concept. He did his best to be fair to me, and we got along personally perfectly well, but not always in agreement. Having said that, I had no doubt he was the best person that Bomber Command could have had. Nobody else of that age group or age level could have done any better, operationally, and no one matched his press-on spirit. He stood up for us against the politicians and all the niggling, and so on, when people wanted to say: 'Stop all the bomb-ing. They're killing women and children. How terrible.' He was able to get up and say: 'Yes, and what did the Huns do to our women and children?' Generally speaking, he put them back in their boxes – not as effectively as I would have liked to have seen, but it was better than nothing.

He put forward very valid arguments against my theories. One was that if you took all your best crews and put them out in front to lead the rest, it would also expose them to greater risk of being hacked down. The losses among your best crews would be so high that it would be prohibitive. We overcame it by adopting tactics that countered this, such as mixing the lead crews with supporters. We also did other things, like setting up diversionary raids to create an element of surprise, but the great exception when we really did suffer was during the Battle of Berlin, which was a scandalous thing. It was a Churchillian doing [announcing our intentions in advance]. They told the Hun we were coming to Berlin every night, and of course we had a terrible time because we couldn't adopt any tactical surprise. If you don't have tactical surprise you get hacked down, it's as simple as that.

The pyrotechnics that we developed to mark the targets were wonderful, made by the fireworks industry of Great Britain, colour screens red, blue, green, purple, white, cascading with delays, without delays, varying heights and varying levels, and so on. And we could ring the changes. We could start with a colour that would make the Hun think that that was where we were going, and then go somewhere else, things like that. Anyway, between the lot of all these changes and innovations we managed to keep our losses down and our results up. We had one outright knife-you-in-the-back antagonist, a very nice chap, but nevertheless the worst enemy we could have had, called Cochrane [Sir Ralph Cochrane, 5 Group Commander, who appointed Leonard Cheshire his own master bomber], who knew nothing at all about technical matters but was out to get Pathfinder Force, largely I think to please the C-in-C. He did things like instructing his squadron commanders to report instantly to him any mistakes made by Pathfinders. Well, the normal channels would have been quite adequate, but he wanted to get his knife in us, and would do everything he could to stop us. He almost ruined the Pathfinder Force through these dirty tricks.

We pressed on and were given a brilliant team of boffins. They told me that they could get a reflection from the ground that would differentiate between land and water and between built-up areas and plain ground. And that they could do this in not more than about 10 years. So I did a bit of shouting, and we got into an aeroplane and went flying straightaway with the boffin in charge. He flew with me by day and by night, and we had a vision of the ground within a couple of days. We were operational within a month, a wonderful effort. They were really a wonderful team of people and they produced H2S, which meant that we could paint a map of the terrain below and the result was that we were dropping blind from 26,000 feet with wonderful results.

By the end of the year the pyrotechnics Bennett had ordered as ground markers were ready for use and, although some crews of Bomber Command still resented the PFF, most were soon converted and glad to discover the markers when they arrived over their bomb delivery area so that they could drop their load and get out of the flak without delay. These innovations were further enhanced when Oboe became operational, on a raid over Flensburg on 20 December 1942. It provided the specific advantage of allowing the crews to bomb blind over target areas hidden in bad weather and fog. One month after the arrival of Oboe, H2S was brought into use, thereby providing crews with a rough map of the ground below on a cathode-ray screen and which, unlike Gee and Oboe, did not depend on transmitters, was not limited by range and could not be jammed.*

Crews themselves were also getting better and better as they bombed the target indicators dropped by the PFF. At the end of the first year of PFF operations, it was estimated (in post-war analysis) that accuracy improved dramatically, with over 40 per cent of bombs dropped reaching their target, and by the time of

---

* It did, however, eventually suffer a severe setback when in July 1944 the Germans developed a monitoring system which made it possible for them to track British bombers through the H2S system throughout their mission. This was discovered in late 1944, and H2S silence had to be imposed.

D-day this had risen to over 80 per cent. Those skills were further enhanced by the creation of the master bomber role, which meant they could be directed to the aiming point over radio transmission while the raid was in progress. The master bomber flew around at low level and called in the aircraft to make their strike.

The addition of the American bombing force fully complemented the British night-time operations with their daytime bombing raids. It was a situation that remained almost to the end of the war that the Americans would bomb only in the daytime. This build-up to virtual round-the-clock bombing of Germany was signalled on 24 January 1943 when Churchill, Stalin and Roosevelt attended the Casablanca conference to put their signatures to an accord on the future progress of the war. It called for Allied forces to achieve 'the progressive destruction and dislocation of the German military, industrial and economic system and the undermining of the morale of the German people to a point where their capacity for armed resistance is fatally weakened'. There was no other force capable of achieving that aim other than Bomber Command and its American counterparts in the 8th US Air Force, a task that was about to be made more effective by the arrival into service of the brilliant Mosquito and, much to the chagrin of the rest of Bomber Command, Don Bennett's Pathfinders were to get priority when the first edition came into service:

> We formed two squadrons of Mosquitos to carry Oboe. They did the job with spectacular results, and I eventually formed 14 Mosquito squadrons. They were wonderful. They could outpace the German fighters, go anywhere in Germany and I had them modified to carry one 4,000-pounder, Blockbuster, the biggest bomb then known. A Mosquito could carry that to Berlin. They were major raids, but on top of that they could also do a very useful purpose connected with the Pathfinder marking. If we were going to a main target with Bomber Command as a whole, in order to put the fighters off and divert any other opposition that might be cropping up, we would send the Mosquitos through the bomber stream on to a target to one side or the other. They would bomb that target with Blockbusters and with markers, the main force having been told to ignore it.

The bombers would go on their way. The Mosquitos would come back to England. The bombers would turn left on to their main target, which had already been marked. By doing that, Mosquitos took the fighters away from the mainstream and saved hundreds of lives. It was a wonderful contribution, and it was quite remarkable that people never really realised the contribution made by the Mosquito force. It was the most cost-effective thing in the war . . . while the heavy bombers, eventually up to 1,200 at a time, each carrying round about 12,000 pounds or 16,000 pounds, were doing enormous damage.

Lancasters were increasingly to figure in these operations as they became the workhorse of the British air fleet, and the first major operation that made them internationally and eternally famous was the next big show Harris pencilled in: an attack on the Ruhr Valley, for immediate action, in accordance with the latest Air Ministry directive. It was territory stacked with important German industry – and some very large dams. They were now to become the focus of attention in what became one of Bomber Command's most talked-about raids of the war: the Dambusters, a story every schoolboy still learns. The Lancaster aircrews were to destroy the walls of German dams with the incredible bouncing bombs invented by Sir Neville Barnes Wallis. No. 617 Squadron was formed at Scampton on 21 March 1943 for the specific purpose of taking on Operation Chastise, the codename for the destruction of the dams. Wing Commander Guy Gibson, already recognised as one of the RAF's most skilled pilots, with long tours of duty in both fighters and bombers, was appointed to command the special unit and was given a free hand to appoint his own men. They were not told the purpose of their mission, although they had a good idea, training for weeks in formation flying at low level over the sea at Margate and Folkestone and reservoirs in Derbyshire.

Nineteen specially modified Lancasters were to carry out the raid, which required Barnes Wallis's 9,250-pound cylindrical weapon to be dropped from an altitude of just 60 feet at a speed in excess of 200 miles an hour. The bomb would be launched from a belt driven by an electric motor inside the aircraft fuselage so that it would hit the water in a reverse spin at a rate of 500 rpm and bounce like a flat stone along the surface to the dam wall and explode. The Mohne, Eder and Sorpe Dams were the prime targets. Gibson assembled his team to carry out this daring raid over an area notoriously heavily defended with flak towers. Among them was Wing Commander Dave Shannon, a native of Unley, South Australia, who at the age of 18 had volunteered for the Royal Australian Air Force and was seconded to the RAF in 1941. He was still only 21 when he was flying bombers:

Having arrived in England, we were first sent to do a further advanced training course at Cranwell, which was completed in about a month or so, and then we were sent to an operational training unit in Scotland at Kinloss. We did a six-month course on Whitleys, and it was from Kinloss that I was posted to 106 Squadron commanded by Guy Gibson. A tour then was considered to be 30 ops; I'd done 36. I wanted to keep flying and I had asked for a posting to the Pathfinder Force with No. 83 Squadron. I'd only been there two or three days when I got a call from Gibson. He had been asked to form a special squadron for a secret operation. Having served with him for so long, I was very happy to say yes. All the crews had volunteered, and we then went into intensive training on an operational station with another bomber squadron who were operating at night there. No one knew what we were training for, and neither did we! So we were all very keen to get on and do it. The accuracy that was required was incredible, and there was only a period of six weeks to achieve it, although it seemed an age at that particular time.

Eventually, it was to become clear that we were to fly from Scampton across the North Sea, crossing the Dutch coast, down into Germany, and then slightly north along the Ruhr Valley, which was a very heavily defended area. So we had the route maps, which had been marked out, and we had the models, which had been built to scale. Before we were shown them, we were sworn to secrecy and finally we had the full briefing. Crews came in and we saw the whole thing for the first time, that the target was the dams that served the Ruhr industries. A full briefing was given by Gibson and by the station commander and by Group intelligence.

We had Barnes Wallis there, who explained in detail the object of this particular operation, how the bombs would work, why we'd had to practise, how we'd had to wait for this time because the object was to hit these dams and breach them when they were absolutely full of water, up to their maximum capacity, to do the most possible damage that we could. Reconnaissance aircraft had been flying over the dams for the previous two months watching them as the water crept up. And we had to wait for the full moon period, which was the only way we could operate flying low. That period hit us in mid-May 1943. Having had the briefing, we all then adjourned back to the mess, had a pre-operational meal and then waited for the takeoff, which was planned for the first wave of aircraft at 21.30, aiming to be over the target at round about midnight to breach the dams. The sequence was that the first nine aircraft would take off for the Mohne and Eder Dams. Immediately after that, flying on a different route, five aircraft took off for the Sorpe Dam for an attack to run concurrently with our raid on the Mohne. So we got 14 off at that stage and then there were another five in reserve, ready for takeoff to attack other dams once we had radioed back the results of ours. So they would not be taking off until around one in the morning.

We flew across the North Sea, quite uneventful until we reached the coast of Holland, and then hit a lot of flak, which continued on all the way to the target. The route also took us across one of the new German aerodromes, and it was there that the first of our aircraft was hit. Bill Astell went down to flak. Once we got to the Mohne Dam, silhouetted there in the moonlight, we could see the target clearly. Gibson said that he would do a reconnoitre, and we were all told to hold off, circling in the hills three or four miles back, to await results. We were all on [radio transmission] so we could hear simultaneously what was going on. Guy went in to make his attack, and it was then that we found out that the Mohne Dam was very heavily defended with a lot of flak guns (a) on the dam wall itself and (b) on the sides on the approach to the dam. Gibson went through and released his mine and there was a tremendous explosion of water and debris up into the air. When it had all subsided, we saw the dam wall was still there.

Gibson now called Hopwood to begin his run-in and he, too, attracted tremendous flak. His plane was under fire all the way in, serious stuff, and he was hit in one of the petrol tanks. His wing on the starboard side caught fire. I think his bomb aimer must have been hit, too, because the bomb was released late and bounced over the wall. There was a tremendous explosion. Hopwood did his best to gain height with a steep climb and got up to about 400 feet when the entire aircraft exploded in mid-air beyond the dam wall. So that was the second bomb and the wall was still standing.

The next chap to go in was Mickey Martin. He was hit several times, but to try and draw off some of the flak Gibson began flying down one side of the lake just out of range of the flak but with his navigation lights on and his spotlights on under the aircraft. It was a bit of spoof but it worked. Martin's bomb was released, as far as we could tell, exactly on site. Again, there was this tremendous, vast explosion of water up into the air, and then when the whole thing had subsided again, the wall was still there. So the next three were called in.

The leader of that group was Squadron Leader Young. And this time, Martin was also flying down one side and Gibson on the other, trying to draw the fire to get some of the flak away, to give the flak gunners three aircraft to shoot at instead of one. Young dropped his mine apparently in the right place. Young called up and said that he thought the wall would go, because as far as he could tell it had been a perfect run. But the wall was still standing. The next one to go was Maltby: the same procedure was carried out again. Maltby had dropped his bomb in exactly the right place, again we had this tremendous explosion of water, it settled down and still the dam wall was there as far as I could see. Gibson then called me in, and I was just starting the run when there were excited yells and cheers over the RT: 'It's gone, it's gone, it's gone.' So Gibson rapidly shouted to me: 'Steer off the run, stand by, stand by, I think it's gone.' And then he came back and said: 'Yes, it's gone.' The whole wall was collapsing and the water had started spewing out down the valley, a great gushing spout that very quickly submerged all in its path.

The job was done and the aircraft that were left were then moved across to the Eder Dam, while Martin and Maltby, both damaged, were told to return to base. By this time it was getting on and the mists were starting to form across the hills and down in the valleys. The Eder Dam, which was even bigger than the Mohne Dam, was not protected by any anti-aircraft defences at all. I think the Germans had thought that its natural surroundings were such that it was quite secure. It was way down at the bottom of a very steep valley. There was a castle which we had to avoid and drop down immediately over the side of the hill, then level out over the water, go over a spit of sand that was jutting out into the lake, and then the dam wall was beyond that. Finally, we had to immediately pull on full throttle and do a steep climbing turn to the right to avoid a vast rock face that was up in the front. I was called in first and I tried, I think, four times to get down, dropping down, and each time was not satisfied with the run that I'd made, and told the bomb aimer not to release. So Gibson said: 'Well, have a rest.' He called in Maudsley, who was leader of the next flight, to come along. He had one dummy run at it, unsuccessfully, and did the same thing that I'd done. He did another run and this time dropped his bomb. Unfortunately, it overshot and bounced over the wall and again exploded below and there was a tremendous flash, a huge ball of flame.

We don't know what happened to Maudsley; his aircraft was never found. Gibson told me to have another go, so I had another dummy run and then I got what I thought was an excellent run down so this time we released the mine. And there was a terrific explosion and there seemed to be a small breach made on the port side, but there was no significant sign of water coming through. Now, there was only one aircraft left, Les Knight, and Gibson called him in – the last chance. He had three or four runs before he could release, and then he released his mine, and I think his mine, together with my mine, was sufficient . . . the dam wall was collapsing.

Shannon's bomb aimer, Len Sumpter, could see the water below gushing out of the breach:

It was getting bigger and bigger all the time as the water washed the sides out. Everybody on the plane and the others were cheering. And there was this wall of water coming through now, just this great flood all the way down the valley. There was a road leading down into it. Cars were going along it and then the lights just vanished underneath the water. You could see them gradually getting dimmer and dimmer and dimmer. And they were either washed away or overcome, or something like that because it was just like the Niagara Falls and it was rolling all the way down the valley. We did a couple of circuits to see how things were going and then Gibson came on the RT and said: 'Right, everybody: home.' We set off back, retracing the same route and ran straight into the flak again. It was as if they were waiting for us. Dinghy Young was shot down. He was nicknamed Dinghy because he'd been shot down three or four times before and always managed to escape by dinghy. Unfortunately, he didn't make the sea this time.

Dave Shannon put on a bit of a spurt and got us out of it, and we landed safely back at Scampton at around 4 a.m. There was a telegram from Harris the next morning, to tell us we'd been awarded an immediate DFM. What I could never understand, though, was that they never sent us back again for a repeat performance and consequently the dams were repaired in about six months.

The Germans couldn't understand it either, as Albert Speer confirmed:

That night, employing just a few bombers, the British came close to a success which would have been greater than they had achieved hitherto . . . but they made a mistake which puzzles me to this day. A few days after this attack, 7,000 men were hard a work repairing the dams. On 23 September, in the nick of time before the beginning of the rains, the breach in the Mohne Dam was closed. We were thus able to collect the precipitation of the winter for the needs of the following summer. The British air force missed its second chance. A few bombs would have produced cave-ins at the exposed rebuilding site and a few firebombs would have set the wood scaffolding ablaze.*

The reason was in fact the high cost of this expedition in which two dams were destroyed. Apart from the 1,800 German lives, of the 19 Lancasters, three failed to complete the sortie and returned home early, and of the remaining 16, eight failed to return. In all, 53 aircrew were killed and three survived to be taken prisoner. Guy Gibson was awarded the Victoria Cross with a citation which read:

Wing Commander Gibson, whose personal courage knew no bounds, was recognised to be an outstanding operational pilot and leader. He served with conspicuously successful results as a night bomber pilot and also as a night fighter pilot, on operational tours. In addition, on his 'rest' nights he made single-handed attacks on highly defended objectives, such as the German battleship *Tirpitz*. Wing Commander Gibson was then selected to command a squadron formed for special tasks. Under his inspiring leadership, this squadron executed one of the most devastating attacks of the war – the breaching of the Mohne and Eder Dams. Wing Commander Gibson personally made the initial attack on the Mohne Dam. He then circled very low for 30 minutes, drawing the enemy fire and permitting as free a run as possible for the following aircraft. He repeated these tactics in the attack on the Eder Dam. Throughout his operational career, prolonged exceptionally at his own request, he has shown leadership, determination and valour of the highest order.†

* Albert Speer; *Inside the Third Reich*, p. 281.
† Following the dams raid, Gibson took an enforced rest in which time he wrote a book about his experiences, entitled *Enemy Coast Ahead*. After visiting America with Winston Churchill, he returned to active service in the autumn of 1944, flying a Mosquito from 627 Squadron. On 19 September, while acting as master bomber in a raid on German positions over southern Holland, his plane crashed, killing both himself and his navigator, Squadron Leader J.B. Warwick.

The Dambuster raid was only part of the Ruhr story, a small part in fact. Bomber Command attacks, which began in March, ran to the third week in July. A total of 23,400 night sorties were flown, almost 60,000 tons of bombs dropped with great loss of life and at a high cost to the Command of over 1,000 aircraft lost or seriously damaged. As the targets diminished, Bomber Command switched its attention to Hamburg for the main thrust of the continued nightly onslaught, and it was here that the results of the new technology and the incoming new machines of the Lancaster and Mosquito breeds began to show results.

Operational Command No. 173, dated 27 May 1943, gave no room for misunderstanding. In a nutshell, it relayed the message: Destroy Hamburg. And while Bomber Command's night raiders began their attacks, so the daylight attacks of the US 8th began to run theirs in unison. The initial sorties were launched on the night of 24 July, when a massive force of 791 bombers unloaded 1,360 tons of high explosives and almost 1,000 tons of incendiaries in a deployment lasting just 50 minutes. Four further raids followed, although the last one went badly awry because of severe weather. Even so, Don Bennett, top dog in an increasingly impressive Pathfinder Force, was unswerving in his recollections of events:

> I would say the proudest time for PFF was Hamburg. We destroyed Hamburg in one week with low casualties to us. It was very effective, one of the most marvellous episodes, and we could have taken Hamburg with a boy scout patrol at that time, they were so taken. Squadron commanders and the leaders of that very rare lot of people who were responsible had put bombs on the aiming points, more exactly and more particularly than anybody else. Now we had a perfect example of that . . .

With up to 50,000 people killed, the raids sent shock waves through Germany and through the Third Reich, and we may defer to Albert Speer once again for a summary of the reaction:

> Rash as this operation was, it had catastrophic consequences for us. First attacks put the water supply pipes out of action, so that in the subsequent bombings the fire department had

no way of fighting the fire. Huge conflagrations created cyclone-like firestorms; the asphalt of the streets began to blaze; people were suffocated in their cellars or burned to death in the streets. The devastation of this series of air raids could be compared only with the effects of a major earthquake. Hamburg had suffered the fate Goering and Hitler had conceived for London in 1940. At a supper in the Chancellery in that year, Hitler had, in the course of a monologue, worked himself up to a frenzy of destructiveness: 'Have you ever looked at a map of London? It is so closely built up that one source of fire alone would suffice to destroy the whole city, as happened once before, 200 hundred years ago. Goering wants to use innumerable incendiary bombs of an altogether new type to create sources of fire in all parts of London. Fires everywhere. Thousands of them. Then they'll unite in one gigantic area conflagration. Goering has the right idea. Explosive bombs don't work, but it can be done with incendiary bombs – total destruction of London. What use will their fire department be once that really starts?' Hamburg had put the fear of God in me. If the air raids continued on the present scale, within three months we shall be relieved of a number of questions we are at present discussing.

CHAPTER TWELVE

Heading for Victory

Fighters, bombers, torpedo carriers . . . and now another vital element had entered the RAF scenario and one which again put pressure on the supply of aircraft and pilots. As the last German units were being booted out of the North African theatre, the next major date in the Allied calendar had been pencilled in – the invasion of southern Italy using Sicily as a stepping stone – an attack that would be led by British paras followed in by the heavily armed airborne units transported in gliders. Preparations were already under way in April 1943 when No. 295 Halifax Squadron was assigned the task of ferrying much-needed giant Horsa gliders from Portreath, Cornwall, to Morocco and then on to Kairouan in Tunisia, a tow of 2,400 miles. By the beginning of July, 27 of the 36 combinations that set off from Cornwall had reached North Africa, the rest having been ditched or crashed en route. The paras and gliders and tugs were an essential element to the capture of Sicily, which was planned as a rapid pincer movement. With General Eisenhower as commander-in-chief of the Allied forces, the Americans were to advance from the west while the British 8th Army, under General Montgomery, moved in from the east coast to block the enemy's escape route across the Strait of Messina.

The task of airborne troops was to capture key bridges, and high ground on the approaches to them, ahead of the arrival of the main force. Three specific targets were vital for the progress of the seaborne assault. On the day before the massive movement of men and machinery, the 1st Air-landing Brigade was assigned to capture the Ponte Grande and clear the way into the port of Syracuse and then the harbour itself. On the evening of 9 July, 2,000 men piled into 137 Hadrian and Horsa gliders towed by 109 American Dakotas and a detachment of 38 Wing RAF and took off from North Africa. The weather was unusually brisk, with winds running up to gale force. Half the gliders were released too early and 78 landed in the sea, leaving the men to swim ashore as best they could; many did not make it. Several others were shot down, and those who managed a landing were miles apart on difficult terrain. Fewer than a dozen gliders in that operation managed to reach the designated landing zones, all towed by RAF aircraft. In spite of the chaotic beginnings, parties of men formed up under the most senior ranks among them and began attacking Axis troops wherever they came across them.

The enemy commanders, totally surprised by the assaults, were thus given the impression that a whole airborne corps had been dropped, which at least helped the seaborne arrivals. They landed virtually unopposed. Nor did the initial target go unattended. A single platoon of one of the glider-borne battalions, the 2nd battalion, South Staffordshire Regiment, captured the Ponte Grande and held it for several hours before they were forced to withdraw under heavy enemy fire. The action was sufficient to hold the Axis troops at bay, and by the afternoon of that day the bridge was retaken with the aid of the 2nd Battalion, Royal Scots Fusiliers, fresh from their beach landing. Around 300 men were lost in this first major airborne operation, most of them drowned in pre-released or shot-down gliders, but the road to Syracuse was secure for the Allied advance.

With the 8th Army now ashore and advancing across the coastal plain towards Catania, the 1st Parachute Brigade was tasked with taking other vital targets, especially where the main road crossed the river, at the Ponte di Primosole. After two postponements, the operation was launched on the night of 13 July, when 113 aircraft and 16 gliders carrying 1,856 men took off from North Africa. Vic Coxen with 1 Para was in the first aircraft:

I was looking out of the window and saw the river; came

back and hooked up. At that moment, the aircraft banked and went out to sea again. I unhooked and went forward and asked what the matter was. The pilot said we were 10 minutes early. I said: 'That doesn't matter a bugger. They know we're here – they're already firing at us. Get in!' As we headed for the dropping zone, the aircraft suddenly bent sideways and climbed sharply. He'd overshot, and there was a bloody great hill in front of him. Everybody went arse over applecart. I went out on my knees. All of my stick got out except the last three, who were tangled up at the back of the plane somewhere. When I came down, it was on the top of a hill. We were in the wrong bloody place. The chap below me broke his leg.

Inexperienced American pilots, the lack of navigators and fear of running out of fuel meant that few of the gliders came down in the right place for the attack on the Primosole bridge. Only 295 officers and men of the brigade came down close enough to the designated dropping zone to form up for the operation. Given the number of paras and glider-borne army units who were tasked for the assault, this first major British use of airborne troops had turned into something of a fiasco, largely because of the untrained American pilots.

On 13 July the first Spitfires roared in from Malta, landing on hastily repaired Sicilian airstrips, and were immediately used to harass the enemy and push their troops towards the sea. Sicily could now be used for frequent bombing raids against targets in southern Italy, while in the north 500 American bombers launched raids on Rome itself for the first time. Pilots were under strict orders to avoid historical buildings and the Vatican, although 4,000-pound bombs shattered the city's railyards, air-fields and industrial areas. From the UK, Bomber Command sent out raids on Milan, Genoa and Turin. They had the desired effect. Mussolini was deposed on 25 July and the new Italian government immediately began secret negotiations for an armistice, eventually declared on 8 September.

The following day, under huge air cover of Spitfires operating from Sicily and Royal Navy aircraft carriers, the Allies landed three divisions into Salerno and, once the bridgehead into the Italian mainland was fully established, Allied forces now began the hard slog north in what would prove to be a monumental series of battles to dislodge the German troops, reinforced by crack units under orders from the Führer not to give an inch. The Allied forces, short of men and machines, moved like 'a bug on one leg', as Churchill put it, and were famously stalled at Monte Cassino, where the retreating Germans turned the Benedictine monastery into an impregnable fortress. There they remained well into the new year, until American Flying Fortresses controversially bombed the religious buildings. Questions were raised in the House of Commons, and Eisenhower, with the approval of President Roosevelt, issued an order that would have far-reaching effects on the remainder of the bombing campaign across Europe: if it is a question of my men getting killed or buildings being destroyed, the buildings must go. Nothing can stand against military necessity.

That philosophy also went for the campaign in Germany, which Bomber Command re-launched with a vengeance in the autumn of 1943 as new aircraft and better techniques finally began to pay dividends. 'Now,' Bert Harris declared on 25 November, 'we shall bomb Berlin until the heart of Nazi Germany ceases to beat.' He kept his promise.

Harris was ready at last to launch an all-out air assault on the German capital, although it must be said that the Germans would put up a more spirited defence than he had bargained for. They had brought on line some new electronics, including a device that enabled fighters to home in on the unsuspecting bombers as they used their radios and at the same time radar systems were upgraded. But one of the most spectacular defensive measures was the building of a dummy suburb of Berlin, 15 miles north-west of the city on the main approaches of the British night bombers. A whole simulated district of streets, houses and shops was laid out and fitted with electronically detonated markers and fire sites aimed at convincing bomber crews that they had arrived over their intended target. Berlin was the focus of a substantial proportion of the effort of Bomber Command. The attacks began on the night of 18 November 1943 with a raid by 440 Lancasters, which were 'brilliantly successful' according to Harris, with only 14 shot down. Four nights later, 764 aircraft were sent out and again losses were kept to a minimum, with 26 failing to return. The skills of Don Bennett's

Pathfinder crews and the use of master bombers, who flew at low level directing their bombers into the attack, was finally paying dividends. Among those in the hot seats was Ivor Broom, whom we last met flying Blenheims in the defence of Malta. On his return to England, he transferred to a Mosquito training unit and subsequently joined the Pathfinders:

> The Mosquito was going into service in Nos. 105 and 139 Squadrons and the big question was: were the Mosquitos going to go into low-level daylight operations or were they going to go into the Pathfinder Force? Don Bennett saw the potential of the Mosquitos as marking aircraft, and so the first squadrons went in with him. As more and more Mosquitos came off the line, so they had two different roles, one for attacking targets in Europe in the bomber ground attack role and the other in the Pathfinder Force leading the main bomber force to their targets. They were also heavily used in diversionary tactics. Bennett formed what was called the Light Night Striking Force and I went into that unit, undertaking various roles. Our main task was to go out with the main bomber force, and when we were within 50 miles or so of its targets we would shoot off in a different direction to confuse the German defences and drop a lot of tin foil, called Window. That would create on the German radar two streams of aeroplanes in the hope that they didn't know which was which. We would then attack the secondary target while the main force went to their designated targets. It was a very effective tactic. Now, when the main force wasn't flying because of the weather, we could still go out. In fact, we had many nights when only the Mosquitos were out over Germany. We used to joke with people that you'd get the freedom of the city when you'd done 21 raids on Berlin. Lots of people did many more than that. My navigator and I did 21 on Berlin. They also had another lovely little catch phrase: that you could go to Berlin and back on a winter evening and still get to the mess before the bar closed. We regularly did Berlin in about four hours or so from Cambridgeshire, whereas the main force would take twice as long. We were never troubled by a night fighter in the 58 raids we did to Germany but we were troubled by flak,

particularly over Berlin. I do remember one attack on Berlin, though, where we really had a rough old night. We were picked up by searchlights very early on in the run-up to what we used to call the big city. We were coned for about 12 or thirteen minutes, and that's a long time, because you've probably covered 100 miles in that time. In and out of the beam, going all over the sky, taking a lot of evasive action because you didn't know if a fighter was going to come on you. When we got out of the searchlights eventually, I turned to my navigator and I said: 'Give me a course for home.' And his classic reply was: 'Well, fly west with a dash of north until I sort myself out.'

I was in No. 571 Squadron initially doing this. Then I was made flight commander, promoted to help form another squadron, 128. Four months later I was acting wing commander and I'm now 24 years of age. Bennett arranged a telephone hook-up with every squadron commander, and he'd give us more background information before we went to brief our own crews. Hardly a week went by but I met Bennett. The difference between Bennett and other commanders was that he was very young and still very much a practising pilot and a practising navigator and a practising operator of Morse code. He was a great aviator, and he couldn't tolerate anything which was second best. That's why he was ideal for the Pathfinders.

If you didn't come up to his high standards, you were no good to him. He really was the right man in the right place at that time, and he had no qualms about what had to be done. We hear a great deal of criticism of the work of Bomber Command nowadays, on the morality of it and another about how effective it was. Well, to the people who question the morality, I would say: What alternative was there? What would you have done after the whole of Europe had been subjugated, and we were on our own? Would you have just defended yourself against attacks? When everyone knows the only best way to defend yourself is to attack the other side. I have no time at all for anybody who says it shouldn't have happened, you shouldn't have bombed civilians, you shouldn't have bombed cities. There were a lot of people who had panacea targets, such as the ball-bearing factories, the power stations, do this and the other and you'll shorten the war. That was proved to be a lot of hooey. I think that on the tremendous destruction of the big cities, you have only to look at Speer's report of this, and take notice of what he said rather than what British people say about the effectiveness of the bomber offensive. So I won't allow anyone to speak to me about the morality without telling me, even with hindsight, a better tactic they would have adopted. It was the only way we had of carrying the war to the enemy.

The raids on Berlin continued through the winter, and on 20 January 1944 the biggest ever bomb load in a single night was dropped on the Nazi capital: 600 Lancasters and Halifaxes delivered 2,300 tons of bombs, starting at least 30 major fires and bringing the total to 17,000 tons in just two months. Hitler ordered the Luftwaffe to muster an immediate response, and the following night British fighter units and home defences were scrambled for the biggest raid in Britain in recent times when a force of 447 German bombers was reported heading their way, though the Spitfires and Hurricanes were waiting to demonstrate that they were gaining air superiority and more than 60 of the incoming attackers were shot down or turned back. Nor could the British count on their own attacks getting any easier either. On the night of 30 March 1944, during a disastrous attack on Nuremberg, Bomber Command suffered its heaviest losses of the entire war: 95 aircraft failed to return from 795 dispatched after being heavily attacked by German night fighters.

Furthermore, a new threat, potentially far more troublesome to Britain, was on the verge of becoming reality: Hitler's much-vaunted secret weapons. For many months, German scientists had been working on the perfection of pilotless flying bombs and rockets, the V-1 and V-2 weapons and the even more secretive V-3, a gun that could fire huge bombs across the Channel, which were all in the final stages of development. Their arrival over England in the early summer of 1944 would temporarily silence the 'morality' debate. The new weapons were designed to terror-ise by their indiscriminate killing of civilian populations.

As early as August 1943, intelligence reports had concluded that the weapons – which the Germans themselves had begun to claim would 'wipe Britain off the map' – were close to reality. The first attacks using the flying bombs and later the V-2 rockets were months away, and indeed would eventually be launched from sites in France and down what became known as Buzz Bomb Alley through southern England and into Greater London. But one of the key rocket research sites had been identified at Peenemünde on the Baltic coast, where both V-1 and V-2 weapons were being developed.

Don Bennett's Pathfinder Force would be called on on numerous occasions in the coming months to guide the bombers to Hitler's secret sites, and undoubtedly delayed the arrival of buzz bombs and rockets over London:

> We were tipped off by some Poles, who told us about the V-2 sites. Lord Cherwell [Churchill's PA] had me in his office on this on a number of occasions long before air staff had heard of them; it was Cherwell, Churchill and myself to start with. The problem: how do you stop a vertical rocket coming down? We all agreed that the only way to stop them was 'abolition' . . . in other words, on the ground before they started, because we could never hope to stop them on a vertical dive. So we laid on the Peenemünde raid with Group Captain John Searby [of No. 83 Squadron] as master bomber. He was one of our leading Pathfinders. It was yet another diversion of effort, the whole Command hitting this one target, and I would have liked to have had surprise to be able to keep my casualties down. Churchill would not allow it so as to avoid civilian casualties as far as possible.

The Pathfinders led in a force of 560 bombers, which delivered a total of 1,800 tons of bombs over Peenemünde, and they had instructions to hit specific targets, including the rocket factory, laboratories and a research station. Searby and the PFF dropped markers on a target area covering less than two miles by one mile to guide the main stream of bombers. At the same time, a diversionary raid was staged by eight Mosquitos from the Light Night Striking Force over Berlin to distract the Luftwaffe night fighters. Even so, they were able to be called to Peenemünde in time to hit Bomber Command hard as the last wave came in, with the resultant loss of 40 Lancasters from the main force. It was a high toll, but one that was felt necessary and worthwhile. Although the research station was back in operation within weeks, the attack undoubtedly saved Britain from a massive onslaught of buzz bombs and rockets before the D-day landings actually got under way.

It was, in fact, just the beginning of something of an impending nightmare, especially when yet a third German secret weapon – the V-3 – was discovered, which was apparently being moved into place in northern France. Its discovery was to lead to a renewed partnership between the bomb maker Barnes Wallis and the Dambusters' squadron, No. 617, this time with Leonard Cheshire at the helm. He was given the task of bombing the sites without causing loss of life to French civilians and, as will be recalled from earlier pages, he had a particular notion about precision bombing which was in direct conflict with Don Bennett's and which he now had a chance to put into effect. The story began in the early summer of 1943, when Cheshire had been taken off operational flying:

I reached a personal crisis in that having done my third tour, I was made a group captain at a very young age and given a station to command. But my heart wasn't in it. I just longed to get back to operational flying, the only thing I knew. Then the current CO of 617 Squadron [the now famous and very independently-minded Dambusters' squadron] was killed. I was asked if I would like to take on 617, and of course I accepted with alacrity. And then suddenly the squadron had a new objective – the V-3 sites, Hitler's virtually unknown secret weapon. It was a new type of heavy gun, which had a series of sequential charges in it which meant that it could throw a 500-pound shell from northern France with accuracy into London. There were three sites, and the prospect of these shells landing in London caused some alarm. So Barnes Wallis was asked to produce a bomb that could penetrate the 50 feet of reinforced concrete. Hitler thought he had a secret weapon that was immune from attack. Barnes Wallis designed his massive bomb, Tallboy, but he required an accuracy of one bomb within 12 metres, from 16,000 feet. When I said that was going to cause us a problem, Barnes Wallis just said: 'Oh well, if you're going to

221

scatter my bombs all over northern France, I don't see why I should take the trouble to build them.' That was a good old Barnes Wallis reply. Anyhow, we had to set about finding a technique for delivering this bomb with great accuracy from 16,000 feet. Clearly, the first thing you had to do was to mark the target point-blank. Any error in the marker would compound the bombing error. Bennett, the expert of all experts – in flying, that is – said it was impossible. So they said: 'Do it at 5,000 feet.' My objection then was that we'd get the worst of both worlds, flak and heavy flak. They just said: 'Well, you've got to do it. It's up to you *how* you do it.' So, fortunately, Mick Martin, my then number two, was the low-flying expert of Bomber Command. So we were given some V-1 sites to bomb initially. They were pretty well undefended. So they were simple targets, and we did our best to mark them at 4,000 to 5,000 feet but never did succeed properly. Then we did a second marking by dive-bombing, releasing at 50 to 100 feet, and every time we did that they were absolutely accurate. We were given the opportunity to try it out. The target we were given was the Gnome Rhône aero engine works outside Limoges. It was referred to the War Cabinet. They said we could do it on condition we took no civilian lives, no French lives. If we took civilian lives, we wouldn't get the opportunity to try it again in France.

Anyhow, we totally obliterated the target and not one bomb fell off the target. So that gave us a whole range of targets in France to try this technique. Now, we proved that in good weather you could drop a pinpoint marker that was extremely accurate and was a single ball of fire. PFF, when necessary, dropped a whole area of markers covering per- haps 10 square miles or even more, and you had to bomb the estimated centre. Now, I'm not criticising Pathfinders, because they were doing the most professional job you could do, given the equipment and given the weather. My proposal suffered from the disadvantage that you could only do it in clear weather. It did work, but I agree that it couldn't substitute for Pathfinders because they had to go night after night and in bad weather.

As for 617 Squadron, everybody really knew what they were doing. All of them had done at least two tours. We had a lot of liberty. We could take decisions on our own that the main force squadron could never take. We had priority in equipment. We did night after night of low-flying practice in our Lancaster bombers, below tree level, and we had a precise objective. A precise objective was a lot better than area bombing. Nobody really enjoyed area bombing. You'd far rather have a precise military target, which you knew you could hit without taking civilian casualties. Well, that's what we had in 617.

We were a mixed squadron. We had Canadians, Australians, New Zealanders. And in a way, they each carried certain national characteristics, especially when we were attacking the V-3 sites. We'd got a whole technique worked out. I went in ahead with my backup marking aircraft, marked the target, flew up, checked whether the marker was accurate: if I thought it was, I asked for confirmation from my number two, while the rest of the aircraft were orbiting 50 miles away, staggered at 50-foot heights. We would call them in and then I would circle round and watch the bombing, and if anything went wrong I could direct operations and if necessary abort and go home. We were attacking one of the V-3 sites and all was going well until the last one to come in, a junior member of the squadron, began to attract all the flak. New Zealander Les Munro, who'd dropped his bombs, saw this. He started to formate on this lad, about three-quarters of a mile to starboard, to attract some of the flak. I called up and said, 'Abandon the attack, Munro, and return to base.' Les says: 'Am not receiving you, sir. Am closing my radio down and carrying on.' It was a good old Munro thing. He couldn't disobey my order. The New Zealanders – largely a farming nation – always did what they set out to do. The Australians had their own characteristics. They were different. They would tend to be a bit more unorthodox and rebellious, but in a nice way. My bomb aimer, Keith Asprey, was an auctioneer, and he was so much the auctioneer that there were times when he just had to go and do some auctioneering. So when this spirit was on him, without telling anybody, he'd disappear off the station, go to Lincoln market and auctioneer. I could send a squad of military policemen, but they wouldn't get him back. So I just had to accept this for two days until he'd get it out of his system, although they weren't all like that.

By March 1944 the Allies' own big secret, the build-up to D-day, was already under way, and by then the British and American air forces were adding substantially to their range and power, whereas the Luftwaffe – under pressure throughout the eastern Mediterranean, the Russian Fronts and the Balkans – were suffering substantial losses in machines and crews. The former were still being replaced as production of the German factories remained surprisingly buoyant in spite of the massive pounding of recent times by Allied bombers on industrial complexes. The shortage of trained pilots, however, was becoming acute, and there were actually machines on the ground which could not be flown because of the lack of crews. In Britain, as D-day approached, however, the Royal Air Force was reaching the historic peak of its manpower of 1,185,913.

The combined strength of Allied aircraft was also becoming increasingly impressive, and efficient. Bomber Command was by now pretty well firing on all cylinders. New aircraft arriving at the front line in recent times had provided a versatility in attack that was unimagined just a few months earlier. These included another superb machine, the Mustang, built in America for the RAF. Although intended as a fighter, its real merits were discovered in ground attack situations, and major opportunities for this role were now opening up as the Allies set about a diverse programme of attacks on German transportation and troop movements prior to D-day. A similar rebirth was in store for the Hawker Typhoon. Also originally designed as a fighter to 1937 specifications, it was now coming into its own as a versatile low-level ground attack and close-support aircraft, capable of dispensing an awesome firepower with four 20-millimetre cannon, two 1,000-pound bombs or eight 60-pound ballistic rockets. Twenty-six squadrons were equipped with the updated version of the Typhoon by D-day, and it proved to be an outstanding addition as the Allied air forces prepared to launch Operation Overlord.

They were used to great effect when the rail infrastructure of northern France was decimated by bombing raids to force all German troop movements on to the roads, where they could be attacked by screaming raids of Typhoons and Spitfires. In addition, the German radar stations, gun emplacements, transport depots, command and control centres, support units and the V-1 sites in the coastal regions of France were subjected to heavy bombardment, and in the three months prior to D-day 70,000 tons of bombs were dropped on almost 100 selected targets. In addition, all kinds of trickery, subterfuge, diversions, mock raids and dummy paratroops were used in the days leading up to D-day and beyond.

Sixteen Lancasters from No. 617 Squadron, for example, flew back and forth on D-day itself distributing very large amounts of Window to give the impression on radar of a massive air attack coming in across the Channel towards Pas-de-Calais, and No. 218 Squadron carried out a similar operation off Boulogne. They were just part of the many ploys now written into history that were used to convince the Germans that the Allied landings in France would be anywhere but the planned invasion area. These combined operations of subterfuge and the all-out bombing of German emplacements, transport and communications facilities, though often overlooked in many accounts of Operation Overlord, were to pave the way for the oncoming Allied forces, and without them the D-day landings could never have been as successful as they were.

And so on 6 June 1944, across the unusually stormy English countryside, the greatest movement of men and machines ever known was under way, with 156,000 men and thousands of tons of heavy metal going ashore in the first 24 hours, followed in the coming weeks by an army of more than two million.

The aircraft involved on the day, or in readiness for movement as the D-day landings progressed, amounted in total to 11,590 Allied aircraft, of which 5,510 were from the Royal Air Force. Their contribution included 61 squadrons of Spitfires, 26 of Typhoons, 12 of Mustangs, 22 of Mosquitos and 13 medium or heavy bomber squadrons. In addition, there was a large contingent of air-sea rescue aircraft from Coastal Command and 406 British and 1,200 American transport aircraft used to drop paratroops and tow the gliders of the airborne units. The para landings were truly an incredible sight, followed by some inspired heroics on the ground. Even so, the 6th Airborne Division alone suffered 786 landing casualties and 1,200 men were dropped or landed in the wrong places, cast adrift in enemy territory.

No one could argue, however, about the impressive sight of the aircraft tugging the giant gliders packed with men, equipment and motor vehicles. Given that there had been little opportunity for intensive training or coordination of the effort, it was a remarkable achievement. The RAF alone flew 5,700 of the 14,674 sorties on the first day, losing 113 aircraft. From then on, and for the next two weeks, the principal task of the air force was to provide round-the-clock cover until the whole invasion force had successfully crossed the Channel in 7,000 ships. Among those aloft was Geoffrey Page, whom we last met at the foundation of The Guinea Pig Club, after suffering terrible burns when he jumped out of his blazing aircraft in the summer of 1940. Now, after much plastic surgery, he was fully operational again and had recently been promoted to commanding officer of No. 132 Fighter Squadron, flying the latest Spitfires:

We were based at an airfield just near Arundel in Sussex called Ford aerodrome, and our task prior to D-day consisted mainly of the very unenjoyable business of two or three times a day attacking the V-1 flying bomb sites, which were based up in the northern part of France in the Pas-de-Calais area, making fighter sweeps and then dive-bombing marshalling yards at places like Arras, Beauvais and Amiens, anything to disturb the German communications and transport system. We were not told of D-day until the night before, when we were confined to camp and the squadron commanders were brought into a conference with the station commander. We were given large documents with all the maps and orders for the invasion. The job of my squadron was to be over the American beaches of Omaha and Utah at first light on D-day and just to keep a fighter patrol over the beaches. Then we'd get relieved after about an hour, come back to England, have a meal, refuel and go back over the beaches again.

It was fascinating, and at times disturbing, to see the troops going into France again and sitting over the beaches at about 1,000 feet. One had really a dress circle view of the whole of the Normandy landings. The landing craft were taking a tremendous pounding from the bad weather conditions. The Channel was rough. I should think a tremendous number of them were ill from seasickness. Our routine was going back out over the beaches several times a day. And in fact it became a little boring after a while, because the Germans thought that the Normandy invasion was a dummy attack and they put up no aircraft resistance at all. We moved after a few days from England into a mud airstrip in Normandy, and we operated from there. Our main task then was attacking anything that moved on the roads in the way of vehicles that were remotely connected with German support. So we were kept busy all day long there, going out attacking, landing again, rearming our guns with ammunition and refuelling, and going out again. So that side of life was much more interesting than the first few days of the actual D-day landing itself. We were getting pretty experienced at shooting at stuff on the ground; the things would just blow up and explode in flames. The only thing that we really couldn't harm were the German panzer tanks, they were so heavily armour-plated. But our Typhoon fighter bombers with their rockets dealt with them very effectively. In fact, the Typhoons I think really made the break-out from the beachhead possible by their destruction of the German armoured corps there.

Meanwhile, many of the fighter-bomber squadrons, as well as some from Bomber Command, had returned to the task of hitting V-1 flying bomb sites. Southern England and London in particular would have had a very rough time if the Allied troops hadn't burst out of the beachhead and captured the Pas-de-Calais. That was a most unpleasant job really, because these flying bomb sites consisted of three basic units. There'd be two small concealed buildings and then there was a thing we used to call a ski jump. Rather like the Olympic Games, where the skiers do their ski jumps. That was the launching ramp for the V-1 itself. So you'd peel off at 12,000 feet when you'd got yourself just about vertically over the target and then scream straight down. But the unattractive part of that operation was that the Germans would put up a cone of light and anti-aircraft fire as you dived down.

You were sitting on top of a 500-pound bomb and you had to go through all this fire, which you could see bursting in puffs of grey smoke. As you went through, you just prayed that your bomb or aircraft wasn't going to be hit. But once you were through that, you released your bomb, then climbed away, with a sigh of relief, and then headed back to England. I think statistics have shown that this wasn't a very effective way of attacking the V-1 sites . In fact, the V-1 sites, because of the smallness of these two little buildings and the ski jump, were difficult targets to knock out. The American lighter bombers tried attacking them in just straight bombing runs but again the success rate wasn't enormous.

Intelligence reports prepared for a meeting of the Chiefs of Staffs Committee on 14 June 1944 indicated that 67 V-1 sites had been identified and a further 10 suspected sites were 'under examination'. It was a gross underestimation. Literally hundreds of the sites were in the process of being installed by German engineers across the whole of northern France (and subsequently other German-occupied territory). In any event, the report was already out of date when the committee met on that day. The previous night, the first 10 V-1s were finally unleashed on southern England, zooming down Buzz Bomb Alley at speeds approaching 400 mph each carrying up to a ton of high explosives. A blanket of secrecy was immediately imposed on where the flying bombs came down and what damage was caused so that the Germans could not use the information to calibrate future efforts. On the night of 15 June, 150 flying bombs reached Britain, 50 of which dropped on the Greater London area. Another 20 were shot down by anti-aircraft batteries and fighters. 'Hitler has started his secret weapon upon London', Churchill wrote to Stalin. 'We had a very noisy night.'

Indeed it was. The whole aura of the flying bomb was the terror it invoked as it reached the point where its fuel ran out, the engine cut out and it dived into the streets and houses below. Warnings were given in newspapers, on radio and in the cinema that people should run for cover if they heard the curious engine noise of the buzz bomb – or doodlebug, as it was more commonly called in the East End. When it stopped, there was little time to seek cover before it upended and hit the ground. On

18 June one of the flying bombs fell on the Guards' Chapel, which was filled with soldiers attending a service. Sixty were killed outright and another 150 injured. The tragedy shocked Britain into the realisation that the secret weapon could be as deadly as Hitler had promised. As one air-raid warden at the time put it: 'As they fly overhead, you pray that it doesn't stop. And then as it passes you feel guilty that someone else is going to get it. Once it stops, the silence is terrifying.'

The attacks grew in intensity almost by the day as the Nazis made their all-out effort in response to D-day. There were now fears that the invasion of France could be in some way negated by the ferocity of the buzz bomb onslaught, which by the end of June had risen to 800 successful arrivals a week, killing more than 2,000 civilians and injuring 7,403. Churchill was grimly informed that the weight of explosives dropped on London in the first two weeks of the attacks was as damaging as during the worst fortnight of the 1940–41 Blitz. Reprisals were being suggested. On 3 July 1944 Churchill told the War Cabinet that they should consider 'publishing a list of, say, 100 of the smaller towns in Germany where the defences are likely to be weak and announce our intention of destroying them one by one by bombing attack . . .'

Several in the Cabinet opposed the idea for fear of reprisals against, for example, captured British troops and especially airmen who were already being mistreated in prison camps. Churchill then suggested consideration of the possibility of using gas against the V-1 installations 'as a reprisal', a suggestion that again met with opposition – not least because Germany probably had far better chemical weapons than Britain – and at a further meeting on 5 July the War Cabinet placed on record its 'general agreement' not to use gas. The flying bomb attacks went on unabated, and Churchill now insisted on urgent action from Bomber Command to hit the V-1 sites and at the same time to reinforce home defences with more guns and fighters even if that meant diverting resources from the thrust into Europe. A line of guns was established on the North Downs so as to avoid shooting them down over London. Additionally, a ring of barrage balloons with nets attached was also created.

By mid-July over 1,200 anti-aircraft guns had been moved into position along the south coast, while 21 squadrons of fighters specifically deployed to shoot down V-1s operated along a

45-mile deep corridor between London and the gun-line. Some of Fighter Command's best aircraft, such as the Spitfire XIV, the Mustang III, the Mosquito and the new Tempest V, were all deployed in the effort to halt the flying bombs, and, difficult though it was to hit them at 400 miles an hour, a large number of interceptions were recorded. Among them were the first success-ful operations by Britain's brand-new experimental jet fighter, the Meteor. On 4 August 1944 a Meteor of No. 616 Squadron, flown by Flying Officer Dixie Dean, downed a V-1 flying bomb by positioning the wing of his aircraft under that of the rocket and tipping it off balance. Minutes later, his colleague, Flying Officer J.K. Roger, also in a Meteor, became the first pilot to shoot down a V-1 by cannon-fire.

Meanwhile, the bombing of the V-1 sites was given new impetus, although, as Geoffrey Page has explained, they were very difficult to hit and even harder to find. One great stroke of good fortune fell to Bomber Command in late July, as Don Bennett revealed:

> The most effective thing of all that we did was the discovery of a dump located at a place called Watten, where we destroyed 10,000 buzz bombs in one night. Had we not done so, they would have been released on the south of England within a matter of weeks and most would have got through and tens of thousands of people within 50 miles of London would have been killed. It could have lost us the war, there's not the faintest shadow of doubt. That was a little diversion of Bomber Command which is hardly ever mentioned.

This stroke of luck apart, even incessant sorties by Bomber Command failed to halt the V-1 bombardment and, even less successfully, the new silent secret weapon, the V-2 rocket, launched from single concrete bunkers, almost invisible from the air, in Germany and Holland. The first hit London in the first week of September. In another War Cabinet meeting in which the weapons were the sole topic of discussion, Churchill reported that the 'best brains' were being employed to try to halt the onslaught. Clearly, they had yet to come up with any foolproof solution. By the end of July more than a million people had been evacuated from London, including 225,000 mothers with children, and 17,000 houses had been destroyed. In August Bomber Command dropped over 100,000 tons of bombs on V-1-and V-2-related sites but still they kept coming.

Gradually, however, rates of interception did improve and coincided with a gradual decline in the number of flying bombs arriving over Britain, especially after the bombing of the Watten store. In all, almost 9,000 flying bombs were launched against Britain (the last on 27 March 1945) before the attacks finally petered out in the wake of the Allies' advance into Germany. Of those, 3,700 were brought down in equal amounts by the fighter squadrons and the gun-line. Another 212 were trapped by the barrage balloons. More than 6,000 people were killed and 28,000 injured – 90 per cent of them in London. More than 1,100 V-2 rockets were launched against Britain, and Belgium was also heavily bombarded.

The ratio of the figures for death and destruction were far higher, however, than conventional bombing. The flying bombs that dropped on Britain represented a tonnage of less than 8,000, whereas in the same period the Allied air force had dropped in the region of 150,000 tons of high explosives over Germany itself. This was over and above the 24,000 tons laid down in bombing raids to ease the break-out of Allied troops from the Normandy bridgehead as they prepared to move the invasion ahead.

Rocket-firing Typhoons played an exceptional role in this stage of the advance from Normandy. In all, 38 fighter-bomber and fighter squadrons, supported intermittently by heavy bombers, were involved, but by early September the Germans were still clinging on to several of the Channel ports. The advance inland meanwhile, continued apace, so quickly in fact that those at the front were running out of supplies. Montgomery wanted to push on to the Rhine, hit the V-1 and V-2 sites and 'end the war by January 1945'. But Eisenhower's staff maintained that the rate of advance could not be sustained because of logistical problems. A compromise was agreed. Elements of Britain's 1st Airborne Division, Poland's 1st Parachute Brigade and America's 18th Airborne Corps, all under the command of an American general, would be airlifted behind German lines to capture vital bridges, which were to be taken progressively, the last during the main bridge at Arnhem. This was assigned to the British contingent, led by Nos. 1 and 2 Parachute Battalions, who, needless to say, had drawn the short straw in terms of danger. Their target was furthest away and the most exposed. Their success depended on the ability of the aircrews to carry out continuous resupply missions and, crucially, the arrival of reinforcements to be supplied by XXX Corps of the British 21st Army, who were 64 miles away.

Thus began one of the biggest cockups of the Second World War . . .

CHAPTER THIRTEEN

The Final Blast

The Bridge Too Far was a tragic disaster in almost every respect, hurried in its conception, driven by the ego of Montgomery and devoid of proper communications (or radios that worked!). Operation Market Garden, as it was called, was launched seven days after Eisenhower gave his formal approval – and was proceeded with in spite of reports from intelligence sources in Holland that a large contingent of heavily equipped SS troops were in the area. Forty-eight hours before the operation was to begin, further reports were more precise: that the 9th and 10th SS Panzer Divisions, crack German outfits, were resting in the area on their way from Normandy. Eisenhower was informed. He passed the buck to Montgomery, who dismissed the report with the wave of a hand. The mission was on: 10,240 men along with Jeeps, wagons, mortars, ammunition, medical teams, engineers and explosives were to be airlifted for the assault. It would have needed 3,790 aircraft – 2,700 for the paras and the rest to tow gliders bearing troops and hardware. As there were only 1,545 planes available, it was decided to perform the operation in three drops beginning on 17 September, while 143 Dakotas and Stirlings were on stand-by to begin the resupply operations – a vital part of the whole adventure because the troops would be so far behind enemy lines.

The first two stages went relatively well, although the Germans soon tumbled to what was happening and resistance was swift in arriving in the form of fighters and especially a large build-up of flak guns. Furthermore, the third day's transport aircraft hit bad weather, failed to make the rendezvous with their fighter escorts and took heavy losses from the Luftwaffe and anti-aircraft fire. What now followed is a story that has remained to the fore in the annals of military history for years. The panzers were indeed in the area and were rushed to the scene. Over the course of the next few days the Allied forces were shot to pieces, as were many of the incoming resupply flights that began on the second day of the operation, coming in low to drop containers of supplies. On the afternoon of the first supply drop, five Dakotas and ten Stirlings were shot down in the space of a couple of hours. Among the pilots in action that day, 19 September, Flight Lieutenant David Lord's Dakota was twice hit when he was three minutes from the dropping zone, but he carried on regardless and began his drops even though his plane was damaged. After the first run, two containers remained on board and, knowing how important they might be to chaps on the ground, he made a second run, aware that his starboard engine was ablaze and the wing might collapse at any moment. Again he faced intense enemy fire as he came in a second time. He dropped his supplies and then ordered his crew to bale out. A few seconds later, the Dakota crashed in flames with its pilot still on board. David Lord was awarded a posthumous Victoria Cross.

But now another catastrophe began to unfold. The beleaguered troops, without adequate communications, had difficulty in signalling either between themselves or to London to notify their new positions to receive the vital supplies of food and ammunition. The RAF were still doing their utmost to get the supplies through, totally unaware that they were dropping in the wrong place. The messages of redirection from divisional headquarters to England had apparently not been received. Desperate attempts were being made from the ground to attract their attention with signals and coloured panels, but they were invisible from the air through the trees, smoke and general mayhem. The supply plane pilots were meanwhile taking terrible risks, some dropping their loads as they headed towards the earth on fire. Army cameraman Mike Lewis reckoned many on the ground were in tears watching the hugely brave efforts of the RAF crews:

They were coming in so low and there was so much flak that the ground shook beneath our feet. And I could see planes, black through the trees, large as houses, pilots fighting to hold their course . . . and bursting into flames . . . One of the few times in the war I wept. I really did. To see those Dakotas and Lancasters going into the Rhine through the trees, and all for what? And from one of them came fluttering down a sheet of paper. One of the men ran over to it. It was that day's newspaper, the *Daily Express*. And the headline read: 'Siegfried Line crumbling – Hitler on the run.' No one could speak at that. Here we were having all kinds of shit knocked out of us and according to this newspaper it was the other way around.

On the worst day, the RAF lost a fifth of its supply aircraft on what were courageous yet hopeless sorties. Many of those that did get through were unwittingly providing the enemy with sustenance and starving their own troops, as John Stanleigh, of the Paras Pathfinder company, recalled:

We weren't told what had gone wrong but we knew something was a bit odd. We realised that with every supply drop the Germans were simply waiting for our supply aircraft to come down low and then shot them down. I think I personally must have seen at least eight or nine being shot down in a very short space of time, just like flies, plucked out of the air, burning, coming down into that area where we'd been waiting. It was terrible. I mean, I can't describe it to you now how we felt to see these boys being shot down. Some [of the crews] escaped by baling out, and these people were just given rifles and helped to man the line. We had to count our ammunition because we had virtually none left. We also had no food. The Germans loved it. They had a feast day after feast day with the food, which was better than theirs. Dropped them right into their lap.

Operation Market Garden was an outright gamble that turned into a failure and a tragedy. Of the 10,240 troops airlifted in, only 2,163 were rescued, and that is not counting the losses of the Polish 1st Parachute Brigade, which were substantial. The

Arnhem-Oosterbeek War Cemetery contains the graves of 3,328 British and Commonwealth soldiers and airmen. The rest went into captivity, many suffering the brutal consequences being meted out to RAF prisoners as revenge against the bombing of German cities.

The Bridge Too Far was eventually overcome in the new year, and before Hitler made a dramatic attempt to save the Third Reich. On 16 December he launched a new offensive on its Western Front into the Ardennes Forest towards Antwerp, preceded by a barrage of V-2 rockets, in what became known as the Battle of the Bulge. Bad weather halted air intervention until Christmas Eve in support of Allied forces but by then the Luftwaffe had pulled in fighters and bombers from all corners of Europe to launch a surprise attack on New Year's Day 1945. More than 800 aircraft were engaged in a massive strike against Allied positions and airfields. It caught the Allied commanders completely off guard, destroying more than 200 aircraft on the ground. But this really was a last-gasp attack, and from then on the eventual outcome was no longer in doubt.

It was this very fact that made the bombing of the historical city of Dresden so hugely controversial. The attack was launched on 13–14 February 1945, St Valentine's Day, and thus an easy connotation to include the word 'massacre' when the issue came up for discussion in the years ahead. In a night and a day of relentless bombardment, first by the RAF's Bomber Command Lancasters and then by the USAAF B-17s, Dresden was reduced to a smoking ruin. The city's peacetime population of 600,000 was expanded by the fact that the Third Reich had moved a large number of civil servants to a city that had little in the way of air-raid defences. Famous for its seventeenth- and eighteenth-century baroque and rococo art and architecture and universally known as the Florence on the Elbe, Dresden was obliterated in the firestorm that came with the pounding of high explosives and incendiary bombs. Estimates of casualties ranged between 30,000 to 60,000 dead with thousands more injured. The city continued to be hit in further raids until 17 April. The Allies justified their decision to bomb Dresden so unmercifully by stating that the city was an important communications network for the German armies on the Eastern Front. In his memoir, recorded for the Imperial War Museum in 1986, Don Bennett repeated that claim and dismissed the criticism 'about a raid which all the do-goody boys are complaining about, along with a bunch of Communists in Berlin, to make out that we went to the trouble to bomb women and children.' He continued:

> This is typical propaganda warfare. We bombed Dresden because it was a prime target on that night. We were called during the day by the Russians, who particularly wanted a raid on Dresden because troops were pouring through the town. There were something like 80,000 at the time, on their way to the Russian Front, only a very short distance away. The Russians were being held up by these troop reinforcements. Could we help? We were put on to Dresden at short notice, and bombed perfectly normally. The fact that it caught fire rather easily was the Germans' fault. They had no air-raid precautions and they didn't believe in building anything other than wooden residences in Dresden.
>
> They also happened to have the German civil service in Dresden more than anywhere else. They'd moved them there out of Berlin for safety. So we did do some heavy bombing, and the next day the Americans did a raid and we did another one. Now OK, a lot of people got killed. But we did stop the troops getting to the Russian Front at a critical moment, and the Russians expressed their thanks to us for that purpose. Today we have many people in this country who believe that we were cruel, horrible people, bombing Dresden because it wasn't even a military target. Of course it was a military target, and it was vitally important to the Russian Front, the Eastern Front, on that particular day.

The controversy over the somewhat extrovert policy of Bomber Command had already passed another milestone when, on 14 March 1945, No. 617 Squadron dropped the first 22,000-pound bomb, known as the Grand Slam, on Bielefeld viaduct in Germany. Senior members of the War Cabinet, not least among them Churchill himself, were among those who expressed concern. After reading a report of the bombing of Dresden from the Air Ministry, Churchill drafted a note to the Chiefs of Staffs Committee questioning the ongoing policy of unremitting bombardment. He wrote:

It seems to me that the moment has come when the question of bombing of German cities simply for the sake of increasing the terror, though under other pretexts, should be reviewed. Otherwise we shall come into control of an utterly ruined land. The destruction of Dresden remains a serious query against the conduct of Allied bombing. I am of the opinion that military objectives must henceforward be more strictly studied . . . the Foreign Secretary has spoken to me on this subject, and I feel the need for more precise concentration upon military objectives, such as oil and communications behind the immediate battle-zone, rather than on mere acts of terror and wanton destruction, however impressive.

In fact the minute was never sent to the CoS committee,* at least not in that form. A toned-down version, drafted by Air Chief Marshal Sir Charles Portal but signed by Churchill, was sent instead, deleting the word 'terror' although still calling for a review of the 'so-called area bombing of German cities'.

The Air Ministry was quick to point out that intelligence reports showed that the Luftwaffe still possessed a large number of serviceable aircraft and that new machines were still coming off the production lines at a considerable rate. With the advance of the ground forces now seemingly unstoppable, however, on 1 April the Air Staff agreed that there was no great advantage to be expected from air attack 'on the remaining industrial centres of Germany'. It was to Churchill's 'grave disappointment' two weeks later to learn that Potsdam had been bombed, on the night of 14 April. He demanded an explanation from Portal: 'What is the point of blowing down Potsdam?'

Portal replied that the Joint Intelligence Committee had learned that the Luftwaffe's operational headquarters had been moved to Potsdam from Berlin and the raid was designed to hasten the 'disintegration of enemy resistance'. He added, however, that as of that date, 20 April, area bombing would be discontinued. It was doubtless difficult for Bomber Command to just end it without being certain it was all over; their lives had been taken over by the determination to succeed. It was suggested to the author that it was impossible to just get up one

* Martin Gilbert, *Road to Victory*, p. 1,257.

morning and say: 'Oh well, we don't have to go in today.' There had been so much given in terms of human effort that those involved simply had to be sure that the lid was closed firm on the Nazi era – if nothing else but for the memory of those who had given their lives and knew that on every mission they flew there was literally only half a chance that they would come back. Of the 111,000 aircrew, 55,564 had been killed and 18,698 wounded or taken prisoner. Of those, 9,919 were Canadian, 5,720 Australian or New Zealand, 929 Polish and 534 others, which included Czech, French and South African pilots. In terms of aircraft, almost 9,000 bombers were lost over Europe alone.

The war with Germany, then, was as good as ended for the Royal Air Force, although there was still unfinished business in the Far East. And, as we will see, it was with incredible irony that Leonard Cheshire, who had won a Victoria Cross for his contribution to the bombing operations while running his own very personal campaign for more precise targeting, was to be Britain's elected participant in the greatest single mass destruction of people and buildings the world has ever seen.

The Far East campaign had begun to swing back in favour of the Allies in the early months of 1943 when Field Marshal Sir William Slim's 14th Army – the Forgotten Army, starved of men and machines for so long – began the long haul towards recovering lost ground. Up to that point, the situation had been miserable and depressing for all concerned. After the fall of Singapore and the retreat from Burma, losing vast numbers of men, aircraft, guns, transport and oil stores, the British and Commonwealth troops, with only limited air cover, battened down the hatches to defend India. As the Japanese launched concerted air raids against Calcutta, additional squadrons began to arrive, and by March the total had improved to 26 squadrons of fighters. These included the new Vultee Vengeance, a dive-bomber which had been ordered from America after the success of the German Stukas but was out of favour by the time of delivery. However, in the Far East new aircraft were a luxury and the RAF would put them to good use. Indeed, regaining control of the air was foremost in the Allied strategy as the second offensive against the Japanese eventually got under way. There were also some new, and hair-raising, experiences for RAF personnel as the British launched their first limited incursions back into the Burmese jungles. These initial raids, in February and March 1943, were in the hands of the newly formed and ultimately famous Chindit special forces, the creation of the controversial Colonel Orde Wingate. The first formation of 3,000 men, of what was officially known as the 77th Infantry Brigade, consisting of British, Indian and Gurkha troops, was launched from Manipur with a vast column of mules, oxen and elephants to carry equipment on long-range penetration missions behind enemy lines in some of the most appalling terrain on earth. They were to split into groups, disappearing into the jungle for up to eight weeks, with an RAF radio operative their only source of contact with the outside world – and their survival rested on his calling in Dakotas to make vital supply drops.

It was a courageous journey into the unknown, questioned by some in post-war writings as downright foolhardy. Although other new formations, such as the Long Range Desert Patrol, the Special Air Service and Special Boat Service, had been careering across North Africa and the European theatres, it was the first time any such operations had been attempted in the ultra-difficult conditions of Burma. The first expedition could at best be classed as experimental and, although numerous targets were successfully attacked, overall this first thrust by the Chindits ended in what can only be termed as a disorganised retreat in which Wingate lost more than a third of his original force, some of whom were lost in the jungle for almost 12 weeks. The expedition did, however, provide some valuable ground rules for future Chindit raids and for the main reinvasion plans of Slim's 14th, in which the RAF were to play a defining role.

The success of the Chindit-style operations was to become apparent as both the Japanese and the Allies formulated their battle plans in South-East Asia for the dry season of 1943–4. The Japanese were preparing a major advance across the Chindwin River, with the aim of occupying the plain of Imphal and placing a strong line of defence in eastern Assam. The Allies, with Lord Louis Mountbatten's South-East Asia Command now in place, planned a four-pronged thrust into Burma: American forces under General Joe Stilwell, which included three Chinese divisions and Merrill's Marauders – the American troops trained by

Wingate on Chindit lines – were to advance on two fronts from the north, and Slim's 14th Army was to launch its XV Corps south into Arakan and its IV Corps east to the Chindwin.

Well aware of the problems of being outflanked by the Japanese in the past, Slim, in conjunction with Sir Richard Peirse, formerly of Bomber Command and now controlling the British air contingent in the Far East, formulated a plan to ensure that his armies would have the support to stand firm against attack, even if they became isolated. Their commanders were assured that they could count both on supplies and reserve troops through airlifts. This promise was made in the knowledge that additional aircraft were now arriving at the theatre in the months of relative inactivity in combat; more than 200 airfields and 71 all-weather strips had been built and more were under construction. The theory was soon to be put to extreme tests.

With only limited support by way of fighter cover, the XV Corps' Arakan operation, launched in November 1943, moved ahead swiftly and achieved most of its objects by the end of January 1944. Then a Japanese counterattack completely surrounded the 7th Indian Division and part of another. Slim's rescue plan was brought into play, with men and supplies being airlifted in by RAF Dakotas, and the Japanese were themselves kept at bay between the Indians and the relieving forces until the Allies were able to secure the Arakan Front. On the central Burmese Front, meanwhile, the Japanese were preparing to launch an offensive towards India, crossing the Chindwin River into Assam, but again they came unstuck through Slim's master plan. Three Japanese divisions advanced towards Imphal, and heavy fighting ensued as they were confronted by four Indian divisions protecting towns ahead of the advance. The Japanese managed to surround the 17th Indian Division by severing road links to their positions, but again reinforcements were airlifted in on a massive scale, including more than 3,000 men of the 5th Indian Division, to halt the Japanese at Kohima. Several Indian divisions moved up, some by air, from the Arakan Front, and with air support Slim's forces now stood firm – according to plan – against numerous Japanese forward and outflanking movements. But the greatest test of these combined operations with the Allied air forces was now to be confronted.

By then, 150,000 British and Empire troops were fighting over an area almost 150 miles from the nearest rail link, and they required a massive input of supplies each day to keep going. At any other time of the war, the odds would have been impossible and retreat almost a certainty. But now, the RAF and RAAF air units swung into action. Starting on 16 March 1944, the greatest airlift operation in the history of the RAF began, with more than 400 tons of stores flown daily into a heavily guarded valley, with only three squadrons of Spitfires available for air defence and six squadrons of Hurricanes for attack. The siege of Imphal lasted three months when, on 22 June, the 14th Army finally broke the Japanese assault towards Assam, and in doing so gained the initiative for its own advance into Burma. The Battle of Imphal cost the British and Indian forces 17,587 casualties, while the Japanese lost 30,500 dead and 30,000 wounded. And while nothing can take away the achievement of the Allied troops, the airlift and air support provided the key to what might otherwise had been a disaster. The rout of the Japanese, combined with successes on other fronts, turned the tide, and by the end of May much of northern Burma was in Allied hands.

Other significant air operations came with the emergence of substantial Chindit campaigns in the autumn of 1943 and on into 1944, now successfully operating on the lines originally planned. This involved deep incursions behind enemy lines, with airdrops to keep them going. Orde Wingate was promoted to acting major-general and given command of airborne troops, though, ironically, as one of the most successful Chindit operations was under way he was killed in an air crash in March 1944. Four brigades of Chindits were landed on previously prepared airstrips to sever Japanese supply lines to the five divisions fighting American and Chinese troops in the north. The airlift, completed in six days, involved the transport of 9,600 troops along with 1,350 mules and oxen, plus more than 100 tons of stores, which were set down safely behind Japanese positions. It was also the first time that helicopters were used in the theatre, with American Sikorsky Hoverflys being used for the evacuation of casualties. There, the Chindits continued their operations in a manner that would be studied, copied and re-enacted many times in conflicts around the world in the years ahead, again with air support a key element.

With fighting now on all major fronts, more and more aircraft were arriving into the South-East Asia Command, and Air Chief Marshal Keith Park replaced Peirse as head of Allied air forces there for the final months of the campaign. But the middle of 1944, 90 Allied squadrons were able to call on a formidable inventory of aircraft, including Spitfires, Hurricanes, Mosquitos and Mustangs, along with two dozen bomber squadrons equipped with Wellingtons, Liberators and Mitchells. The work-horses, however, were the Dakotas and Hudsons of the 12 transport squadrons, which had now adopted the motto: 'Our business is moving.' As further squadrons released from Europe arrived in the remaining months of the year, air supremacy was totally assured. The Japanese were on the run.

Weeks of difficult conflict still lay ahead as the Allies launched their main offensive to regain central Burma and then on to Rangoon. On the northern tip of the Burmese Front, a three-pronged drive by American and Chinese forces southwards from Myitkyina to the Irrawaddy River by General Stilwell was under way. Although only partially successful, elements of his force linked with Slim's 14th Army as he began his surge south through central Burma. His forward troops picked out Japanese positions for air attacks, targets that ranged from defensive bunkers, troop concentrations, bridges or stores dumps. With air superiority already established, the likes of Wing Commander Jack Rose's No. 113 Squadron, based at Palel and equipped with Hurricane fighter-bombers, initially flew from a single airstrip 20 miles south of Imphal over terrain that rose to between 9,000 and 10,000 feet. No. 17 Squadron's Spitfires under Squadron Leader Ginger Lacey kept a watchful eye on the bomber units as they dived in to release their bombs or to shoot their 20-millimetre cannon at ground targets. Rose recalled:

Although at that stage we were relatively free from the threat of enemy fighter opposition, the hazards associated with low-level attacks on defended targets in broken country were ever present. One aspect of the air fighting over Burma which contrasted with operations over occupied Europe was the likely fate of a pilot unlucky enough to be taken prisoner. The stories of the inhuman treatment of their captives by the Japanese were legion. Their reputation was even further debased by intelligence photographs which circulated at the time showing a row of captured aircrew, kneeling and blindfolded, in the act of being beheaded by a Japanese soldier while a group of his grinning fellows looked on.

Slim, meanwhile, thrust on through the centre of Burma and aimed for Meiktila, which lay east of the Irrawaddy and was central to Japanese communications between Mandalay and Rangoon to the south. To achieve his objective, he sent one of his corps on a diversionary movement towards Mandalay, a 300-mile trek, while another corps moved ahead, again supported by air operations and supply flights. Indeed, the whole of the movement south, lasting almost five months, required a massive and constant airlift of supplies to keep this army of more than a quarter of a million men on the move. The RAF's No. 232 Group was a key element in the operation, and all told some 17 squadrons of Dakotas of what was now known as the Combat Cargo Task Force were involved. It was an incredible undertaking over the worst of terrain, setting down on strips of earth that might sink below them. Throughout these months, they were responsible for ferrying reinforcements to units under pressure, carting every kind of cargo imaginable and, most trying of all, securing the heavy plant and vehicles that were required to build airfields as the army progressed south. It was a gargantuan task that became ever more stressful for the crews and ground staff as the 14th drove further on.

Meiktila was taken on 3 March 1945 and was held against fierce counterattacks. Next, Slim took Mandalay after 10 days of bitter fighting, and the whole area was under his control by the end of the month. The Burmese capital of Rangoon was the next stop, and with the monsoon about to close in, which would have halted the advance, Slim sent in a combined operation of paratroops and an air- and sea-landed Indian division on 1 May 1945. Rangoon was taken without opposition, so Burma was effectively recaptured. Japanese resistance had virtually crumbled in the wake of devastating attacks by Allied fighter-bombers, and the final days of the campaign saw 10,000 Japanese troops killed while trying to escape from Burma in an attack lasting nine days, spearheaded by aircraft of the US 10th Air Force.

It was perhaps a sad irony that the British representative to participate in the final acts of the Second World War, leading to the surrender of Japan, was none other than Leonard Cheshire, who had, throughout the proceedings, been an advocate of precision bombing and an opponent of area bombing. As we have seen, he had been awarded the Victoria Cross for his work with Bomber Command in which he had flown more than a hundred missions and had been the master bomber of the elite volunteers of No. 617 Squadron. There was to be a note of severity and melancholy as he recalled in his tape-recorded memoir what happened next:

I was sent for by Field Marshal Lord Maitland-Wilson at the Joint Chiefs of Staff's mission in Washington on 17 July 1945, the day after the successful test explosion of an atomic bomb in the New Mexico desert. Well, I then went out to Tinian in the Marianas, where the fly-by-night bombardment group, the attack unit, that was to carry the bomb was based. My job was to report back to Churchill on the operational use of the bomb and its consequences for the future of aerial warfare. That's how I understood my brief. Lord Penny was dealing with the technical side. I had to understand something about what was involved in getting an atomic bomb off the ground and on to the target. There were quite a lot of problems. For one thing, nobody could be quite certain whether it would detonate when dropped from the air or if, after the first one had been dropped, whether the Japanese could have succeeded in detonating the second in the aircraft by radio signals, so the weapons system people had to be alert to that possibility. There were various other technical problems which were encountered on the way because it wasn't like a high-explosive bomb that's just static until the detonator goes off. It had its own electrical circuits. And things could go wrong with those circuits and in fact, on the Nagasaki attack, did, and the guy who was in charge of that had to take an inspired guess as to what was the correct action to take.

In the absence of a Japanese surrender by the time of a deadline set by the Allies, the Americans started the countdown for the world's first atomic bombing, destined to be carried by the B-29 bomber Enola Gay, and dropped on the city of Hiroshima in

Japan. This mission was performed on 6 August 1945, producing an explosion equivalent to 15,000 tons of TNT. The combined heat and blast vaporised everything in the explosion's immediate vicinity and wiped out an area of some 4.4 square miles, killing 75,000 people on the spot and countless thousands more later. Behind the Enola Gay, three days later, came another B-52 carrying a second atomic bomb destined to arrive over the city of Kokura. Cheshire was on that mission:

So there were operational problems getting the bomb there. Indeed, the attack was beset by them. There was bad weather on the way, which meant that the aircraft couldn't keep in formation. There were three taking part, one carrying the bomb, one carrying scientific observing instruments, monitoring instruments, and the third carrying cameras. The primary target, which was Kokura, was obscured by bad weather. The orders were: 'Visual drop only.' In other words, they were not allowed to drop the bomb unless they had the aiming point in their sights. They couldn't do that at Kokura. By the time they got to Nagasaki, the secondary target, they only had enough fuel for one run before landing on Okinawa, which is the nearest point to Japan. And on the run-in they didn't think they were going to sight the aiming point, but at the last moment the bomb aimer did see it. He shouted out: 'I've got, I've got it.'

But the delay led to an error of two miles in the drop. I remember that although the sun was shining, the flash just lit the cockpit. We all turned round and at that time, the moment I first saw it, it was like a ball of fire, 3,000 feet high, because it was detonated 3,000 feet above the ground, to maximise the blast and minimise radiation. It was like a boiling sort of fire. But the fire rapidly died down and became a . . . I don't know how to describe it . . . a cloud, a churning, boiling, bubbling cloud, getting larger and larger and rocketing upwards, and balanced on this column. I would think that within two or three minutes it was at 60,000 feet. It's a guess. We were 39,000 feet. It was above us. We can't really judge, but I estimate the cloud remained stationary at 60,000 feet. It seemed to me to be about two miles in diameter.

It was still bubbling. It was a frightening sight. But what I found, well, the most frightening, was its symmetry. All high-explosive detonations that I've seen are ragged. But here you had a finely sculpted shape – a mushroom head, a delicate column reaching right through 60,000 feet of space, of air, then fanning out into a big pyramid at the bottom. The column seemed to be slowly gyrating. There was a break at somewhere near the top and it had a sort of a sleeve. It gave me the impression of an immensely powerful man under control. And he's much more frightening than a powerful man who's lost his temper, who's out of control. I know that's a subjective reaction, but that's the effect on me. I thought, this is of an order completely different from anything I've known before, not just in terms of power, but of its nature. I think that if there was a first impression that I had, it was that you cannot fight this weapon. If your enemy has this weapon, then you cannot fight it. It convinced me that the war was finished. I know that Hiroshima three days previously hadn't finished the war. We now know what happened and why it happened. We didn't know that on Tinian. But I know that when I saw that, when I saw it with my own eyes, I thought this has to be the end of the war. I couldn't believe that any nation could go on fighting that weapon.

Well, then I had other things to think of . . . my job. I had to remember what I was there for. I found myself then thinking of the people underneath that cloud. You see, the base of that column was like a pyramid. I would imagine that also was two to three miles in diameter. And that was completely black. You could actually see particles of black soot or dust – I don't know what they were – being sucked up into the air by the heat of the explosion. It was impenetrable. You couldn't see what was underneath. But all round the periphery were starting up spontaneous little fires. I couldn't understand why at the time. Now I know that it was because of the heat. The heat at the moment of the explosion, 20 million degrees, I don't know what it was – something approximating the external heat of the sun – was just generating these fires, combusting these fires.

The thing is, conventional bombing was going on and on

and on. You knew it had to be. You knew there was no other way of carrying the war to Germany. I think that position is defensible now – that had it not been for the bomber offensive, there would have been no re-entry into Europe in 1944. But the bomber offensive acted as a second front, because of the amount of personnel and equipment that it was diverting to the defence of Germany. Most important of all, the fact that it forced the Luftwaffe to come up and fight. And we defeated them. So that at D-day we had total mastery of the skies. I would submit that if we'd not had it but had had to fight for it over the beaches, D-day, Normandy, might well not have succeeded. My point is that you knew that the bomber offensive was necessary. You couldn't afford to let yourself give too much of your thoughts to the people on the ground. For one thing you have so many people dying. We know that an average of 10,000 a day were dying in the concentration camps. We didn't know that number then. But we had an idea that something like that was happening. So if you start giving too much of your sympathy to the people you've got to attack, you wouldn't do it. You've either not got to do it or do it.

And there's something else I've got to say, again of a personal nature: that in the conventional bombing of Germany, the odds were against us. We were suffering far more casualties proportionately than the Germans were on the ground. The average we were losing was four and a half to five per cent a night. So 20 trips is about all you could hope for – 20 to 25. And I know this doesn't stand in logic, but it felt fair. Nagasaki didn't feel fair. Not in the sense that it shouldn't have been done. Because I maintain to the end that it had to be done to end the war. But at a personal level I didn't like it. We were well above flak, well above the fighters; nothing could touch us. They had no warning of what was coming. They'd been warned in general, but it meant nothing to them. So at that level I didn't like it and I felt uneasy. But that's a purely subjective level.

Did the dropping of the bomb subsequently affect the course of my life? I can't tell you. I know that before the war was over I'd made up my mind that if I survived I must try and do something to help prevent another war. But how do

The place is RAF Wyton, the date 24 June 1958 and (*bottom*) a crew from Britain's V-Bomber Force demonstrate their readiness to scramble. (*Right*) Vulcan bombers from RAF Waddington in flight. (*Inset*) Blue Steel training missiles being loaded into a Vulcan.

The RAF entered the jet age as early as 1944. In August a Meteor of No 616 Squadron became the first to bring down a V-1 rocket by cannon-fire.

A rare photograph of the prototype of the ill-fated TSR2 which was scrapped but left the legacy of its advanced technology.

Advances in missile form also arrived for operations involving the RAF Regiment, as with this Rapier missile being test-fired on a range in November 1999.

During the Cold War, encounters with the 'enemy' were not uncommon: (*above*) in 1963 when a Lightning F6 of No 23 Squadron intercepted a marauding 'Bear' of the Russian Air Force high over the North Sea. From the 1970s, the RAF commitment included the Phantom air defence fighter/inceptor (*right*) such as this F4J of No 74 Squadron and (*below*) the Jaguar of No 41 Squadron.

The aerobatics of the RAF jet teams have been thrilling crowds for half a century: this formation is of Lightnings from the Firebirds team of No 58 Squadron in 1963.

Still going strong: the world famous Red Arrows.

Hunters of No 43 Squadron aerobatics team pictured in 1955.

The giant Hercules (*above*), for so long a workhorse in the vital transport and logistics role, ferrying troops and supplies as well as participating in countless humanitarian operations, as captured here (*right*) by Sergeant Jack Pritchard as a crew drops tents and blankets for Kosovan refugees in March 1999.

Another vital role among support aircraft – the air-to-air refuelling process – made famous by 26-hour non-stop round-trip flights to the Falklands, demonstrated here in Corporal John Cassidy's photograph of an RAF TriStar of No 216 Squadron giving sustenance to Tornado F3s.

Kevin Capon captured this scene as members of 1 Para Regiment prepare to embark into the Chinook helicopters of the RAF's No 27 Squadron on the Kosovan border in June 1999.

Puma Helicopters provided by No 33 Squadron landing in a scenario of noise and swirling dust, reminiscent of the film *Apocalypse Now,* and brilliantly captured by Kevin Capon as paratroops wait to be airlifted from the road to Pristina, in June 1999.

A sign of the times, with Harrier units of the RAF and the Royal Navy set to merge: here Harriers in the Gulf region in 1998 were operating from the carrier, HMS *Invincible*.

Running repairs during operations in the Gulf: a member of ground crew of No 14 Squadron inspects the trailing edge of a Tornado GR1 at Ali al Salem airbase in Kuwait, in 1998.

Also in Kuwait was Royal Air Force policewoman Corporal Lorna Anderson, from Galashiels, pictured on the day she celebrated her first wedding anniversary, 14 February 1998, half a world from home.

In the visibly shimmering heat, Harrier GR7s of No 1 (F) Squadron taxi out of an airbase in Southern Italy during the Kosovo crisis in 1999, each loaded with four cluster bombs and two AIM-9L Sidewinder missiles

At the same airbase, SAC Carol Robinson (*left*) checks a 1,000lb Paveway bomb mounted beneath a Harrier GR7 bound for the former Yugoslavia.

Also during the Kosovo crisis, Corporal Peter Morgan (*below right*) of No 1 (F) Squadron, RAF Wittering, leads a team of armourers fitting a Thermal Imaging and Laser Designator pod to a Harrier GR7 at the Italian air base.

you do that? The bomb was a terrible thing. I know that. But when you compare it with the totality of the casualties, it's relatively small. If you divide casualties, which they estimated at 55 million by the days of the war, you get a Nagasaki on average every two days of the war. Of those 55 million casualties, two-thirds were civilian. Of the 25 million casualties in the First World War, 17 million were civilian, the indirect consequence of war. So my point is that modern war, quite apart from atomic weapons, over built-up areas of Europe, will inevitably cause huge numbers of civilian casualties. The only conclusion you can come to is that from now on we cannot allow war between major powers, whether conventional or nuclear. However dreadful the atom bomb was, it wasn't that that turned my mind towards working against the root causes of war. It was the war as a whole. Obviously, Nagasaki played a part.

What surprised me when I returned to Japan after the war was how little its people knew . . . there was a total lack of knowledge, historical knowledge about the Second World War. They knew nothing of the attacks on Manchuria, or that the Japanese military killed 5.8 million civilians in China through the most horrible methods. They didn't know that they'd launched an attack across South-East Asia. And they certainly knew nothing about the fanatical determination of the military to fight to the last inch of soil even after Hiroshima. When we bombed Nagasaki, the Emperor intervened for the second time and they agreed to his face but went back to military headquarters and said: 'Go on fighting.' When he finally ordered them on 14 August, he only succeeded because he brought up this argument: 'This is not surrender to a human enemy. You cannot fight this bomb. Therefore your army is undefeated. You may lay down your arms with honour, for the peace of the world.' And so the Japanese never, in their eyes, surrendered, and if they had not had a way of saving face there would have been an absolute catastrophe. The Japanese people, the media, knew nothing of this. Questions they asked me didn't even relate to this. Nor did they know that the fate of every PoW was sealed the day that the Allied offensive to regain South-East Asia opened and Field Marshal Terauchi, who commanded

South-East Asia, had ordered every PoW to be killed. Every PoW in Japan was doomed. I was so surprised by this lack of knowledge that I didn't quite know how to cope with it.*

Thousands of Allied servicemen, of course, died in horrific circumstances while in captivity – starved, diseased, brutalised, tortured, worked to death, shot, beheaded, mutilated beyond recognition – for which the Japanese have never formally apologised. Fortunately, in the immediate aftermath of the end of hostilities, the RAF, with so many transport aircraft to hand, were able to fly in immediate aid to the many camps holding Allied prisoners, scattered far and wide across the region. Many of those who survived this cold-blooded barbarism were barely alive but were gathered up and flown out to safety or hospitalised locally if they were too weak to travel. In the six weeks to the end of September 1945, 53,700 prisoners and internees were evacuated from the region by air or sea.

In 2002 the remaining survivors of this era, when the Japanese gave lessons in the capacity of man's inhumanity to man, continued their campaign to hear the word 'Sorry'.

---

* Leonard Cheshire suffered from nervous exhaustion after the war. On recovery, his wartime experience, along with a new-found faith in Roman Catholicism, made him decide to devote the rest of his life to the relief of suffering. He founded the now world-famous Cheshire Foundation Homes for the sick in many countries. In 1959 he married Sue, Baroness Ryder, who founded the Sue Ryder Foundation for the sick and disabled of all age groups.

CHAPTER FOURTEEN

Airlifts and Uprisings

As with all the services, the Royal Air Force faced massive logistical problems at the end of the war, with more than a million men and women from the United Kingdom and the Dominions and no fewer than 55,469 aircraft scattered across the world. The 'hostilities only' personnel were, like all the others from whatever country they fought for, anxious to get home to their families and hopefully resume a normal life. But because of its ultra-mobility, suddenly with all those empty aircraft available for transportation, the RAF became the workhorse of the world, and thousands of chaps both at home and in far-flung parts hoping for an early release were to be disappointed. To begin with, No. 2 Group of Bomber Command, along with the 2nd Tactical Air Force, joined the British Forces of Occupation, with the immediate task of disarming the Luftwaffe, while a special team was charged with gathering up vast collections of files, records and scientific material relating to German aircraft and rocket production.

The sheer weight of transportation needs turned the RAF into something of an international airline. In fact, the RAF was at the helm of some quite remarkable humanitarian efforts even before the war ended, both in Europe and the Far East, ferrying out prisoners of war and arranging food drops to beleaguered civilians and prison camps. The most dramatic was on the doorstep of Europe itself. Holland, which had suffered dire food shortages ever since the German occupation, was severely hit by the actions of German troops as they fled back across their own borders ahead of the advancing Allied forces. They ordered 7,000 inhabitants of the Wieringermeer Polder in northern Holland out of the area before blowing the dykes and flooding tens of thousands of acres of land and more than 500 farms in an attempt to slow down the Allies. With the Allies warning the Germans that they would be held accountable for deaths as a result of this disaster, the German governor of occupied Holland, still *in situ*, agreed to secret negotiations and eventually arranged local cease-fires so that food drops could be made to the starving Dutch. Lancasters from No. 115 Squadron began immediate trials for what became Operation Manna, and by the end of April 600 tons of food was being shifted by 253 Lancasters, flying in terrible weather and freak blizzards. Each aircraft carried 3,280 family ration packs consisting of tea, coffee, egg powder, flour, chocolate and other essentials to which some RAF and Allied crews added some of their personal stores, such as cigarettes. The relief flights continued into May and beyond, and in all 500 aircraft of Bomber Command and 300 from the US air bases in the UK distributed 7,500 tons of food over Holland until the regular flow of supplies was running by road, rail and ships.

Elsewhere, demands on the RAF were considerable, and by the beginning of 1946 an average of 9,000 passengers a month were being carried back and forth from the Far East alone. Initially, at least 60 per cent of the flights were to assist in the repatriation of prisoners of war of all nationalities, some still being found virtually starving to death in remote locations. The RAF was also involved in a tremendous effort to distribute food and resources across the entire Far East. There was also a great deal of activity handling the many diplomatic and military missions to cities where once those European nations wielded significant power and influence, not merely to re-establish connections. Great swaths of heavily populated areas, not least among them Singapore, were now devoid of police and judicial systems as well as most of the other administrative services. Many servicemen among the occupying forces, including the RAF, found themselves co-opted into these roles, acting as anything from the local magistrate to the chief of police. Similar demands arose across virtually every other theatre of war, where life had been decimated either by enemy action or occupation. Air transport requirements to and from Germany and other centres was especially busy, with every kind of passenger or cargo ranging from lawyers for the war crimes tribunals to flying back to Britain the most sensitive material among the hundreds of tons of secret scientific data and equipment being plundered by the Allies from occupied territories. The tasks at hand were immense and involved great numbers of military and civilian personnel, many of whom were soon to be engaged in the preliminary arrangements for securing decent and honourable burial sites for the millions of casualties of the war.

India, on the other hand, was to be the scene of mass evacuation of another kind. The jewel in the Empire crown had finally managed to sever ties with the British, having been granted independence, which was to become effective in 1947 with partition from the newly created state of Pakistan. In the build-up to this event, thousands died as Muslim-Hindu violence flared, particularly in Calcutta where bodies were piled high in the streets. This centre of British wartime operations saw the need for a further influx of battle-weary British troops as murderous violence spread across the subcontinent, in which an estimated 400,000 had died by Christmas 1947 as the greatest migration in history was under way, with some 8,500,000 refugees moved to resettle on either side of the Indo-Pakistan border. For the RAF, this additional requirement of supporting the military operations ran parallel with its contribution to the dismantling and carting away the last remains of centuries of the British Raj.

Almost immediately, nationalist and Communist groups in other countries, such as Malaya and Indo-China, who had fought alongside the Allies to defeat the Japanese, began laying their own plans to turn against former colonial rulers. Palestine was also on the brink of conflagration as the Allies produced recommendations in May 1946 for the partition of the Holy Land, the resettlement of displaced European Jewish communities and eventually the creation of the state of Israel. Those troubles were already becoming a reality, but in the meantime the vast and complex logistical operations confronting the RAF – along with the massive task of reorganising their own resources – would keep almost 800,000 personnel employed well into 1947. With political pressure mounting to speed up the demobilisation of remaining 'hostilities-only' personnel, the figure was down to 325,000 by the spring of 1948, with a target to reduce the overall manpower of the RAF to fewer than 200,000 by the end of the decade. Already, the strain was beginning to show.

As elements of Fighter, Bomber and Coastal Commands were being decommissioned, the RAF's Transport Command would bear the brunt of the movement of personnel and stores. It was organised into 42 squadrons operating approximately 1,500 transport aircraft of various kinds, distributed across the world: Dakotas, Liberators, Douglas Skymasters, Halifaxes and Sunderland flying boats.

Among the hundreds of pilots, crews and ground staff engaged in these operations was Group Captain Dick Arscott, who had reached his twenty-first birthday in 1945. He had joined the RAF in 1942 and, after training in the UK and Canada, volunteered for special duties. He was posted to the Far East with No. 358 Squadron which was one of two special duties squadrons engaged in dropping agents across the Far East theatre of war, mainly in support of the clandestine activities associated with the Special Operations Executive. There he found himself flying Liberators on long-haul flights, 14 to 22 hours at a time, over what was then Siam and French Indo-China, dropping dozens of agents and civilian officials into Japanese-held territory. The experience, in which he saw service predominantly over Indo-China, dropping French agents, would serve him well for his post-war experiences:

The agents would come out to us mostly without experience of flying, let alone jumping out of an aircraft. They would arrive at our base east of Calcutta on day one, and our job was to show them how to jump out. We used to have a tower in which they used to practise jumping, and the following day we would take them out. We'd be up before dawn, because the trips were going to be long. In the back of the Liberator we used to have a children's slide to the back hatch, which we used to help the 'Joes', as we called them, make their exit. When the green light came on over the dropping zone, the dispatcher pushed them down the slide. He also had a stick to hit their knuckles if they grabbed the side, which they often did. Out the back they went. The dropping zones were literally the size of a cricket square and you certainly didn't want to go round again in the conditions we had to drop in – hence the slide for quickness and no delays. Get them all out as quickly as possible. Their jobs were to raise sabotage groups, and once they were in it was our responsibility to resupply them. The major problem was the appalling weather and the lack of maps as we flew low over what really was suicidal terrain. We had a 78 per cent casualty rate on the squadron, although only one aircraft was actually shot down by the Japanese. We also got to know where the prisoner-of-war camps were located and used to drop what food we could, and bundles of magazines.

With this experience, Dick Arscott returned to the UK in December 1945 and joined No. 46 Squadron on transport Dakotas, one of several squadrons engaged on what became scheduled air shuttle services throughout Europe, with diplomatic runs to cities such as Berlin, Warsaw, Frankfurt, Vienna, Hamburg and Hanover carrying personnel as well as top-security diplomatic bags:

> It was very interesting, because the battle now was with the weather. Flying aids were still fairly rudimentary. You used your eyes and a stopwatch going in. British European Airways were doing similar runs, and so it became a challenge for us to get through when BEA were grounded. We never cancelled going into Warsaw or Vienna, so I was accustomed to European flying when the airlift to Berlin first started.

The Berlin airlift began on 28 June 1948, the official onset of the Cold War that was to heavily engage the frontline of the Royal Air Force for the next 40 years. In April the Russians had walked out of the joint council set up by the Allies to govern Germany, complaining that meetings had been held in London without Soviet involvement. In truth, the Russians were unhappy that they had control of the poorer part of Germany – the east. The Ruhr was very much in British hands, and they wanted the Allies out of Berlin. By June Stalin had imposed a total blockade on the city, and the massive airlift to save its people from starvation was launched. Heavy bombers were flown in from America to take up positions on nearby American bases to counter any threat from the Soviets while the Royal Air Force led the Western Allies into an airlift of food and essential supplies, a mammoth undertaking that eventually embraced a number of private concerns as well as the Allied air forces and lasted for almost two years. Two large US air bases were brought into the operation, while the RAF established flights from six airfields in the British zone, with all aircraft destined to go to just two crowded reception airfields in Berlin, at Gatow in the British sector and Tempelhof under American control. Dick Arscott was among the pilots involved:

The idea of the airlift was an RAF one. Air Commodore Waite, who was a planner over there at the time, decided it could be done. He did his sums and wrote a paper on how you could get aircraft going into Berlin and what was needed to sustain the Berliners on a military diet. Originally, it was a contingency plan to sustain the British garrison, so he extended it and sold it to the military commander at the time of the blockade on the basis that the Americans were thinking about going up the autobahn shooting. The irony of the chaps who not long before had been coming out to flatten Berlin and were now lending a helping hand didn't really apply. There were chaps in my squadron who had bombed Berlin, but the general view among them was that the Luftwaffe had fought according to the rules of war, even if the likes of the Gestapo hadn't. We were now transport, pushing commodities around Europe.

I was actually doing the Dakota run into Bückeburg when the Soviet military closed all traffic and began searching everything. It was quite impossible to move. When I returned to Oakington, I was told that I was going back into Germany immediately because there was trouble. One other aircraft and myself were going to augment the Anson that ran from Bückeburg to Berlin on a daily basis, to keep communications going, not only in freight but VIPs as well. I was still doing that when the Berlin airlift started and I continued on it until August the following year. The whole of the squadron went into Wunstorf to begin flying food into Gatow. They posted in an army unit of captain, staff sergeant and 20 soldiers to load 48 aircraft, which was clearly quite impossible. They eventually brought local civilians to help. The ground crews used what facilities were available. Accommodation was non-existent. There was an officers' mess, but with 48 aircraft with four-man crews there were simply not enough beds or facilities. Fifty of us were sleeping in the attic.

Initially, there was no organisation as such. We used to go down to the flight line and to the maintenance huts to see if there was a serviceable aircraft that had got a load on it, then we'd just take it and fly into Berlin and come back and look for another. Usually, in a day you could get three flights in, sometimes four, and that was the pattern for the first few weeks. Then the rest of Transport Command was mobilised and the York four-engined transports came in and, being heavier, caused absolute chaos.

We were moved off to another Luftwaffe station, and they were actually able to organise things much better. They had a rail link outside, and they were able to bring trains in 24 hours a day. They organised a local labour force, about 6,000 of them, who were loading the coal in to bags. We flew coal for a long time, and naturally it was a very dirty and dusty business. By then the routine had been set down: 10 hours on, 10 hours off, flying day and night, with a day off every seventh day and every fifteenth day; we went home to England on a 48-hour pass. Then the Americans came in force and took over from us while the Dakotas moved up to Lübeck. The same procedure continued. It was a very interesting time, because the economists were now deciding what we were going to take (in order to achieve the best weight, i.e. with no waste products at the other end). We carried boneless meat, real coffee because it produced more coffee at the other end, and so on.

On return trips, the Dakotas brought out children and the elderly who would either go to stay with relatives or be brought out to go into hospital, because there were no facilities in Berlin. So we were bringing children out and that was terribly sad. You would bring a load of about 30 children with one adult and take them to Lübeck. The administration there did not necessarily come to collect them. The children, who had probably been very sick all over

257

the aircraft, had to wait until they had been cleared. So we had a lot of contact with the civilians we were bringing out.

We also began taking in raw materials so that the Berliners could actually manufacture goods to keep the economy going. We were now taking in every kind of commodity as well as food, including timber, heavy goods such as steel plates, and even tar. There was a notorious case where a consignment of steel plates was mistakenly loaded on to a Dakota when it was supposed to go on to a York, and not surprisingly the pilot had some difficulty getting off the end of the runway. The Yorks also flew in a bulldozer in parts and a complete generating system, because the Russians used to close down the generators in their sector when they thought it would embarrass us most. It was by then so organised that, when we landed, a lorry would back up and a shift of labourers would swoop in to unload just in time for you to get out, and perhaps give you time to have a cup of coffee at the Malcolm Club, which was on the hard standing. We got it off to such a fine art that you might only be on the ground for 20 minutes.

Although the emphasis was on how well we did, you have to remember that the Germans themselves suffered intolerable conditions. Berlin itself was almost a flattened city, and there wasn't much food anyway. Without their determination not to give in to the Russians, the thing would have collapsed.

It was indeed a tremendous achievement by all concerned. The blockade-running forces embraced large contingents of British and American aircrews from both military and private sectors. When the Russians finally lifted the restrictions, on 12 May 1949, the RAF aircraft alone had flown over 18 million miles in 50,000 flights. In total, more than 300,000 tons of goods and materials had been flown into Berlin, and more than 70,000 passengers airlifted in and out of the city. The end of the blockade was merely the beginning of the tense war of nerves that put RAF squadrons in the very front line of vigilance for years hence and, as we will see in ensuing chapters, the arrival of the airborne nuclear deterrent in the emerging era of jet aircraft.

★ ★ ★

Before going on to the latter event, however, it will be as well to examine a succession of overseas operations between 1945 and the early 1960s which saw the Royal Air Force returning to scenes familiar in the inter-war years when it had fulfilled the role of a mobile police force engaged in peacekeeping and anti-terrorist operations. The first of these erupted in the vast and inhospitable Dutch East Indies even as the Japanese were pulling out, leaving dozens of camps filled with thousands of unattended prisoners of war and internees. It would take months before many of them could be reached.

In one of their last acts before surrender, the Japanese had created the Independent Republic of Indonesia, and with the Dutch unable to restore any form of control and administration in the region the South-East Asia Command was forced to send in the RAF and ground troops, first to locate and rescue the prisoners of war and then to attempt to quell insurrections that were breaking out across the whole of the region. A division of troops, including Indian and Gurkha battalions from the 14th Army, was dispatched to the main island of Java in the autumn of 1945, followed by an RAF headquarters formation from No. 221 Group, Burma, and a ground party of airmen numbering more that 2,500. As the trouble flared out of the control of such a small force, additional air support was ordered. Over the coming weeks, Nos. 60 and 81 Squadrons, flying Thunderbolts arrived, followed by Mosquitos from Nos. 84, 47 and 110 Squadrons. No. 31 Squadron came in with Dakotas for search, rescue and supply operations, along with a Spitfire for photographic reconnaissance.

As fighting escalated in central Java, where a Gurkha detachment was temporarily isolated against superior numbers, air support in the way of ground strafing and bombing became a vital ingredient against the Indonesian positions. The Dakota crews, meanwhile, were completing around 30 trips a day picking up prisoners of war and other detainees scattered over a wide area. The Mosquitos provided cover for those taken out by road who faced a gauntlet of resistance from Indonesian rebels. It took 16 months before the situation was stabilised, during which time the ground forces' casualties amounting to 480 killed and more than 600 injured. The dead included 13 officers and 26 other ranks from the RAF contingent, while another 40 were injured. Almost all the RAF losses were incurred in search and rescue missions to save the prisoners of war – and in the entire operation 24,436 flying hours were recorded during the airlifting of 127,000 passengers. Nor was this to be the last the British would hear of President Sukarno, who was elected President of Indonesia after Queen Juliana of the Netherlands signed a treaty ending Dutch colonial rule in December 1949.

By then, another flare-up was under way. What became known as the Malayan Emergency, a Communist-led revolution against Imperialist rule, had been simmering since the end of the war and came to the boil on 16 June 1948 when Chinese Communists murdered three British rubber planters. The perpe-trators of the crimes were Britain's former allies, once known as the Malayan People's Anti-Japanese Army. Now it was called the Malaya Races Liberation Army but was still run by its Communist Chinese leader, Ching Peng, MBE, who apart from getting a medal from King George VI had also marched in the 1946 London Victory Parade. He declared war on the British following the formation of the Federation of Malay States in February 1948 under a British High Commissioner. Ching had behind him a well-disciplined organisation and an army of 5,000 men run on formal military lines, backed up by a fair stock of arms dropped by the British during the war to fight the Japanese. The British government ordered an immediate state of emergency, which was declared the day after the murders. The 'emergency', as it was known – never referred to as a 'war' – was going to be over by Christmas but lasted almost 12 years against an enemy known as Communist terror-ists – CTs for short – who were the forerunners of a long line of such warriors who gave Western governments a real run for their money through the 1950s and 1960s, culminating in the costly, tragic and unwinnable conflict in Vietnam that engaged the Americans and Australians for so long.

At the start of the emergency, six battalions of Gurkhas were massed in Malaya, to be joined by various elements of other British and Commonwealth forces over the coming years to participate in the long and monotonous game of hide-and-seek. It developed into one of the most arduous and difficult cam-paigns of this post-war era, running from June 1948 to July 1960 in what British troops in Malaya nicknamed the Green Hell.

Stretching 400 miles between Thailand and Singapore, the peninsula had a hot and wet climate and four-fifths of the land area was covered with dense tropical rainforest. Apart from the terrorists, this grossly inhospitable terrain harboured all kinds of nasties, including leeches, ticks, scorpions and snakes, which troops regularly encountered as they hacked their way through creepers and vines or waded waist-deep in mosquito-blown swamplands.

The air forces missed most of these ground-level unpleasantries but faced no less an arduous campaign which, during its 12-year run, maintained the attentions of numerous squadrons of the Royal Air Force, the Royal Australian Air Force and the Royal New Zealand Air Force under the auspices of the Far East Air Force headquarters based in Singapore. They were supplemented from time to time by fighter, bomber and transport squadrons based in the UK and the Middle East, who between them flew operations using virtually every kind of aircraft available during that time, including Spitfires, Mosquitos, Lancasters, Sunderland flying boats, helicopters and then, as the jet age prospered, several of the new jet-powered fighters and bombers.

But on the ground there was no replacement for the sheer hard slog of the jungle, and again an impressive list of combatants over the period amounted to the equivalent of 26 infantry battalions drawn from the Gurkhas, general British regiments, paratroops, commandos, the SAS, the SBS and units from Australia, New Zealand, Africa and Fiji. These were in addition to thousands of Malayan Home Guard and police forces.

By March 1950 the CTs had taken a hefty toll – 863 civilians, 323 police officers and 154 soldiers had been killed. The terrorists had also suffered, and their casualty figures were 1,138 killed, 645 captured and 359 surrendered for the same period. Even so, within a year terrorist incidents were running at over 600 a month.

Coincidentally, in Hong Kong at that time was a British staff officer who had served in Burma at the time of the Chindit operations. In May 1950 Brigadier 'Mad Mike' Calvert, who had finished the war as commander of an SAS brigade, was sought out by General Sir John Harding, Commander-in-Chief of Far East Land Forces, to make a detailed study of the problems

261

facing troops in Malaya. Calvert took off for the jungle and made a 1,500-mile tour, unescorted and along routes infested with terrorists. The result was an ambitious plan to close down 410 Malayan villages, most of them shanties, to stop terrorists from drawing food and supplies. More than 400,000 Chinese Malays were moved into fortified regions, thus out of contact with the terrorists, to enable ground forces to embark on their own guerrilla-style long-range patrols supported by air reconnaissance and supply drops, as in the Chindit operations.

The patrols began almost instantly, with particular emphasis on operations that established a pattern for special forces of the future, with the Gurkhas and a newly formed unit under Calvert called Malaya Scouts (SAS) being sent into the jungle for weeks at a time, which meant they were totally reliant on accurate airdrops by RAF crews. By mid-1952 the long-range patrols, combined with general military operations, were beginning to make some headway into tracking and arresting the elusive CTs. Reliance on transport aircraft became of paramount importance for troop movements and supplies. In spite of the array of aircraft ultimately used in the campaign, the increasing successes on the ground were aided in no small measure by, initially, the Dakotas flown by Nos. 48, 52 and 110 Squadrons from Changi and later with Valettas and Whirlwind helicopters. They flew in appalling weather conditions, with hazardous cloud and mists that could envelope higher areas without warning. Donald Cox spent three years flying Dakotas for No. 52 Squadron:

The main work was communications, transport of troops and personnel, and supply drops for troops in the jungle. This could be in the jungles or in the central highlands of Malaya, where the hills rose to between 5,000 and 6,000 feet, often across territory for which no maps existed. Troops would report in about where they thought they were and would request a supply drop at a certain time at a certain point. The army would load the aircraft with supplies, and we were given the task of going out to find them. The troops in the jungle would lay out a marker if they could find enough space to do it. Dakotas were the most suitable aircraft for the task at the time. They were very agile and fairly safe for the low flying involved, sometimes down to

100 feet. The only problem was you had to push the supplies out of the side, rather than the back. The packs were big things, weighing up to 270 pounds each, usually in wicker baskets with parachutes fastened to the top of them, or canvas packs thrown out through the door. There were only two losses I can remember in my time: one Dakota from 48 Squadron crashed on a border patrol. Another aircraft was out searching for a lost Spitfire in northern Malaya and unfortunately hit a mountain.

The airdrops of supplies did not always go according to plan, especially those for the Gurkhas who, because of their religion, could receive only 'live' meat, as Major Dal Bahadur Gurung explained:

I went to my regiment in November 1953, 6th Gurkha Rifles. Quite soon afterwards, I had two new experiences: the jungle and a ride in a helicopter, which was quite exciting for a young man who was only just past his seventeenth birthday. The Royal Air Force had new Whirlwind helicopters, which took us deep into the Malayan jungle, where we set up camp and began our patrols. That operation lasted for 51 days. We normally carried enough rations for five days, fairly meagre food carefully measured each day. After that, fresh supplies came by way of an airdrop from a Dakota. We would have to radio our position, chop away the undergrowth and create a drop zone. Now, there are certain aspects of the Gurkha soldiers' religion that affect what we eat – no beef – and how it is slaughtered. So they dropped us live chicken in the baskets. Well, most of the time they became entangled in the trees. Sometimes, the baskets broke open and the chickens would come fluttering down, squawking, and we were all running around trying to catch them. Other times, the baskets were just hanging there, high in the branches, and the birds were going cock-a-doodle-do and we had to climb up and get them down. One of the baskets was hanging from a very tall tree, high in the ceiling of the jungle. We tried to chop it down, but we couldn't and one of our men had to climb up and release the chickens. It wasn't funny at the time!

Those mishaps apart, the Royal Air Force, over time, contributed much to the Malayan campaign and tried out a number of innovations of their own. Although initially only conventional aircraft were used in the Malayan campaign, jet fighters were introduced in the region after 1950. The first were the Meteor Fighter Reconnaissance aircraft, the FR10, and then the photographic reconnaissance fighter-bomber came into service there. The Meteor Mk I, as already noted, was the first British jet fighter, brought into service with No. 616 Squadron in July 1944, although at the time it was no faster than conventional fighters. The Mark I and all later models carried fuselage-mounted 20-millimetre cannon. The de Havilland Vampire, the RAF's second jet fighter, was also deployed over Malaya, having entered operational service in 1946–7. By 1950 five regular squadrons were flying the Vampire in the UK and another five were to receive them for service in the Middle East. Again, although jet-powered it bore none of the sophistication of contemporary jets (see Chapter Fifteen). Canberras and limited operations by elements from Britain's new V-bomber force were also used.

Running alongside the unrest in Indonesia and Malaya was the outbreak of war in Korea when the Chinese-backed north invaded the south in June 1950. Already heavily committed to the emergencies in the Far East and still with a large presence in the Middle East and Cyprus, where the EOKA terrorist campaign was just beginning to surface, the Royal Air Force would have only a limited involvement in the Korean War. It sent three Sunderland flying boat squadrons, Nos. 88, 205 and 209, on attachment to the USAF, and individual volunteers, mostly seconded into the Royal Australian Air Force's No. 77 Squadron flying Meteors. The Royal Navy's Fleet Air Arm were also involved alongside the Americans who had overall command of the UN-backed force in support of South Korea.

First to operate over Korean waters was No. 88 Squadron, which only a short time earlier had managed to pull off a daring flight to put a doctor and medical supplies aboard the Royal Navy frigate HMS *Amethyst* after she was famously ambushed by Chinese batteries on 30 July 1949 and trapped for four months on the Yangtze River. As tensions mounted with the advance of the Chinese Communist forces, No. 88 Squadron then evacuated large numbers of British civilians from Shanghai to Hong Kong.

The Sunderlands were based at Iwakuni on the southern tip of Japan and initially operated in support of Royal Navy warships. As the fighting in Korea grew more intense, all three squadrons of Sunderlands were formed into a wing under the control of the American navy flying boat depot ship USS *Curtis* moored in Iwakuni Bay. In addition to supporting the attempted blockade of Korean ports, the Sunderlands flew very long patrols along each coast of Korea as well as joining anti-submarine operations in conjunction with both the Royal Navy and the American navy, often in appalling weather with many operations flown in temperatures as low as minus 20 degrees Celsius. The Sunderland squadrons also provided cover for invasion forces during Allied amphibious landings on the mainland of Korea and in all notched up a total of 1,100 missions with 12,500 flying hours, with the loss of one flying boat which came down between Iwakuni and Hong Kong, killing 14 crew and passengers.

As the campaign progressed, the Royal Australian Air Force began to suffer heavy losses flying Meteors against the superior Russian-built MiG-15 fighters, and the call went out across the Royal Air Force for volunteers. Among the 29 who were accepted for service by the RAAF – as well as another 21 who served with the USAF – was Squadron Leader I.L. Schweiger, who had passed out of the Royal Air Force College at Cranwell in August 1951 in front of the reviewing officer, who was Princess Elizabeth, and converted to Meteors:

> I subsequently joined No. 226 OCU in Suffolk, where I was taught the practicalities of fighter reconnaissance, air-to-air firing, air-to-ground firing and a further course in reconnaissance photography. I was then posted to No. 208 Squadron in Egypt, equipped with the Meteor FR9, which had a wide-ranging role in fighter/reconnaissance including a daily examination of the Egyptian army [whose manoeuvres the British were coming to deeply mistrust]. At about this time a signal came to the squadron for volunteers to go and reinforce the Royal Australian Air Force's No. 77 Squadron in Korea. They had been there since the beginning, and had lost a number of pilots. Many of them had done two or three operational tours. Myself and a good friend of mine both volunteered and, with others, flew out to Japan to

report to the RAAF HQ for a conversion course to firing rockets, which was the role of 77 Squadron. Most of us hadn't had any experience of that. After 10 days we had done our training and had a briefing about the area and set off to an operational area near Seoul, about 11 miles behind the front line where there was a fair amount of fighting going on.

After a couple of trips getting to know the local area, crossing the bomb line to have a look at salient map points, we were put on operations and carried out a number of strikes on North Korea with high-explosive rockets or napalm rockets. Napalm rockets were developed by the Australians – jellified petroleum in five-gallon canisters – and they were extremely effective in destroying the targets we attacked. We used to fly 16 aircraft to attack one target, which were generally speaking described as troop concentrations by American intelligence, and we utterly and completely destroyed a village with the napalm rockets.

This limited RAF force won seven medals between them for distinguished action, including the shooting down of seven MiGs. But, like the Australians, the British team suffered heavy losses – 11 RAF aircrew were killed in the campaign. The performance of the Meteors in the role of front-line fighters also confirmed what many in the Air Ministry suspected – that they were vastly inferior to the Russian fighters – and almost immediately the call went out to the Americans for the loan of more than 400 Sabres.

Nor were the MiGs far away as the next significant action loomed on the horizon for the RAF as President Nasser of Egypt got into bed with the Russians. He began urging the British to depart his country and to give him back the Suez Canal, in which the British bought a controlling interest in 1888. In 1954 Nasser agreed not to press the matter further if the British on their part agreed to a gradual withdrawal of all remaining forces of what once formed a 70,000-strong British Army of the Nile. This arrangement seemed to calm the heightening tension between Nasser and the West but it didn't last. By early 1955 more Russian MiG fighters and copious amounts of other hardware from the Soviet bloc arrived in Egypt on a £200 million buy-now-pay-later arrangement for which Nasser mortgaged his entire cotton for the next five years. The West responded by withdrawing from negotiations to finance Nasser's dream project, the Aswan High Dam, which he was desperate to build to improve the nation's irrigation, and therefore crop production, as well as to generate hydroelectric power. Backed into a corner, the then toughest operator in the Middle East came out punching, and on 26 July, one month after the last of the British troops had been pulled out under the 1954 agreement, Nasser announced he was nationalising the Suez Canal without compensation to the Imperialists. That night there was dancing in the streets of Cairo.

What is generally referred to as the Suez Fiasco now began to unfold. The British and the French began to put together an invasion plan to reclaim the Canal Zone, but the impetus drifted somewhat because it would take at least three months to assemble adequate forces and drawn up a battle plan. By the time the task force was ready to move, it was clear that the international community, and America in particular – currently in the throes of re-electing Eisenhower for a second term – would not support any heavy-handedness, given that the Soviets were hovering in the background. Notwithstanding this lack of support, British Prime Minister Anthony Eden and his French counterpart pressed on and secretly accepted the offer of some side-action from one of their few supporters in this venture, Israel. In spite of Eisenhower's pleadings not to endanger peace in the volatile region, Israeli Prime Minister David Ben-Gurion gave the order for his troops to invade Egypt on 29 October, and thus provided the Anglo-French forces with a carefully prearranged excuse to zip across the Mediterranean and take possession of the Canal Zone. A joint British and French ultimatum called on the Egyptians and the Israelis to pull back from the Canal Zone within 12 hours. Israel agreed on condition that Egypt did the same, but Nasser naturally rejected the call.

And so the invasion of Suez moved towards its catastrophic finale. The British contribution to the assault was a task force of 18 squadrons of Canberra and Valiant bombers, to be flown out of Malta and Cyprus, along with seven fighter squadrons, three photographic reconnaissance squadrons, eight paratroop transport squadrons bearing elements of the 16th Parachute Brigade, and a contingent of seaborne Royal Marines. Originally, the entire parachute brigade of three battalions and a headquarters unit was to be dropped on strategic targets, but the RAF had sufficient transport aircraft available to carry only 668 men, who were to be from 3 Para. This meant that 1 and 2 Para would now have to go in by sea, along with Royal Marine Commandos in a convoy of 20 ships.

On the afternoon of 29 October Israeli paratroops were duly dropped 30 miles east of Suez, their forward advance supported by drops of arms and food from French aircraft. As this diversion took hold, Eden pressed the button for the British attack to begin. It entailed a two-phase air assault to bomb all Egyptian airfields, using the Canberras of Nos. 10 and 12 Squadrons and the Valiants of No. 148 Squadron. They took off from Cyprus on the afternoon of 31 October and arrived over Egypt as dusk was closing in. Flares dropped by Pathfinders marked the targets, which were hit relentlessly with 500-pound and 1,000-pound HE bombs as the RAF pilots dodged anti-aircraft fire but saw little opposition from Egyptian MiGs.

Despite warnings over the BBC World Service, the Egyptians seemed unprepared. More than 200 planes were destroyed on the ground, and one of the Canberra pilots interviewed at the time, Flight Lieutenant John Slater, said: 'We could clearly see the lights of Cairo and adjoining areas were lit up but then, after my aircraft passed, the lights suddenly went out.' Although the air attack went in on 31 October, the naval task force was still six days away, which was far more time than the RAF needed to ensure air superiority. In fact, it gave the Egyptians time to regroup and prepare their troops for the incoming ground forces.

On 5 November 750 British and French paratroops were dropped on Port Said by Hastings and Valettas from Cyprus to secure the landing area for the arrival of the seaborne invasion force the following day. These troops went hard to their given targets, or at least as hard as they could, given that there was virtually no ground transport, as Gordon Burt of 3 Para painfully recalled: 'Each platoon in my company was told to go out and see what transport they could commandeer. One platoon came back with a bus, another with a tip-up truck and I'm afraid mine came back with a horse and cart. Anyway, we all piled on the bus and motored off down towards the Canal.'

It was no easy route through for the ground troops either, their arrival having been well signposted or, as one 'pissed-off para' put it: 'They might just as well have hung a trailer from a Canberra announcing our time of arrival.' The Egyptians were by then well dug in and had machine-gun sniper nests all over the place. Commandos being flown in by Royal Navy helicopters did so into the teeth of machine-gun fire as they came in to land on the beaches of Port Said. Elsewhere, some brand-new SU100 self-propelled artillery units made life difficult, but the biggest and most upsetting pieces were lorry-mounted batteries of rockets that would come hurtling over as the paras and Commandos proceeded to their given targets. In spite of these setbacks, there was no doubt that the task force, along with RAF air support in the way of strafing attacks on opposing positions, would achieve all its given objectives on the first day. By nightfall there was word that Port Said was ready to capitulate, and the three commanders of the land, naval and air forces took to a boat from their offshore HQ, HMS *Tyne*, and set off to receive the surrender – only to be fired on as they approached. They quickly hightailed it back to their ship. Clearly, there was to be no surrender that night, and in fact quite the reverse happened.

At midnight on 6 November, a cease-fire was declared in London. The task force was to pull back immediately. The United Nations Security Council, meeting in New York, had received a US-sponsored resolution calling for a cessation of force and 'to refrain from giving aid to Israel'. Eisenhower was piling on the pressure. Sterling was in free fall, and the British government faced a crisis of monumental proportions which, as history records, cost Anthony Eden his job and saw the British troops pulled out ignominiously, to be replaced by a 6,000-strong United Nations peacekeeping force.

Meanwhile, when the Royal Air Force began bombing Egypt and drew the focus of international attention, the Russians had seized the opportunity to prepare an invasion of their own. On 5 November, the same day that the paras landed on Egyptian soil, Red Army tanks rolled into Budapest and crushed Hungarian hopes of freeing themselves from Soviet domination. The last words on Radio Budapest before it was silenced were addressed to the Western world: 'Help . . . Help . . . Help.' The UN also passed a resolution the following day ordering the Soviets to pull out. It took them 33 years to comply.

Those two events, Suez and Hungary, in many ways epitomised the shaping of world events and the future role of the Royal Air Force in British defence policy. Suez was a defining moment in the future of British presence overseas. In the coming decade, apart from their considerable contribution towards resolving the Indonesia confrontation when President Sukarno attempted to expand his empire on the island of Borneo, the RAF found itself in regular fire-brigade roles. Overseas bases drenched in RAF history, such as Iraq and Aden, were to be successively given up to regimes hostile to the West and to the United Kingdom in particular. The end of an era was in sight as the Royal Air Force provided the cover for the hastening withdrawal of British presence from the traditional strongholds of influence across that vast arena of the Middle and Far East that the RAF had policed for so long.

By then, they were already engaged in a war of nerves with the Soviets – closer to home, and face to face with nuclear weapons drawn.

CHAPTER FIFTEEN

'What Happens If . . .?'

Fighter Command had a certain reputation to live up to in post-war years, especially as the plethora of post-war movies began to appear in the cinema, and Brylcreemed heroes became the role model of every schoolboy. In reality, there was little chance of the Battle of Britain being won again when international tensions were high, simply because Britain's capacity to meet such a challenge in that austere age had been seriously diminished by an economic straitjacket. The cost of rearming the Royal Air Force, along with what was still a huge commitment overseas, plus the mounting expense of equipping the bases across Germany against the threat of invasion from the Warsaw Pact countries, weighed heavily on the RAF's own aspirations. Furthermore, as was demonstrated from some of the skirmishes in the international trouble spots, Britain's current crop of fighters, namely the early Meteors and the Vampires, were no match for the Soviet MiG-15s. Later marks would get better and both proved to be popular with the crews. In the short term, however, only the arrival of the American-designed Sabres, built under licence for Britain in Canada, provided a temporary stopgap until the newer types began to arrive at the Royal Air Force front-line squadrons in Britain and Germany. The Sabres had a top speed of 700 mph and were actually supersonic in a shallow dive.

This urgent need for decent aircraft for both fighter and bomber squadrons became more glaring when the Soviets exploded their first atomic bomb in 1951, which threw the West into a blind panic about how this threat could be met. The grand plan had already been categorically established by the post-war Labour Prime Minister Clement Attlee: that the answer to an atomic bomb on London was an atomic bomb on another great city, which thus became a headline: 'Bomb must be answered by bomb.' But in reality Britain could not afford to put a battle force into the skies that would match the might of the new perceived enemy, the Soviet Union. Indeed, one of the main reasons why Eisenhower uttered a mouthful of f-words when Britain and France began its ill-fated raid on Egypt was his fear that the Soviet Union might get involved. That night, the United States Air Force was placed on the highest state of alert.

In an age of food rationing and urgent rebuilding of Britain's bomb-damaged cities, money was simply not available for re-equipping the nation with implements of war. Although the government had established an expensive and comprehensive plan for the creation of Britain's own atomic deterrent, which would be placed solely in the hands of the RAF, with what became known as the V-Bomber Force, it would not become a reality until the late 1950s. Britain therefore could only match the new Soviet air fleet with a force of somewhat mixed ability until the newer aircraft arrived on the scene.

In the years immediately after the war, the decline in Britain's air power was dramatic. The home-based Bomber Command, after decommissioning wartime equipment, was reduced from 1,700 aircraft to a mere 150 and, as a stopgap measure to fill the long-range bomber requirement in the Cold War, Boeing B-29D Washingtons began entering service with Bomber Command squadrons during August 1950 until Britain's first post-war jet bomber, the twin-engined Canberra, came into service with No. 101 Squadron at Binbrook, Lincolnshire, in 1952. The Canberra was a versatile and much-loved aircraft, which became one of the most successful and, partly because of the cancellation of other projects, the longest-serving aircraft type the RAF had ever possessed.

The Canberra was developed through numerous versions, which extended its capabilities from conventional bombing to the use of rockets, guns, photographic reconnaissance and eventually as a nuclear-strike bomber. It did, however, have its limitations, as did the array of sleek and – at the time – much-admired jet fighters that came on stream in the 1950s when Britain's defence chiefs were faced with a gap of several years before that Labour-invoked policy of nuclear deterrence became a reality. Yet, on the edges of a great arc across the world, the menacing influence of the Soviet Union and their Communist allies, now backed by The Bomb, was causing the military planners in the West many sleepless nights. In the absence of a significant response to possible Soviet aggression – apart from that provided by the Americans – the defence of Britain became an equally contentious issue, and equally vital was the strengthening of air defences in the front-line force in Germany, the 2nd Tactical Air Force. Air Chief Marshal Sir Joseph Gilbert, later to become one of NATO's senior planners and deputy head of Strike Command, began his service as a fighter pilot in 1952 when all these deliberations, constant changes of mind and much wringing of hands over money and policy were uppermost in the minds of the political and military hierarchy. Although somewhat detached from this ultra-secret world of 'What happens if . . .?', the general atmosphere of controlled fear filtered down to the men at the sharp end at the time:

> I was commissioned in 1952 and within a year I was in a front-line fighter squadron, mainly because people were being trained urgently for the Korean War. The fighter squadrons I flew with were involved in the air defence of the UK; ours was the pure task. If the UK came under air attack, we were there for that role. Air defence was a fairly narrow role. It was great fun to fly the aircraft but had it come to conflict it would have been our task to shoot down enemy aircraft; it was as simple as that. We were flying Meteors to begin with and then for a short time the Hawker Hunter [introduced in 1954]. Next came the Gloster Javelin [1956], and we went into the 1960s with the English Electric Lightning. All of them were good from a pilot's point of view, except for the Javelin, which was a great big delta-winged aircraft alleged to be supersonic, but, you had to throw it at the ground from a great height to get it to go supersonic.
>
> The other aircraft were more exciting, especially the

Lightning, this in spite of the fact that it was an engineer's nightmare. It was a very difficult aircraft to maintain, but once in the air the sheer performance was outstanding. There were lots of vices with these early aircraft. The Javelin had a hydraulics system which was impenetrable to understand and if it went wrong you were supposed to sit there and try to determine the fault. The Lightning was prone to catch fire because the fuel system was a bit leaky. Now, you might think this would have put the pilots off, but it didn't. You will meet quite a lot of Lightning pilots whose aircraft had caught fire under them. But notwithstanding that, it was an aircraft that everyone loved. It was also an aircraft that, if it went wrong in the air, the only thing to do was get out of it because you couldn't easily get it back on to the ground. You couldn't land it, for example, with the undercarriage up. I had my fire, and it all happened so quickly that it was all over in two or three minutes just after takeoff. I had a great deal of difficulty in getting the wheels down and on to the ground.

Although most of the aircraft were not incapable of fighter-to-fighter combat, they were primarily there to shoot down enemy bombers. In the early stages [of the Cold War] the only real way of attacking an enemy bomber was with guns, specifically the 30-millimetre Aden cannon, and the only thing to do was what you did in the Second World War, which was to get immediately behind the bomber aircraft and fire at it from as close a range as you could. Later on, of course, with air-to-air missiles, you could stand off at a greater distance and you needn't necessarily be behind the aircraft. We knew quite a lot about enemy bombers and had quite a lot of intelligence on their capabilities; we were very well served with intelligence information and we knew how to attack. Unlike our own aircraft, which didn't have any form of active defence, the Soviet air force did have active defence, with rear-mounted turrets and things of that sort.

The tension surrounding world events heightened progressively, and the prospect of an attack by Soviet bombers on the United Kingdom became the central plank in home defence and deliberations on future planning. As always, there could be no short-term measures and decisions on the type and cost of new aircraft, and the rapidly improving technological advances and armoury were to become confusingly disrupted by intermittent changes of government policy, and of governments. Expansion under one might quickly turn into contraction, and vice versa, or defence studies would throw up new thinking for the future, as indeed happened in 1958. The then Conservative Defence Minister, Duncan Sandys, issued a white paper, *Outline of Future Policy*, that became infamous in the annals of the RAF. It predicted a dramatic shift in defence requirements. He reiterated the belief in the deterrent effect of the V-bombers as underpinning future policy, but maintained that interceptor fighters would play a lesser role. Their place would increasingly be taken by surface-to-air missiles (SAMs). Even though Britain's capacity in the latter was virtually nil at the time, he ordered some swingeing cutbacks in the numbers of fighter squadrons based in Britain. The number of aircraft in Fighter Command was reduced from its 1956 peak of 600 aircraft to 326 in 1958, falling to 272 in 1960 and just 140 by 1962. Outrage and uproar followed across all levels of the RAF, well justified to some extent by the failure of the missile system that was to replace them (see Chapter Sixteen).

Meanwhile, the Soviets themselves piled on the pressure in a tense game that increasingly involved electronic monitoring systems which, fortunately, were one of the areas in which Britain excelled and in any event had upgraded the home defence early-warning and radar systems that could now track incoming aircraft at 200 miles at heights of up to 40,000 feet. The big question now was: could the RAF respond in sufficient strength to do anything about it? It appeared not. The Soviets were keeping close watch, both manually and electronically, and dispatched numerous 'spy' trawlers around British waters to constantly monitor air defence activities and exercises, as well as actually flying into British airspace on photographic reconnaissance missions, as Joseph Gilbert remembers:

It became a regular occurrence for Soviet aircraft to probe the UK by coming round the North Cape. They would quite often enter our air defence region and then have to be intercepted and shepherded out by our own aircraft. It was a very real threat, and there is no question that the UK would have been a prime target [in any war situation between the Soviets and the West]. Much later, when I was involved in matters of policy, I discovered that contrary to what was popularly believed, we actually underestimated what the Soviet Union was capable of doing. We now know that there were perceptions by the Soviet leadership later on that NATO was girding itself for war, but this had more to do with the Soviet's perception of NATO military exercises. In the Second World War there was always the fear of bombers launching a knockout blow and now that persisted in a different way.

Whereas there was area bombing then, it was recognised in the Cold War that what one needed to do in the attack – and this is thought to be what the Soviets had in mind – was to knock out key aspects of state power. Clearly, this could be done with nuclear weapons, and the Soviet capability was growing enormously.

There were to be occasions, without question, when we felt that the situation was becoming dangerous and that an attack by the enemy might be pending. There were definitely times when things were extremely tense. I was a very young squadron leader in the personnel side of the MoD during the Cuban missile crisis of 1962. I seriously considered moving my wife and family away from near London, where we lived, to the West Country. That was probably the worst occasion, but because the preponderance of Soviet military power was so great there was always a fear of an attack with little or no warning, perhaps within 48 or 72 hours. Although there would have been warning indicators, the actual immediacy of the attack could be very great indeed. There were a number of occasions when we brought our air defence forces up to a higher state of readiness because we thought this might happen.

Attack from the air is very quick, whereas an attack by sea requires the warships to be deployed and get out there. Attack from the air can arrive with minimal warning. We know ourselves as civilians that we can get in our jet aircraft and fly from Heathrow to Prague and we're there in a matter of a couple of hours. As regards the satellite nations of the

Soviet bloc, I don't think they would have been able to do anything other than take full part in it; events would have overtaken them and they would have been drawn in. There was always lingering hope in NATO that they would not be as belligerent as the Soviet Union itself, but fortunately we never had to find out. We had to plan for an attack from any direction, and they certainly had the range to do so, but the majority of our air defences were located on the east coast of England. We were confident in our own ability and the air defence system that we had. What worried us was that sheer numbers would overwhelm us.

It was a totally different scenario to the Battle of Britain but it was a close-run thing in the same sort of way. Dowding is quoted as saying what he needed was more and more pilots. I think if [Soviet] attacks had persisted, we would eventually have had to succumb because we simply didn't have enough fighter aircraft or pilots to be able to avoid being overwhelmed. Historical study was made of past events, but what tended to happen was that we took part in large-scale exercises to bring the scenario up to date; in other words our bomber aircraft would come in to attack the United Kingdom; we had regular air defence exercises and this was the basis of our confidence. You've got to remember, however, that the scale of the mock attack that we mounted against ourselves was a good deal less than what we would actually face from the Soviet Union. In a sense these exercises took place daily in the normal exercising of fighter operations but specific exercises were staged regularly, half a dozen times a year or more.

Similar procedures and systems were operating in West Germany, where the RAF had a presence first in their commitment to the British Forces of Occupation and subsequently as the 2nd Tactical Air Force which formed part of the NATO structure for the defence of Europe. Events elsewhere in the world led the NATO commanders to call for a major expansion of the British contribution, and from the early 1950s 2TAF became a further, but necessary, drain on RAF resources when the existing 16 squadrons were scheduled to double, and then some. Part of the expanded force would consist of light bombers that would, according to NATO planners, be used to carry any war into the Warsaw Pact countries. The armoury for such aircraft was initially conventional weapons, but they were soon to receive tactical nuclear weapons supplied by the Americans, along with air-to-air and surface-to-air missiles.

Other squadrons flew fighters whose sole role was the interception of bombers, while others were equipped for fighter reconnaissance and photographic reconnaissance – vital work in the West German theatre, with aircraft constantly on patrol. Nigel Walpole, in his memoir recorded for the Imperial War Museum in 1997, recalled his experiences of all of them as a fresh young pilot in Germany, where the tension heightened progressively and a constant routine of patrols and exercises was maintained to meet any potential threat. He joined the RAF in 1951 as short-service officer to become a navigator but instead went to the Royal Air Force College and trained as a pilot. His first operational squadron was No. 26 day fighter squadron based in northern Germany, flying Hunter 4s equipped with 30-millimetre Aden cannon:

> At that stage it was all medium to high-level work, between 30,000 and 50,000 feet. The threat from the Warsaw Pact was strategic and tactical bombers that we would have had to intercept. We practised this scenario continuously in the middle to upper airspace. I did two years on No. 26 Squadron before being posted to No. 79 Fighter Reconnaissance Squadron flying Swift FR5s at Gütersloh. This was an entirely different type of flying – all at low level, all at very high speeds. The Swift was very stable, had wonderful ailerons and would fly almost hands-off even in turbulence. The Swift carried three cameras, one in the forward facing station and one either side of the nose, which enabled us to take excellent photography at the very high speeds and low level we were operating at. It was a strip-aperture camera, ideal for its purpose, and outclassed anything that was available for other air forces. The way we operated depended entirely on the target and how close you were to it, how high and what speed you were. We had no form of sighting equipment and it was a matter of experience. We just learned it very quickly.

The targets would be the forward edge of the [supposed] battle area to help the army to find out what was ahead of them. Therefore, we looked for which routes the enemy would use advancing on us, whether we had struck the bridges that were crucial to the campaign, whether there was helicopter deployment and indeed where the troop concentrations were. The system of pilots providing an in-flight report was also vitally important. It provided instant intelligence to a terminal on the ground and would enable the army to know instantly what was going on immediately ahead of them. The speed we were travelling would be 480 knots, perhaps 560 in hostile areas. Only if we were short of fuel would we come down to 420, but even at those speeds I can assure you that we could pick up the crucial elements of the target array by the naked eye and report it back instantly, provided you have the facility, that the communication isn't jammed and the terminal on the ground is ready to take that information and pass it on.

The other advantage of visual over photographic reconnaissance was that there was a great delay in getting back to base and the possibility of not being able to get back to a base that has the processing ability. Assuming you could get to those facilities, you would only be on the ground for 10 minutes before wet negatives would be available for interrogation. The problem is getting back: 20 or 30 minutes, during which time the army could be on the move and if you haven't got your report through from your visual sighting, your photographs might be of little use.

The scenarios always envisaged massive conventional land force penetration by the many well-known units within the Warsaw Pact, which depended on the diverse terrain. We obviously attempted to guess where they would penetrate and try to concentrate our attention on those areas, but we were also well prepared to take on the unexpected should an Ardennes situation occur in the Third World War. We were very, very good at wheedling our way around at ultra low level in the generally appalling low cloud of northern Germany. We learned to live and fly with those very difficult weather conditions. We were better at it than some of our allies, who were more strictly regulated. Some of our chaps

279

might boast they didn't need a map, because they had flown over northern Germany so much, but of course when you were in a battle situation you needed maps, because at that time we had absolutely nothing in the tactical roles in the way of intelligence electronics.

The importance of the reconnaissance role in West Germany was further enhanced by the formation of three squadrons – Nos. 69, 58 and 542 – flying the latest Canberra bomber equipped for photographic reconnaissance. They were especially useful for high-level intelligence missions over Warsaw Pact territory for which they were regularly used. Nor was it generally known at the time that the squadrons of the new Canberra bombers which followed the PR7s into Germany were to include the first British aircraft in West Germany to have nuclear strike capability. The Canberra B(1)6 – an interim version of the B(1)8 – was based at Brüggen under the command of Wing Commander Dick Arscott, whom we last met flying the blockade into Berlin. In the meantime he had held a number of senior posts, which included the setting up of training systems for all photographic reconnaissance pilots. The Canberras were flown as a tactical nuclear strike force:

We were equipped initially with a free-fall bomb that was released in a climb, and you rolled off the top and got out of the way as quickly as you could. Eventually, we changed over to lay-down bombs, which were far more effective and accurate and had a parachute behind it so that you were able to fly directly over the target and drop it. You could get it within 20 feet, whereas with a toss bomb you had difficulty in getting it as close as 200 yards. The bombs that we were using were the American bombs, so that we had American custodians at Brüggen who were looking after the bomb. We had two aircraft on QRA [Quick Reaction Alert] at all times, and there were white lines around the aircraft because the bomb was aboard it. American soldiers guarded the planes constantly and they were told by their superiors: 'You shoot if anyone puts a foot over the white line.' One day one of their custodians was showing some Americans around and he told them: 'If I put my foot across the white line, that soldier will shoot it.' And he did, there and then, and he was shot in the foot.

The Americans were in charge of the armoury, or the nuclear bomb dump, and were responsible for servicing the nuclear weapon. We did exercises at least once a month. They brought the bombs from the bomb dump on their side of the airfield on RAF trailers with American guards who used to stay with the bombs. The trailers were brought to the aircraft and RAF armourers would put them up, but they were always supervised by the American custodians. Once they were loaded up, each aircraft had an American custodian attached to it, and if you started up the aircraft engine without clearance the custodian, rather than shoot anybody, was under orders to literally throw his rifle into the engine and of course shatter all the blades. That was their brief.

We never actually flew with a live bomb, only with dummies. Only the QRA, which could get off in three minutes, was always loaded. Then you had to generate [load them up] the next two in half an hour, the next two in an hour, and so on until the whole squadron was in the air. We had an exercise once a month when the station commander blew the whistle, as it were, and then once a year we were tested by a NATO inspection team who would arrive on the station and make sure we were up to standard at generating at this minimum speed. We were very quick. We had some splendid ground crew who used to work like slaves and generate the whole squadron in something like five hours.

We used shaped dud bombs the same size as the real thing, which we dropped on the practice range in northern Germany. To watch this shape come out of the bomb bay was incredible. It was an interesting time. I also had the only B(1)6 squadron; all the others were the B(1)8s with a single navigator. The B(1)6 had two navigators, which was a great advantage, one of them was in the nose map-reading. Come the war, we always reckoned that we were more likely to get to the target than anyone else, because you had the chap at the back with his radar, and so forth, but you had the man with his eyeballs and stopwatch up in the front.

The Canberra had at least kept the somewhat demoralised

Bomber Command ticking over, having to some extent lost its sense of purpose in the decade after the war. The arrival of the much-vaunted V-Bomber Force, however, provided the Command with the major defensive role it had been seeking – along with the awesome responsibility of carrying Britain's primary nuclear deterrent. The original specification for the bombers called for four-engined aircraft capable of reaching a target at 1,500 nautical miles' range, flying at 40,000 to 50,000 feet at a speed of 500 mph. Later, however, this was upgraded to carry a 10,000-pound bomb over a range of 4,000 miles. The force that began arriving in 1956 eventually consisted of 175 Valiants, Victors and Vulcans to be deployed on 10 main bases and a minimum of 30 dispersal airfields. The Victor and Vulcan were of more stringent design than the earlier Valiant, which was the first to enter service but had to be withdrawn within six years because of structural fatigue problems caused by low-level flying. The numbers were made up by further additions of the Vulcan squadrons.

The organisational structure of Bomber Command Groups Nos. 1 and 3 was retained, and some of the V-bomber squadrons actually found themselves stationed at pre-war bases with box-like hangars and attractive Lutyens-style messes and married quarters: No. 83 Squadron at Scampton and 44 and 50 Squadrons at Waddington were stationed there in September 1939 flying Hampdens and took part in the first operations of the war. The difference now was that the place was strung around with a tight cordon of security, the strictest of operational procedures and a stern-faced opening-day lecture on the challenge ahead in the scenario of an ever-growing Russian ballistic missile threat capable of penetrating sophisticated effective air defence systems.

Air Vice-Marshal Eric Macey joined the V-Bomber Force in 1958, his previous squadron having been disbanded under the white paper defence cuts. He had entered the RAF as a National Service conscript and signed on almost immediately for a short-service commission and then a permanent commission. It was the beginning of a long and illustrious career in the Royal Air Force. His first posting was with No. 263 Squadron at Wattisham, which became No. 1 Squadron with Hunter IIs and Vs, and later moved to Cyprus during the Middle East troubles of the mid-1950s. He recalls that there were something like 60 Hunters on the ground at Nicosia, where he was given first introduction to rat and terrier low-level interception and to cover ground convoys during the era of tacking EOKA terrorists on the island during the emergency of the 1950s. On his return to the UK he was accepted for conversion to the V-Bomber Force and in early 1959 was posted to No. 214 Squadron at Marham, to become co-pilot to Wing Commander Michael Beetham, who went on to become Marshal of the Royal Air Force and Chief of Air Staff. Macey's recollections provide a fascinating and detailed journey back into the dark days of a threatening nuclear holocaust:

> The squadron at that stage consisted of eight crews, one of which was commanded by the CO, five were commanded by squadron leaders and only two by flight lieutenants. It was a very high-powered unit, because most of those who had been selected had Second World War experience, or immediately post-war, on the Lancaster, the Lincoln and perhaps the Canberra force. They were seasoned, experienced people, and 214 was a fully operation squadron very much involved in high-level nuclear bombing. It was equipped with the first-generation UK nuclear weapon, called the Blue Danube, a hefty beast and free-falling bomb which virtually filled the bomb bay. Its main stream was high-level bombing, but 214 at that time was primarily involved in a series of trials in in-flight refuelling techniques and rendez-vous techniques, which were utterly fascinating. It was principally concerned with perfecting the air-to-air approach and making the contact and then take on the fuel.
>
> All crews joining the squadron were required to be converted on to the in-flight refuelling role initially as members of a competent tanker crew. So one had to learn the techniques of trailing the hose, maintaining the balance of the hose, monitoring the flow and monitoring the contact with the Valiant tanker. Each Valiant on the squadron had the capability of being a tanker, and its internal plumbing had been adapted so that the fuel could be consumed by its own engines or funnelled out to the hose drum unit mounted in the bomb bay, from which a 90-foot hose culminating in a conical drogue could be released. As the trials proved the concept, we were required to put it to

the test by a series of non-stop flights around and across the world, and the one that sticks in my mind was the first ever non-spop flight to Singapore which I flew with a crew captained by John Garston. We took off from Marham at about 5 p.m. one evening intending to take on fuel at three locations, landing in Changi 15 and a half hours later. At that stage the Vulcan force was expanding more rapidly in 1 Group. So it was decided that I should change horses and I duly arrived on No. 101 Squadron at Waddington in February of 1961 and remained with them for the best part of four years. Like the Valiant, the Vulcan was principally employed as a high-level bomber equipped with later-generation British weapons. In addition to the Blue Danube, there was a weapon called the Yellow Sun, which came in two versions, and these were all free-falling weapons.

While primarily equipped for weapons of that range, it was still equipped with the old-fashioned iron bombs. The Vulcan carried 21 of these and the Victor 35. Mostly we carried scaled-down dummies, but just now and then we were required to train with the real thing and indeed to release them. This exercise was usually conducted on the desert range at El Adam in Libya, and it is no exaggeration to say that the aircraft did lurch somewhat as nine and a half tons of bombs fell away simultaneously. Our primary role, however, remained as part of the UK's national nuclear deterrent, initially at high level but ultimately at low level and indeed ultra low level. This change came about very soon after Gary Powers' U2 was shot down by a Soviet ground-to-air missile [in May 1960]. It didn't take a thinking man long to appreciate that we were very vulnerable. The Vulcan could reach a height of 49,000 feet over the target, and Gary Powers was considerably in excess of that when he was shot down. So low level was then on the menu.

All the V-bombers were originally finished in a white high-gloss anti-radiation paint, but with the switch to low level a dark green camouflage paint was used to the upper surfaces. But the boffins had failed to appreciate that to a fighter loitering above we now stood out like the proverbial sore thumb when flying perhaps over a snow-covered terrain of Northern Europe or the Soviet Union, which was our presumed hunting ground. Nor at low level could we use the blackout curtains that had previously been zipped up – a curtain right across the whole of the pilot's windscreen canopy – and there were also little shutters to put over the side portholes against nuclear flash. Now, we couldn't use these at low level because we needed to look out, and so we were issued with and were required to wear a standard black medical eye patch and in the event of being blinded we were to switch it over to the other eye. That was our primary aid against nuclear flash at that time.

While Bomber Command was responsible for maintaining the strategic nuclear deterrent pre-Polaris, a proportion of the force was held on permanent standby with weapons loaded in the posture known as QRA [Quick Reaction Alert]. The aircraft were usually positioned on a dispersal bay close to the end of the runway with sleeping and feeding facilities for both aircrews and ground crews close by. Our accommodation in those very early days was in five-berth caravans with very thin aluminium walls, no privacy attached; the bunks were very narrow, and tall chaps like me regularly rolled off. An aircrew buffet was established on each of the V-force stations to provide for crews of QRA a full breakfast, a lunch and a dinner in addition to the in-flight packs that we carried to ensure that those condemned to escape and evasion did so on full stomachs.

The operational side of QRA was termed Readiness 15, which meant we were to be capable of getting airborne within 15 minutes whatever our location on the station. We had our dedicated transport, which were initially the somewhat unreliable Morris J2 vans that didn't start terribly well in the winter. The next Highest Readiness state was 05, with crews strapped in to the cockpit with the door closed and perhaps even repositioned on the forefinger of the ORP [Operational Readiness Platform] at the end of the runway.

The very highest state of alert was for crews to start the engine and move to the end of the runway if not already on the ORP to await political authorisation to get airborne. In times of tension – and there were one or two – the entire force would be put on to alert and flights of two or four aircraft – and here I'm embracing the whole of the V-force, including the Valiants and the Victors – would disperse to some 30 military or civilian airfields throughout the UK. Our intelligence people believed that we would get a minimum of four minutes' warning of an incoming missile attack, within which time all 90 or so bombers could get airborne from those 30 runways in the time taken by just four aircraft to scramble from one airfield. This simple but very effective plan considerably strengthened the credibility of our nuclear posture. We maintained this constant state of readiness for many years on end and were properly established to do so.

All the V-bombers had a five-man crew consisting of two pilots, two navigators and an air electronics officer concerned with communications and radio. The original Vulcan catered for just one pilot, but A.V. Roe was asked to fit two ejector seats side by side in the extremely small cockpit. It also had a very tightly curved roof, which is why many of us who flew the Vulcan have a permanent crick in the neck. Because of this, the rule that pilots should wear protective helmets was relaxed because there just wasn't headroom. The crews usually formed up at the conversion unit, and ideally it would remain as a cohesive unit for the entire length of the tour – usually about three years. Early weeks were spent consolidating aircraft systems and handling, and practising airborne navigation, bombing, communication and electronic defence procedures until it had reached a standard declared Combat Ready. From that point on, crews spent a great deal of time locked in windowless rooms on target study, material prepared for our war missions. Nominated targets were within certain countries of the old Warsaw Pact, and contrary to much speculation they were not one-way missions. There were two plans. One was NATO-generated, when Bomber Command's missions would be integrated with other strike forces operating under the NATO aegis; the other plan was a purely national effort.

Each crew would be required to study perhaps five NATO-developed targets and two national ones and be extremely familiar with those targets to the extent that if all aids failed [they would] hopefully reach the target and release their load in the specific area.

Much of this sensitive and very specialist indoctrination was completed when rostered for QRA. One had to fill the time somehow, and that was a good opportunity. It was complemented by ever-more demanding flying and ground training for the entire crew while the pilots spent many additional hours rehearsing drills in the flight simulator. To maintain an individual combat rating, all members of the crew had to complete a minimum number of exercises pertinent to their specialisation while the crew was judged as a team. Progression to the highest category [was through ratings of] Combat, Combat Star, Select and ultimately Select Star. The training period was six months, so the earliest a crew could achieve Select Star, the highest category, was two years. We could certainly be expected to perform at a much higher standard all round than the basic combat-ready crew, and it was the great aspiration to become Select Star. Both pilots were required to be instrument-rated and latterly what was called a procedural endorsement to conform to civil requirements, because when we did detach overseas we invariably went along the civil airways structure.

A massive training programme constantly being updated put the crews and ground staff of the V-Bomber Force through every possible scenario, from enemy attacks by missiles, fighters and bombers to testing the crews' reactions to in-flight failures, such as double engine failures, collapse of communications, degraded navigational aids, bird damage, the aircraft being 'bounced' by fighters, and so on. Many of these training sorties were carried out over the UK, but for more wide-ranging tests of the crews' ability and bombing practice, the V-force would deploy to air bases in Canada and America, where environmental restrictions on noise and overflying were not as strict, especially on low-level bombing training. Participation in the American Red Flag exercises at Nellis Air Force Base in Nevada allowed the virtually unrestricted operation of all penetration aids and electronic counter-measures, such as jamming ground stations. The introduction to low-level flying was 500 feet by day and 1,000 feet by night; later on, as the aids became more sophisticated, the crews flew at progressively lower levels to 300 or even 250 feet.

Crews preselected for **Red Flag** had to satisfy their superiors that they were fit and safe to perform these low-flying operations before they were detached. Crews on QRA were also frequently brought to Highest Readiness state for simulated scrambles, usually in the middle of the night. They would rush to the aircraft, unlock the door, climb up the ladder and begin procedures up to the point of takeoff with engine start initiated externally by technicians with their start trolley. Like many crews engaged on nuclear-linked operations, Eric Macey also remembers vividly where he was at the time of the Soviet missile crisis:

My sobering experience in October 1962 was when a Soviet freighter thought to be carrying nuclear missiles to Cuba was ordered to turn back in the face of President Kennedy's naval blockade. The QRA posture of being able to get airborne in 15 minutes had been tightened to cockpit readiness, 05, while the number on alert was considerably strengthened. At the critical time, my crew was strapped in and poised to start engines with a nuclear weapon loaded in our bomb bay. Had we been scrambled, we were to fly east into the unknown. What is pretty certain, I suppose, is that the face of Lincolnshire would have been unrecognisable had we been fortunate enough to return. I can honestly say that nobody was more relieved when that freighter did an about-turn than those members who had been sitting in cockpits like myself and my colleagues on the squadron.

The bomber controller would have required the political authority to initiate these procedures. In case there was a maverick on the end of the telescramble transmitter at High Wycombe, he was required to authenticate his message and we were required to validate it with codes that we carried in the aircraft. If the codes didn't match up, we didn't move. The bomber controller himself would receive the authorisation direct from No. 10 Downing Street.

Events elsewhere, however, had already cast doubt on the future of the V-bombers, whose development, etched in 1950s thinking, was now dating rapidly amid advances in ballistic missiles in the Soviet Union and America. The much-hated white paper of Duncan Sandys on future strategy had already caused deep divisions among military analysts. Many supported his theory that the age of heavy-duty warplanes was over and in their place would come unmanned missile-delivery systems; others said this was too futuristic by half. In the long term, Sandys and his MoD advisers were to some extent proved right. Of course, there would remain a role for a strong air fleet, but the writing was already on the wall for the large forces of big bombers. At the time, however, they were all that Britain possessed. Attempts to find a viable alternative rumbled on with an air of panic well into the 1960s as the cash-strapped Ministry of Defence looked at numerous ways in which to develop a home-grown ballistic missile programme.

It finally settled on the Blue Streak intermediate-range ballistic missile (IRBM), but the much-publicised project collapsed after two years without a missile in place. It was discovered that the liquid-fuel system could not be launched in under 20 minutes and was vulnerable to a pre-emptive strike by the hundreds of Soviet missiles now pointing in the direction of the United Kingdom. With no suitable missile in sight, the British government accepted the invitation of the Americans to site their IRBMs in the UK. The RAF was to undertake responsibility for this new addition to the British nuclear armoury, and the roundel was emblazoned on the side of each one.

By the early 1960s, 60 of the massive Thor IRBMs, with a 1,500-mile range, had been sited on RAF bases, the first going to No. 77 Squadron at Feltwell, Norfolk. The rest were allocated to 23 squadrons at bases in East Anglia, Lincolnshire and Yorkshire, each squadron having five launch crews, under the operational control of Bomber Command. Almost 1,500 men and women were employed at the sites to form a 24-hour ready-to-fire rota system. Each missile carried a megaton-class warhead, supplied by the Americans, and, as with the nuclear bombs, US custodians were posted to each launch site.

The British also had to agree that no launch could take place without the approval of the Americans, who had authentification officers on each base. However, even as the sites and rocket launch pads were being built, there was concern – not least among local residents and anti-nuclear protesters in particular – that Thor carried dangerous implications. Like the cancelled Blue Streak, it needed a 15-minute preparation time and was sited above ground, thus providing an open invitation to the Russians to strike first if conflict arose. The Americans themselves realised this vulnerability, and little more than three years after the last of the expensive Thor missiles was sited in Britain, the project was scrapped and all the missiles and warheads were collected up and returned to the US.

They were to have been replaced by another US missile, the air-to-ground Skybolt missile that ostensibly could be carried by the B.2 versions of the Vulcan and Victor bombers, which would have allowed the British government to honour its 'second-strike' commitment to NATO. But then the US government suddenly cancelled Skybolt after serious problems during testing; in any case the Americans had developed other systems that were more suitable to their own requirements. This left the RAF high and dry at a time when the V-bomber armoury of Blue Steel Mk I nuclear missiles, plus Yellow Sun Mk II and WE 177 nuclear bombs, was already beginning to look very uncompetitive.

The solution to all these problems lay in top-secret developments in America that had been instigated in a paper by a high-powered American think-tank, which believed that MAD (Mutually Assured Destruction) was no longer applicable because all Allied nuclear installations were vulnerable to a surprise attack, after which retaliation would be impossible. Intelligence analysts were convinced that across Europe, Allied bases, missile sites, airfields and dockyards were permanently targeted by lines of Soviet missiles. The solution arrived hand in hand with the development of nuclear-powered submarines, which could stay submerged for months without having to surface or reveal their whereabouts. This, together with the arrival of inertial guidance systems, meant that long-range submarine-launched ballistic missiles could supposedly be delivered from beneath the ocean with incredible accuracy to targets 1,500 miles away. Thus, the Polaris submarine-launched ballistic missile system was born to secure a 'second-strike' capability.

Britain's Chief of Defence Staff Lord Louis Mountbatten, who had secured agreement from the Americans to supply a power plant for Britain's first nuclear submarine, *Dreadnought*, now flew off to persuade the Americans to sell Polaris to the British. The upshot was a meeting between Prime Minister Harold Macmillan and President John Kennedy in the Bahamas on 21 December 1962, two months after the Cuban crisis. What became known as the Nassau Agreement would enable the US to provide the complete weapon system to equip four British Resolution-class nuclear submarines and assure the UK's deterrent potential for years ahead.

Delivery of the first submarines was achieved by 1968 and all four were completed by 1969, at which point the Royal Navy assumed recognition as holder of the British nuclear deterrent. The V-Bomber Force remained bearer of the nuclear deterrent in the meantime but was gradually cut back and Blue Steel was taken out of service in 1969–70. The Victors were successively converted to strategic reconnaissance and tanker operations. By the end of 1970 the V-Bomber Force had shrunk to six Vulcan B.2 units (Nos. 9, 35, 44, 50, 101 and 617) operating in the free-fall bomber role with conventional and/or nuclear weapons as part of the UK's air commitment to NATO. By 1982 the remaining Vulcans were to be retired, although the Falklands War led to a heroic last gasp of fame (see Chapter Sixteen). Eric Macey, meanwhile, had returned to No. 101 Squadron to command it before moving on to a series of influential appointments before retirement in 1991. The last one had a touch of irony about it – that of Assistant Chief of Defence Staff (Policy) with responsibilities for both briefing Prime Minister Margaret Thatcher on her nuclear function and on the development of the Trident submarine-launched system that was to become the nation's sole nuclear deterrent for the new millennium.

CHAPTER SIXTEEN

Strike Command!

The Royal Air Force had been given early warning of its forth-coming loss of the primary deterrent role and used the interven-ing years to take an inward look at itself, assess the future and set its stall out accordingly. Some of the best brains and planners were tapped for their views on the way forward, and of course the Chiefs of Staff, Whitehall and NATO would ultimately have their say. Several of those whose recollections are recorded in these pages were involved in these deliberations over the next decade. Not least among them was Dick Arscott, whom we last met in Germany heading a Canberra nuclear strike squadron. After other appointments, he was subsequently called in to become involved in the planning of the most radical shake-up in the history of the Royal Air Force. 'It was a very interesting time,' he recalled with unassuming reference to this mission, continuing:

I had been on the air-warfare course and became an air planner at Bomber Command. There were just two of us, and we were somewhat surprised to discover that the pair of us were assigned the task of incorporating all the Com-mands into what was to become known as Strike Command. We had to prepare all the papers on each one of the Commands – Fighter, Bomber, Coastal and Signals – to bring them together into one unit. It was an exceedingly busy time. The pair of us would come into work at seven in the morning. I would go home about nine o'clock at night, while my group captain went on until ten o'clock. This we did for about two years with an open door to the C-in-C on a daily basis.

The new umbrella organisation, which would ultimately lead to a shrinkage in overall manning and aircraft, would come into effect in 1968, not without howls of protest that the great traditions of the Royal Air Force were 'being sacrificed on the altar of Mammon'. Some commentators more pointedly asserted that successive governments had blighted the RAF with indecision and mismanagement and had continuously failed to understand the long-term needs of the RAF, while politicians reversed the process and blamed the RAF for its bureaucracy, old boy network and a wilful waste of taxpayers' money. Elements of both contributed to what was an unhappy time for the RAF, and morale among all levels of personnel was low.

The ill-fated TSR2 'wonder plane' became a central plank in this friction. It was the great white hope to lead the RAF into the 1970s and beyond, and needless to say reputations were at stake, politically, industrially and within the service. This was to be a supersonic strike and reconnaissance aircraft designed as a replacement for the Canberra but with a far higher profile in terms of the huge technological advances that came with it. Great expectations were also afoot in terms of export orders. The TSR2 was of revolutionary design, on the lines of Concorde which followed it, and was based on highly complex specifications originally drawn up in 1959. It was intended as the ultimate long-range nuclear strike aircraft that could also perform virtually every other task from close air support to reconnaissance. Everything about the TSR2 was new. The design called for Mach 2 at medium height, a fully automatic navigational system and automatic terrain-following radar.

Sadly, the technology became bogged down by an unwieldy management structure that allowed too many people to have a say, and a bureaucratic nightmare descended around the project. In an attempt to get back on schedule, the design was frozen in 1962. No further alterations were to be made, and work went ahead towards building a prototype. Already, the TSR2 was well behind schedule with the delivery date put back to 1968. By 1963 over £200 million (or £2.5 billion at 2002 prices) had been spent on research and development alone. Squadron Leader I.L. Schweiger who had been on Canberras and Vulcans, then found himself posted to the Air Ministry as project officer for the TSR2:

> This multi-role, high-performance and quite extraordinary aeroplane was being developed by British Aerospace and the engine by Hawker Siddeley. My job was to oversee the specifications, with regular visits to the manufacturers, of whom there were a great many. The reason I had been selected was my experience in the various roles that the TSR2 was to be used. The aeroplane was subjected to a great deal of political attack as being too expensive and not required, and a great deal of my time was spent briefing ministers and giving presentations to officers of other nations' services with the object of trying to get them to buy the aircraft. But then, somewhere along the line Hawker Aircraft at Kingston produced a design of another aircraft called the P1127, or Kestrel, and I was asked to take on this role as well. It became obvious that this was a most promising project. It was impossible to give justice to both, and I was moved solely on to the P1127. I spent a great deal of my time in discussion with the planners and the designer, Sir Sydney Camm,* and others. Out of this programme came the famous Harrier Vertical/Short Take-Off and Landing [V/STOL] fighter [which became one of Britain's most successful aircraft, the only fighter ever sold to four air forces and which remains in service today]. A tripartite squadron of UK/US/Germany was formed to do trials with nine aircraft based in the UK. I went to the Pentagon to try to persuade them to consider buying it, which the US Marine Corps did, with their version. The Harrier went ahead and Hawker then produced plans for the supersonic P1154. The Air Staff decided they needed this aircraft and again I acquired this responsibility. At the same time, Armstrong Whitworth had produced a vertical

---

* Designer of some of the most famous aircraft, including the Hurricane, Typhoon, Hunter and Tornado.

and short takeoff transport aircraft called the AW681, and so there were three projects on which the RAF seemed to depend at that time – the TSR2, the P1154 and the AW681. A great deal of political discussion went on and in 1964, when the Labour government of Harold Wilson seemed certain to win the election, the Air Staff, knowing the political feeling of the Labour Party, had to rethink its policy. It was decided at senior level not to press for the P1154, not to press for the AW681 but to keep the TSR2 at all costs. This fight for the other two, if I might say so, was rather given up before the battle was even joined. In fact, the new Labour government scrapped the TSR2 because of the cost, and looking back I think it was the right decision. At the time I thought it was a magnificent aircraft, terrifically advanced weapon system, but I think it was for a role that, by then, the UK didn't have. The research was not wasted. Its weapons systems are used in the Tornado, and the aerodynamic design and the engines were used in Concorde.

A great many people who had spent years on the TSR2 and who also had hopes for the P1154 and AW681 were left bewildered and disillusioned, Schweiger included. He subsequently took redundancy and a small pension. It was the case, however, that apart from the delays and rising costs to the TSR2 project, the logistics of nuclear strike planning had altered dramatically. Polaris had been thoroughly proved in the US, and the also very expensive Resolution-class submarines, which were to carry the system for Britain, were already under construction. And so the future of the TSR2 was already in doubt when it had its maiden flight on 24 September 1965 and soon thereafter drifted off into history. The cancellation of the TSR2, the Hawker P1154 and, a short while later, an Anglo-French project for a variable geometry aircraft exacerbated the gap in the RAF's anticipated inventory. There was now nothing in the pipeline to replace the now virtually obsolete Hunter and the Lightning, the last all-British supersonic combat aircraft, which were also due to be phased out gradually from the early 1970s.

Initially, the RAF ordered 55 American F-111s as a stopgap, but this order was subsequently cancelled in favour of the

McDonnell Phantom FGR2. Its arrival was also delayed when the government required the incoming aircraft to have British Rolls-Royce Spey engines fitted, adding £3 million to the cost of each plane, and it finally came progressively into service from 1968, first with No. 226 OCU at RAF Coningsby. Other Phantom variants were to follow. In the meantime, the RAF was persuaded by Mountbatten, who had never wanted the TSR2 either, to take 50 Buccaneer S2s from the Fleet Air Arm as the Royal Navy was forced to run down the aircraft carrier fleet. The RAF, which had at first derided the navy's hand-me-downs, soon came to love this sturdy striker, especially for its 'superb ride'. Both Phantom and Buccaneer became popular and long-serving members of the strike force, and the younger of the two, the Phantom FGR2 ground attack version, went on to become one of the longest-serving post-war combat aircraft, with almost 120 aircraft being delivered to the RAF over two decades to 1992.

The starting points for all these setbacks and developments were crammed in to a three- to four-year period at the end of the 1960s and early 1970s, and for a while the RAF was unhappily sitting under a cloud of budget restrictions and reorganisation. There was one more major break with historic traditions that set in tow the closure of virtually all the overseas bases. It came with the final withdrawal of British troops from the protectorate of Aden under the terms of independence negotiated by Harold Wilson's government which then decreed it wanted the British all out in a hurry. After 128 years of British rule, the divided country was left in the hands of the People's Republic of South Yemen. For the RAF, the withdrawal presented a massive operation for its Transport Command, which oversaw the largest airlift of personnel, families and stores since the Berlin airlift.

The final restructuring of bringing all commands under one roof as Strike Command brought overall reductions in both personnel, bases and airfields. The new organisation initially contained four groups covering specific roles of operations. Eventually, as new tasks replaced obsolete operations and aircraft such as the V-bombers and the Canberra dropped out of the reckoning, they were contained in three groups: 1 Group was strike attack aircraft, offensive support, tactical and strategic reconnaissance, support helicopters; 11/18 Group was for air defence, surface-to-air missiles, the ballistic missile early-warning radar station at Fylingdales, air defence radar and communications, maritime reconnaissance, anti-submarine warfare, search and rescue; and 38 Group, originally designed as a go-anywhere, ready-for-anything operation, comprised transport aircraft, helicopters, Phantoms and Harrier ground attack aircraft for overseas operations and the Royal Flight.

Whenever an emergency blew up outside the UK, 38 Group would draw the short straw, dealing with anything from humanitarian airlifts to reinforcing ground troops in Belize when Guatemala threatened to attack. In fact, 38 Group became over time something of a model for the future, the kind of versatile forces that were generally recognised as becoming increasingly necessary: highly mobile, multi-capable, immediate deployment, the type that the UK eventually sought to have. Ironically, 38 Group itself was scaled back in terms of its operational aircraft in the 1990s, with certain operations being transferred to other groups. It thus became a more focused group, containing air transport, air-to-air refuelling and the RAF Regiment.

Thus, after one of the most difficult periods in the RAF's peacetime history, harping back in some ways to the post-war deficiencies, the RAF had put in place operational systems that were to carry it forward into the next century, as Air Chief Marshal Sir Joseph Gilbert recalled:

Strike Command was an example of the Royal Air Force reducing in size and therefore slimming down its structure. All the groups were pulled together into Strike Command, eventually to include the rump of Royal Air Force, Germany, so that there became one operational command. The advantages are obvious in that you can have total control over operations. One of the key things that happened was the building of a huge bunker underground at High Wycombe, a headquarters for the air force to withstand nuclear attack. It is still there of course, enormously deep and complex. I mention that because what was created there was a headquarters from which military operations could be commanded worldwide. In the Gulf War [see Chapter Seventeen], for example, that was the headquarters used for commanding the British force and proved itself not simply as a Cold War vehicle but as a headquarters from which you could control operations as far away as the Gulf. The essence of Strike Command is simply that: you can coordinate and pull together air operations in a way that has never really happened in the past.

Nor was the RAF's long experience in the field of nuclear weapons delivery and targeting put aside when the nuclear deterrent role switched to the Royal Navy:

In 1968, under Denis Healey as Defence Minister, there was a return to a more mature consideration of the use of conventional force and a period of conventional operations. On the whole nuclear question, I was sent in 1968 to join the then new defence policy staff and the then Air Vice-Marshal, Neil Cameron, later Marshal of the RAF and Chief of Defence Staff. This developed out of something Healey had set up called a programme evaluation group. I went as a staff officer and was asked to concern myself with the NATO planning group, which started a whole new and really quite intellectual part of my military career. I came back to it in several guises and appointments and was deeply involved in the planning of the acquisition of nuclear weapons, in other words what the British nuclear deterrent should be, what it should consist of. I was involved in policy planning and to some extent the targeting of Polaris missiles, and later I was involved in thinking through the Trident problem, whether to acquire it or not, and the whole issue of how and in what respect nuclear weapons should be used, and what nuclear weapons should be acquired.

This was a whole new dimension, if you like, to thinking the unthinkable. I was quite keen on placing myself before audiences that were not very receptive, usually university audiences . . . and I do believe that the Western nuclear deterrent did work, and any British government now would have to be extremely careful in abandoning a nuclear weapons capability. So far there has not been a government prepared to do that. One had to respect the arguments of those who were against nuclear weapons in any shape or form if it was a purely pacifist argument. But usually one found that people had not had the opportunity that I and others had had to think these things through in coming to the rather ready conclusions they'd come to. All this may be sounding rather trite, especially now when we do not perceive any real nuclear threat, but we don't know, do we? With the possibility of the development of nuclear capability in perhaps Iran or Libya or Iraq we may find that as time goes by we may have to become more concerned with this over the next few years.

The Cold War still dominated operational programmes of defensive measures on the home front and nuclear strike, attack and reconnaissance in Germany. Over the decade of the 1970s, in addition to the underground nuclear-proof bunker at High Wycombe from which the nation's entire air defence network and operational functions were controlled, 12 radar installations around the British Isles were regularly upgraded to keep abreast of threats from supersonic interlopers and the continued incursions of Soviet spy planes into the airspace of the United Kingdom. In addition to all these improvements in the offensive and operational systems, the RAF's inventory of versatile aircraft was further enhanced by the arrival of Anglo-French SEPECAT consortium's Jaguar, which began to enter service in 1973 with the GR1 version and went on to establish itself as one more classic aircraft to add to what was at last becoming a very formidable line-up. Many of the Jaguars would be earmarked to fulfil Britain's role in Germany, which itself underwent a complete overhaul through the 1970s, both in the air and on the ground. Bloodhound surface-to-air missiles were deployed along with the RAF Regiment equipped with Rapier missiles to cover the main air bases of Brüggen, Laarbrüch, Wildenrath and Gütersloh. Nigel Walpole, whom we first met flying fighter reconnaissance aircraft, was impressed:

In 1977 I became Jaguar Force OCU Wing Commander, Operations, at the very big Strike Attack Jaguar base then forming at RAF Brüggen. I arrived in April to a base which had been almost completely rebuilt, one of the first to be fully hardened and aircraft accommodated in hardened aircraft shelters to accommodate four big Jaguar squadrons, 15 each at their peak, with a combat operations centre fully hardened and filtered. I was No. 2 to station commander. There were hardened and filtered facilities for all the pilots, pilot briefing facilities and a very large QRA force compound at one corner of the airfield (fully survivable in a nuclear, biological or chemical environment). The airfield was optimised for contemporary operations and envied by all around us, from all the nations from the 2nd Allied Tactical Air Force. We were now in the strike and attack role, unprecedented in the RAF for a single-seat aircraft.

In the past, nuclear operations had been conducted with two men in the crew with all the validation processes involved. So it was particularly demanding for the crew to be fully prepared and extremely well rehearsed for tactical nuclear weapons as well as conventional operations. The nuclear operations took up a great deal of our time, checked and double-checked continuously by the tactical evaluation team. It was amazing to me how well the single-seat crews coped with this additional burden. Validation was carried out on the ground between the pilot and officers before he got airborne, but of course when he got airborne his finger was on the trigger. They were relatively low-yield weapons for specific preplanned targets, and the procedures were such that they could not be abused or released for delivery accidentally or on purpose by a man who had lost his wits.

My very dramatic and impressive station commander had a notice put up at Brüggen saying: 'Our purpose is to train for war and don't you forget it.' Everything was done to that end, totally realistic. The Jaguar was fairly limited in its weapons at that time: two effective 30-millimetre guns and the 1,000-pound bomb. A cluster bomb unit was the other anti-armour, anti-personnel weapon in support of ground forces. The Jaguar had been developed from a training aircraft, and we had made it into a very successful ground attack aircraft, then for day use only, but later converted to night flying.

There were four categories of evaluation: alert and readiness, operations, support functions and survival to operate. We had a surface-to-air missile site and headquarters on the eastern side of the airfield and our own short-range Rapier missile on an RAF Regiment squadron. Evaluating all these elements on the base, we were the first to be given gradings of one in all four categories. I was brand new to a new facility, new to the Jaguar, but known to others in other aeroplanes called the head-up display in which a lot of weapons and navigation symbology is reflected on the windscreen. It would show you all the usual things, such as height, rate of descent, target, direction, speeds, without you having to go head down into the cockpit as we had to in other aeroplanes in the past. The great advantage was that you could look out while you were looking at your heading and your bank angle, you could see perhaps the possibility of a collision with another aeroplane, a radio mast, birds, etc. So that was invaluable for flight safety and target acquisition.

In my own case, the value was evident on my very last Jaguar trip when I was flying south to north on the edge of the Rhine Valley on the plateau, and as I turned on to the northerly heading I noticed I had a fault with my navigational equipment, and it was while I was head down into the cockpit to remedy this defect that I almost collided with two Dutch 104s which were crossing me from right to left. I do believe as I yanked back on the stick to climb into low cloud I heard the noise of these two 104s. When I pushed forward and came out of the cloud, the 104s were heading on their way. I'm sure they saw me. I saw them too late, and it was a salutary experience not to keep your head into the cockpit more than you absolutely have to. The value of head-up display was very well illustrated there.

The Jaguar was an interesting aeroplane, very pleasant provided you kept to the higher speeds. Down into the lower speeds it was harder to manage, particularly in difficult terrain, and I was particularly unhappy with the reconnaissance version and the huge pod that was slung underneath which affected its manoeuvrability.

Nigel Walpole left Brüggen in 1979, after being promoted to group captain, to go back to the Ministry of Defence, responsible for operational training for the whole of the RAF. To his great delight he was returned to Germany and Rhinedalen in 1982 to become group captain for the offensive operations of two Harrier squadrons, four Jaguar strike attack squadrons at Brüggen, a Jaguar recce squadron at Laarbrüch and two Buccaneer overland strike attack squadrons:

> To me the most important contribution I made to finish my career was the final tour in the same building and the same sort of tag and responsible for offensive operations as Assistant Chief of Operations (Offensive) into 2ATAF under a British three-star officer, a German two-star officer, an American one-star officer, and in company with seven other assistant chiefs responsible for the various arms and support functions, typically air defenders, intelligence, exercisers, and so forth. My job was to coordinate the wartime plans and policy as handed down from above and bring them into practical application and rehearse them in live and paper exercises. For those exercises we deployed our whole staffs of 2nd Allied Tactical Air Force into the wartime headquarters, caves underneath the border between Belgium and Holland at Maastricht [since closed], plus a mobile headquarters which would be deployed into the field to act as a backup if our static war headquarters was destroyed. This to me was an ideal way to finish my career . . .

By the early 1980s, therefore, the structure and the way forward for the Royal Air Force were more or less in place. There was one other important element that had progressed rapidly through the ranks of operational aircraft: the helicopter. Its use advanced dramatically, as did the technology and tactical usage as the RAF prepared to meet the demands of modern times, especially in the area of internal security within the United Kingdom. There was already a wealth of experience to draw on, dating back to the first multiple use of helicopters for casualty evacuation and supply drops in difficult terrain during the Malayan emergency in the late 1940s. From that beginning, they were extensively deployed on the anti-terrorist campaigns in Cyprus and other trouble spots such as Aden and the Radfan mountains in the Middle East. Similarly, helicopters were the only way to travel on deployments over the jungles and the wild terrain of Borneo during what was termed the 'confrontation', which lasted from 1963 to 1966. They proved invaluable for troop insertions in areas where there were no facilities for conventional landings and were soon adopted as an essential tool in Special Forces' operations.

These deployments, generally over impossible landscapes, became the proving grounds for the Wessex on a multitude of tasks in cooperation with the British army, including surveillance, troop insertions, rat and terrier operations against terrorists, casualty evacuation and supply drops. Their versatility became legendary, particularly on those occasions when a particular airlift required a swift landing and a sharp exit, perhaps under fire. The American experience in Vietnam added further to the development of helicopters as gunships and fighting machines suitable for a variety of ground support and combat roles, which were extended further when deployed from ships.

From the RAF's standpoint, these early operations provided, above all, vital experience for the formation of tactics for internal security operations that was soon to confront them in Northern Ireland on a daily basis, in conjunction with army, Royal Marines and Special Forces' units, for decades hence. Thus, when the Troubles flared in 1969, RAF crews – little did they know it then – participated in launching what became the longest and largest continuous deployment of helicopters combined with ground forces on live operations anywhere in the world. That is not a record the RAF is keen to boast about, but it is a fact none the less that RAF Aldergrove performed a significant role as operational base for the squadrons who came and went over the years, working with impartiality at the sharp end of those difficult years.

The base that the RAF has latterly shared with the Army Air Corps is close to Belfast's own civilian airport and was first opened in 1918. It became a fully operational flying station in 1925 and has been involved in the ups and downs of life in Northern Ireland ever since. For much of the time, it has also doubled as a vital Coastal Command station, especially during the Second World War, when Atlantic convoy protection, anti-submarine work and search and rescue operations for distressed mariners were on Aldergrove's doorstep.

It was, then, with more than a touch of irony that many of the crews who returned to the UK expecting a relatively peaceful time after the humdrum of the colonial troubles of the Middle East in 1960s found themselves back in the frontline, in their own country. They were soon to be engaged in situations where, at best, people on the ground considered it something of a sport to take pot shots at passing helicopters of military origin and, at worst, possessed a predilection for blowing them up. In the countryside of Northern Ireland, it would also become something of a challenge not dissimilar to Cyprus.

Helicopters had already made their appearance in Northern Ireland in the 1950s at a time – as is often overlooked in accounts of the Troubles – when the IRA was continuing post-war actions in the province. A mere three Sycamores used for search and rescue by Coastal Command at Aldergrove were formed into No. 118 Squadron to operate with the Royal Ulster Constabulary but were subsequently withdrawn back to the mainland in 1962 when the IRA declared a cease-fire. The return to duties in Northern Ireland was signalled in the summer of 1969 when growing tension within the Catholic and Protestant communities flared into open warfare in Londonderry in the wake of the Apprentice Boys' March. Battles continued for three days in which five people were killed and almost 1,000 injured. The escalation of the conflict has been well documented, but it is worth remembering that in the summer of 1969 there was only a small garrison of 500 British troops in Ulster. By 1972 there were 20,000 uniformed soldiers on the streets of the province, a year which was the province's bloodiest ever with 468 people killed and 5,000 injured.

RAF helicopters came back in the first year of violence, first with a flight of six Westland Wessex HC.2 helicopters of No. 72 Squadron from Odiham. They remained on detachment to Aldergrove. The detachment remained on an *ad hoc* basis for many months. By the end of 1971 a permanent RAF deployment became necessary, working in conjunction with Coastal Command, the Army Air Corps and eventually the Royal Navy's helicopter squadrons as Royal Marines and SBS personnel were drawn in. The RAF's involvement in Northern Ireland thereafter remained on a permanent footing, and in 1981 the Wessex squadron moved its headquarters to Aldergrove to take the commitment to the province into the new millennium. The Wessex tactical transport ground assault helicopter, flown by a crew of three and capable of carrying 16 soldiers, soon became a familiar sight over the troubled areas of Northern Ireland, and was hated by the local people for its noise and by the warring paramilitaries for its intervention in their affairs. The Wessex became the workhorse of many major operations, and its versatility was demonstrated by the various tasks the RAF crews had to perform during those most desperate years of conflict. These included not only the transport of troops but missions exposing the crews to considerable danger in the border territory, known to all as bandit country. The use of helicopter transport at all levels became a crucial element as the IRA began to put great effort into mining roads and laying booby traps along routes likely to be taken by the army's own ground transport. The skill with which these acts were performed was apparent at the scene of the infamous Warrenpoint massacre, aimed at the Parachute Regiment in the wake of Bloody Sunday.

On the afternoon of 27 August 1979 the IRA set up an ambush on the shores of Carlingford Lough, marking the border with the Republic, and followed a style the IRA had perfected over the previous two years. First, they planted a massive 1,000 pounds of explosives under a stone gateway leading to Narrow Water Castle, a medieval building near a stretch of dual carriageway. The bomb had a fuse that could be detonated by a signal from the type of equipment used to control model aeroplanes. The site of the bomb was carefully selected. The IRA men could keep the spot under observation from a hide across the border, 200 yards away, and detonate the bomb at the required moment.

To create the incident that would lure an army force to the spot, the IRA used a second bomb, hidden in a hay lorry. As one of the officers of 2 Para described: 'At this point, the IRA got lucky. They would have blown up any suitable target that came along the road. What in fact did come along was a small convoy from 2 Para – about 30 men travelling in two four-ton trucks and a Land Rover, on a routine movement along the coastal road from Ballykinder en route for A Company's base at the border town of Newry.' The bomb in the hay trailer was detonated from the IRA hide as the third vehicle of the convoy passed, completely destroying one of the four-ton army vehicles. Six soldiers were killed instantly and several others were wounded, two of them very seriously. Ammunition in the blazing lorry was also now exploding, and after tending the wounded the men had to take cover to avoid possible sniper fire. The explosion could be heard for miles, and a detachment of Royal Marines on patrol in Warrenpoint radioed A Company's base at Newry.

Two A Company machine-gun patrols, hearing the radio alert, headed for the explosion site, as did A Company's commander, Major Peter Fursman, who gathered some men and sped off in two Land Rovers. At the same time, the 1st Battalion, The Queen's Own Highlanders, based at Bessbrook, County Armagh, ordered an emergency reaction team into the air, consisting of two RAF Wessex helicopters carrying an assault team and three medics. By the time they reached the scene, the A Company machine gunners had set up roadblocks and the helicopters, which landed on the central reservation, began to bring forward the wounded for evacuation. A third helicopter, a Gazelle, carrying the commanding officer of the 1st Battalion, Queen's Own, Lieutenant-Colonel David Blair, landed in a field. He disembarked and ran to meet Major Fursman, whose two Land Rovers were parked at the gatehouse – at the very spot where the main IRA bomb had been planted. The IRA ambush team, in their hillside hide, had sat it out for 25 minutes after the first explosion. Now they detonated their second bomb and opened up with rifle fire, and this time the carnage was even worse – 12 more servicemen killed and many more seriously injured.

No members of the army forces deployed in Northern Ireland could escape such acts of appalling violence and for many years the RAF crews flew into the very teeth of such operations along with their army colleagues. The Warrenpoint massacre exacerbated the necessity as helicopters became even more widely deployed, especially in area surveillance after an explosion or even a suspected incident had occurred.

As heat-seeking equipment, imaging sensors and other ground-scanning equipment came into use, much of it designed especially for use in Northern Ireland, aerial surveillance became a crucial role of the helicopter squadrons. These involved direct surveillance sorties over meetings and gatherings, such as the showpiece IRA funerals where helicopters were the only form of aircraft that could be used for video and photographic work. Communications and liaison were also a vital area in the positioning of troops, and as in the jungles of Malaya the resupply of outposts and remote operations could be achieved only by helicopters. Casualty evacuation was also a major task, again often under fire or flying into potentially booby-trapped areas or potential ambush sets. Fortunately, the helicopters seemed generally impervious to ground fire, although a Gazelle was shot down near Newry and the crew killed in 1978. Over the 30 years of deployment in Northern Ireland, the RAF helicopters came up against just about every scenario imaginable, and along with army crews they were often applauded by ground forces as the unsung heroes of many operations.

Similar accolades have also been earned aplenty by the helicopter crews of Coastal Command and its successor, RAF Search and Rescue. A winter does not pass without gripping footage of their spectacular missions, usually in appalling and dangerous conditions, appearing on television news bulletins. The number of lives saved by the SAR squadrons now runs into thousands. In 2001, their sixtieth anniversary year, they received 1,095 call-outs involving 745 people and 2,064 flying hours. Finally, the progressive expansion of helicopter operations across the whole spectrum of RAF activity was to be graphically demonstrated in many diverse ways during combat, peacekeeping and humanitarian operations in the second half of the twentieth century, with a range of equipment that has included the Wessexes in their various guises, Pumas, Chinooks and Sea Kings deployed, at their peak, in five squadrons.

CHAPTER SEVENTEEN

Put to the Test

Spending cuts were again on the agenda at the turn of the 1980s, when Margaret Thatcher and her Defence Secretary John Nott made it known to all three services that some trimming had to be made. Among those elements on which the axe was about to fall was the Royal Navy's sole bearer of the White Ensign in the southern hemisphere – the ice-patrol vessel HMS *Endurance* – which would save just £3 million a year from a multi-billion-pound budget, and something of a national debate opened up. The Argentinians were listening and the head of the Argentine military junta, General Leopoldo Fortunato Galtieri, took this to mean that the British no longer cared about its furthest-flung outpost, the Falkland Islands, and used it as an excuse to launch an invasion, stir up some nationalism at home and get him out a spot of difficulty with his domestic economy.

It was time for his nation to reclaim what his people believed was their territory and bestow on the islands their correct title of the Malvinas. Many in the Falklands were expecting this to happen, and some did not even care because, of late, Britain had become something of an absentee landlord to the 1,950 inhabitants of this remote sheep-farming community, although there were signs that this would change because someone had mentioned the word 'oil'. A British embassy military attaché in Buenos Aires had been warning for some time that Argentina was planning an invasion and even predicted – almost to the day

– when it would happen. No one paid much heed, and nor were the appeals to keep the *Endurance* on patrol successful, despite the reports of vastly increased radio traffic monitored by its captain, Nick Barker, RN. He and others had correctly read the signs, and the pleas to keep the *Endurance* in those waters were turned down. Minds were changed only at the very last minute when a group of Argentinian scrap dealers landed on South Georgia – which was not part of the Falklands – and hoisted up their national flag. Galtieri's brave lads would surely soon follow.

Whitehall mandarins went into a rapid huddle. What could be done from 9,000 miles away? According to one who was there, interviewed by the author for a 'previous work on the SBS, the first unit to get ashore, some 'mad, mad schemes were being bandied about . . . one of them quite astonishing: that the British should made a very loud bang in the South Atlantic by Friday 9 April 1982', whatever that meant. Sir Joseph Gilbert was Assistant Chief of Defence Staff (Policy) at the time:

> The war started for different people in different ways. It found me trying to take a bird-watching holiday in the West Country, and I'd just checked into a hotel with my wife when the news came in. We'd had slight inclines beforehand. I'd attended Defence Operations Executive meetings because we were concerned about what the Argentinians were getting up to. I went back to Whitehall and whereas my horizon had been stretched up to 10 years ahead on defence policy planning, it then became maybe a week ahead. It was given to the Defence Policy Staff to determine what we should be doing and how we should go about it. Meanwhile, the operators were doing everything they could to prepare for whatever the government decided. We wrote a paper for the Chiefs of Staff Committee with 14 military options that could be pursued. We had to think laterally, and my recollection is that seven of those options were used. I won't be around for the release of papers in 30 years' time, but the staff colleges of the day will have a field day, forgetting entirely [the procedures] that most of the papers presented to the Chiefs of Staff Committee then were . . . [the result] of the Assistant Chief of Defence Staff (Policy) – i.e. me – being invited to write a paper on thus and thus and thus and

presenting it 24 hours later – or that they had received the paper and had invited me to revise it in the light of their comments and they would take it again in four hours' time. There were no word processors and only one in the CoS secretariat. The only way of doing this was for me to get on to that word processor and type in the essential bits myself, and my staff would provide the ancillary papers.

The Prime Minister herself took command and stated that she wanted to be kept closely informed of the decisions made by the military. It was she personally who announced that a task force of 40 ships was being assembled to carry troops. They would include an advance party of the SBS, SAS and Royal Marines, followed by the 2nd and 3rd Battalions of The Parachute Regiment, the Gurkhas, the Blues and Royals, Scots Guards, Welsh Guards and other famous elements of the British army. The big question, however, was what could the RAF do from such a distance and, indeed, because their contribution received little attention among the welter of other activity at the time, it is often assumed that the RAF weren't greatly involved. In fact, although only peripheral, their actions had a significant impact both on the war itself and in the future operations, especially in the area of in-flight refuelling, which was vital for the Falklands and then the Gulf War at the end of the decade. The way it emerged for the Falklands adventure is one of the great untold stories of that conflict, masked by the drama of the war itself.

Until the Falklands, there had been no projected scenarios in which the Royal Air Force – or its NATO allies generally deployed in the European anti-Cold War measures – would ever need any great capacity for refuelling other than for fighters or bombers. But the Falklands were 9,000 miles away, and there was only one base between the UK and the place of conflict – Ascension Island, roughly halfway. The Vulcan air-to-air refuelling system described in Chapter Fifteen had been out of action for many months in view of the planned retirement of the Vulcan bombers, and although Phantom, Harrier, Sea Harrier and Buccaneer were equipped for refuelling, only the Victor K2 tankers were available to supply fuel en route. The ability to get any large force to the Falklands by air – and keep them flying once there – was therefore impossible at the time of the Argentine invasion.

Aircraft would have to go by sea, using the Royal Navy's Sea Harriers and Sea King helicopters, plus a small number of RAF Harriers, which were taken aboard the task force carriers.

The first detachment of five Victors arrived at Ascension in mid-April to begin operations, with another four coming up behind. They were in for a busy few months. They could receive and dispense fuel and thus, by using a fleet of them, it would be possible to begin limited operations in support of the task force as it began its journey south. First, the Victor tankers flew a succession of three 15-hour radar reconnaissance missions close to the Falklands between 19 and 25 April. Each sortie required four tankers outbound and the same number for the return to Ascension Island.

On the intelligence gained depended the success of an operation intended to deliver a firm message to the Argentinians: that the British were coming. It was a complete success, and on 25 April Special Forces and Royal Marines, who were sent on ahead of the main group, some travelling by nuclear submarine, repossessed the island of South Georgia. It was not actually part of the Falklands but it was of sufficient importance for Mrs Thatcher to come dashing out of No. 10 Downing Street shouting 'Rejoice! Rejoice!' into the waiting television cameras. Six days later, at 4.25 local time on 1 May, the next major shock for the Argentinians was launched when two Vulcan bombers set off from Ascension, each carrying 21 1,000-pound bombs, to attack the Falklands' only airstrip in Port Stanley. One aircraft was designated for the attack and the second was sent as a reserve. To achieve this target would require 11 Victor tankers, in part to dispense fuel to each other and then to the Vulcans. They took off at the rate of one every two minutes and were ordered to maintain radio silence until clear of Ascension because a Soviet spy ship was monitoring operations just a few miles off the end of the runway. One Victor was sent up in reserve and would be needed, because one of the main force had trouble disgorging the fuel hose and had to pull out of the operation. A second casualty followed when the cabin of the Vulcan earmarked for the attack developed pressurisation problems and had to return to base, leaving Flight Lieutenant Malcolm Withers in the reserve Vulcan flying on to Port Stanley with 10 Victor tankers for company in what became the first trial run to get a heavily laden aircraft – in this case 6,000 pounds overweight – into the Falklands.

All seemed to be going to plan until the first fuel transfer an hour and three-quarters after takeoff from Ascension, approximately 850 miles south. Four Victors and the Vulcan filled their tanks from the four Victors that were now to turn back, and it was while going through this process that a severe miscalculation in the amount of fuel required to complete the operation was discovered. The aircraft had used considerably more fuel than expected because an overweight Vulcan flying in formation with tankers meant that neither could operate at optimum efficiency. Only a small differential in fuel consumption over such a distance could, and did, have an enormous effect on consumption. There were now fears that the whole mission was threatened. To ease the deficiency, the four Victors turning back gave fuel from their own reserves to allow the aircraft continuing on to be topped up with the maximum possible. This led to further problems. The aircraft returning to base would do so with a fuel tank that bore no room for manoeuvre. When they arrived back to the sometimes cloud-engulfed Ascension, they would have to go straight in and in the event it was a nerve-jangling, touch-and-go situation.

Nor had the problems going south been resolved. Four more fuel transfers, tanker to tanker and tanker to Vulcan, took place, with the Victors progressively falling out of the formation to fly home. Two of the transfers had been completed in violent weather, using even more fuel than anticipated to get above the storm at about 31,000 feet. With only one Victor remaining, the final fuel transfer was due at 400 miles north of Port Stanley, and for the tanker pilot, Squadron Leader Robert Tuxford, there was to be a tough lesson in crisis management as the two aircraft approached the PNO (Point of No Return – and this became a familiar term on the Falklands run in the months ahead). Tuxford discovered that if he gave Malcolm Withers the fuel he required to make the attack and return to Ascension, the Victor would have insufficient to get home; he would crash into the sea around 600 miles south of the island. It was his decision: they either both turn back then or Tuxford could pass on the fuel and risk getting close enough to Ascension for a relief tanker to come out to meet him. He chose the latter option. Fortunately, he radioed in early enough for a rescue mission to be launched, and a further Victor tanker took to the air to refuel him in good time for him to get home.

Meanwhile, four other Victor tankers had already embarked on progressive takeoffs from Ascension to rendezvous with Malcolm Withers for the return journey after he had dropped his bombs on Port Stanley. This was achieved with a measure of success, leaving a large crater in the airstrip. Although the airstrip was out of action for only a short while, the commanders back at the Royal Navy bunker at Northwood, the command and control headquarters of the war, were delighted, as Joseph Gilbert confirmed:

> Although it was only one crater, it must have had an enormous impact on the Argentinians to have this Vulcan come out of the sky – think of the thousands of miles involved, the fuel and the planning to get it there – and to be bombed out of nowhere. They then realised: 'We're in for it.' So it had a remarkable effect, especially on the morale of the troops.

With the additional tanker that was sent out to meet Tuxford, the number of Victors required to get the Vulcans to the target and back was 15. Withers landed safely back at Ascension after a flight lasting 16 and a half hours. The Northwood commanders were delighted with the result and ordered two more attacks, one on 4 May and one on 11 June, although again the amount of damage was insignificant when compared with the effort involved. By then, Nimrod Mk 2 surveillance and reconnaissance planes were also operating as the Task Force headed south, having been fitted with refuelling gear and their crews trained for air-to-air refuelling in 48 hours. This allowed them to penetrate close to the Argentine operations and provide vital surface surveillance from high level as the British ships approached. The Nimrods flew sorties lasting 20 hours a time, and they, too, were kept aloft by a continuous fuel service from the Victors.

Meanwhile, the RAF was also tasked to send Harrier GR3s to join the task force. These came from No. 1 Squadron from RAF Wittering, then the only UK-based Harrier unit, which began carrier takeoff and landing exercises on RNAS *Yeovilton*. The initial party of nine Harriers, accompanied by Victor air-to-air refuelling tankers, then set off for the forward base at Wideawake airport on Ascension. From there, six were loaded on the container ship *Atlantic Conveyor* for the journey south and were eventually transferred to the aircraft carrier HMS *Hermes*. The Harriers were deployed with the Royal Navy's own larger contingent of Sea Harriers, operating from the carriers of the task force to provide cover for the ships as well as ground attack and close support to the first elements of the 10,000 land forces as they stormed ashore towards their own battle start-lines.

Air activity was considerable as the Sea Harriers sought to assert air superiority as quickly as possible, although that had by no means been achieved when the first land forces went ashore on 19 May. During the campaign as a whole, the Harriers recorded 20 Argentine aircraft shot down, with the loss of eight of their own brought down or damaged by ground fire. Replacements were urgent by the end of May, and now the only way forward was to fly down the four RAF Harriers waiting at Ascension. Two were dispatched on this incredible journey on 1 June using the Victor tankers for air-to-air refuelling with Nimrods performing search and rescue backup in the event that the Harriers were forced to ditch. The remaining two GR3s left by the same route on 8 June.

On 29 May the Harriers already *in situ* were being used for offensive air support and were, for example, a welcome addition overhead as 2 Para launched its heroic assault on Goose Green. Even so, 17 paras were killed, including Lieutenant-Colonel H. Jones, commanding officer of 2 Para, who was posthumously awarded a Victoria Cross after leading a charge on a submachine-gun post which was holding up their advance. A replacement was appointed to take command of the battalion, Colonel Jones's good friend and long-time colleague, Lieutenant-Colonel David Chaundler, who was at that time working in Whitehall at the Ministry of Defence. He would have to be literally parachuted into the Falklands after he was first flown to Ascension Island, where he was put aboard one of the giant RAF Hercules C130 transport freighters that were now operating from Wideawake air base:

It was a very interesting journey. I was the only person in the back, apart from a parachute jump instructor, who was there to get me out of the aircraft when the time came, and two army dispatchers, who were the throw my kit out of the aircraft in the sea after I'd jumped (and who incidentally slept for the entire journey south). The in-flight refuelling process was absolutely riveting as the pilot had never done it for real before. The maximum speed of the Hercules is slower than the minimum speed of the Victor tankers which were refuelling us. So the whole thing had to be done downhill* so that the C130 could get up enough speed to get the nozzle into the cone to receive the fuel. We had two goes at it, and I didn't like to ask what would happen if they couldn't get it in. We refuelled twice, and it took three tanking aircraft to get the Hercules down to the Falklands.

When we reached the Falklands, it was dusk and the weather was appalling. There were white horses on the sea and a high wind. The parachute jump instructor looked out and said: 'I can't allow you to jump in these conditions because you're not water-trained.' That was true, but I replied: 'Look, I've just spent 12 hours flying down here and I'm not going to spend another 12 hours flying straight back again – I'm jumping. So out I went and landed a mile from the frigate that was supposed to pick me up. I spent half an hour in the sea, with a leaky suit, before a little boat from the frigate finally found me and plucked me out, very wet and cold.

Similar operations were necessary when a signal was received from one of the three nuclear submarines operating in the Falklands, *Splendid*. She had developed problems with one of her two turbogenerators. A spare part was packed in a timber case at the home base and was to be parachuted to a given rendezvous from a Hercules freighter – again going through the same refuelling procedures that David Chaundler had witnessed. Unfortunately, when the timber case hit the waves, it splayed open and the machinery sank to the bottom. A replacement was sent by the same route a week later, but that became contaminated by seawater during the drop. In the end, the submarine's engineers carried out emergency repairs themselves.

* The RAF tanker crews call it a toboggan manoeuvre.

The long haul south would become a daily routine for Hercules crews over the coming months to airlift thousands of tons of supplies, vehicles and personnel, eventually engaging Nos. 24, 30, 47 and 70 Squadrons from RAF Lyneham. Several of the Hercules were themselves hurriedly converted into fuel-carrying tankers, while others had their standard fuel tanks substantially enlarged so that greater quantities of fuel could be carried and to resolve technical problems that arose from the Victor-to-Hercules transfers. Long-time people carrier and general-purpose pilot, Flight Lieutenant John Rowlands, originally a specialist in the tricky old Hastings transports which he used to drop supplies to troops in the jungles of Borneo back in the 1960s, had recently converted to Hercules:

In 1982 I joined Hercules as the aircraft were being converted to make long-range flights for supply drops down to the Falklands. We began by learning the AAR [air-to-air refuelling] procedure behind a Victor tanker. It was incredible. I never thought I'd be able to do it, just putting the probe into the hole while flying this giant at 200 knots chasing a Victor. I was able to manage quite successfully after the second attempt, over several hours. Other people took a longer time, but once you've mastered it it's like riding a bike. The procedure was that the Hercules would take off with a maximum weight of fuel, wait for it to burn down and then take some more fuel on from a Victor tanker. But we discovered that taking on fuel from the Victor tanker could be a tricky manoeuvre. You had to go through the Victor's slipstream to take up your receiving position and until you got there, in the slipstream, you took quite a bit of rough. Once inside the slipstream, it's fairly calm unless there's turbulence or you start swinging a bit. Then it's terrible. We also hit another problem which we resolved with the toboggan manoeuvre. Often, you couldn't stay plugged in because as we gained weight we had difficulty in remaining straight and level as the aircraft dropped in height. The Victor, being much faster, came down as slow as it could, to about 210 knots, while we were at full throttle, but that didn't resolve the problem. We had to get the Victor tanking aircraft to descend during the tanking procedure.

317

A typical freighter flight to and from Ascension would involve six Victors to progressively fuel each other and the Hercules, which would take on board between 18,000 and 22,000 pounds of fuel, depending on the winds. A typical contact would entail the Victor trailing his hose, and the Hercules would come in with the co-pilot talking the captain into position – up, left, right – until contact was made. The final transfer would take 20 to 25 minutes at around 23,000 feet. As the toboggan operations began, the two aircraft would zoom down, descending at an alarming rate of around 500 feet a minute, to perhaps 12,000 or even 8,000 feet, depending on the weather. The lowest in-flight toboggan drop recorded was down to around 6,800 feet, which everyone agreed was too close for comfort. This procedure was also necessary in the early stages of Hercules tanker operations and was made even more uncomfortable when the crew of the tanker had to put on oxygen masks and open up the back end of the aircraft to trail the fuel hose. The crews were very glad when need for the toboggan procedure was substantially reduced by the introduction in August of Hercules C1Ks, which had been hurriedly converted with long-range tanks and the refuelling hose leading out through a sealing door. Sixteen freight-carrying Hercules were also modified into the receiver-only mode, some with extra-large tanks to extend their range. Even so, there were some hair-raising moments as the journeys back and forth were stepped up, and a number of aircraft arrived back at Ascension with their fuel tanks virtually empty, as John Rowlands recalls:

On Ascension, we saw a huge amount of activity. When we first went there in June, all round there were boxes of munitions, torpedoes, missiles, everything you could think of . . . It was bullets and buns – food and ammunition – with dozens of ships coming in with supplies and troops to be ferried down to the Falklands, and initially it was necessary for the Hercules freighters to drop the load without landing [as with David Chaundler and the submarine spares]. Even after the war had ended and the runway at Stanley repaired, we might find it was impossible to get in because of the weather and would simply have to turn round and come back again. That was often the case when you arrived over

318

Port Stanley until they finally managed to install precision-approach radar.

It was one of the most amazing places I've ever been to, where you could have four seasons in a day. The record for the longest flight was held by Flight Lieutenant Lock, who was in the air for 28 and three-quarter hours from Ascension and back. Later on, arrangements were made to enable us to divert to refuelling stations in South America if necessary – except of course when we were carrying VIPs. Margaret Thatcher went down with one of my friends; I refuelled the plane carrying her. I also took the governor of the Falklands, Sir Rex Hunt, back, and later the Secretary of State for Defence, Michael Heseltine, and his party. That was the most interesting one I'd ever flown out of Ascension. We had seven aircraft airborne to accompany us: three Victor tankers with one in reserve and two Hercules tankers with one in reserve to support my long-range Hercules freighter, which had a couple of extra tanks. The total fuel involved was 400,000 pounds. The freighter could land with a maximum amount of fuel, 62,000 pounds so that if we couldn't get in (because of bad weather) we could turn round and comfortably begin our return journey back to Ascension, because it wasn't deemed a good idea at that time to take the VIPs to the South American mainland. The aircraft was fitted with a VIP pack, a portable cabin with special seats, a proper loo, a first-class steward who had mustered up some Chablis, and there was everything you could wish for on a trip of that nature. There were a few extra people on board, about 19 in all, and they all came to the flight deck when we were carrying out the AAR; you couldn't move. I don't think they had been adequately briefed about the journey, because some of them quite clearly didn't know what to expect. They were quite amazed when they saw the tanker aircraft right in front of them – just a few feet away.

In all I did about 2,000 hours flying freighters and tankers down to and around the Falklands, sometimes refuelling fighters over the period of the next year, and there were quite a few hairy moments, because sometimes it was quite difficult for the freighter to make contact with the tanker because of the weather or cloud. One of the RVs [rendez-vous points] was often in a bunch of cloud, which tended to be rather exciting. There were occasions when the aircraft lost each other or missed the RV altogether because of foul conditions. Fortunately, there were never any accidents. We were very lucky considering the massive amount of traffic flying back and forth. There were, however, some interesting incidents of airmanship. I was trundling along in the tanker one day when the accompanying aircraft came past and got on ahead. This was rather strange since I was his refuelling station, and most people prefer to stay behind and keep the tanker in sight. Anyhow, he disappeared into the distance and later he rang up and said: 'Can't you go any faster?' I said I could if I dumped his fuel, because we were far heavier than him. You could see a 'thinks' bubble in the distance and the gap between us started decreasing.

The Hercules also became a lifeline in communications for the troops themselves, arranging mail drops and pick-ups. An ingenious system was invented whereby two poles were erected with wire strung between them with another wire hanging down with a mailbag attached. The Hercules would fly low over the area, drop the mail and then wind a hook out of the back of the aircraft and come in again to snatch the mailbag before flying home. During the course of the campaign itself, the Hercules squadrons, along with a private concern flying ex-RAF Short Belfasts, shifted 7,000 tons of supplies and 5,500 personnel. The Hercules transport flights were to run for many months, and again intensified when the new airfield was being constructed with Air Vice-Marshal Eric Macey, the former Vulcan pilot, involved in the development.

In fact, trips were still being made two years later when six crews went to participate in another major humanitarian mission, Operation Bushell, to being much-needed relief to the starving millions of Ethiopia, hit by a great famine in the autumn of 1984. The mission was in response to revelations of the horrific scale of the crisis, revealed in a BBC television report by Michael Buerk, and the sight of emaciated children clinging to their dying parents brought an incredible response from the British public. The RAF crews were first there, setting up a tented headquarters outside Addis Ababa, which was ironically in the midst of a lavish celebration marking the creation of a Communist state. The crews first carried out reconnaissance missions to get the lie of the land, and then began moving grain, tents and medical supplies around the country. After frustrating delays by local bureaucracy, they were soon running an effective system of daily deliveries, with aircraft loaded with grain which had arrived the night before and flown the next morning throughout the blighted area before the international relief agencies took over. Later came the aid resulting from worldwide efforts as Bob Geldof's famous pop concert under the title of Live Aid. It was the forerunner of several humanitarian efforts involving RAF transport squadrons over the next couple of decades.

The Falklands conflict had been one that involved the forces of the United Kingdom in a purely national effort, in that it involved no other allied forces, other than cooperation from the Americans' intelligence-gathering over their satellite system. This was an ongoing facility shared among the five-nation linkup in electronic surveillance under the UKUSA Agreement involving the US, Britain, Canada, Australia and New Zealand set up during the Second World War. Britain's NATO partners were not called on. Nor did the Falklands diversion diminish the attention of the Royal Air Force in its front-line commitment to Cold War duties, either at home or in Germany. This was a one-off excursion outside the European operations on which the RAF had been directly focused since the pull-out from the Middle East. Had anyone in the various planning committees suggested at that stage that the end of the Cold War was in sight, they would have been recommended for psychiatric treatment. There were no signs of a thaw in East–West relations, and in fact President Ronald Reagan even turned up the pressure when he famously dubbed the Soviet Union the 'evil empire' and two days later revealed his controversial 'Star Wars' defence programme.

NATO was therefore in the middle of attempting to achieve even deeper affiliation among its member nations in which Britain played a leading role. For the Royal Air Force the 1980s saw a consolidation and expansion of the work achieved under the banner of Strike Command during the previous decade. This was especially marked by the arrival of another of the operational stars of the next decade and beyond, the brilliant Tornado developed by the international consortium of Panavia, which delivered its first version to a training establishment at Cottesmore for the three nations involved in its development: Britain, Germany and Italy. In 1982 No. 9 Squadron became the first to fly the GR1 strike-attack version, followed by No. 617 Squadron, and progressively over the next six years seven squadrons in Germany were equipped with Tornados, followed by seven squadrons in the UK, who took delivery of the Air Defence Variant, the Mark II, and subsequently the definitive F3, gradually replacing the Phantoms. These changes brought virtually every arm of the Royal Air Force up to peak performance, and when the time came to put it to the test it was thankfully not the Soviet Union who were on the opposing side, but the iniquitous and callous Middle Eastern dictator Saddam Hussein who would draw the firepower of an international coalition of daunting weaponry.

The West had been well warned about the madness of Saddam. First he bombarded his enemy with mustard gas during the Iran–Iraq War in 1984 when thousands of casualties were gathered up from the battlefields. Then, in March 1988 he launched his infamous genocidal attack on his own people, which intelligence experts believed was an experiment to test the effectiveness of his chemical and biological weapons, manufactured, incidentally, with materials and technology bought from America, Britain, Germany and Italy. The result was catastrophic, and the world would soon see the result with the publication of horrific photographs of some of the 4,000 men, women and children in Kurdish villages who were killed. Another 20,000 people were seriously affected by the poisons, which consisted of mustard gas, nerve gas and hydrogen cyanide.

When a United Nations investigation team arrived, the death toll had risen to 5,500. Yet in spite of professed outrage, the West did nothing and continued to do business with Iraq simply because it was the enemy of Iran. A few weeks later, Britain even approved £400 million a year new trade credits for exports to Iraq from a dozen household-name companies. America also carried on trading with Saddam Hussein, France lent him the money to buy Mirage F1EQs and the Russians were more than happy to sell him some MiGs.

Now, that grave error of judgement was returning to haunt the world leaders who sat back and allowed the Iraqi psychopath to acquire materials to build a vast armoury of chemical weapons, set up the beginnings of a nuclear weapon plant and amass a substantial collection of Scud missiles, not to mention arming the world's fourth-largest army and an air force flying 250 combat aircraft. The Iraqis possessed a strong surface-to-air force, with 6,000 SAMs and 10,000 anti-aircraft guns. When suitably equipped, and with his troops and air force back to strength after the war with Iran, Saddam Hussein invaded Kuwait on 2 August 1990.

And so the RAF prepared to return to old stamping grounds that had been vacated almost 30 years earlier and where, in fact, some of the buildings erected for them in times past were still standing. With Saudi Arabia threatened by the massive build-up of Iraqi troops, President George Bush began to muster support of the nations of the world who eventually sent troops to form the coalition forces for Operation Desert Storm. Much has been written on the unfolding events of those few months, and this narrative will therefore focus predominantly on the RAF's role while recognising that they were just one relatively small element of the massive coalition response to the Iraqi invasion.

The High Wycombe underground fortress of Strike Command was immediately designated the operational control centre of all British operations under Air Chief Marshal Sir Patrick Hine. Britain and America mobilised their air forces to send operational patrols – including 12 Tornado F3s – over north-eastern Saudi Arabia. Within a month, allied air forces had put more than 1,200 aircraft into the region, while naval forces were heading towards the Persian Gulf. There followed a period of political and diplomatic activity during which time Saddam Hussein's forces brutalised the citizens of Kuwait, took thousands of them away to Iraq, many of whom were never seen again, and took Western hostages whom he threatened to chain to the military installations if the allied aircraft violated Iraqi territory. While the United Nations deliberated on an American-led resolution to order Iraq to quit Kuwait or suffer the consequences, coalition forces began to pour into the tented cities set up around the region in preparation for a war, a massive movement of men and machines that took almost four months to complete. Conflict became inevitable when Iraq failed to respond to a UN deadline to get out of Kuwait by midnight on 15 January 1991.

By then, 720,000 men and women from 30 countries had been assembled, along with 2,420 ground-based and carrier aircraft, 530 attack helicopters and 150 warships and four submarines armed with cruise missiles. The RAF contribution to the coalition as hostilities began was 18 Tornado F3 fighters, 46 Tornado GR1 strike/attack and reconnaissance aircraft, 12 Jaguar fighter-bomber aircraft, 12 Chinook helicopters and 19 Puma helicopters capable of lifting 20 men at a time. Additionally, Buccaneers and Tornados came in later. Three Nimrods from Kinloss were in operation over the Gulf from 10 September to enforce a United Nations embargo of certain goods getting into Iraq and in that role carried out almost 400 sorties even before hostilities began.

As ever, there was massive involvement from the RAF's air transport using their own aircraft from seven strategic transport squadrons: Nos. 24, 30, 47 and 70, operating Hercules freighters and tankers, No. 101 flying VC10s, No. 206 with TriStars and No. 55 with their ancient Victor tankers. Air transport also oversaw the involvement of dozens of commercial aircraft, ranging from Boeing 707s to the ex-RAF Belfast heavy-lift planes, brought in to join the huge logistical operation of ferrying thousands of tons of materials and troops, while 17 heroic AAR tankers comprising seven Victors and 10 VC10s or TriStars, small in number though they were, were highly praised throughout the campaign in supplying fuel to combat aircraft from whatever air force needed it and often over enemy territory. During the course of the campaign, RAF transport moved 25,000 passengers, 54,000 tons of freight and flew more than 50,000 hours. The RAF Regiment was also deployed with the Wing HQ, two Rapier Squadrons and four Light Armour Field Squadrons, bringing the total RAF personnel involved to 7,000, including those operating out of Cyprus.

Another small but vital force that began operations even before the firing started was a flight of Tornado GR1A reconnaissance aircraft. Six were based at Dhahran from 14 January and importantly possessed a night-time recce ability. They flew singly and unarmed at 200 feet and at speeds in excess of 600 knots deep into enemy territory. They were particularly relied on for post-attack reconnaissance, line searches and hunting Scud-missile sites and returned with valuable recorded material for analysis.

Once under way, the first ever major war shown live on television produced frighteningly spectacular footage of the first night of the assault on Baghdad on 16–17 January. First, the shadowy American Stealth bombers hit key command centres in the heart of the Iraqi capital while helicopters attacked early-warning systems. Then came the launch of 62 Tomahawk cruise missiles from US navy ships in the Red Sea, followed by wave after wave of attacks from 700 coalition aircraft across the whole of Iraq.

For the British Tornados, the principal task was in the counter-air role, leading raids on the key airfields among 24 heavily fortified main operating bases, including the largest, Tallil air base in south-east Iraq, which was twice the land area of London's Heathrow Airport. All the major airfields were surrounded by efficient defence systems and well protected by a largesse of SAMs and anti-aircraft emplacements. The Tornado GR1s were tasked specifically to bomb more than a dozen Iraqi main runways at low level, a risky business which the Americans did not much care for and in fact were not equipped to do. US fighters swooped in first to brush aside the Iraqi air defences and launch HARM anti-radiation guided missiles to attack ground missile sites, anti-aircraft radars and early-warning systems. Even so, the Tornado crews were still confronted by intense anti-aircraft fire as they flew towards their targets. A more effective method of attacking the airfields was quickly established, with Tornados using conventional 1,000-pound 'toss' bombs backed up with aircraft equipped with the JP233 multi-munitions weapon, originally designed for attacks on Warsaw Pact airfields in Europe. It came in a dual package slung beneath the fuselage of the Tornados and was dropped simultaneously to release 215 area-denial bombs and 30 others causing craters in the runways. Additionally, ALARMs (Air-Launched Anti-Radiation Missiles) were rushed into use by the RAF Tornados shortly before the war began for suppression of enemy air defences (SEAD) operations. Attacks continued virtually around the clock, with Tornados flying by night and Jaguars involved in daylight sorties. Tornado

F3s mounted continuous combat air patrols close to international borders with VC10 and Victor tankers in support for refuelling.

These attacks, combined with those of all allied air contingents, rapidly knocked down Iraqi air power in key areas, putting eight airfields out of action and damaging a number of others. As surface-to-air defences were effectively put out of operation, the Tornados were able to resort to daylight operations above the reach of Iraqi anti-aircraft fire, which had remained the Iraqis' most effective defence. Within four days of the commencement of operations, Saddam Hussein's air force was effectively knocked out, with many aircraft destroyed and others flown off into hiding – some even in Iranian territory. The RAF played a significant role in this better-than-expected rout, with a loss to themselves of four Tornados.

Tornado GR1s flying medium-level now began sorties using free-fall bombs to attack assorted Iraqi ground targets and were soon to be joined by Buccaneers of the OCU, Lossiemouth, equipped with Pave Spike laser-guided designators whose accuracy and those of similar smart-bomb systems in use by the Americans were soon amazing television viewers. This success was joined in mid-February with the arrival of brand-new thermal-imaging laser weapons for use by Tornados, and the ability to put a laser-guided bomb through the front door of an Iraqi storage dump added a new dimension to the term 'precision bombing.'

With air superiority established, Tornados began hitting Iraqi supply lines. Of particular interest was the main highway between Baghdad and Basra, which contained 30 bridges that became the scene of utter carnage at the end of the war as troops tried to make their escape back to the capital. The highway was a favoured target of Tornados and Buccaneers, and many of the bridges were destroyed before launching the attack on the Iraqi air bases to thwart any attempt by the remnants of the enemy air force to return to the fray. Southern airfields in particular were blasted during a four-day onslaught as well as military bases to the battle front. By then, two-thirds of the Tornado sorties were made with laser-guided bombs with considerable success.

The Jaguar bombers had also resorted to attacking supply dumps and surface-to-air missile sites but were particularly active against Iraqi shipping and coastal installations using their newly introduced CVR7 high-velocity rocket equipped with an anti-armour warhead. The Jaguar was capable of carrying four launchers each containing 19 rockets. Its flat and exceedingly accurate trajectory was used in strikes against Iraqi naval targets and virtually cleared out all enemy ships along the coast, sinking 15 in 10 days of operations. They then moved on to attacks on Silkworm missile sites, SAM and artillery emplacements lining the Kuwaiti coast, although again the Jaguars had to dodge a hail of anti-aircraft fire. An area bombing strategy was introduced to allow the Jaguars to operate above the range of the guns, this time using a weapon new to them, the CBU87, which was an American cluster bomb containing more than 200 armour-piercing fragmentation bomblets. Up to five of these weapons could be carried on a Jaguar, and they were used with what RAF reports described as 'spectacular results'.

The air sorties continued relentlessly until the war commanders were ready to launch the ground war on 24 February, when Puma and Chinook helicopters came into their own, with army units carrying out resupplies, troop insertion and special forces operations, airlifting equipment and, later, evacuating casualties and prisoners. The advance of allied tanks and ground troops behind a devastating artillery barrage supported by swarms of allied aircraft literally queuing up to attack the Iraqi bunkers, dugouts and tanks put Saddam Hussein's army to flight. Within three days it was all over: the 100-hour ground war was won, facilitated by a month of unremitting allied air operations. The allies had launched between 2,000 and 3,000 sorties a day throughout the conflict, with an average of one bombing sortie occurring every minute of every day in spite of poor weather and the smoke from the 167 Kuwaiti oil wells set ablaze by retreating Iraqi forces. Over 110,000 sorties were flown by coalition aircraft during the entire campaign, of which 6,327 were carried out by the Royal Air Force for the loss of six Tornados. More than 88,000 tons of bombs were dropped during the campaign, 7,500 of which were precision-guided. Overall, the coalition lost just 41 aircraft with another 33 accidentally written off.

Much of Iraq's strategic installations lay in ruins, and Iraqi losses included 3,700 tanks, 2,400 armoured personnel carriers, 2,600 artillery pieces, 14 warships and 11 auxiliary vessels. The

Allies estimated that Iraq suffered 150,000 casualties, with over 100,000 taken prisoner, but controversially they did not include Saddam Hussein himself, and as a result the RAF would soon be back in action over this forlorn land.

Chapter Eighteen

Busier Still

Confirmation that the Cold War was as good as over came with the failure of a plot by Communist hardliners to overthrow Soviet President Mikhail Gorbachev, author of *glasnost*, in August 1991, and the fear among Western leaders of a return to the bad old days proved to be unfounded. Boris Yeltsin won the first free presidential elections in Russia's 1,000-year history, signalling the anticipated dismantling of the Soviet Union and all the military hardware stacked up against the borders of the NATO allies. There were, however, concerns about long-term instability as the Soviet republics and remaining Communist-aligned Warsaw Pact nations made their dash for independence. As it turned out, only Yugoslavia, with its dictatorial clone of a fading era, Slobodan Milošević, would present any lasting problems.

He first demonstrated his intent on maintaining the status quo when he ordered his police force to open fire on his own people during an anti-Communist demonstration by 100,000 people in Belgrade's Republic Square, which he had personally banned. Thereafter, he attempted to maintain the status quo in Yugoslavia as member nations within his empire began to press for independence. This, along with his personal belligerence, set the region on a course of events escalating into appalling ethnic violence. The result was that along with unfinished business in Iraq, which called for considerable intervention from Britain and the United States, the Royal Air Force was embarking on one of its most consistently demanding periods since the Second World War. Ironically, it coincided with the arrival of two major reviews of defence policy and spending, in 1990 and 1994, both of which would result in what modern terminology would describe as further downsizing.

The first of these, called *Options for Change*, which was presented by Margaret Thatcher's then Defence Secretary, Tom King, a week before the Iraqi crisis began, was drastic. The strength of the three services would be cut by 18 per cent and the British Army of the Rhine and RAF Germany would be halved. The Cold War, which had engaged such a large percentage of service personnel for so long, was officially declared over. The whole structure of the RAF would come under the microscope, although it was clear from the outset that a number of squadrons would be axed as the overall manning level was reduced from 89,000 to 75,000. Phantoms and Buccaneers were listed for retirement and their squadrons were to be either disbanded or transferred to Tornados. There were other fairly comprehensive changes at the top of the RAF structure, along with a judicious pruning of training establishments and other services within the organisation to reflect the decrease in the numbers coming through.

The Gulf War did not change political minds, and the downsizing went ahead in spite of a sudden emergence of further trouble in Iraq and disconcerting developments in Yugoslavia. The first of these unsavoury events began in April 1991 when it became apparent that Saddam Hussein's leadership of Iraq remained as firm as ever and he made it clear that anyone who thought otherwise would be shot – as indeed many were, including some from his own family. The only group who attempted to complete what President George Bush had refused to contemplate were Kurds of northern Iraq. They launched an unlikely attempt to overthrow Saddam Hussein, and in the true gangster style for which he has become renowned the dictator turned his battle-weary troops against the unarmed Kurdish people, resulting in a mass exodus of terrified communities. More than two million people fled into the mountainous regions of northern Iraq, southern Turkey and even across the border into Iran. Without food, water or shelter and in appalling weather conditions, a human tragedy of gargantuan proportions began to unfold. President Bush, who was bumbling along towards being ousted himself, refused to let America get involved. From a fishing trip in Florida, he declared that no parent wanted to risk 'precious American lives in what is ostensibly an Iraqi civil war', which of course it wasn't. Margaret Thatcher, now out of office herself, stepped in angrily, declaring: 'Surely it is not beyond the wit of man to get planes there with tents, food and water.'

Prime Minister John Major responded by ignoring Bush's gutless dismissal of the Kurds' plight and put up £20 million in aid. The RAF was told to stand by for a humanitarian effort ahead of the Prime Minister's personal solution to the crisis, that of establishing a United Nations safe haven for the Kurds protected by an international force. The UN moved as swiftly as its bureaucracy would allow and within a week approved a resolution in line with Major's suggestion, warning Saddam Hussein of severe repercussions if he harassed the Kurdish communities any further. Thus, George Bush was shamed into recommitting American troops to resume hostilities if it became necessary, 'although only as a last resort'. What in fact happened was the establishment of a no-fly zone over which Iraqi aircraft would be shot down, and to cap it all an unseemly row developed between Downing Street and the White House when the Americans claimed that 'safe haven' was their idea.

British, French, Turkish and American forces were deployed to enforce it and to begin flying in aid and shelter. Five thousand Royal Marines and French paratroops were among troops flown in to protect the Kurds and to help organise the logistical problems in feeding and sheltering the starving hordes. RAF Jaguar GR1s of Nos. 6, 41(F) and 54 Squadrons and American A-10s supported by Victor tankers from No. 55 Squadron based at Akrotiri, Cyprus, moved up to cover the arrival of the aid and to shoot down any Iraqi aircraft that strayed into the no-fly zone. They were later joined by Harriers from the UK. Meanwhile, a fleet of coalition transports, including Hercules from RAF Lyneham, began hauling tons of supplies to the refugees, whose plight had moved from appalling to absolutely desperate. Their efforts were aided locally by RAF helicopters diverted from their intended route back to the UK after service in the Gulf War. The no-fly zone was also extended to cover the Shiahs in the south, who also came under attack from Iraqi aircraft, and although both situations eventually returned to comparative normality in that time frame, it was by no means the end of the commitment. Saddam Hussein would provide the RAF with some side action for the rest of the decade and into the next millennium.

Even as the RAF were cleaning out the backs of the Hercules and giving the aircraft a much-needed service, further tasking for the RAF was already being signalled by the end of the year. Throughout 1991, the Balkans had flared into bloody inter-ethnic strife, which grew more threatening to the stability of the region as each month passed. Both Slovenia and Croatia, following the lead of former Communist-dominated states in Eastern Europe, declared independence from the iron hand of Milošević's Serbian-led Federal Socialist Republic of Yugoslavia. The unravelling of the states unwillingly thrown together after the First World War – which was sparked by the assassination of the heir to the Austro-Hungarian throne by a Serb on the streets of Sarajevo in June 1914 – was of great concern to the nations of the European Union, but they shied away from serious involvement.

By July, expatriates of most of the EU nations were being advised to leave the country immediately and, sure enough, full-scale fighting broke out first between the Slovenians and the Serb-controlled federal army and then between the Croats and Serbs. The EU proposed to send in a European peacekeeping force to manage a cease-fire but then backed down because of dissension among the nations, and the whole powder-keg situation blew up again. As Dubrovnik came under siege, the United Nations Security Council became involved and ordered a cease-fire that would be monitored by a UN peacekeeping force. The warring factions ignored both.

The countdown to what history shows was the beginning of almost a decade of the most brutal of wars, punctuated by crimes against humanity of a kind not seen since the Second World War, was being played out against the backdrop of the final curtain for the Soviet Union. All year, since the plot to dethrone Gorbachev, tension had mounted between the republics that formed the Soviet Union. On 8 December Russia, the Ukraine and Byelorussia agreed to the formation of the Commonwealth of Independent States. Two weeks later the Soviet Union ceased to exist, Gorbachev as its President found himself out of a job and Boris Yeltsin, as President of Russia, became the second most powerful man in the world. All that remained was to resolve the question of whose finger was on the trigger of the 27,000 nuclear weapons that now no longer had any central control.

Milošević was out on his own as one of the last remaining Communist leaders of Eastern Europe, and in 1992 he made it clear that he was determined to keep his act together in spite of a referendum in Bosnia-Herzegovina in which 62 per cent of the population, mostly Muslims, were in favour of independence. The minority Serbs, who controlled more than 60 per cent of the territory, voted against, and another war, the longest and bloodiest of them all to date, began to reach television news and the front pages of newspapers around the world. At its heart, the beautiful city of Sarajevo gradually descended into bitter fighting and, ultimately, ruin. In one month from the declaration of independence, 300 civilians were killed.

In May the United Nations Security Council voted to impose sanctions on Serbia as Bosnian Serbs, backed by Milošević, launched a fierce attack on Sarajevo to put the city under siege. On 8 June 1992 the UN authorised a humanitarian airlift to carry food into the beleaguered city under the protection of a 1,000-strong blue-helmeted UN force as a preliminary to the gathering of a 20,000-strong force to move in during the winter of 1992 with the RAF involved in logistics and transport. In August John Major announced a British contribution to support the United Nations High Commission for Refugees operations but time was needed to assemble and prepare such a force, and it was winter before the 1st Battalion, Cheshire Regiment, and a reconnaissance team from 9/12 Royal Lancers moved in under the overall command of 1st Cheshire CO Colonel Bob Stewart to join the UNProFor operations. The UN role, filled with complexities, restrictions, local opposition and with one arm tied behind its back, was for the most part impossible from the start because, as Bob Stewart strongly observed in his autobiography, 'The Cheshire group . . . were not there to "make peace"; we were not enforcers of it. Helping to create conditions for peaceful resolution of disputes was one thing, but forcing a cessation of hostilities was certainly outside our charter. Peacekeepers have to react to events while enforcement troops may have to create them.'

The same applied to the Royal Air Force in its eventual role. The aircraft flying in the humanitarian aid were mostly civilian transport planes to begin with, hired by the United Nations because Britain and America, at that point, were in no hurry to get involved. On 2 July 1992, however, a heavily armed, blue-helmeted Canadian infantry battalion of the advance UN force seized control of the airport, and now the UN called for military transport to step up the aid flights to eight a day. Once again, the RAF Hercules squadrons came to the rescue, along with aircraft of other nations, to join what became the longest airlift of food and supplies in history, running from July 1992 to January 1996.

During that time, the RAF Hercules carried 26,577 tons of aid in more than 2,000 flights into Sarajevo out of the total of 160,000 tons flown in under the UN banner usually under perilous conditions from both the weather, locked in by the surrounding hills, and the snipers hiding in the dense countryside. The airport itself was still a dangerous place, a front line almost, with Muslims on one side and Serbs on the other firing at each other across the runways as the relief planes came in to land. Some pilots adopted the effective but hazardous Khe Sanh approach, perfected during the Vietnam War, in which the pilot makes the steepest possible approach to landing to remain above the small-arms fire until almost touchdown.

Running as a parallel operation to the relief flights, the RAF also began surveillance operations over the Adriatic Sea in 1993 in support of NATO warships enforcing a UN arms embargo against all the states previously joined at the hip in the Federal Socialist Republic of Yugoslavia. The RAF were flying their new Boeing Sentry E-3 airborne early-warning aircraft delivered in 1991 and based at RAF Waddington as well as forming part of the NATO Airborne Early Warning Force in Germany. This version, built on the old Boeing 707 airframe, could operate on station for up to six hours, cruising at 40,000 feet and up to 1,000 miles from base – which in this case was in northern Italy. The Sentry carries on-board radar and transmits a constant array of digital data to ground and shipboard stations. The detachment remained on this task for almost two years and was in the skies for a total of 9,000 hours' flying time. The United Nations extended these operations later in the year by introducing a no-fly zone over Bosnia, banning all but NATO military aircraft. Operation Deny Flight was policed by a large NATO force, which included RAF Tornado F3s and Jaguars from the UK, flying from the Gioia del Colle air base in southern Italy. Over the next 14 months the Tornados clocked up 7,200 hours on CAPS (combat air patrols), while the Jaguars flew 3,000 attack and reconnaissance sorties. They were supported by RAF TriStar refuelling tankers based in Sicily, while E-3 Sentry and Nimrod maritime patrol aircraft continued to provide surveillance over the region. As the international attempts to halt the civil war, which Bob Stewart described as one of the most vicious ever, increasing numbers of troops from many countries were drawn in. Even so, the unforgettable television pictures of starving prisoners of war, the massacres, the mass graves, the sheer terror of the civilian populations as they went about their daily lives continued unabated, and frustrated commanders in the UN force could do nothing about it. Even with these glaring human rights abuses staring the world in the face, peace efforts stalled time and time again and the sheer desperation of the peace negotiators showed on the desolate faces of the Vance–Owen teams as they tried repeatedly to persuade the Serbs to stop the killing.

In the summer of 1995 international attempts to instigate a halt to the fighting finally became more determined. Limited force was authorised by the UN and joined by NATO nations in spite of remaining fears among some of becoming drawn into a Vietnam-type situation. In August 1995, therefore, selected air strikes under Operation Deliberate Force were joined by the air forces of several NATO nations against Serb positions. British Special Forces were among those on the ground covertly obtaining intelligence over a period of several weeks for target selection, a task that needed care in that many Serbian guns were deliberately placed in the middle of civilian areas. However, the use of precision weapons enabled effective strikes on Serb positions, stores and supply lines. The attacks were stepped up in September when numerous operations launched by NATO were joined by RAF Harriers and Jaguars, pounding the Serbian positions with rockets, laser-guided weapons and 1,000-pound free-fall bombs.

Within two weeks the Serbs agreed to further talks, and the Dayton Peace Initiative was forged in October 1995, supported by all the major Western powers under the NATO alliance, which set in motion the groundwork for a total cessation of hostilities. NATO would provide 60,000 troops, including 20,000 Americans and 10,000 British – this time as enforcers. D-day was nominated as 18 January 1996, when UNProFor would join incoming forces under the command of NATO's Allied Command Europe, Rapid Reaction Corps (ARRC). RAF transports and helicopters were also concerned, of course, with the movement of ground forces and supplies, including covert operations by the British Special Forces, who were tasked to provide advance intelligence for incoming troops across a wide area where flash points of resistance might occur. Air cover, reconnaissance and surveillance were maintained throughout this tense period of immense activity on the ground. The cease-fire held and the weeks turned into months, only stumbling when the War Crimes Commission in The Hague published a list of names of Bosnian-Serb leaders and officers whose arrest was sought to stand trial for crimes that included the massacre of civilians. The two most prominent were the leader of the Bosnian Serbs Radovan Karadžić and his army commander, General Ratko Mladić. At the time of writing, six years later, they had not been taken into custody.

Even as the Bosnian crisis was being resolved, the RAF was to become involved in a revival of missions over Iraq which would engage its Tornados throughout the latter years of the 1990s and into the new millennium, after Saddam Hussein declared in September 1996 that the no-fly zones imposed on him after the Gulf War were 'null and void'. He ordered his air force to shoot down any aircraft patrolling the area. Western intelligence sources reported that he had moved his tanks deeper into the northern Kurdish areas, whereupon the US launched a missile strike from two B-52 bombers along with 27 cruise missiles from the US destroyer *Laboon* in the Gulf. Many of America's allies in NATO and in the Middle East condemned the attack and only Britain seemed prepared to back the Americans. France briefly lent its support but pulled out at the end of 1996 after an outbreak of fighting between rival Kurdish factions, one of which was backed militarily by Saddam Hussein. By then, Britain had ordered RAF contingents on a rotating basis to join the Americans in daily combat patrols over Iraq. Between February 1997 and February 1998 alone, RAF aircraft flew a total of 2,000 sorties and clocked up 5,980 hours. But this was only the beginning of what became a substantial commitment for the RAF, now the sole supporter of the American action.

A further irritant to the campaign came later in that year of 1998 when Iraq expelled the United Nations team investigating intelligence reports that Saddam Hussein was once again stock-piling weapons of mass destruction, including chemical and biological weapons, and possibly attempting to build a nuclear capability. As Richard Butler, head of the UN Special Commission for Disarmament, withdrew, the Pentagon, backed by Britain, staged a four-day blitz against Iraq, during which it fired 425 Cruise and Tomahawk missiles, 90 more than during the whole of the Gulf War. At the UN Security Council, Russia and China demanded a halt to these actions, claiming that the US–UK operations were not covered by the UN resolution originally approved for the no-fly zones and was a violation of international law. Saddam Hussein repeated his warning that he would shoot any 'invading' aircraft down but, although he made several attempts, failed to do so because his ground-to-air systems were inadequate. The US–UK alliance pressed on with their raids on Iraq and in December 1998 launched Operation Desert Fox, to which the RAF committed 12 Tornado GR1s to a base in Kuwait and the Anglo-American force began 100 hours of non-stop bombing of Iraq. After the first joint attack, the RAF produced video footage demonstrating the present capability of its strike force, using what a Ministry of Defence spokesman said were the most accurate bombs ever used by the RAF.

The footage showed the bombing of Iraqi aircraft hangars, radar installations and radio antennae, and in the first grainy infra-red negative picture the beam of a laser-aiming device from a Tornado GR1 ground attack aircraft was seen hovering over an aircraft hangar in the desert near Basra in southern Iraq. The Tornado swooped down to the hangar, and the image remained steady until dense black and a bright flash revealed a direct hit by a 2,000-pound British Paveway III. An RAF commentary said: 'If there were any aircraft in the hangar they will not be flying today.' The next target was described as a radar installation for an anti-aircraft missile system surrounded by sand bunkers. The laser target designator was locked on, and again the structure disappeared in a huge explosion. Another part of the video footage filmed an aircraft hangar being hit by a bomb set with a delayed fuse which allowed it to crash through the roof of the hangar before exploding, blowing the whole building apart. The Tornados had flown in pairs to allow the maximum number of precision weapons to be carried and all returned safely in spite of heavy anti-aircraft fire from Iraqi ground defences. General Sir Charles Guthrie, then Chief of Defence Staff, said that only smart bombs were used by the Tornados, including Paveway II 1,000-pounders and Paveway III 2,000-punders. George Robertson, the then Defence Secretary, said that one of the hangars at the Tallil airfield was thought to house unmanned drones built specifically to spray biological or chemical weapons.

Operation Desert Fox would become an ongoing commitment for the RAF, but in that autumn of 1998 a far greater challenge was already looming on the horizon. The Bosnian crisis had calmed, but the Yugoslav President, Slobodan Milošević had embarked on parallel lines of conflict in the province of Kosovo, attempting to ethnically cleanse the towns and villages of the Albanian Kosovans. As with Bosnia, the current troubles dated back to the end of the Cold War when Milošević dissolved the Kosovo assembly and ethnic Albanian legislators in the province responded by declaring independence, which the Serbs refused to recognise. Tens of thousands of ethnic Albanians lost their jobs as Milošević ordered a clampdown in the province and the shadowy Kosovo Liberation Army (KLA) made its presence felt by admitting responsibility for a number of bombings and attacks against Serbian police and state officials.

Fast-forwarding to March 1998, the situation had stumbled through several phases of internal crisis until the international community acknowledged, finally, that a repeat of Bosnia was already unfolding in Kosovo. Serbian police fired on a student demonstration and conducted a series of raids in the Drenica region of Kosovo. Houses were burned, villages emptied and dozens of ethnic Albanians killed. Thousands of refugees from Serbian brutality were already on the move when US envoy Richard Holbrooke flew to Belgrade in June to meet Milošević and try to end the conflict. The Serb leader gave no promises and the following day UN Secretary-General Kofi Annan cautioned

NATO that it must seek a Security Council mandate for any military intervention.

All summer long, diplomatic activity swung back and forth and the Kosovans, meanwhile, were being brutalised. First reports of mass graves and many instances of the burning of houses and clearing of villages were appearing. On 24 September 1998 NATO approved two contingency plans, one for air strikes and the second for monitoring and maintaining a cease-fire agreement if one was reached. The UN High Commissioner for Refugees, meanwhile, announced on 29 September that 200,000 civilians had already been displaced within Kosovo since fighting began in February. International mediators continued their efforts, but months passed during which there were promises by Milošević which were never kept, peace talks that didn't happen, of NATO air strikes which were postponed, and the general air of impending doom deepened. The refugee problem had by now long ago passed crisis point and was heading for catastrophe as the winter weather set in and thousands more were heading for the borders.

Observers on the ground in Kosovo reported that the speed with which the refugee crisis developed appeared to indicate that there was a plan to ethnically cleanse at least the KLA strong-holds, if not the entire province, of its Albanian population. By February 1999 the humanitarian situation had significantly deteriorated and reports of atrocities were widespread as Serbian troops advanced into the countryside. The UNHCR reported a total of 333,000 displaced Kosovans and the figure was rising. By 23 March 23 major cities were being targeted by Serbian forces. The emptying of Kosovska Mitrovica had begun with thousands of homes and businesses looted and torched. With thousands of refugees still heading for the borders, Western leaders proposed an airlift to take 100,000 Kosovans to NATO countries. NATO also released imagery taken by RAF surveillance aircraft of 500 people surrounded by Serb forces in the town of Glodane. There was also evidence of mass graves in Drenica, Malisevo and Pagarusa. Approximately 150 bodies were discovered in Drenica, and Serbian forces reportedly locked the members of an entire family into a house in a village in Drenica and burned them alive. Further RAF imagery corroborated refugee reports of mass burials at Pusto Selo. Against this background, further frantic diplomatic efforts were under way, with talks arranged in Paris and a peace deal hammered out that seemed to present an eleventh-hour hope of a solution. Milošević refused to sign it.

On 24 March NATO finally launched its air war with the assembled aircraft of 14 nations. Wide-ranging targets pre-selected by Special Forces and agents on the ground and imagery from surveillance aircraft would take the allied bombers across Kosovo and into Serbia and Montenegro. Belgrade itself was rocked by bombs on the first wave of attacks. Dozens of Tomahawk cruise missiles were launched by warships and submarines – mostly American, but including one Royal Navy nuclear submarine, *Splendid*. Then, six USAF B-52 bombers temporarily based at RAF Fairford, Gloucestershire, delivered the heaviest airborne bombardment. The RAF began its contribution to the campaign when six Harrier GR7 fighter-bombers took off an hour after the initial bombardment was launched. They had been tasked to attack an ammunition dump used by the Ministry of Interior Police during their repression of the Kosovan Albanians. Four aircraft were armed with Paveway laser-guided bombs, while the other two acted as escorts. Unfortunately, the Harriers did not achieve the success they had hoped for. They formed part of the third wave of attacks on the position but because of explosions, fire and smoke caused by the earlier strikes the Harriers had difficulty in seeing and maintaining a lock on their targets. Paveways released by the lead aircraft fell short of the target on open ground and the remaining Harriers aborted their attack and returned to their base in Italy without releasing their weapons. Thereafter, RAF fortunes did improve to make a significant contribution to the NATO effort, although the weather curtailed their best intentions in the early stages. With heavy cloud locked in by the Balkan mountains, the Harriers temporarily switched tactics in mid-April and dropped 2,000-pound bombs for the first time since the conflict began. The laser-guided Paveway IIIs were capable of striking at Serb tanks hidden deep in tunnels in the Kosovo mountains. RAF armourers loaded them on to a pair of Harriers at the Gioia del Colle air base in southern Italy shortly before 10 a.m. on the day of the attack. They were back at base two hours later after successfully knocking out a major road bridge in Kosovo as part of NATO's continued attempts to cut Serbian military supply lines. A second pair of Harriers hit an ammunition dump using RBL755 cluster bombs.

The Harriers continued to take advantage of the good weather, flying back-to-back missions throughout the day, with avionics technicians and armourers working in shifts to rearm and refuel the jets for fresh sorties. The *Daily Telegraph* reported that the decision to use the 2,000-pound Paveway IIIs, accurate to within six feet and capable of penetrating rock or reinforced concrete, was seen as part of a fresh NATO strategy to get to grips with Serbian forces on the ground in Kosovo.

The RAF contingent was constantly on call and would be asked for operations on every one of the 80 days of the campaign and, as it extended over a much longer time frame than analysts had anticipated, additional aircraft of all types were committed by the RAF, eventually to the extent of 16 Harrier GR7s, 12 Tornado GR1s, three Sentry E3s, one Nimrod and four TriStar tankers. In addition, Hercules transports were also engaged in a huge airlift of food, blankets and tents for the refugees as the exodus of new arrivals on the border as the air bombardment raged over them reached the crisis level of 20,000 a day. They were now being openly herded out of towns and villages by the Serbian forces and used for protection on roads. Based on accounts from refugees, the UNHCR reported that the Djakovica region 'undoubtedly has been one of the most violent and cruel in the whole of Kosovo, turning it at times into a virtual killing field'.

One month into the bombing campaign, the UN human rights observers estimated that 1.2 million Kosovan Albanians had been displaced from their homes since the conflict escalated in March 1998, and 400 towns and villages were reportedly damaged or destroyed by Serbian forces since mid-March 1999. There were also reports of considerable collateral damage occurring, and NATO faced increasingly hostile daily press briefings to explain these occurrences and, conversely, why the bombing campaign had not been more effective in achieving its aims. Analysts who were prepared to consider the history of bombing campaigns, from the Second World War to modern times, would point out that there was no consistent evidence that air power alone could destroy national willpower, and dictators especially had no track record of being affected by it.

There was already a ground swell of 'stop-the-bombing' opinion but the alternatives were bleak: to allow the savage human rights abuse to continue or to send in a substantial ground force, a course clearly unacceptable to NATO and the Americans in particular, given the potential for great loss of life among the troops on both sides. The end game in this case was to degrade Serbian military capacity for oppression to such an extent that ground forces could move in to assert a political agreement. There was, however, no question that the air campaign was highly sensitive to civilian casualties, which in turn induced caution initially over targeting.

After a month of operations, NATO aircraft had flown 8,000 sorties, of which 2,500 had been attack missions. The RAF had carried out around 12 per cent of that total, with Harrier GR7s dropping laser-guided bombs, Paveway and cluster bombs, Tornado GR1s dropping laser-guided bombs and the Royal Navy's Sea Harrier FA2s flying Combat Air Patrol missions from HMS *Invincible*. Since 16 February the RAF's air transport fleet of Hercules had flown 270 sorties, in addition to numerous VC10 and TriStar sorties.

There was, however, no sign of Milošević buckling under the pressure, and clearly air strikes against military facilities and strategic targets were gaining even more momentum with daily sorties averaging 650, which carried far greater risk of collateral casualties. In Belgrade, the main TV station, the headquarters of the Yugoslav army, the federal Interior Ministry, a police building and the Chinese embassy were struck (the last by mistake), some of them by cruise missiles fired from HMS *Splendid*. Fighter-bombers were out looking for tactical targets, such as groups of military vehicles, fuel bowsers, and tank and surface-to-air missile sites. This RAF daily operations report was typical:

Ten missions and RAF Harrier GR7s dropped a number of RBL755 cluster bombs on a military vehicle compound and a barracks near the border. Six RAF Tornados, operating from RAF Brüggen, also successfully attacked an ammunition plant in Serbia. Support sorties were also flown by TriStar and VC10 tankers which so far in the campaign have flown over 120 sorties and provided 3,500 tons of fuel to other aircraft. As well as refuelling RAF and RN aircraft, they have refuelled combat aircraft from France, Italy, Germany, Spain, Canada and the United States. The air transport fleet has also moved over 5,000 troops and 20,000 tons of freight to the theatre.

It was along these lines that the air campaign proceeded against, it must be said, increasingly vocal detractors. There was also some stinging media criticism, especially after some serious errors caused traumatic civilian casualties. On 11 May John Keegan, the knowledgeable defence editor of the *Daily Telegraph*, upset Defence Secretary George Robertson when he suggested that Milošević was not suffering any backlash in his own country, in what was an interesting analogy with events of 1940:

> Unsuccessful air wars make the target country and its leader look good, while making whoever is launching the bombs look bumbling, if not bullying. That was certainly the effect of Germany's bombing campaign against Britain in 1940, with which analogies can increasingly be drawn. The Battle of Britain rightly remains a national epic. It was, moreover, a genuine victory, in which the RAF defeated the Luftwaffe, so successfully defending this country against German invasion. It is important, however, to remember what the RAF was defending. Its own airfields, of course, and the fighting power of the Royal Navy. Yet in the last resort it was defending the English Channel. As long as the RAF's fighters flew over the Channel, the Germans dared not launch their enormous army on to the waves. The more the Germans bombed, moreover, the worse they made themselves look in the eyes of neutrals, particularly in American eyes, and the better – because braver – they made the British look. It was [Churchill's] magnificent articulation of Britain's determination to resist the Luftwaffe's bombing which both inspired his own people to do so and won him moral superiority over his much stronger political opponent. Yet it was in Britain's inaccessibility that his real superiority lay. Milošević also enjoys geographical inaccessibility. It is provided not by the sea, for Serbia is landlocked, but by the Balkan mountains. Yet, by NATO's analysis, the mountains are equivalent to a sea: a sea of ambush places, natural anti-tank obstacles, firetraps and every other sort of terrain favourable to Serb defence and

unfavourable to NATO attack. So NATO, in its under-
standable anxiety to check Serb aggression against Kosovo's
Albanians, decided to bomb. It is still bombing and still
insisting that bombing will break the will of Milošević and
the Serbs, without the necessity to commit ground troops.
This seems, again by analogy with 1940, a faulty analysis.

The bombing continued, although targets were becoming scarce,
but NATO commanders believed their policy was vindicated
when, at the beginning of June, Milošević agreed to meet negotiators and subsequently accepted cease-fire terms. By then,
ground troops were already being brought to the edges of the
conflict, with the RAF organising 20 or so troop-carrying flights
a day, 17 with RAF aircraft, the remainder with civilian charter
flights as part of the UK's contribution of 11,000 troops to the
KFOR peacekeeping force, which would enter Kosovo under the
terms of the cease-fire. Chinook and Puma support helicopter
forces had also arrived, operating from Macedonia, while RAF
attack aircraft remained at a high level of readiness to resume
operations if required. They weren't, and within a week the air
forces of the 14 nations were being stood down as British
paratroop and Gurkha battalions led a 40-mile column of troops
cautiously into the ravaged countryside of Kosovo, strewn with
mines left by Serbian forces and unexploded ordnance from the
NATO cluster bombs. It was the latter that subsequently killed
two members of The Queen's Own Gurkha Engineers while
clearing unexploded material from around a village school at
Orlate, south-west of Priština airfield. During the night of
11–12 June the RAF also suffered its first loss of the operation
when a Hercules transport was involved in an accident at Kukes
airfield. There were three injuries among the 12 personnel on
board.
    In the aftermath, some of the criticisms of the campaign were
taken up and examined in the course of intensive studies of the
day-by-day operations of the campaign as part of a massive
'lessons learned' exercise launched by the Ministry of Defence
almost as soon as the war in Kosovo ended. According to the
Daily Telegraph, an analysis prepared for the RAF acknowledged
failings in intelligence, training, weapons and other hardware.
Intelligence reports about Serb troop and equipment locations

took up to three days to reach front-line attack squadrons, by which time the Serbs had changed position. Many pilots found themselves bombing old tank tracks or civilians as a result. American intelligence 'bureaucracy' was blamed. Secure communications were also inadequate, meaning that vital information could not be passed to RAF attack units for fear of the Serbs hearing it, and it was alleged that some weapons developed 'unexpected and extremely difficult' characteristics in flight and especially during bad weather or smoke from the ground, making it harder than anticipated to drop them accurately.

The paper, said the *Telegraph*, provided a 'detailed British account of the hitherto unknown reasons behind the West's almost complete failure to hit Serb forces in Kosovo.' In the political arena, however, a number of former service chiefs and a Conservative opposition spokesman joined forces to call for a public inquiry into the campaign. One of the most sensitive issues was that of political interference, so evidently apparent given that there were 14 nations involved in the campaign. It was raised by the then Conservative defence spokesman, Iain Duncan Smith, who said: 'This is why we need an inquiry, because we need politicians to accept their share of the blame for any failures.'

It was not the first time such as issue had been raised. Memories of the Falklands War would be revived by those involved, and in his memoir for the Imperial War Museum, tape-recorded in 1997, Sir Joseph Gilbert had made remarks highly pertinent to that question:

> The principal lesson learned from the Falklands which this country forgets at its peril: the government has to determine and set out what it is that it wishes to be done. Of course, it has to be consulted as to how the military are going to do this – in case what the military propose is unacceptable for a whole variety of reasons – but having decided what and approved of how, leave the military alone to get on with it and do not interfere. When I talked to the Pentagon about the Falklands, before I ever arrived they said please come here and say that. Remember how they'd had the hostage crisis in Iran and how badly that had gone. The military headquarters in this country was at Northwood. An admiral was put in charge and around him he had the army and navy

people he needed and was left alone. It has been said that when the forces landed in the Falklands and seemed to be bogged down, it is said then there was interference and urgings to get on by HMG, i.e. the Prime Minister [Margaret Thatcher]. I have no first-hand knowledge of whether that was true, but by and large and partly because of the lack of communications, when satellites were not available, the military were allowed to get on with it. The advent of modern communications means that there is a grave danger of political interference all the time during a military operation. It is better, having set out what is required, to let the military get on with it.

The politics of war, however, continued to reign supreme and were never more apparent than when the RAF and the USAF resumed operations over Iraq and were given a fresh impetus under the incoming president of the United States, George W. Bush, picking up where his father had left off. Between December 1998, when Desert Fox was launched, and December 2001, the joint air operations of the air forces of two nations amounted to more than 40,000 sorties. The Royal Air Force is ultimately answerable to the politicians for whom it has always had the responsibility of providing the plan – the means by which political decisions could be carried through, and in this case it was what to do about Saddam.

On this occasion the Americans were supplying the answers and the RAF became part of the instrument that was to deliver the big stick and thus carry some of the burden of criticism that began to mount around the world. Numerous challenges to the US–UK action were presented to the United Nations Security Council with Russia and China predominantly among the detractors, claiming that the bombing was illegal. Worse still from the British point of view was the fact that in a region where Tony Blair claimed to have achieved some influence, there was mounting sympathy for the Iraqis and a noticeable swing in public opinion, inspired to some extent by television pictures of dead and wounded Iraqis broadcast into millions of Arab homes by several Arabic satellite channels. Public opinion sways politicians, and Middle Eastern leaders, who were once willing partners with the West in their war on Iraq, became noticeably less vocal in their support, turning instead towards the view that trade sanctions imposed on Saddam should be ended. That movement of opinion was halted, if only temporarily, by the events of 11 September 2001 and the resultant war on international terrorism declared by Bush and Blair. It was well known in the Arab world that Saddam had long supported the Palestinian *intifada* in words and deed, sending truckloads of food and medicine to the Palestinians and a substantial cash sum to the families of the martyred Palestinians killed in the 'golden effort to liberate their nation'.

None of this, of course, ought to have a bearing on the men and women of the Royal Air Force, who are there to keep the aircraft flying and do their masters' bidding, but it is never as clear cut as that, nor was it ever. The insidious nature of twenty-first century politics impacts on their lives in a way that it never has before, and the challenge to perform well and do the job to the best of their ability becomes even greater.

Even as these words were being written, almost all elements of the Royal Air Force were involved in activity of a deeply uncomfortable, dangerous and demanding nature in some of the most inhospitable parts of the globe at a time when its overall manpower had been reduced to the lowest level since the 1930s. This was particularly so for the specialist trades of the air force, the vast body of men and women who provide the logistical and electronic services that keep the planes in the air and facilitate their landing in remote parts where local infrastructure is limited or non-existent. The Tactical Communications Wing, for example, is a behind-the-scenes unit with a staff of almost 450 that is required to service virtually every overseas operation undertaken by the RAF. The Wing, as it is known throughout the service, is a modern-day version of the signals group. It installs, operates and maintains vital communications and information systems in support of RAF squadrons and units. The detachments overseas invariably involve long hours, usually in very basic – sometimes dire – living conditions and extremes of climate, the combination of which provides significant technical and personal challenges. This world-wide commitment may be in support of national interests, United Nations operations or as part of their ongoing role servicing NATO Reaction Forces.

Their mission requires the regular exercising and evaluation of their ability to support these operations in the environment in which they are expected to operate – such as bombed-out airfields in Afghanistan, perhaps under hostile conditions. Apart from establishing satellite communications for headquarters staff posted to remote locations, the Wing provides the facilities for fixed-wing aircraft, mainly the Harrier and F3 Tornados, and their support teams to operate from wherever they are required. They are trained to meet and overcome the most extreme circumstances, such as setting up a landing base on a strip of grass or dusty landscape where there are no communications, navigational aids or lighting. They also support air-to-air refuelling, maritime reconnaissance and transport operations, which include providing communications and landing-light facilities at staging airfields for major logistic and troop movements.

One of Wing's growth areas in the 1990s was in support to No. 1 Air Control Centre, based at RAF Boulmer, which operates mobile radar and fighter control communications as well as the Tactical Air Control Centre. At the time of writing the Wing's mandate called for its ability to support thirteen deployed sites simultaneously, and these included exceedingly busy 'live' situations in the early months of 2002 – in Kosovo, the Gulf, Afghanistan and Africa. It was a situation aptly described by their motto, *Ubique Loquimur* or 'We Speak Everywhere'.

All of the most extreme challenges were, of course, confronting RAF personnel who took part in operations in Afghanistan in support of the Allied action against the Taliban. This included RAF TriStar and VC10 tanker aircraft from RAF Brize Norton which were deployed to become an integral part of the US bombing sorties. American warplanes and carrier-borne aircraft are all compatible with British systems and the RAF now possesses the largest air-to-air refuelling tanker force in the world after the United States. Other RAF aircraft supporting the air and ground activities of the Allied troops included sophisticated E-3D Sentry AEW1 surveillance and control aircraft, Nimrod R1 and MR2 and Canberra PR9 photographic reconnaissance aircraft. The reconnaissance and surveillance roles were especially vital in Afghanistan in that, as well as observing possible enemy activity, their technology can seek out the location of concentrations of displaced people who might require humanitarian assistance. The vintage Canberra photographic reconnaissance aircraft proved once again to be a particularly useful tool in this respect.

RAF helicopters were to the fore in the early stages in operations with the British Special Forces, which included contingents from both the SAS and SBS. Later, they were joined by members of No. 27 Squadron flying Chinook helicopters in support of the British Commando battle-groups operating with American forces to clear the remaining Taliban from remote regions of the country. As well as providing a significant combat support force, the RAF contributed fully to the International Security Assistance Force of 5,000 men from nineteen nations. RAF specialist units were engaged at various centres in Afghanistan setting up temporary facilities for incoming aircraft and troops and restoring existing airfields to working order. First in were operatives from the RAF No. 5131 Bomb Disposal Squadron, based at RAF North Luffenham, who joined army units in making Kabul airport safe by exploding a considerable amount of loose ordnance before undertaking a succession of other similar tasks. The RAF Regiment, as ever, fulfilled a multitude of tasks, ranging from security and protection of airfields to the overseeing of rebuilding and refurbishment projects. No. 34 Squadron, for example, took command of a large force of local labour to reinstate damaged runways at Kabul to receive incoming VIPs, troops and aid flights. They also supervised repairs to the airport buildings, even down to buying material to recover chairs in the airport waiting areas. As stability was gradually restored, RAF Lyneham moved rapidly into action, with round-the-clock operations flying their Hercules transports loaded with both humanitarian aid and supplies to meet the needs of the many hundreds of British troops and personnel established in the region.

Throughout the emergency resulting from the terrorist attack on New York on 11 September 2001, the RAF maintained a full complement of personnel for its commitments elsewhere, including a continuing role in support of KFOR forces in Kosovo and full participation with the Americans in monitoring the no-fly zones in the north and south of Iraq. In the latter, the first three months of 2002 saw several incidents of aircraft being fired upon from the ground, and tensions once again ran high. The two sectors were monitored by Jaguar GR3s of No. 6 Squadron in the north and Tornado GR4s of No. II (AC) Squadron and Tornado F3s of No. 25 Squadron in the south, operating from Kuwait and

Saudi Arabia respectively, again with full back-up of support services and the RAF Regiment. Additionally, RAF surveillance and reconnaissance aircraft were retained in the region after an exercise following President George W. Bush's warning in the autumn of 2001 that he intended to strike once again at Iraq in an effort to depose Saddam Hussein, unless the UN inspectors of weapons of mass destruction were allowed back into the country.

Prime Minister Tony Blair was pretty much a lone voice among Western leaders in aligning the United Kingdom to America's declaration of intent over Iraq; and, given the commitments already to hand in May 2002, the RAF found it necessary to issue a compulsory call up order for forty-nine reservists from the Royal Auxiliary Air Force to 'assist with the war on terrorism'. A number of analysts came quickly to the view that the Royal Air Force, under the British New Labour Government, was being edged closer into the long-ago discredited role of world police-man. Only time will tell. But, as we leave this account of RAF current activity, there were serious concerns over the RAF's ability to maintain its efficiency in the wake of contraction of manpower in the previous decade.

APPENDIX

Into the Twenty-First Century

In April 2000 a review of Britain's strategic and military policy brought a further rationalisation of the overall structure of the Royal Air Force to provide two commands – Strike Command and Personnel and Training Command – while logistical support for all three services was reorganised into the Defence Logistics Organisation, which in turn led to the merging of vital areas of aircraft deployment to which the British army and the Royal Navy also contribute. The headquarters of the RAF's Strike Command remained at High Wycombe and its mandate to react to crises and undertake expeditionary operations remained unchanged.

However, the strike capability was substantially improved by the establishment of tri-service groups, principally the Joint Rapid Reaction Force, a Joint Helicopter Command and Joint Force Harrier. RAF Strike Command continued to be based on three groups, but with this streamlining of the command and control structure, and to take account of inter-service cooperation, the three previous main groupings of its aircraft and services were reorganised so that No. 11/18 Group, originally created from No. 11 Group (famed for its Battle of Britain role), No. 18 Group (formerly maritime operations) and No. 38 Group (which operated the Hercules, VC10 and TriStar) were all disbanded. In their place came three new commands, updated to coincide with the cross-service roles of the helicopter, Harrier and rapid reaction forces.

No. 1 Group takes in all strike attack and offensive support

351

aircraft, including Tornado F3 units originally with No. 11/18 Group. With the exception of the Harrier, the re-formed No. 1 Group will operate all the RAF's front-line aircraft, including, in the future, the Eurofighter.

No. 2 Group operates all the aircraft and force elements that support front-line operations. These include the air transport and air-to-air refuelling aircraft formerly in No. 38 Group and the Nimrod R and Sentry aircraft from No. 11/18 Group as well as the RAF Regiment and ground-based air defence systems.

No. 3 Group, which originally controlled the V-Bomber Force of the 1960s, operates the new Joint Force Harrier. The group also includes Nimrod maritime patrol aircraft, search and rescue helicopters and the RAF's mountain rescue teams. The Harriers and Sea Harriers were to be headquartered at RAF Cottesmore and RAF Wittering as a joint force capable of operating either from land or from the Royal Navy's aircraft carriers. For the first time since the dissolution of the Royal Naval Air Service in the First World War, the Air Officer Commanding, a naval officer, was appointed to the role of heading the joint force of RAF and naval aircraft, the first incumbent being Rear-Admiral Scott Lidbetter.

RAF Innsworth, headquarters of the Personnel and Training Command and originally created on 1 April 1994, consolidated its wide-ranging role covering recruitment, training, career management, welfare, conditions of service, resettlement and pensions for all RAF regular and reserve forces. All RAF policy management staff involved in every aspect of personnel are based here. As of 2001, they were operating to a budget of £800 million, and the Command had a headquarters staff of 1,500 which overall managed the employment of 17,000 people, including 4,000 civilians at more than 30 locations. It is also responsible for 500 training aircraft, of which 150 are gliders. An integral part of the PT Command includes the RAF Training Group Defence Agency, which in turn comprises nine RAF stations as well as administering the RAF aerobatic team, the Red Arrows.

Royal Air Force Flying Stations

The stations of the Royal Air Force are widespread and complex units, many in remote locations away from centres of population for specific tasks such as night flying. The front-line stations themselves have over the years taken on the appearance of small towns to accommodate aircrew, maintenance, electronics and armaments experts, air-traffic control and a dozen other vital services. They have been developed as far as possible as self-contained and self-reliant units providing accommodation, catering, banks, shops and post offices.

Aldergrove
First opened in 1918 for a year, Aldergrove became a fully operational flying station in 1925. Operating as an important Coastal Command station throughout the Second World War, Aldergrove is now home to a mixed force of Wessex and Puma helicopters operating in support of the British army, from No. 72 Squadron and No. 230 Squadron, although there are regular detachments from other Puma and Chinook squadrons. No. 3 Squadron of the RAF Regiment are the field squadron based at Aldergrove. Two army air corps units are also based at Aldergrove.

Barkston Heath
The primary function of RAF Barkston Heath is as a relief landing ground for the flying training activities at RAF Cranwell. The airfield originally opened in 1941 and was home to the 61st Troop Carrier Group of the 9th USAF during the Second World War. Now it accommodates the Joint Elementary Flying Training School, which operates 18 Firefly II two-seater trainers.

Benson
Opened in 1939 as part of the RAF's expansion programme, Benson was home to No. 1 Photographic Reconnaissance Unit throughout the Second World War. Currently, 15 Pumas of No. 33 Squadron, the London and Oxford University Air Squadrons, with Tutor T1s, and No. 6 Air Experience Flight are based at Benson, along with two Royal Auxiliary Air Force/RAF reserve units in the form of the Helicopter Support Squadron and the Mobile Meteorological Unit, plus Merlin HC2s operated by No. 28 Squadron.

Boscombe Down
Home of the Aircraft and Armament Experimental Establishment, the RAF presence at Boscombe Down comprises the

Empire Test Pilots School, the Strike/Attack Operational Evaluation Unit and the Southampton University Air Squadron.

Brize Norton
This is the largest RAF station in the UK and the nerve centre of the RAF's air transport. Opened in 1937, the station was used to train airborne forces before being handed over to the USAF in 1950. Strategic Air Command based B-29 and B-47 bombers here before the station was handed back to the RAF for use as a tanker and transport base. Also based at Brize Norton is No. 1 Parachute Training School, which includes the RAF Parachute Display Team, the Falcons. No. 99 Squadron and its Boeing C-17 Globemaster transport aircraft arrived here in 2001.

Chivenor
Originally a civil airfield opened in the 1930s, the RAF took over the site from May 1940 for use as a Coastal Command station. Post-war, the station was largely used for training, particularly weapons training as the home of No. 2 Tactical Weapons Unit from 1980 until fixed-wing flying ceased in 1994. The only units now based at Chivenor are A Flight of 22 Squadron, with two helicopters for search and rescue duties, and its HQ Flight, and No. 624 Volunteer Gliding School, operating Vigilant T1 motor gliders.

Coltishall
Famous as a night fighter station since May of 1940, Coltishall was first to operate the English Electric Lightning all-weather jet fighter and is currently home to the entire RAF Jaguar fleet of aircraft.

Coningsby
Originally a heavy bomber base as part of No. 5 Group, Bomber Command, Coningsby maintained its link with the heavy bomber force until 1964, when the Vulcan squadrons moved to Cottesmore. Coningsby became the first RAF station to operate the Air Defence Variant of the Tornado, the major type still based here. Units based at Coningsby are No. 5 Squadron, No. 56 (Reserve) Squadron, The Tornado F3 Operational Conversion Unit, the Tornado F3 Operational Evaluation Unit and the world-famous

Battle of Britain Memorial Flight, which operates five Spitfires of various Marks, the only flying Lancaster in Europe, two Hurricanes, a Dakota and two Chipmunks. At nearby Woodhall Spa is located the RB199 engine repair facility, which, as well as maintaining the engines of Coningsby-based aircraft, provides services for the other Tornado F3 units.

Cosford

Cosford is principally involved in the training of RAF ground tradesmen, as it has been since it opened in 1938. Units currently based at Cosford are No. 1 School of Technical Training, the Birmingham University Air Squadron and No. 633 Volunteer Gliding School, with Vigilant T1s.

Cottesmore

A wartime expansion airfield with a considerable history, Cottesmore has been used variously as a bomber, training, troop carrier and electronic counter-measures base. In 1976 the station was upgraded to operate the Interdictor Strike version of the Tornado in a unique way. For 20 years until April 1999, the major operational unit based at Cottesmore was the Tri-National Tornado Training Establishment, with Tornado GR1s, supervising all conversion training for the British, Italian and German air forces. But with the decision to relocate Tornado training to member nations, the TTTE was disbanded. Within weeks, however, flying returned to the station when, in preparation for the station becoming the home to all front-line RAF Harrier squadrons, Nos. 3 and 4 Squadrons moved from RAF Laarbruch in Germany after it was closed. A few months later, No. 1(F) Squadron left nearby Wittering after 31 years for Cottesmore, bringing its 12 Harriers. The Royal Navy's Sea Harriers were scheduled to move here from Yeovilton, making Cottesmore one of the busiest stations in the RAF. Also based here is the Offensive Support Squadron manned by members of the RAAF.

Cranwell

Originally HMS *Daedalus*, a Royal Naval Air Service training and airship base, the site was taken over by the RAF in 1918 for officer cadet training, and continues to this day at the famous

RAF College. Currently based at Cranwell are the RAF aerobatic team, the Red Arrows, along with No. 3 Flying Training School. Also based on the main airfield is the RAF College Air Squadron and Cranwell Gliding Club, part of the RAF Gliding and Soaring Association. The Air Warfare Centre is also based here.

Kinloss
Used for training heavy bomber crews during the war, RAF Kinloss began a long association with Coastal Command with the arrival of six Operational Training Units for Beaufighters and Mosquitos. Lancasters and Shackletons followed, before the Nimrod entered service at Kinloss in 1971. Kinloss is now home to the entire RAF fleet of 21 aircraft, split between Nos. 120, 201 and 206 Squadrons.

Leeming
A bomber station from July 1940 operating Whitley, Stirling, Halifax and Lancaster aircraft, the station became a night fighter base, equipped initially with the Mosquito and then with the Meteor and Javelin before becoming a Training Command airfield in 1961. The station underwent a major overhaul in the 1980s and reopened in 1988 as a main operating base and is today home to squadrons of the UK's air defence fighter force, attached to both the UK's Joint Rapid Reaction Force and NATO's Immediate Reaction Force (Air). Leeming is also home to two other high-readiness units with both national and NATO commitments – No. 34 Squadron RAF Regiment and No. 2 RAF Tactical Survive To Operate HQ. Also at Leeming is No. 100 Squadron, equipped with target facilities aircraft along with exercise and training support, and the Joint Forward Air Controllers Training and Standards Unit. Other units at Leeming include the Air Defence Support Squadron, an RAAF unit, Northumbrian Universities Air Squadron and No. 11 Air Experience Flight. The station also has a mountain rescue team consisting of five permanent staff and 20 volunteers.

Leuchars
With a history dating back to balloon flying in 1911, the station was then home to RNAS fleet fighters and was later a

Coastal Command airfield. After the Second World War, Leuchars became a fighter command station and continues in this role today as one of the RAF's air defence bases, with 22 Hardened Aircraft Shelters (HAS), currently housing the Tornado F3s of Nos. 13 and 111 Squadrons. Aberdeen, Dundee and St Andrews University Air Squadrons also operate from the airfield, as does a mountain rescue unit and the Air Transportable Surgical Unit.

Linton-on-Ouse

Classed as one of the busiest training airfields in the RAF, it has been used as a bomber, transport and fighter airfield since it opened in 1937. Since 1957 the main role of the station has been pilot training, initially with the Jet Provost but now with the Tucano T1. No. 1 Flying Training School operates no fewer than 78 of these aircraft, providing basic flying instruction. Also at Linton is No. 642 Volunteer Gliding School, equipped with Vigilant T1s.

Lossiemouth

Home to Bomber Command's No. 20 Operational Training Unit and No. 46 Maintenance Unit during the war, the station became a satellite of RAF Milltown in Coastal Command before becoming HMS *Fulmar* of the Royal Navy in 1946 for Fleet Air Arm operations. With the impending demise of aircraft carriers, the RAF returned here in 1972 and the station steadily expanded as a versatile centre. Aircraft types flown here have included Whirlwind, Jaguar, Shackleton, Sea King, Hunter, Buccaneer and Tornado, employed in various roles including search and rescue, airborne early warning, operational conversion unit, tactical weapons unit and maritime strike/attack. Ground-based units have included the air and ground defence, airfield damage repair and airfield support roles. Today, it is one of the RAF's leading stations, with its present Tornado GR1/4 complement of three operational units – Nos. 12, 14 and 617 Squadrons – and one operational conversion unit – No. XV (Reserve) Squadron; its helicopter search and rescue unit, – D Flight, No. 202 Squadron – and two ground defence units – No. 51 Squadron and No. 2622 (Highland) Squadron, RAF Regiment.

Lyneham

The station became the first RAF airfield to operate jet transports when the first Comet C2s arrived in 1956. Now the RAF's major tactical transport station, the airfield is home to the Hercules aircraft operated by Nos. 24, 30, 47 and 70 Squadrons. The original Hercules are now being replaced by the second-generation C130J in RAF service with the stretched C4 and the standard C5 versions.

Marham

With a history dating back to the First World War, Marham has been used as both a heavy bomber and fighter station before it became the RAF's major reconnaissance base in 1993. Currently operating from Marham are No. II (AC) Squadron and No. 13 Squadron, both equipped with Tornado GR1As and GR4As, as well as No. 39 (1 PRU) Squadron, which operates the last of the Canberras. No. 2620 (County of Norfolk) Squadron, RAAF, is also based here.

Northolt

A key base for the defence of London during the Battle of Britain, Northolt became the major airport for London in 1946, until the opening of Heathrow. Transport Command took Northolt to provide VIP air transport, with No. 32 (Royal) Squadron, and incorporates the aircraft of the former Queen's Flight.

Odiham

Odiham opened in 1936 as an army cooperation base and later became a base for tactical reconnaissance and fighter aircraft until the switch to transport duties, particularly helicopters, that continues to this day. Currently based at Odiham are Nos. 7, 18 and 27 Squadrons, flying Chinook HC2s.

St Athan

A major RAF maintenance base for the Harrier, Tornado, Jaguar, Hawk, Dominie and VC10, all of which are the responsibility of the Engineering Division. Other units are a mountain rescue team, the University of Wales Air Squadron and No. 634 Volunteer Gliding School, with Viking TX1s.

St Mawgan
The base was opened for Ferry Command to receive aircraft from the US and Canada in the Second World War. In 1951 the station reopened as a Coastal Command base and now operates largely as a search and rescue base. Nimrods and Tornados regularly detach to St Mawgan to exercise the defence of the south-west approaches. All maintenance for the RAF Sea King fleet is carried out at St Mawgan, and the airfield is home to No. 3 Maritime Headquarters Unit. Two field squadrons are also based here: No. 1 Squadron, RAF Regiment, and No. 2625 (County of Cornwall) Squadron, RAAF.

Shawbury
A training airfield since 1917, it has also accommodated the central Air Traffic Control School since 1944. All the flying training here is now rotary-winged. In April 1997 this became the tri-service Defence Helicopter Flying School (DHFS) operating Squirrel HT1 and Griffin HT1 helicopters. The unit also includes the helicopter element of the Central Flying School.

Valley
Located on Anglesey, Valley was considered ideal for its dual role of fighter base, protecting Liverpool and the north-west, and ferry reception airfield during the war. Since 1957 it has become established as an important training base, with No. 4 Flying Training School, which operates 71 aircraft and incorporates the Central Flying School Advanced Training Unit. Valley is also home to C Flight of No. 22 Squadron, Sea King search and rescue and training units.

Waddington
A Royal Flying Corps field in 1916, it became a bomber base in 1926 and remained as such until the withdrawal of Vulcans in 1984. Waddington now fulfils two main roles in the RAF: that of electronic reconnaissance, carried out by the Nimrod R1s of No. 51 Squadron, and airborne early warning, provided by the six Sentry AEW1s of Nos. 8 and 23 Squadrons. Ground and air defence of the airfield is provided by No. 26 Squadron, RAF Regiment, with its Rapier FSC surface-to-air missiles, and No. 2503 (County of Lincoln) RAAF Field Squadron. NATO

aircraft of many nations also use Waddington as a temporary base during exercises in the North Sea air combat range.

Wittering

Dating back to 1916, the Central Flying School was based at Wittering until it became a fighter base in 1935, the role it still fulfils as 'The Home of the Harrier'. Currently home to the Operational Conversion Unit for the Harrier, No. 20 (Reserve) Squadron, the Sea Harriers of the navy's Operational Conversion Unit will move to Wittering from Yeovilton as part of the joint RAF/Royal Navy Joint Force Harrier team.

Akrotiri, Cyprus

The Sovereign Base Area of south-eastern Cyprus includes the airfield of Akrotiri, which was first opened in 1956. The RAF now uses the airfield as a staging post for transport aircraft and as a temporary operating base for aircraft carrying out armament practice camps. Permanently based at Akrotiri is No. 84 Squadron, with Wessex HC2s, who perform search and rescue duties as well as a support role for the UN peacekeeping forces on the island.

Ascension Island

A staging base during the Falklands War, it remains as such today, a duty it performs for both the RAF and the USAF. Regular flights from RAF Brize Norton link the island to the UK.

Brüggen, Germany

The station was rapidly built on drained marshland within a heavily forested area in 1953 to house the expanding NATO forces. From 1953 to 1957 it operated as a fighter station; from 1967 to 1998 in the strike/attack role and from April 1998 has operated in the attack role. During the fighter phase, No. 23 Squadron, Belgian Air Force, and Nos. 67, 71, 112 and 130 Squadrons, Royal Air Force, operated from Brüggen. It then became a Canberra station with the arrival of Nos. 80 and 213 Squadrons in the summer of 1957. From 1969 to 1975 the station operated Phantoms in the strike/attack role, before changing to Jaguars in 1975. Royal Air Force Brüggen underwent a complete

change of aircraft between 1984 and 1987 with the Jaguar
Squadrons being replaced by Tornado Squadrons. The base
became the largest Tornado base in NATO and home to two
RAF Tornado GR1 attack squadrons (IX(B) and 31 Squadrons),
both of which took part in the Gulf War. The two Tornado
Squadrons were declared to NATO as Main Defence Forces and
Reaction Force (Air) assets. RAF Brüggen was tasked by NATO
to mount offensive air operations against the former Republic of
Yugoslavia on 28 March 1999. The first mission from RAF
Brüggen consisted of six Tornado GR1s and three VC10 tankers
and was launched on 4 April 1999. RAF Brüggen was also home
to the Rapier surface-to-air missile squadron, No. 37 Squadron,
RAF Regiment, and 12 Flight, Army Air Corps. No. 37 Squadron, RAF Regiment, formed part of the UK contribution to the
Immediate Reaction Force (Air). Brüggen consisted of four
operational squadrons (three Tornado and one Rapier) supported by a large three-wing structure: operations, engineering
and supply and administration. At the end of March 1999, RAF
Brüggen's population included 222 RAF officers and 1,881 airmen, 55 members of the other services and 590 civilian employ-
ees. When some 3,452 dependent personnel were included, the
total population of the base was 6,100. The last act of Brüggen's
illustrious history was acted out in June 2001 when a parade was
held to mark the official closure of the station, thus bringing an
end to the last remnants of the RAF's Cold War past. The
Tornado squadrons returned to the UK before the base was
handed over to the British army.

Gibraltar
Although forming part of Headquarters, British Forces Gibraltar,
no aircraft are now stationed on The Rock, although Hercules,
Nimrod and Tornado GR1B aircraft make regular visits.

Goose Bay, Canada
A team of RAF personnel is stationed at Goose Bay, a large
military airfield in Labrador, to support RAF fast jet aircraft
carrying out low-level flying training over Labrador's vast snowy
wastes. The fast jets are usually accompanied by VC10, TriStar or
Hercules aircraft, providing AAR or transport support. Use of
Goose Bay reduces the volume of training undertaken over the

UK and hence cuts down on jet noise disturbance.

Mount Pleasant, Falkland Islands
An airfield purpose-built in 1984 to establish a fighter and transport presence following the Falklands War, Mount Pleasant houses regular flights of Tornado F3s, VC10s and Hercules as well as Nos. 5, 7, 303 and 751 Signals Units and a Rapier detachment from the RAF Regiment.

Index

Vessels are given in *italic*. References to footnotes are shown 'n'

Home Guard 132
Hopkins, Dr J.C.F. 65–6
Hopwood (Dambuster pilot) 206
Hornchurch 136
Hornchurch Wing 165
humanitarian operations 320–1,
    331, 334
Hungary, Russian invasion of
    269–70
Hunt, Sir Rex 319

Immediate Reaction Force (Air)
    356
Immelmann, Max 31
Immelmann turn 31, 34
Imperial Airways 157
Imphal, Battle of 241–2
India 81, 239–40
    independence 253
Indomitable, HMS 189
Indonesia 259–60
Inglis, Donald 38
Inskip, Sir Thomas 97
interrupter gear 30
Invincible, HMS 342
Iran 322, 326
Iran–Iraq War 322
Iraq 84, 90, 322–8, 336–8, 349, 350
Irvine jacket 106
Ismay, Hastings, Lord 138
Israel 253
Italian air forces 176–7
Italy, armistice declared in 215
Iwakuni 265

Jameson, Flight Lieutenant Pat
    107–8
jammers
    Mandrel 198
    Tinsel 198
Johnson, Johnnie 163–5
Joint Elementary Flying Training
    School 353
Jones, Lieutenant Colonel H. 315
JP233 weapon 325

Karadžić, Radovan 336
Keegan, John 343–4
Kennedy, John F. 290
The Kids Who Couldn't Miss (film)
    39
King, Tom 330
Kingsnorth, RNAS 46–8
Kinkaid, Sam 'Kink' 70–1
Kinloss 356
Kirton-in-Lindsey 163
kites 11
    see also airships; balloons
Kitty Hawk, North Carolina 9
Knapsack power station raid 3–7,
    166–7
Knight, Les 207
Kohat 81–2
Kohima 241
Kokura 246
Korea 264–6
Kosovo 338–45
    see also Balkans
Kota Baharu 187, 188
Kurds, Iraqi 330–1
Kut-el-Amara 42n
Kuwait 323, 349
    see also Gulf War

Laboon, USS 336
Lacey, Squadron Leader Ginger
    243
Laffan's Plain 20
Lambert, Count de 12
Larkhill 21
Latham, Hubert 12
Lawrence of Arabia 82
Lazaretto, Malta 184
Leeming 356
Lend-Lease Act 159
Lerwell (observer) 23–4
Leuchars 356–7
Lewis, Mike 234–5
Lewis machine gun 28–9
Light Night Striking Force 217,
    220
    see also Pathfinder Force (PFF)
Lilbourne Training Camp 34–5